LOGISTICS ENGINEERING AND MANAGEMENT

PRENTICE-HALL INTERNATIONAL SERIES
IN INDUSTRIAL AND SYSTEMS ENGINEERING

W. J. Fabrycky and J. H. Mize, Editors

BEIGHTLER, PHILLIPS, AND WILDE *Fundamentals of Optimization*, 2/E
BLANCHARD *Logistics Engineering and Management*, 2/E
BLANCHARD AND FABRYCKY *Systems Engineering and Analysis*
BROWN *Systems Analysis and Design for Safety*
BUSSEY *The Economic Analysis of Industrial Projects*
FABRYCKY, GHARE, AND TORGERSEN *Industrial Operations Research*
FRANCES AND WHITE *Facility Layout and Location: An Analytical Approach*
GOTTFRIED AND WEISMAN *Introduction to Optimization Theory*
HAMMER *Product Safety Management and Engineering*
KIRKPATRICK *Introductory Statistics and Probability for Engineering,
    Science, and Technology*
MIZE, WHITE, AND BROOKS *Operations Planning and Control*
MUNDEL *Motion and Time Study: Improving Productivity*, 5/E
OSTWALD *Cost Estimating for Engineering Management*
SIVAZLIAN AND STANFEL *Analysis of Systems in Operations Research*
SIVAZLIAN AND STANFEL *Optimization Techniques in Operations Research*
THUESEN, FABRYCKY, AND THUESEN *Engineering Economy*, 5/E
TURNER, MIZE, AND CASE *Introduction to Industrial and Systems Engineering*
WHITEHOUSE *Systems Analysis and Design Using Network Techniques*

LOGISTICS ENGINEERING AND

2nd edition

BENJAMIN S. BLANCHARD

*Virginia Polytechnic Institute
and State University*

PRENTICE-HALL, INC., *Englewood Cliffs, New Jersey* 07632

Library of Congress Cataloging in Publication Data

BLANCHARD, BENJAMIN S
  Logistics engineering and management.

  (Prentice-Hall international series in industrial
and systems engineering)
  Bibliography: p.
  Includes index.
  1. Systems engineering. 2. Logistics. I. Title.
TA168.B57 1981   658.7   80-24070
ISBN   0-13-540088-0

Dedicated to my wife, DOROTHY,
my children, BECKY, BENJAMIN, *and* LISA,
*for their tolerance
and encouragement in this endeavor.*

*Editorial production supervision
and interior design by Karen Winkler.
Manufacturing buyer: Anthony Caruso.*

Printed in the United States of America

10   9   8   7   6   5   4   3   2   1

PRENTICE-HALL INTERNATIONAL, INC., *London*
PRENTICE-HALL OF AUSTRALIA PTY. LIMITED, *Sydney*
PRENTICE-HALL OF CANADA, LTD., *Toronto*
PRENTICE-HALL OF INDIA PRIVATE LIMITED, *New Delhi*
PRENTICE-HALL OF JAPAN, INC., *Tokyo*
PRENTICE-HALL OF SOUTHEAST ASIA PTE. LTD., *Singapore*
WHITEHALL BOOKS LIMITED, *Wellington, New Zealand*

CONTENTS

5 Functional Analysis and Allocation 116

6 Logistics Support Analysis 138

9 Production and/or Construction 258

10 System Operation and Support 288

11 Logistic Support Management 312

APPENDICES

PREFACE

Logistics is by no means a new subject area. Historically, the concept of logistics stems from specific facets of military and industrial management. In the military sense, logistics is concerned with the various aspects of maintenance and system/product support, particularly from the point in time when systems are in operational use. In the industrial or commercial sector, logistics has been defined to include such activities as material flow, product distribution, transportation, warehousing, and the like. In both situations, however, logistics has been considered as a "downstream" effort, and the requirements for logistics have not been very well defined or integrated.

In recent years, systems and products have become more complex as technology advances, and logistics requirements have increased in general. Not only have the costs associated with system/product acquisition increased significantly in the past decade, but the costs of logistic support have also been increasing at an alarming rate. At the same time, the current economic dilemma of decreasing budgets combined with upward inflationary trends results in less money available for both the procurement of new systems and for the maintenance and support of those items already in use.

In view of these trends, one of the greatest challenges facing industry, businesses, government agencies, and the general consumer of products and services today is to meet the growing need for more effective and efficient management of our resources. The requirement to increase overall productivity in a resource-constrained environment has placed emphasis on *all* aspects of the system/product life cycle, and logistics has assumed a major role comparable to research, design, production, and system performance during operational use. The need to address total system life-cycle cost (in lieu of acquisition cost only) is evident, and experience has shown that logistic support is a major contributor to life-cycle cost. Further, experience has indicated that a great deal of the impact on the projected life-cycle cost for a given system or product stems from decisions made during the early stages of advance system planning and conceptual design. Decisions at this point have a major effect on activities and operations in all subsequent phases of the life cycle. Given the "cause and effect" relationships and the fact that logistics costs may assume major proportions, it is essential that logistic support be considered (as part of the decision-making process) in the early phases of system/product planning and design.

In essence, logistics, which includes the integration of many activities and elements, has become significant in each phase of the life cycle. Logistics requirements must be initially planned and subsequently integrated into the system/product design process. The ultimate objective is to develop, produce, and operate a system incorporating the necessary logistic support capability both effectively and efficiently.

The purpose of this book is to provide a new emphasis in logistics—the emphasis on logistics in the total system design and development process. The design of a system or product for supportability has a tremendous impact on what resources will later be required to support that system. Through the proper planning and emphasis on logistics early in the system life cycle, the necessary characteristics can be incorporated to ensure that the resultant product can be effectively and economically supported from the time that the product is initially introduced until retirement and phase-out occurs. Logistic support should be a major consideration in the establishment of system requirements, in the development of design criteria, and in the evaluation of alternatives leading to the selection of a firm design configuration. The object is to develop a system that will fulfill its mission at the lowest overall life-cycle cost.

This book provides an introduction to logistics engineering and management, and the material presented herein may be categorized in three basic areas. Chapters 1 and 2 focus on the language, definitions, principles, and some of the quantitative measures of logistics used in prediction and analysis. Coverage includes systems engineering, cost/system effectiveness, reliability and maintainability, and the application of statistical techniques in logistics. These chapters constitute an introduction to the subject matter. Chapters 3 through 10 apply the principles of logistics to the system/product life cycle commencing with the identification of a need and extending through system operational use and ultimate retirement. These chapters are presented in the order of progression one would expect in the development and use of a system (i.e., definition of operational requirements and maintenance concept, system functional analysis, detail design and development, test and evaluation, production or construction, and operational use). As the reader progresses through the text, he or she should be able to readily apply the principles of logistics to a real world situation. Finally, Chapter 11 presents a total management overview covering all phases of a program and integrating the functions discussed in the earlier chapters. Although management is inherent throughout the book, Chapter 11 emphasizes the major considerations involved.

This book is designed for use in the classroom (at either the undergraduate or graduate program levels) or by the practicing professional in industry, business, or government agency. The concepts and techniques presented are applicable to any type of system, and the functions discussed may be "tailored" to meet the needs of both large- and small-scale programs. Many practical problems are introduced, and numerous excellent references are included. In addition, the text material is arranged in such a manner as to guide the practicing engineer on a day-to-day basis in the performance of his or her job, and to serve as an authoritative source for those in management who must direct and control logistic support activities.

I wish to thank Dr. Wolter J. Fabrycky, Dean of the Research Division, Virginia Tech, for his encouragement in the preparation of this text, and Mr. Elmer L. Peterson (Teledyne Ryan Aeronautics) and Mr. William Rogers (Martin Marietta-Denver Division) for their review and comments associated with the text material.

BENJAMIN S. BLANCHARD

INTRODUCTION TO LOGISTICS

A "system" may be considered to be a nucleus of elements structured in such a manner as to accomplish a function to satisfy an identified need.[1] The elements of a system include all equipment, related facilities, material, software, data, services, and personnel required for its operation and support to the degree that it can be considered a self-sufficient entity in its intended operational environment, throughout its planned life cycle. Logistics relates to the support of a system and includes the elements of test and support equipment, supply support, personnel and training, transportation and material handling, special facilities, data, and so on, necessary for the accomplishment of material flow and distribution functions, as well as the sustaining life-cycle maintenance support of the system throughout its period of use.

In the development of systems, the past has been replete with instances where the prime equipment has been designed, with the logistic support requirements evolving after the design is established as being "fixed." On

---

[1] A system may vary in form, fit, and function. We may be discussing a worldwide communication network, a group of aircraft accomplishing a mission at a designated geographical location, or a small ship transporting cargo from one location to another. The system, oriented to a function, is discussed at various levels throughout this text. Also, refer to B.S. Blanchard, and W.J. Fabrycky, *Systems Engineering and Analysis*, Prentice-Hall, Inc., Englewood Cliffs, N.J., 1981, for definition and classification of systems.

1

numerous occasions, this practice has been costly—with the prime equipment lacking in design for supportability, and the various elements of logistic support not being compatible with the prime equipment or with each other. In addition, many of the necessary items of support have not been available on a timely basis; that is, items were delivered either too early or too late. In essence, improper attention to logistics has been predominant in the past, and the elements of the system have been fractionated and not well integrated in the development process.

With the advent of new technologies and the increasing complexities of systems today, combined with limited resources and reduced budgets, it is essential that all facets of a system be addressed on an integrated basis. If the results are to be effective, logistics must be considered on an integral basis with all other elements of the system. Logistic support must be initially planned and integrated into the overall system development process to assure an optimum balance between the prime equipment and its related support. This balance considers the performance characteristics of the system, the input resources required, the effectiveness of the system, and the ultimate life-cycle cost.

The area of logistics is experiencing rapid growth and has undergone considerable change in recent years. The objective of this chapter is to provide the reader with a basic understanding of the need for logistics, the scope of logistics, logistics in the system life cycle, and some of the terms most commonly used in the language of logistics.

1.1. Scope of Logistics

Historically, the concept of logistics stems from specific facets of military and industrial management. In the military sense, Webster defines logistics as

> The procurement, maintenance, and transportation of military material, facilities, and personnel.[2]

Further, a United States Air Force technical report defines logistics as

> The science of planning and carrying out the movement and maintenance of forces. In its most comprehensive sense, logistics pertains to those aspects of military operations which deal with (a) design and development, acquisition, storage, movement, distribution, maintenance, evacuation, and disposition of materiel; (b) movement, evacuation, and hospitalization of personnel; (c) acquisition or construction, maintenance, operation, and disposition of facilities; and (d) acquisition or furnishing of services.[3]

In essence, logistics from a military view has primarily been oriented to "system/product support" and has included the elements of maintenance planning, test and support equipment, supply support, transportation and handling, facilities, personnel and training, and technical data.[4]

In the industrial or commercial sector, logistics, often called "business logistics" or "industrial logistics," has been defined to include such activities as material flow, product distribution, transportation, purchasing and inventory control, warehousing, customer service, and the like. More specifically, Magee has offered the following definition:

> The art of managing the flow of materials and products from source to user. The logistic system includes the total flow of materials, from the acquisition of raw materials to the delivery of finished products to the ultimate users. . . .[5]

---

[2]*Webster's Seventh New Collegiate Dictionary*, G. & C. Merriam Company, Publishers, Springfield, Mass., 1963, P. 497.

[3]Gluck, F., ed., Technical Report No. 5, *A Compendum of Authenticated Logistics Terms and Definitions*, School of Systems and Logistics, U.S. Air Force Institute of Technology, WPAFB, Ohio, 1970.

[4]DOD Directive 4100.35, "Development of Integrated Logistics Support for Systems/ Equipment," Department of Defense, Washington, D.C., October 1970.

[5]Magee, J. F., *Industrial Logistics*, McGraw-Hill Book Company, New York, 1968.

Bowersox offers a comparable definition:

> The process of managing all activities required to strategically move raw materials, parts and finished inventory from vendors, between enterprise facilities, and to customers.[6]

The activities associated with business (or industrial) logistics have in the past been primarily oriented to production operations and the physical distribution of goods and services by the producer. On the other hand, emphasis of the military or defense environment has been placed on the sustaining life-cycle support of the system or product while in use by the consumer. In both situations, logistics has been considered as a "downstream" effort, and the overall requirements for logistics have not been very well defined or integrated.

More recently, logistics has been viewed on a much broader scale and the field of logistics has been growing at a rapid pace, stimulated primarily by the technological, sociological, and economic trends in our world today. Systems and products have become more complex as technology advances, and logistics requirements have increased in general. Not only have the costs associated with system/product acquisition increased significantly in the past decade, but the costs of logistic support have also been increasing at an alarming rate. At the same time, the current economic dilemma of decreasing budgets combined with upward inflationary trends result in less money available for the acquisition of new systems and/or for the maintenance and support of those items already in use.

In view of these trends, one of the greatest challenges facing industry, businesses, government agencies, and the general consumer of products and services today is the growing need for more effective and efficient management of our resources. The requirement to increase overall productivity in a resource-constrained environment has placed emphasis on *all* aspects of the system/product life cycle, and logistics has assumed a major role comparable to research, design, production, and system performance during operational use. The need to address total system *life-cycle cost* (in lieu of acquisition cost only) is evident, and experience has shown that logistic support is a major contributor to life-cycle cost—at least on the basis of those costs which are visible! Further, experience has indicated that a great deal of the impact on the projected life-cycle cost for a given system or product stems from decisions made during the early phases of advance system planning and conceptual design. Decisions at this point have a major impact

---

[6]Bowersox, D. J., *Logistics Management*, Macmillan Publishing Co., Inc., New York, 1974. Two additional references that cover the area of "business logistics" are (a) Ballou, R. H., *Business Logistics Management*, Prentice-Hall, Inc., Englewood Cliffs, N. J., 1973, and (b) Heskett, J. L., Glaskowsky, N. A., and Ivie, R. M., *Business Logistics*, 2nd ed., The Ronald Press, Company, New York, 1973.

on activities and operations in all subsequent phases of the life cycle. Given the "cause-and-effect" relationships and the fact that logistics costs may assume major proportions, it is essential that logistic support be considered (as a part of the decision-making process) at the early stages of system/product planning and design.

In essence, logistics, which includes the integration of many activities and elements, has become significant in each phase of the life cycle. Logistics requirements must be initially planned, and subsequently integrated into the system design process. The ultimate objective is to develop and produce a system incorporating the necessary logistic support capability in an effective and efficient manner.

Considering the current trends where the scope of logistics is expanding, the spectrum of activity included in business logistics and military logistics (as defined earlier) is less than desirable if one is to view logistics in terms of the total system life cycle. In other words, the field of logistics has become much broader than initially defined. In an attempt to respond to the dynamics of the situation, the Society Of Logistics Engineers (SOLE) has expanded the definition of logistics to

> The art and science of management, engineering, and technical activities concerned with requirements, design, and supplying and maintaining resources to support objectives, plans, and operations.[7]

This definition is *conceptual* in nature, and supports the life-cycle approach to logistics. It includes both business logistics considerations and military logistics considerations. In addition, it addresses the establishment of requirements in the early phases of the life cycle and the subsequent design activities that precede production operations, product distribution, and the various aspects of sustaining system support during consumer use.

In summary, the field of logistics has evolved from several different categories of activity into a wide range of functions spread throughout the system life cycle. Logistics is broader than what was included in "business logistics" or "military logistics" in the past. In essence, one must employ a life-cycle approach in dealing with logistics today.

1.2. Logistics in the System Life Cycle

Logistics in the context of the system life cycle involves planning, analysis and design, testing, production, distribution, and the sustaining support of a system (or product) throughout the consumer use period. Logis-

---

[7]This definition was established by the Society Of Logistics Engineers (SOLE), August 1974.

tics includes both the economic support of large systems being developed for consumer use in the field over a relatively long period of time and the support of various products from the standpoint of material flow and production operations. In other words, we are actually dealing with two different areas within the broad spectrum of logistics: the business logistics area of activity and the sustaining consumer support area, which is related to military logistics described earlier. These areas, although the emphasis is somewhat different in each instance, are an inherent part of the life cycle, must be addressed in each phase of the life cycle, must be dealt with on an integrated basis, and fall within the broad definition of logistics assumed herein.

The major facets of logistics as related to various program phases are highlighted in Table 1-1.

The intent of this text is to address all of the logistics-related activities identified in the table, and to provide emphasis on logistics in the engineering development process. This emphasis is illustrated in Figure 1-1, and the steps identified in the process are highlighted below.[8] A step-by-step analysis of the system development process depicted in Figure 1-1 is as follows:

1. Given a specific need, the system operational characteristics, mission profiles, deployment, utilization, effectiveness figures of merit, maintenance constraints, and environmental requirements are defined. Effectiveness figures of merit may include factors for cost effectiveness, availability, dependability, reliability, maintainability, and so on. Using this information, the system maintenance concept is defined. Operational requirements and the maintenance concept are the basic determinants of logistic support resources (Figure 1-1, blocks 1 and 2).

2. Major operational, test, production, and support functions are identified, and qualitative and quantitative requirements for the system are allocated as design criteria (or constraints) for significant indenture levels of the prime equipment as well as applicable elements of support (i.e., test and support equipment, facilities, etc.). Those requirements that include logistics factors also form boundaries for the design (Figure 1-1, blocks 3 and 4).

3. Within the boundaries established by the design criteria, alternative prime mission equipment and support configurations are evaluated through trade-off studies, and a preferred approach is selected. For each alternative, a preliminary logistic support analysis is accomplished to determine the anticipated required resources associated with that alternative. Through

---

[8]It should also be noted that much of the discussion throughout this text will be related to the life-cycle support of systems and products in use by the consumer. This area of logistics has not been covered in the literature to any great extent, whereas the area of business logistics has been covered rather extensively (refer to the bibliography in Appendix F).

Table 1-1. MAJOR LOGISTICS FUNCTIONS BY PROGRAM PHASE*

Program Phase	Major Program Functions
Identification of need (consumer)	"Want or desire" for systems or products due to deficiencies or problems made evident by consumer(s).
Advance planning and conceptual design	Market analysis, feasibility studies, mission requirements analysis, operational requirements, maintenance concept, quantitative and qualitative logistics effectiveness factors, design criteria, and logistics planning. (Identification and rank ordering of competing alternatives.)
Advance development and preliminary system design (validation)	Allocation of logistics requirements. System analysis, optimization, synthesis, trade-offs, and definition. Design support, predictions, and preliminary logistic support analysis. (Selection of "preferred" alternative.)
Detail design and development (full-scale development)	Detail system/product design (prime equipment, elements of logistic support, software, etc.). Design support analyses, predictions, and design review. Logistic support analysis. Provisioning and acquisition of logistic support elements for production operations and for consummer life-cycle support. System test and evaluation. Data collection, analysis, and feedback for corrective action (as required).
Production and/or construction	Production and/or construction of system. Material flow, procurement and inventory requirements, packaging, warehousing, physical distribution, transportation and traffic management, commucations, data processing, customer service, and logistics management (i.e., "business logistics activities") Provisioning and acquisition of logistic support elements for consumer and for system life-cycle support. Assessment of logistic support capability. Data collection, analysis, and feedback for corrective action (as required).
System use and life-cycle support (consumer)	System operation in the field. Sustaining maintenance and logistic support—supply support, test and support equipment, personnel and training, facilities, transportation and handling, data processing, customer service, and logistics management. Assessment of logistic support capability. Data collection, analysis, and feedback for corrective action (as required).
System retirement	System retirement, material phase-out and recycling and/or disposal, and logistic support requirements.

*The program phases indicated in Table 1-1 are considered typical, but many vary from program to program depending on the type of equipment and extent of design and development required. The purpose is to convey that logistics is significant in each program phase.

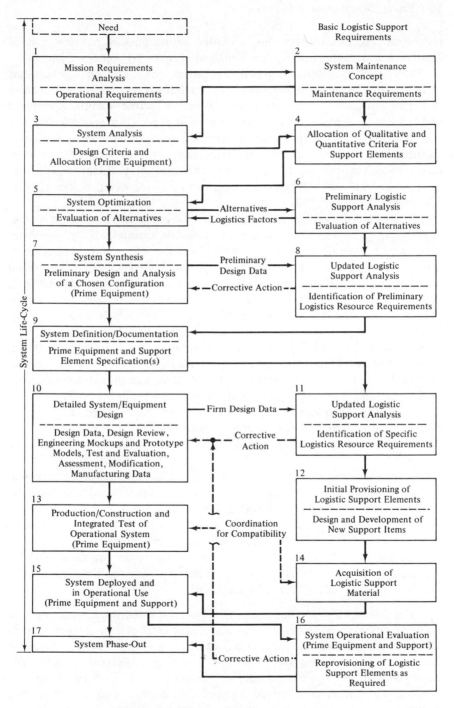

Figure 1-1. System development process.

numerous trade study iterations, a chosen prime mission equipment configuration and support policy are identified (Figure 1-1, blocks 5 and 6).

4. The chosen prime mission equipment configuration is evaluated through a logistic support analysis effort which leads to a gross identification of logistics resources. The system configuration (prime mission equipment and support elements) is reviewed in terms of its expected overall effectiveness and compliance with the initially specified qualitative and quantitative requirements (i.e., its capability to cost-effectively satisfy the statement of need). The ultimate output leads to the generation of a system specification (and lower-level specifications) forming the basis for detail design (Figure 1-1, blocks 7 through 9).

5. During the design process, direct assistance is provided to design engineering personnel in areas such as reliability, maintainability, supportability, and human factors. These tasks include the interpretation of criteria; accomplishment of special studies; participation in the selection of equipment and suppliers; accomplishment of predictions (reliability and maintainability); participation in progressive formal and informal design reviews; and participation in the test and evaluation of engineering models and prototype equipment. An in-depth logistic support analysis, based on released design data, results in the identification of specific support requirements in terms of tools, test and support equipment, spare/repair parts, personnel quantities and skills, training requirements, technical data, facilities, transportation, packaging, and handling requirements. The logistic support analysis at this stage provides (a) an assessment of the prime equipment design for supportability and potential cost/system effectiveness, and (b) a basis for the provisioning and acquisition of specific support items (Figure 1-1, blocks 10 through 12).

6. Prime mission equipment items are produced and/or constructed, tested, and deployed or phased into full-scale operational use. Logistic support elements are acquired, tested, and phased into operation on an as-needed basis. Throughout the operational life cycle of the system, logistics data are collected to provide (a) an assessment of system cost effectiveness and an early identification of operating or maintenance problems, and (b) a basis for the reprovisioning of support items at selected times during the life cycle (Figure 1-1, blocks 13 through 16).

Consideration of the basic steps in Figure 1-1 is essential in the development of any system. However, the extent and level of activity within each block is "tailored" to the specific requirement (e.g., type of system, extent of development, associated risks, mission and operational needs, etc.). The presentation in the figure represents a "thought process" covering the system engineering process and logistic support considerations as a part of that process.

1.3. The Language of Logistics

With the objective of further clarifying the field of logistics, it seems appropriate to direct attention toward its language. A few terms and definitions are discussed to provide the reader with the fundamentals necessary to better understand the material presented in this text. Additional terms are introduced throughout subsequent chapters.

A. SYSTEM ENGINEERING

The application of scientific and engineering efforts to (1) transform an operational need into a description of system performance parameters and a preferred system configuration through the use of an iterative process of functional analysis, synthesis, optimization, definition, design, test, and evaluation; (2) integrate related technical parameters and assure compatibility of all physical, functional, and program interfaces in a manner that optimizes the total system definition and design; and (3) integrate reliability, maintainability, logistic support, safety, producibility, security, survivability, structural integrity, human factors, and other related specialities into the total engineering effort.

The systems engineering process, in its evolving of functional detail and design requirements, has as its goal the achievement of the proper balance between operational, economic, and logistics factors. The process employs a sequential and iterative methodology to reach cost-effective solutions. The information developed through this process is used to plan and integrate the engineering effort for the system as a whole.

B. LOGISTIC SUPPORT

Logistic support is viewed as the composite of all considerations necessary to assure the effective and economical support of a system throughout its programmed life cycle. It is an integral part of all aspects of system planning, design and development, test and evaluation, production and/or construction, consumer use, and system retirement. The elements of support must be developed on an integrated basis with all other segments of the system. The major elements of logistic support are described below.

1. *Maintenance planning.* This includes all planning and analysis associated with the establishment of requirements for the overall support of a system throughout its life cycle. Maintenance planning constitutes a sustaining level of activity commencing with the development of the maintenance concept and continuing through the accomplishment of logistic support analyses during design and development, the procurement and acquisition of support items, and through the consumer use phase when an on-going system/product

capability is required to sustain operations. Maintenance planning is accomplished to integrate the various other facets of support.

2. *Supply support.* Supply support includes all spares (units, assemblies, modules, etc.), repair parts, consumables, special supplies, and related inventories needed to support prime mission-oriented equipment, software, test and support equipment, transportation and handling equipment, training equipment, and facilities. Supply support also covers provisioning documentation, procurement functions, warehousing, distribution of material, and the personnel associated with the acquisition and maintenance of spare/repair part inventories at all support locations. Considerations include each maintenance level and each geographical location where spare/repair parts are distributed and stocked; spares demand rates and inventory levels; the distances between stockage points; procurement lead times; and the methods of material distribution.

3. *Test and support equipment.* This category includes all tools, special condition monitoring equipment, diagnostic and checkout equipment, metrology and calibration equipment, maintenance stands, and servicing and handling equipment required to support scheduled and unscheduled maintenance actions associated with the system or product. Test and support equipment requirements at each level of maintenance must be addressed as well as the overall requirements for test traceability to a secondary or primary standard of some type. Test and support equipment may be classified as "peculiar" (newly designed and/or off-the-shelf items peculiar to the system under development) or "common" (existing items already in the inventory).

4. *Transportation and handling.* This element of logistics includes all special provisions, containers (reusable and disposable), and supplies necessary to support packaging, preservation, storage, handling, and/or transportation of prime mission equipment, test and support equipment, spares and repair parts, personnel, technical data, and mobile facilities. In essence, this category basically covers the initial distribution of products and the transportation of personnel and materials for maintenance purposes.

5. *Personnel and training.* Personnel required for the installation, checkout, operation, handling, and sustaining maintenance of the system (or product) and its associated test and support equipment are included in this category. Maintenance personnel required at each level of maintenance are considered. Personnel requirements are identified in terms of quantity and skill levels for each operation and maintenance function by level and geographical location.

Formal training includes both *initial* training for system/product familiarization and *replenishment* training to cover attrition and replacement personnel. Training is designed to upgrade assigned personnel to the skill levels defined for the system. Training data and equipment (e.g., simulators, mock-ups, special devices) are developed as required to support personnel training operations.

6. *Facilities.* This category refers to all special facilities needed for system operation and the performance of maintenance functions at each level. Physical plant, real estate, portable buildings, housing, intermediate maintenance shops, calibration laboratories, and special depot repair and overhaul facilities must be considered. Capital equipment and utilities (heat, power, energy requirements, environmental controls, communications, etc.) are generally included as part of facilities.

7. *Data.* System installation and checkout procedures, operating and maintenance instructions, inspection and calibration procedures, overhaul procedures, modification instructions, facilities information, drawings, and specifications that are necessary in the performance of system operation and maintenance functions are included herein. Such data not only cover the prime mission equipment but test and support equipment, transportation and handling equipment, training equipment, and facilities.

8. *Software.* This facet of support refers to all computer programs, condition monitoring and diagnostic tapes, and so on, necessary in the performance of system maintenance functions.

For large-scale systems, the logistic support requirements throughout the life cycle may be significant. The prime-mission-oriented segment of the system must be designed with support in mind, and the various elements of logistic support must be designed to be compatible with the prime mission equipment. Further, these different elements of logistic support interact with each other and the effects of these interactions must be reviewed and evaluated continually. A major decision or a change involving any one of these elements could significantly affect other elements and the system as a whole.

On the other hand, the logistics requirements for relatively small systems (or products) may entail only the functions of product distribution for the consumer and initial system installation and checkout, while the sustaining life-cycle maintenance support will be minimal. In this instance, the emphasis on logistic support (and the design for supportability) will not be as great as for large systems. The specific support requirements must be tailored accordingly.

C. Integrated Logistic Support (ILS)

ILS is basically a management function that provides the initial planning, funding, and controls which help to assure that the ultimate consumer (or user) will receive a system that will not only meet performance requirements, but one that can be expeditiously and economically supported throughout its programmed life cycle. A major ILS objective is to assure the integration of the various elements of support (i.e., test and support equipment, spare/repair parts, etc.).

D. Logistics Engineering

Logistics engineering includes those support-related engineering activities that deal primarily with system design and development. Such activities include the initial establishment of logistic support requirements (i.e., criteria and constraints), the development of the maintenance concept, the allocation of support requirements, logistic support analysis (LSA), the design for system supportability, the design and development of new elements of logistic support (e.g., test equipment, facilities, etc.), and the test and evaluation of the system support capability. In essence, logistics engineering covers (1) the design of the prime mission equipment for supportability, and (2) the design of the overall support capability for the system.

E. Logistic Support Analysis (LSA)

LSA is an iterative analytical process by which the logistic support necessary for a new system is identified. LSA constitutes the application of selected quantitative methods to (1) aid in the initial determination and establishment of logistics criteria as an input to system design, (2) aid in the evaluation of various design alternatives, (3) aid in the identification and provisioning of logistic support elements, and (4) aid in the final assessment of the system support capability during consumer use. LSA is a design analysis tool employed throughout the early phases of system development and often includes the maintenance analysis, life-cycle cost analysis, and logistics modeling. An output of LSA is the identification of and justification for logistic support resources: spare/repair part types and quantities, test and support equipment, personnel quantities and skill-level requirements, and so on.

F. Reliability (R)

Reliability can be defined simply as the probability that a system or product will perform in a satisfactory manner for a given period of time when used under specified operating conditions. This definition stresses the elements of *probability*, *satisfactory performance*, *time*, and *specified operating conditions*. These four elements are extremely important, since each plays a significant role in determining system/product reliability.

Probability, the first element in the reliability definition, is usually stated as a quantitative expression representing a fraction or a percent signifying the number of times that an event occurs (successes), divided by the total number of trials. For instance, a statement that the probability of survival (P_s) of an item for 80 hours is 0.75 (or 75%) indicates that we can expect that the item will function properly for at least 80 hours, 75 times out of 100 trials.

When there are a number of supposedly identical items operating under similar conditions, it can be expected that failures will occur at different points in time; thus, failures are described in probabilistic terms. In essence, the fundamental definition of reliability is heavily dependent on the concepts derived from probability theory.

Satisfactory performance, the second element in the reliability definition, indicates that specific criteria must be established which describe what is considered to be satisfactory system operation. A combination of qualitative and quantitative factors defining the functions that the system or product is to accomplish, usually presented in the context of a system specification, are required.

The third element, *time*, is one of the most important since it represents a measure against which the degree of system performance can be related. One must know the "time" parameter in order to assess the probability of completing a mission or a given function as scheduled. Of particular interest is being able to predict the probability of an item surviving (without failure) for a designated period of time. Also, reliability is frequently defined in terms of mean time between failure (MTBF), mean time to failure (MTTF) or mean time between maintenance (MTBM); thus, the aspect of time is critical in reliability measurement.

The *specified operating conditions* under which we expect a system or product to function constitute the fourth significant element of the basic reliability definition. These conditions include environmental factors such as the geographical location where the system is expected to operate, the operational profile, temperature cycles, humidity, vibration, shock, and so on. Such factors must not only address the conditions for the period when the system or product is operating, but the conditions for the periods when the system (or a portion thereof) is in a storage mode or being transported from one location to the next. Experience has indicated that the transportation, handling, and storage modes are sometimes more critical from a reliability standpoint than the conditions experienced during actual system operational use.

The four elements discussed above are critical in determining the reliability of a system or product. System reliability (or unreliability) is a key factor in the frequency of maintenance, and the maintenance frequency obviously has a significant impact on logistic support requirements. Reliability predictions and analyses are required as an input to the logistic support analysis.

Reliability is an inherent characteristic of design. As such, it is essential that reliability be adequately considered at program inception, and that reliability be addressed throughout the system life cycle. Figure 1-2 illustrates reliability (*R*) and maintainability (*M*) activities in the life cycle. These activities will be discussed further in subsequent chapters.

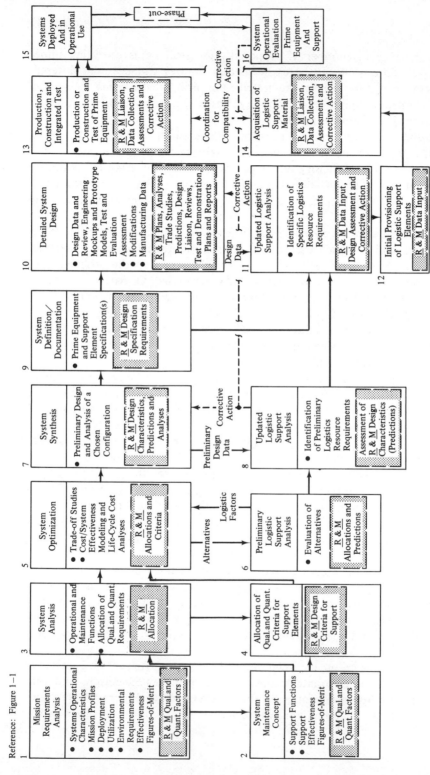

Figure 1-2. Reliability and maintainability interfaces.

G. MAINTAINABILITY (*M*)

Maintainability, like reliability, is an inherent characteristic of system or product design. It pertains to the ease, accuracy, safety, and economy in the performance of maintenance actions. A system should be designed such that it can be maintained without large investments of time, cost, or other resources (e.g., personnel, materials, facilities, test equipment) and without adversely affecting the mission of that system. Maintainability is the *ability* of an item to be maintained, whereas maintenance constitutes a series of actions to be taken to restore or retain an item in an effective operational state. Maintainability is a design parameter. Maintenance is a result of design.

Maintainability can also be defined as a characteristic in design that can be expressed in terms of maintenance frequency factors, maintenance times (i.e., elapsed times and labor-hours), and maintenance cost. These terms may be presented as different figures of merit; therefore, maintainability may be defined on the basis of a combination of factors, such as:

1. A characteristic of design and installation which is expressed as the probability that an item will be retained in or restored to a specified condition within a given period of time, when maintenance is performed in accordance with prescribed procedures and resources.[9]
2. A characteristic of design and installation which is expressed as the probability that maintenance will not be required more than *x* times in a given period, when the system is operated in accordance with prescribed procedures. This may be analogous to reliability when the latter deals with the overall frequency of maintenance.
3. A characteristic of design and installation which is expressed as the probability that the maintenance cost for a system will not exceed *y* dollars per designated period of time, when the system is operated and maintained in accordance with prescribed procedures.

Maintainability requires the consideration of many different factors involving all aspects of the system, and the measures of maintainability often include a combination of the following:

1. MTBM—mean time between maintenance, which includes both preventive (scheduled) and corrective (unscheduled) maintenance requirements. It includes consideration of reliability MTBF and MTBR. MTBM may also be considered as a reliability parameter.
2. MTBR—mean time between replacement of an item due to a maintenance action (usually generates a spare-part requirement).

---

[9] MIL-STD-721B, "Definitions of Effectiveness Terms for Reliability, Maintainability, Human Factors, and Safety," Department of Defense, Washington, D.C., August 1966.

3. $\bar{M}$—mean active maintenance time (a function of $\bar{M}ct$ and $\bar{M}pt$).
4. $\bar{M}ct$—mean corrective maintenance time. Equivalent to mean time to repair (MTTR).
5. $\bar{M}pt$—mean preventive maintenance time.
6. $\tilde{M}ct$—median active corrective maintenance time. Equivalent to equipment repair time (ERT).
7. $\tilde{M}pt$—median active preventive maintenance time.
8. $MTTR_g$—geometric mean time to repair.
9. M_{max}—maximum active corrective maintenance time (usually specified at the 90% and 95% confidence levels).
10. MDT—maintenance downtime (total time during which a system/ equipment is not in condition to perform its intended (function). MDT includes active maintenance time ($\bar{M}$), logistics delay time, and administrative delay time.
11. MMH/OH—maintenance manhours per equipment operating hour.
12. Cost/OH—maintenance cost per equipment operating hour.
13. Cost/MA—maintenance cost per maintenance action.
14. Turnaround Time (TAT)—that element of maintenance time needed to service, repair, and/or check out an item for recommitment. This constitutes the time that it takes an item to go through the complete cycle from operational installation through a maintenance shop and into the spares inventory ready for use.
15. Self-test thoroughness—the scope, depth, and accuracy of testing.
16. Fault isolation accuracy—accuracy of equipment diagnostic routines in percent.

Maintainability, as an inherent characteristic of design, must be properly considered in the early phases of system development, and maintainability activities are applicable throughout the life cycle. Figure 1-2 illustrates this point.

H. HUMAN FACTORS[10]

Human factors pertain to the human element of the system and the interface(s) between the human being, the machine, and associated software. The objective is to assure complete compatibility between the system physical and functional design features and the human element in the operation, maintenance, and support of the system. Considerations in design must be given to anthropometric factors (e.g., the physical dimensions of the human being), human sensory factors (e.g., vision and hearing capabilities), physiological factors (e.g., impacts from environmental forces), psychological factors (e.g., human needs, expectations, attitude, motivation), and their

---

[10]This area of activity may also be included under such general terms as "human engineering," "ergonomics," "engineering psychology," and "systems psychology."

interrelationships. Human factors (like reliability and maintainability) must be considered early in system development through the accomplishment of functional analysis, operator and maintenance task analysis, error analysis, safety analysis, and related design support activities. Operator and maintenance personnel requirements (i.e., personnel quantities and skill levels) and training program needs evolve from the task analysis effort. Maintenance personnel requirements are also identified in the logistic support analysis (LSA).

I. MAINTENANCE

Maintenance includes all actions necessary for retaining a system or product in, or restoring it to, a servicable condition. Maintenance may be categorized as corrective maintenance or preventive maintenance.

1. *Corrective maintenance*—includes all unscheduled maintenance actions performed, as a result of system/product failure, to restore the system to a specified condition. The corrective maintenance cycle includes failure localization and isolation, disassembly, item removal and replacement or repair, reassembly, and checkout and condition verification. Also, unscheduled maintenance may occur as a result of a "suspected" failure, even if further investigation indicates that no actual failure occurred.

2. *Preventive maintenance*—includes all scheduled maintenance actions performed to retain a system or product in a specified condition. Scheduled maintenance includes the accomplishment of periodic inspections, condition monitoring, critical item replacements, and calibration. In addition, servicing requirements (e.g., lubrication, fueling, etc.) may be included under the general category of scheduled maintenance.

J. MAINTENANCE LEVEL

Corrective and preventive maintenance may be accomplished on the system itself (or an element thereof) at the site where the system is used by the consumer, in an intermediate shop near the consumer, and/or at a depot or manufacturer's plant facility. Maintenance level pertains to the division of functions and tasks for each area where maintenance is performed. Task complexity, personnel-skill-level requirements, special facility needs, and so on, dictate to a great extent the specific functions to be accomplished at each level. In support of further discussion, maintenance may be classified as "organizational," "intermediate," and "depot."

K. MAINTENANCE CONCEPT

The maintenance concept (as defined in this text) constitutes a series of statements and/or illustrations defining criteria covering maintenance levels (i.e., two levels of maintenance, three levels of maintenance, etc.), major functions accomplished at each level of maintenance, basic support policies, effectiveness factors (e.g., MTBM, $\bar{M}$ct, MMH/OH, cost/MA, etc.), and primary logistic support requirements. The maintenance concept is defined at program inception and is a prerequisite to system/product design and development. The maintenance concept is also a required input to logistic support analysis (LSA).

L. MAINTENANCE PLAN

The maintenance plan (as compared to the maintenance concept) is a detailed plan specifying the methods, resources, and procedures to be followed for system support throughout the life cycle during the consumer use period. The maintenance plan is developed from logistic support analysis (LSA) data.

M. SYSTEM EFFECTIVENESS

System effectiveness is often expressed as one or more figures of merit representing the extent to which the system is able to perform the intended function. The figures of merit used may vary considerably depending on the type of system and its mission requirements, and should consider the following

1. *System performance parameters*, such as the capacity of a power plant, range or weight of an airplane, destructive capability of a weapon, quantity of letters processed through a postal system, amount of cargo delivered by a transportation system, and the accuracy of a radar capability.
2. *Availability*, or the measure of the degree a system is in the operable and committable state at the start of a mission when the mission is called for at an unknown random point in time. This is often called "operational readiness." Availability is a function of operating time (reliability) and downtime (maintainability/supportability).
3. *Dependability*, or the measure of the system operating condition at one or more points during the mission, given the system condition at the start of the mission (i.e., availability). Dependability is a function of operating time (reliability) and downtime (maintainability/ supportability).

A combination of the foregoing considerations (measures) represents the system effectiveness aspect of total cost effectiveness. By inspection, one can see that logistics impacts the various elements of system effectiveness to a significant degree, particularly in the areas of availability and dependability. System operation is highly dependent on support equipment (handling equipment), operating personnel, data, and facilities. Maintenance and system downtime are based on the availability of test and support equipment, spare/

repair parts, maintenance personnel, data, and facilities. The effect of the type and quantity of logistic support is measured through the parameters of system effectiveness.

N. LIFE-CYCLE COST (LCC)[11]

LCC involves all costs associated with the system life cycle, to include:

1. *Research and development (R&D) cost*—the cost of feasibility studies; system analyses; detail design and development, fabrication, assembly, and test of engineering models; initial system test and evaluation; and associated documentation.
2. *Production and construction cost*—the cost of fabrication, assembly, and test of operational systems (production models); operation and maintenance of the production capability; and associated *initial* logistic support requirements (e.g., test and support equipment development, spare/repair parts provisioning, technical data development, training, entry of items into the inventory, facility construction, etc.).
3. *Operation and maintenance cost*—the cost of sustaining operation, personnel and maintenance support, spare/repair parts and related inventories, test and support equipment maintenance, transportation and handling, facilities, modifications and technical data changes, and so on.
4. *System retirement and phase-out cost*—the cost of phasing the system out of the inventory due to obsolescence or wearout, and subsequent equipment item recycling and reclamation as appropriate.

Life-cycle costs may be categorized many different ways, depending on the type of system and the sensitivities desired in cost-effectiveness measurement.

O. COST EFFECTIVENESS (CE)

The development of a system or product that is cost effective, within the constraints specified by operational and maintenance requirements, is a prime objective. Cost effectiveness relates to the measure of a system in terms of mission fulfillment (system effectiveness) and total life-cycle cost. Cost effectiveness, which is similar to the standard cost–benefit analysis factor employed for decision-making purposes in many industrial and business applications, can be expressed in various terms (i.e., one or more figures of merit), depending on the specific mission or system parameters that one wishes to measure. The prime ingredients of cost effectiveness are illustrated in Figure 1-3.

---

[11]Refer to Blanchard, B. S., *Design and Manage to Life Cycle Coast*, M/A Press, International Scholarly Book Services, Inc., Forest Grove, Oreg., 1978.

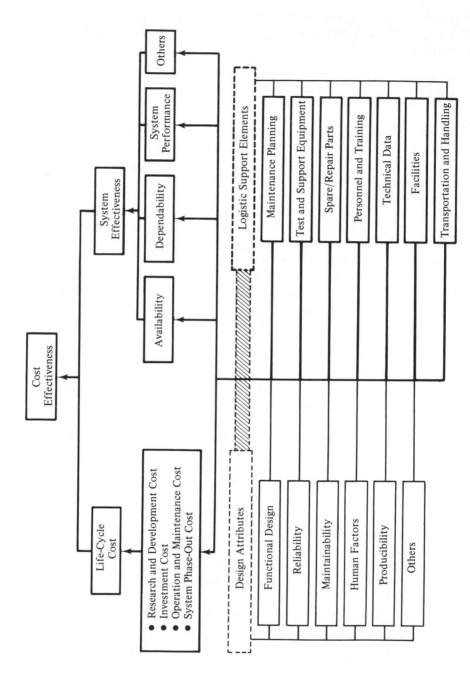

Figure 1-3. The basic ingredients of cost effectiveness.

Although there are different ways of presenting cost effectiveness, this illustration is used for the purposes of showing the many influencing factors and their relationships. Further discussion of cost effectiveness is presented in Chapters 2 and 6.

QUESTIONS AND PROBLEMS

1. How would you define "logistics"? How is "business logistics" related to "military logistics"? Identify some of the functions in each approach that are comparable. Define ILS.

2. Select a system of your choice and develop a flow diagram showing the evolutionary steps of design, development, test and evaluation, production and/or construction, operational use, and phase-out. Identify logistic support functions.

3. Why is logistics important in the system design and development process?

4. What is the relationship (impact of one on another) between reliability and maintainability? Maintainability and human factors? Reliability and logistic support? Maintainability and logistic support? Human factors and logistic support?

5. What is the relationship (impact of one on another) between the following: Test/support equipment and facilities? Test/support equipment and spare/repair parts? Personnel/training and technical data? Facilities and personnel? Personnel-skill-level quantity requirements and training?

6. What is the relationship between system engineering and logistic support?

7. What is the difference between maintainability and maintenance?

8. What information is included in the maintenance concept? Maintenance plan?

9. Describe the logistic support analysis (its content and purpose). How does it relate to the maintenance concept and to the maintenance plan?

10. How do the elements of logistic support influence system effectiveness? How do these elements affect cost effectiveness?

11. What is the significant difference between MTBM and MTBF? MTBM and MTBR? MTBR and MTBF?

12. Define what is meant by "life-cycle cost." How may life-cycle costs be categorized?

13. How may life-cycle costing be employed in the decision-making process throughout system design and development?

MEASURES OF LOGISTICS

Logistics is viewed as the composite of all considerations necessary to assure the *effective* and *economical* support of a system throughout its programmed life cycle. It is an integral part of all aspects of system planning, design and development, test and evaluation, production and/or construction, consumer use, and system retirement. The elements of logistics must be developed on an integrated basis with all other segments of the system.

To ensure that logistics is properly addressed throughout the system life cycle, one must establish the appropriate logistic support requirements in the early stages of advance planning and as part of conceptual design. Logistics requirements must be initially specified, both in quantitative and qualitative terms. As system development progresses, the configuration defined must be evaluated against the specified requirements, and modification(s) for improvement must be incorporated as needed to ensure effective results. This evaluation task, which is an iterative process, is accomplished through a combination of predictions, analyses, and physical demonstrations.

Intuitive in the process of requirements definition, specification, and system evaluation is the aspect of identifying the appropriate quantitative measures of logistics for a given system configuration. Those measures may, of course, vary from system to system, as the consumer need and mission requirements will vary from one application to the next. Further, there may be multiple factors for any given situation. Thus, it is impossible to cover

2

all conditions and certainly not feasible within the confines of this text. Nevertheless, the quantitative measures of logistics must be addressed.

The intent of this chapter is to introduce some of the more commonly employed quantitative factors applicable in the development and evaluation of a logistic support capability for a system. Of particular significance are reliability and maintainability factors, supply support factors, test and support equipment factors, organizational factors, facility and transportation factors, economic factors, and effectiveness factors. Knowledge of the material presented in the various sections of this chapter is essential if one is to plan for, design, produce, and implement a logistic support capability in an effective and efficient manner. Since much of the material included herein is presented in terms of an "overview," the review of additional text material as listed in Appendix F is recommended for more detailed coverage.

2.1. Reliability Factors

In determining system support requirements, the frequency of maintenance becomes a significant parameter. The frequency of maintenance for a given item is highly dependent on the reliability of that item. In general, as the reliability of a system increases, the frequency of maintenance will decrease, while unreliable systems will usually require extensive maintenance. In any event, maintenance and logistic support requirements are highly influenced by reliability factors. Thus, a basic understanding of reliability terms and concepts is required. Some of the key reliability quantitative factors used in the system design process and for the determination of logistic support requirements are briefly defined herein.

A. THE RELIABILITY FUNCTION

Reliability can be defined simply as the probability that a system or product will perform in a satisfactory manner for a given period of time when used under specified operating conditions. The reliability function, $R(t)$, may be expressed as

$$R(t) = 1 - F(t) \tag{2.1}$$

where $F(t)$ is the probability that the system will fail by time t. $F(t)$ is basically the failure distribution function, or the "unreliability" function. If the random variable t has a density function of $f(t)$, then the expression for reliability is

$$R(t) = 1 - F(t) = \int_t^\infty f(t)\, dt \tag{2.2}$$

Assuming that the time to failure is described by an exponential density function, then

$$f(t) = \frac{1}{\theta} e^{-t/\theta} \tag{2.3}$$

where θ is the mean life, t is the time period of interest, and e is the natural logarithm base (2.7183). The reliability at time t is

$$R(t) = \int_t^\infty \frac{1}{\theta} e^{-t/\theta}\, dt = e^{-t/\theta} \tag{2.4}$$

Mean life (θ) is the arithmetic average of the lifetimes of all items considered. The mean life (θ) for the exponential function is equivalent to mean time between failure (MTBF). Thus,

$$R(t) = e^{-t/M} = e^{-\lambda t} \tag{2.5}$$

where λ is the instantaneous failure rate and M is the MTBF. If an item has a constant failure rate, the reliability of that item at its mean life is approximately 0.37. In other words, there is a 37% probability that a system will survive its mean life without failure. Mean life and failure rates are related in Equation (2.6).

$$\lambda = \frac{1}{\theta} \tag{2.6}$$

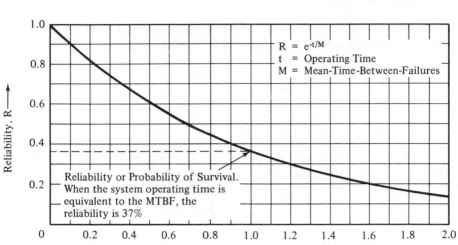

Figure 2-1. Basic reliability curve.

Figure 2-1 illustrates the exponential reliability function where time is given in units of t/M.

The illustration presented here primarily focuses on the reliability function in terms of the exponential distribution, which is commonly used in many applications. Actually, the failure characteristics of different items are not necessarily the same. There are a number of well-known probability density functions which in practice have been found to describe the failure characteristics of different equipments. These include the binomial, exponential, normal (or Gaussian), Poisson, gamma, and Weibull distributions. Thus, one should take care not to assume that the exponential distribution is applicable in all instances, or the Weibull distribution is the best, and so on.[1]

B. THE FAILURE RATE

The rate at which failures occur in a specified time interval is called the failure rate during that interval. The failure rate (λ) is expressed as

$$\lambda = \frac{\text{number of failures}}{\text{total operating hours}} \tag{2.7}$$

The failure rate may be expressed in terms of failures per hour, percent failures per 1,000 hours, or failures per million hours. As an example, suppose

---

[1]Two excellent references covering the application of reliability distributions are (a) Kapur, K. C. and Lamberson, L. R., *Reliability in Engineering Design*, John Wiley & Sons, Inc., New York, 1977; and (b) Calabro, S. R., *Reliability Principles and Practices*, McGraw-Hill Book Company, New York, 1962.

that 10 components were tested under specified operating conditions. The components (which are not repairable) failed as follows:

—Component 1 failed after   75 hours.
—Component 2 failed after 125 hours.
—Component 3 failed after 130 hours.
—Component 4 failed after 325 hours.
—Component 5 failed after 525 hours.

There were five failures and the total operating time was 3,805 hours. Using Equation (2.7), the calculated failure rate per hour is

$$\lambda = \frac{5}{3,805} = 0.001314$$

As a second example, suppose that the operating cycle for a given system is 169 hours, as illustrated in Figure 2-2. During that time six failures occur at the points indicated. A failure is defined as an instance when the system is not operating within a specified set of parameters. The failure rate, or corrective maintenance frequency, per hour is

$$\lambda = \frac{\text{number of failures}}{\text{total mission time}} = \frac{6}{142} = 0.0422535$$

Assuming an exponential distribution, the system mean life or the mean time between failure (MTBF) is

$$\text{MTBF} = \frac{1}{\lambda} = \frac{1}{0.0422535} = 23.6667 \text{ hours}$$

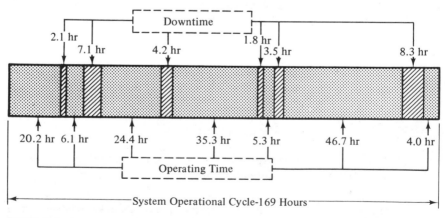

Maintenance Actions

Figure 2-2. Operational cycle.

Figure 2-3 presents a reliability nomograph (for the exponential failure distribution) which facilitates calculations of MTBF, λ, $R(t)$, and operating time. For example, if the MTBF is 200 hours ($\lambda = 0.005$), and the operating time is 2 hours, the nomograph gives a reliability value of 0.99.

When determining the overall failure rate, particularly with regard to estimating corrective maintenance actions (i.e., the frequency of corrective maintenance), one must address all system failures to include failures due to primary defects, failures due to manufacturing defects, failures due to operator and maintenance errors, and so on. The overall failure rate should cover all factors that will cause the system to be inoperative at a time when satisfactory system operation is required. A combined failure rate is presented in Table 2-1.

Table 2-1. COMBINED FAILURE RATE

Consideration	Assumed Factor (*instances/hour*)
(a) Inherent reliability failure rate	0.000392
(b) Manufacturing defects	0.000002
(c) Wearout rate	0.000000
(d) Dependent failure rate	0.000072
(e) Operator-induced failure rate	0.000003
(f) Maintenance-induced failure rate	0.000012
(g) Equipment damage rate	0.000005
Total combined factor	0.000486

When assuming the negative exponential distribution (Poisson), the failure rate is considered to be relatively constant during normal system operation if the system design is mature. That is, when equipment is produced and the system is initially distributed for operational use, there are usually a higher number of failures due to component variations and mismatches, manufacturing processes, and so on. The initial failure rate is higher than anticipated, but gradually decreases and levels off during the "debugging" or "burn-in" period, as illustrated in Figure 2-4. Likewise, when the system reaches a certain age, there is a "wear-out" period where the failure rate increases. The relatively level portion of the curve in Figure 2-4 is the constant failure rate where the exponential failure law applies.

Figure 2-4 illustrates certain "relative" relationships. Actually, the curve may vary considerably depending on the type of system and its operational profile. Further, if the system is continually being modified for one reason or another, the failure rate may not be constant. In any event, the illustration does provide a good basis for considering failure-rate trends on a relative basis.

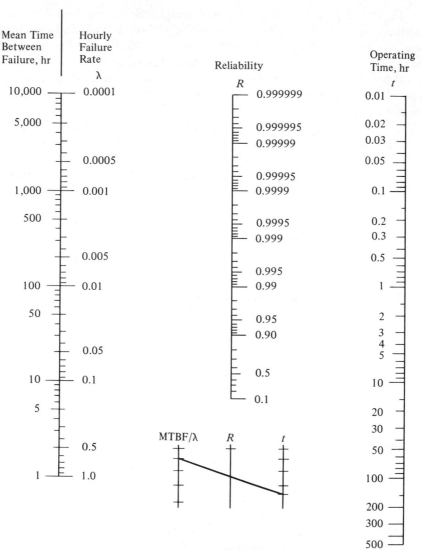

Given Equipment Mean Time to Failure or Hourly
Failure Rate and Operating Time, Solve for
Reliability. Connect "MTBF" and *t* values With
Straight Line. Read *R*.

Figure 2-3. Reliability nomograph for the exponential failure distribution. (NAVAIR 00-65-502/NAVORD OD 41146, *Reliability
Engineering Handbook*, U.S. Navy, Revised March 1968, Washington, D.C.)

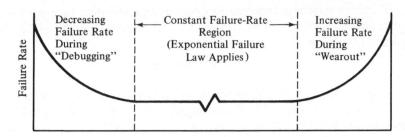

Figure 2-4. Typical failure-rate curve.

C. RELIABILITY COMPONENT RELATIONSHIPS[2]

Given the basic reliability function and the measures associated with failure rate, it is appropriate to consider their application in series networks, parallel networks, and combinations thereof. These networks are used in reliability block diagrams and in static models employed for reliability prediction and analysis. Reliability prediction is a necessary input for logistic support analyses.

1. Series networks. The series relationship is probably the most commonly used and is the simplest to analyze. It is illustrated in Figure 2-5. In a series network, all components must operate in a satisfactory manner if the system is to function properly. Assuming that a system includes Subsystem *A*, Subsystem *B*, and Subsystem *C*, the reliability of the system is the product of the reliabilities for the individual subsystems and may be expressed as

$$\text{reliability } (R) = (R_A)(R_B)(R_C) \tag{2.8}$$

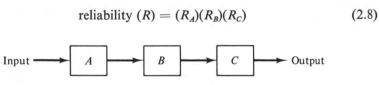

Figure 2-5. A series network.

As an example, suppose that an electronic system includes a transmitter, a receiver, and a power supply. The transmitter reliability is 0.8521, the receiver reliability is 0.9712, and the power supply reliability is 0.9357. The overall reliability for the electronic system is

$$R_s = (0.8521)(0.9712)(0.9357) = 0.7743$$

---

[2]Much of the information on reliability component networks is taken from Blanchard, B. S. and Fabrycky, W. J., *Systems Engineering and Analysis*, Prentice-Hall, Inc., Englewood Cliffs, N.J., 1981.

If a series system is expected to operate for a specified time period, its required overall reliability can be derived. Substituting Equation (2.5) into Equation (2.8) gives

$$R_s = e^{-(\lambda_1 + \lambda_2 + \lambda_3 + \cdots + \lambda_n)t}$$
(2.9)

Suppose that a series system consists of four subsystems and is expected to operate for 1,000 hours. The four subsystems have the following MTBF's: Subsystem A, MTBF $= 6,000$ hours; Subsystem B, MTBF $= 4,500$ hours; Subsystem C, MTBF $= 10,500$ hours; Subsystem D, MTBF $= 3,200$ hours. The objective is to determine the overall reliability of the series network where

$$\lambda_A = \frac{1}{6,000} = 0.000167 \text{ failure per hour}$$

$$\lambda_B = \frac{1}{4,500} = 0.000222 \text{ failure per hour}$$

$$\lambda_C = \frac{1}{10,500} = 0.000095 \text{ failure per hour}$$

$$\lambda_D = \frac{1}{3,200} = 0.000313 \text{ failure per hour}$$

The overall reliability of the series network is found from Equation (2.9) as

$$R = e^{-(0.000797)(1,000)} = 0.4507$$

This means that the probability of the system surviving (reliability) for 1,000 hours is 45.1%. If the requirement were reduced to 500 hours, the reliability would increase to about 67%.

2. Parallel networks.   A pure parallel network is one where a number of the same components are in parallel and where all the components must fail in order to cause total system failure. A parallel network with two components is illustrated in Figure 2-6. The system will function if either A or B, or both, are working, and the reliability is expressed as

$$\text{reliability } (R) = R_A + R_B - (R_A)(R_B)$$
(2.10)

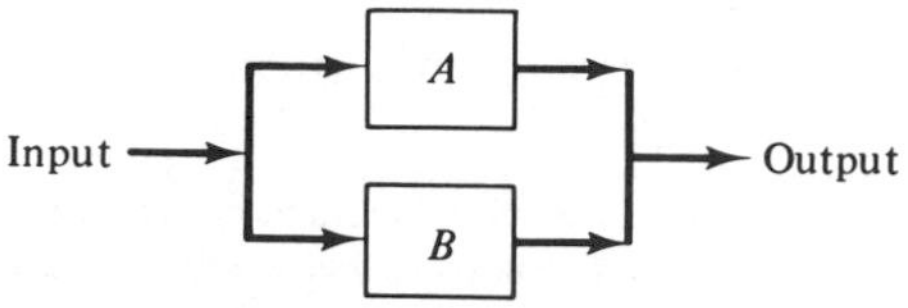

Figure 2-6. A parallel network.

Consider next a network with three components in parallel as shown in Figure 2-7. The network reliability is expressed as

$$\text{reliability } (R) = 1 - (1 - R_A)(1 - R_B)(1 - R_C) \qquad (2.11)$$

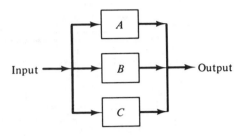

Figure 2-7. Parallel network with three components.

If components A, B, and C are identical, then the reliability expression for a system with three parallel components can be simplified to

$$\text{reliability } (R) = 1 - (1 - R)^3$$

For a system with n identical components, the reliability is

$$\text{reliability } (R) = 1 - (1 - R)^n \qquad (2.12)$$

Parallel redundant networks are used primarily to improve system reliability as Equations (2.11) and (2.12) indicate mathematically. For instance, assume that a system includes two identical subsystems in parallel and that the reliability of each subsystem is 0.95. The reliability of the system is found from Equation (2.10) as

$$\text{reliability } (R) = 0.95 + 0.95 - (0.95)(0.95) = 0.9975$$

Suppose that the reliability of the system above needs improvement beyond 0.9975. By adding a third identical subsystem in parallel, the system reliability is found from Equation (2.12) to be

$$\text{reliability } (R) = 1 - (1 - 0.95)^3 = 0.999875$$

Note that this is a reliability improvement of 0.002375 over the previous configuration, or that the *un*reliability of the system was improved from 0.0025 to 0.000125.

If the subsystems are not identical, Equation (2.10) can be used. For example, a parallel redundant network with two subsystems with $R_A = 0.75$ and $R_B = 0.82$ gives a system reliability of

$$\text{reliability } (R) = 0.75 + 0.82 - (0.75)(0.82) = 0.955$$

3. Combined series–parallel networks. Various levels of reliability can be achieved through the application of a combination of series and parallel networks. Consider the three examples illustrated in Figure 2-8.

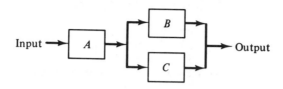

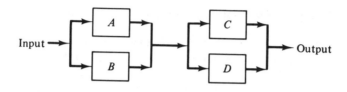

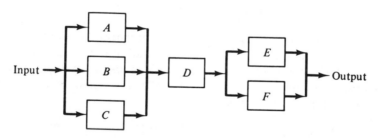

Figure 2-8. Some combined series-parallel networks.

The reliability of the first network in Figure 2-8 is given by the equation

$$\text{reliability } (R) = R_A(R_B + R_C - R_BR_C) \tag{2.13}$$

For the second network, the reliability is given by the equation

$$\text{reliability } (R) = [1 - (1 - R_A)(1 - R_B)][1 - (1 - R_C)(1 - R_D)] \tag{2.14}$$

And for the third network the reliability is given by the equation

$$\text{reliability } (R) = [1 - (1 - R_A)(1 - R_B)(1 - R_C)][R_D]$$
$$[R_E + R_F - (R_E)(R_F)] \tag{2.15}$$

Combined series–parallel networks such as those in Figure 2-8 require that the analyst first evaluate the redundant (parallel) elements to obtain series or unit reliability. Overall system reliability is then determined by finding the product of all series reliabilities.

2.2. Maintainability Factors

Maintainability is an inherent design characteristic dealing with the ease, accuracy, safety, and economy in the performance of maintenance functions. Maintainability, defined in the broadest sense, can be measured in terms of a combination of elapsed times, personnel labor-hour rates, maintenance frequencies, maintenance cost, and related logistic support factors. The measures most commonly used are described in this section.

A. MAINTENANCE ELAPSED-TIME FACTORS

Maintenance can be classified in two categories:

1. *Corrective maintenance*—the unscheduled actions accomplished, as a result of failure, to *restore* a system to a specified level of performance.
2. *Preventive maintenance*—the scheduled actions accomplished to *retain* a system at a specified level of performance by providing systematic inspection, detection, servicing, condition monitoring, and/or replacement to prevent impending failures.

Maintenance constitutes the act of diagnosing and repairing, or preventing, system failures. Maintenance time is made up of the individual task times associated with the required corrective and preventive maintenance actions for a given system or product. Maintainability is a measure of the ease and rapidity with which a system can be maintained, and is measured in terms of the time required to perform maintenance tasks. A few of the more commonly used maintainability time measures are defined below.

1. Mean corrective maintenance time ($\bar{M}ct$). Each time that a system fails, a series of steps is required to repair or restore the system to its full operational status. These steps include failure detection, fault isolation, disassembly to gain access to the faulty item, repair, and so on, as illustrated in Figure 2-9. Completion of these steps for a given failure constitutes a corrective maintenance cycle.

Throughout the system use phase, there will usually be a number of individual maintenance actions involving the series of steps illustrated in Figure 2-9. The mean corrective maintenance time ($\bar{M}ct$), or the mean time to

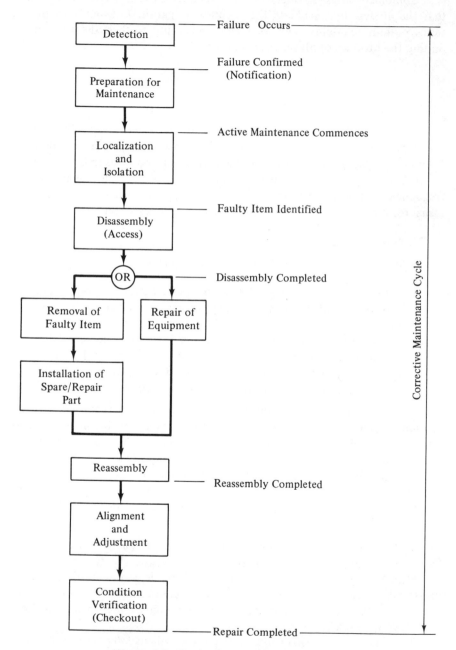

Figure 2-9. Corrective maintenance cycle.

repair (MTTR), which is equivalent, is a composite value representing the arithmetic average of these individual maintenance cycle times.

For the purposes of illustration, Table 2-2 includes data covering a sample of 50 corrective maintenance repair actions on a typical equipment item. Each of the times indicated represents the completion of one corrective maintenance cycle illustrated in Figure 2-9.

Table 2-2. CORRECTIVE MAINTENANCE TIMES (Minutes)

40	58	43	45	63	83	75	66	93	92
71	52	55	64	37	62	72	97	76	75
75	64	48	39	69	71	46	59	68	64
67	41	54	30	53	48	83	33	50	63
86	74	51	72	87	37	57	59	65	63

Based on the set of raw data presented, which constitutes a random sample, a frequency distribution table and frequency histogram may be prepared as illustrated in Table 2-3 and Figure 2-10, respectively.

Table 2-3. FREQUENCY DISTRIBUTION

Class Interval	Frequency	Comulative Frequency
29.5–39.5	5	5
39.5–49.5	7	12
49.5–59.5	10	22
59.5–69.5	12	34
69.5–79.5	9	43
79.5–89.5	4	47
89.5–99.5	3	50

Referring to Table 2-2, the range of observations is between 97 minutes and 30 minutes, or a total of 67 minutes. This range can be divided into class intervals, with a class interval width of 10 assumed for convenience. A logical starting point is to select class intervals of 20–29, 30–39, and so on. In such instances, it is necessary to establish the dividing point between two adjacent intervals, such as 29.5, 39.5, and so on.

Given the frequency distribution of repair times, one can plot a histogram showing time values in minutes and the frequency of occurrence as in Figure 2-10. By determining the midpoint of each class interval, a frequency polygon

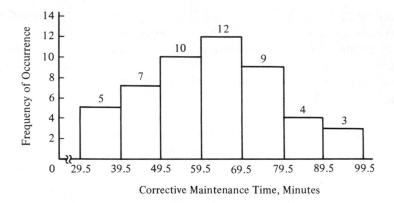

Figure 2-10. Histogram of maintenance actions.

can be developed as illustrated in Figure 2-11. This provides an indication of the form of the probability distribution applicable to repair times for this particular system.

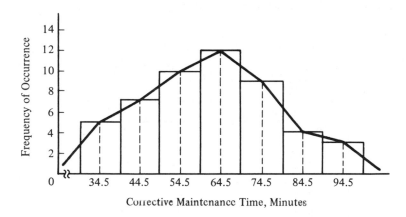

Figure 2-11. Frequency polygon.

The probability distribution function for repair times can usually be expected to take one or two common forms:

a. The *normal* distribution, which generally applies to relatively straight-forward maintenance tasks and repair actions, such as simple remove and replace tasks, which consistently require a fixed amount of time to accomplish with very little variation.
b. The *log-normal* distribution, which applies to most maintenance tasks and repair actions where the task times and frequencies vary. Exper-

ience has indicated that in the majority of instances the distribution of maintenance time for complex systems and equipment is log normal.

As additional corrective maintenance actions occur and data points are plotted for the system in question, the curve illustrated in Figure 2-11 may take the shape of the normal distribution. The curve is defined by the arithmetic mean ($\bar{X}$ or $\bar{M}ct$) and the standard deviation (σ). From the maintenance repair times presented in Table 2-2, the arithmetic mean is determined as follows:

$$\bar{M}ct = \frac{\sum_{i=1}^{n} Mct_i}{n} = \frac{3{,}095}{50} = 61.9 \quad (\text{assume } 62) \qquad (2.16)$$

where Mct_i is the total active corrective maintenance cycle time for each maintenance action, and n is the sample size. Thus, the average value for the sample of 50 maintenance actions is 62 minutes.

The standard deviation (σ) measures the dispersion of maintenance time values. When a standard deviation is calculated, it is convenient to generate a table giving the deviation of each task time from the mean of 62. Table 2-4 illustrates this for only four individual task times, although all 50 tasks should be treated. The total value of 13,013 docs cover all 50 tasks.

Table 2-4. VARIANCE DATA

Mct_i	$Mct_i - \bar{M}ct$	$(Mct_i - \bar{M}ct)^2$
40	-22	484
71	$+ 9$	81
75	$+13$	169
67	$+ 5$	25
etc.	etc.	etc.
Total		13,013

The standard deviation (σ) of the sample normal distribution curve can now be determined as follows:

$$\sigma = \sqrt{\frac{\sum_{i=1}^{n} (Mct_i - \bar{M}ct)^2}{n - 1}} = \sqrt{\frac{13{,}013}{49}} = 16.3 \text{ minutes} \quad (\text{assume } 16) \qquad (2.17)$$

Assuming normal distribution, the characteristics displayed in Figure 2-12 will hold true. It can be stated that approximately 68% of the total

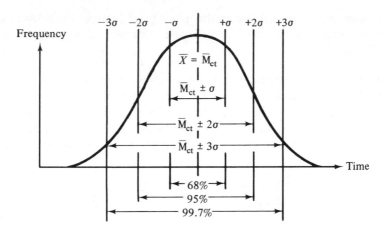

Figure 2-12. Normal distribution.

population sample falls within the range 46 to 78 minutes. Also, it can be assumed that 99.7% of the sample population lies within the range of $\bar{M}ct \pm 3\sigma$, or 14 to 110 minutes.

As an example of a typical application, one may wish to determine the percent of total population of repair times that lies between 40 and 50 minutes. Graphically, this is represented in Figure 2-13.

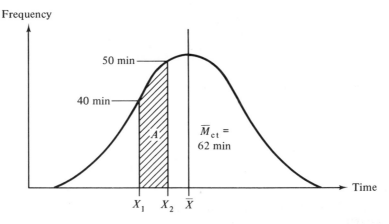

Figure 2-13. Normal distribution sample.

The problem is to find the percent represented by the shaded area. This can be calculated as follows:

a. Convert maintenance times of 40 and 50 minutes into standard values (Z), or the number of standard deviations above and below the mean of 62 minutes:

$$Z \text{ for 40 minutes} = \frac{X_1 - \bar{X}}{\sigma} = \frac{40 - 62}{16} = -1.37 \quad (2.18)$$

$$Z \text{ for 50 minutes} = \frac{X_2 - \bar{X}}{\sigma} = \frac{50 - 62}{16} = -0.75 \quad (2.19)$$

The maintenance times of 40 and 50 minutes represent 1.37 and 0.75 standard deviations below the mean since the values are negative.

b. Point X_1 $(Z = -1.37)$ represents an area of 0.0853 and point X_2 $(Z = -0.75)$ represents an area of 0.2266, as given in Appendix E, Table E-1.

c. The shaded area A in Figure 2-13 represents the difference in area, or area $X_2 - X_1 = 0.2266 - 0.0853 = 0.1413$. Thus, 14.13% of the population of maintenance times are estimated to lie between 40 and 50 minutes.

Next, confidence limits should be determined. Since the 50 maintenance tasks represent only a sample of all maintenance actions on the equipment being evaluated, it is possible that another sample of 50 maintenance actions on the same equipment could have a mean value either greater or less than 62 minutes. The original 50 tasks were selected at random, however, and statistically represent the entire population. Using the standard deviation, an upper and lower limit can be placed on the mean value ($\bar{M}$ct) of the population. For instance, if one is willing to accept a chance of being wrong 15% of the time (85% confidence limit), then

$$\text{upper limit} = \bar{M}\text{ct} + Z\left(\frac{\sigma}{\sqrt{N}}\right) \quad (2.20)$$

where $\sigma/\sqrt{N}$ represents the standard error factor.

The Z value is obtained from Appendix E, Table E-1, where 0.1492 is close to 15% and reflects a Z of 1.04. Thus,

$$\text{upper limit} = 62 + (1.04)\left(\frac{16}{\sqrt{50}}\right) = 64.35 \text{ minutes}$$

This means that the upper limit is 64.4 minutes at a confidence level of 85%, or that there is an 85% chance that $\bar{M}$ct will be less than 64.4. Variations in risk and upper limits are shown in Table 2-5. If a specified $\bar{M}$ct limit is established for the design of an equipment (based on mission and operational requirements) and it is known (or assumed) that maintenance times are normally distributed, then one would have to compare the results of predictions and/or measurements (e.g., 64.35 minutes) accomplished during the

Table 2-5. RISK/UPPER LIMIT VARIATIONS

Risk	Confidence	Z	Upper Limit
5%	95%	1.65	65.72 minutes
10%	90%	1.28	64.89 minutes
15%	85%	1.04	64.35 minutes
20%	80%	0.84	63.89 minutes

development process with the specified value to determine the degree of compliance.

As indicated earlier, the maintenance task times for many systems and equipments do not fit within the normal curve. There may be a few representative maintenance actions where repair times are extensive, causing a skew to the right. This is particularly true for electronic equipment items, where the distribution of repair times often follows a log-normal curve, as shown in Figure 2-14. Derivation of the specific distribution curve for a set of maintenance task times is accomplished using the same procedure as given in the preceding paragraphs. A frequency table is generated and a histogram is plotted.

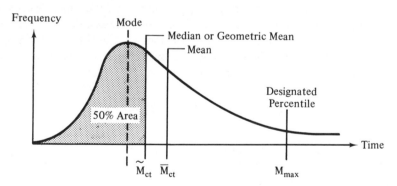

Figure 2-14. Log-normal distribution.

A sample of 24 corrective maintenance repair actions for a typical electronic equipment item is presented in Table 2-6. Using the data in the

Table 2-6. CORRECTIVE MAINTENANCE REPAIR TIMES (Minutes)

55	28	125	47	58	53	36	88
51	110	40	75	64	115	48	52
60	72	87	105	55	82	66	65

table, the mean is determined as

$$\bar{M}ct = \frac{\sum_{i=1}^{n} Mct_i}{n} = \frac{1,637}{24} = 68.21 \text{ minutes}$$

When determining the mean corrective maintenance time ($\bar{M}ct$) for a specific sample population (empirically measured) of maintenance repair actions, the use of Equation (2.16) is appropriate. However, Equation (2.21) has a wider application:

$$\bar{M}ct = \frac{\sum (\lambda_i)(Mct_i)}{\sum \lambda_i} \tag{2.21}$$

where λ_i is the failure rate of the individual (*i*th) element of the item being measured, usually expressed in failures per equipment operating hour. Equation (2.21) calculates $\bar{M}ct$ as a "weighted average" using reliability factors.

It should be noted that $\bar{M}ct$ considers only active maintenance time or that time which is spent working directly on the system. Logistics delay time and administrative delay time are not included. Although all elements of time are important, the $\bar{M}ct$ factor is primarily oriented to a measure of the supportability characteristics in equipment design.

2. Mean preventive maintenance time ($\bar{M}pt$). Preventive maintenance refers to the actions required to retain a system at a specified level of performance and may include such functions as periodic inspection, servicing, scheduled replacement of critical items, calibration, overhaul, and so on. $\bar{M}pt$ is the mean (or average) elapsed time to perform preventive or scheduled maintenance on an item, and is expressed as

$$\bar{M}pt = \frac{\sum (fpt_i)(Mpt_i)}{\sum fpt_i} \tag{2.22}$$

where fpt_i is the frequency of the individual (*i*th) preventive maintenance action in actions per system operating hour, and Mpt_i is the elapsed time required for the *i*th preventive maintenance action.

Preventive maintenance may be accomplished while the system is in full operation, or could result in downtime. In this instance, the concern is for preventive maintenance actions which result in system downtime. Again, $\bar{M}pt$ includes only active system maintenance time and not logistic delay and administrative delay times.

3. Median active corrective maintenance time ($\tilde{M}ct$). The median maintenance time is that value which divides all of the downtime values so that

50% are equal to or less than the median and 50% are equal to or greater than the median. The median will usually give the best average location of the data sample. The median for a normal distribution is the same as the mean, while the median in a log normal distribution is the same as the geometric mean illustrated in Figure 2-14. $\tilde{M}ct$ is calculated as

$$\tilde{M}ct = \text{antilog} \frac{\sum_{i=1}^{n} \log Mct_i}{n} = \text{antilog} \frac{\sum (\lambda_i)(\log Mct_i)}{\sum \lambda_i} \qquad (2.23)$$

For illustrative purposes, the maintenance time values in Table 2-6 are presented in the format illustrated in Table 2-7. The median is computed as follows:

$$\tilde{M}ct = \text{antilog} \frac{\sum_{1}^{24} \log Mct_i}{24}$$

$$= \text{antilog} \frac{43.315}{24} = \text{antilog } 1.805 = 63.8 \text{ minutes}$$

Table 2-7. CALCULATION FOR $\tilde{M}ct$

Mct_i	Log Mct_i	$(\text{Log } Mct_i)^2$	Mct_i	Log Mct_i	$(\text{Log } Mct_i)^2$
55	1.740	3.028	64	1.806	3.262
28	1.447	2.094	115	2.061	4.248
125	2.097	4.397	48	1.681	2.826
47	1.672	2.796	52	1.716	2.945
58	1.763	3.108	60	1.778	3.161
53	1.724	2.972	72	1.857	3.448
36	1.556	2.241	87	1.939	3.760
88	1.945	3.783	105	2.021	4.084
51	1.708	2.917	55	1.740	3.028
110	2.041	4.166	82	1.914	3.663
40	1.602	2.566	66	1.819	3.309
75	1.875	3.516	65	1.813	3.287
Total				43.315	78.785

4. Median active preventive maintenance time ($\tilde{M}pt$). The median active preventive maintenance time is determined using the same approach as for calculating $\tilde{M}ct$. $\tilde{M}pt$ is expressed as

$$\tilde{M}pt = antilog \frac{\sum (fpt_i)(log\ Mpt_i)}{\sum fpt_i} \qquad (2.24)$$

5. Mean active maintenance time ($\bar{M}$). $\bar{M}$ is the mean or average elapsed time required to perform scheduled (preventive) and unscheduled (corrective) maintenance. It excludes logistics delay time and administrative delay time, and is expressed as

$$\bar{M} = \frac{(\lambda)(\bar{M}ct) + (fpt)(\bar{M}pt)}{\lambda + fpt} \qquad (2.25)$$

where λ is the corrective maintenance rate or failure rate and fpt is the preventive maintenance rate.

6. Maximum active corrective maintenance time (M_{max}). M_{max} can be defined as that value of maintenance downtime below which a specified percent of all maintenance actions can be expected to be completed. M_{max} is related primarily to the log-normal distribution, and the 90th or 95th percentile point is generally taken as the specified value, as shown in Figure 2-14. It is expressed as

$$M_{max} = antilog\ [\overline{log\ Mct} + Z\sigma_{log\ Mct_i}] \qquad (2.26)$$

where $\overline{log\ Mct}$ is the mean of the logarithms of Mct_i, Z is the value corresponding to the specific percentage point at which M_{max} is defined (see Table 2-5, $+1.65$ for 95%) and

$$\sigma\ log\ Mct_i = \sqrt{\frac{\sum_{i=1}^{N} (log\ Mct_i)^2 - (\sum_{i=1}^{N} log\ Mct_i)^2/N}{N-1}} \qquad (2.27)$$

or the standard deviation of the sample logarithms of average repair times, Mct_i.

For example, determining M_{max} at the 95th percentile for the data sample in Table 2-6 is accomplished as follows:

$$M_{max} = antilog\ [log\ \tilde{M}ct + (1.65)\sigma_{log\ Mct_i}] \qquad (2.28)$$

where, referring to Equation (2.27) and Table 2-7,

$$\sigma\ log\ Mct_i = \sqrt{\frac{78.785 - (43.315)^2/24}{23}} = 0.163$$

Substituting the standard deviation factor and the mean value into Equation

(2.28), we obtain

$$M_{max} = \text{antilog} \,[\log \tilde{M}ct + (1.65)(0.163)]$$
$$= \text{antilog} \,(1.805 + 0.269) = 119 \text{ minutes}$$

If maintenance times are distributed log normally, M_{max} cannot be derived directly by using the observed maintenance values. However, by taking the logarithm of each repair value, the resulting distribution becomes normal, facilitating usage of the data in a manner identical to the normal case.

7. *Logistic delay time (LDT).* Logistics delay time refers to that maintenance downtime that is expended as a result of waiting for a spare part to become available, waiting for the availability of an item of test equipment in order to perform maintenance, waiting for transportation, waiting to use a facility required for maintenance, and so on. LDT does not include active maintenance time, but does constitute a major element of total maintenance downtime (MDT).

8. *Administrative delay time (ADT).* Administrative delay time refers to that portion of downtime during which maintenance is delayed for reasons of an administrative nature: personnel assignment priority, labor strike, organizational constraint, and so on. ADT does not include active maintenance time, but often constitutes a significant element of total maintenance downtime (MDT).

9. *Maintenance downtime (MDT).* Maintenance downtime constitutes the total elapsed time required (when the system is not operational) to repair and restore a system to full operating status, and/or to retain a system in that condition. MDT includes mean active maintenance time ($\bar{M}$), logistics delay time (LDT), and administrative delay time (ADT). The mean or average value is calculated from the elapsed times for each function and the associated frequencies (similar to the approach used in determining $\bar{M}$).

B. MAINTENANCE LABOR-HOUR FACTORS

The maintainability factors covered in the previous paragraphs relate to elapsed times. Although elapsed times are extremely important in the performance of maintenance, one must also consider the maintenance laborhours expended in the process. Elapsed times can be reduced (in many instances) by applying additional human resources in the accomplishment of specific tasks. However, this may turn out to be an expensive trade-off, particularly when high skill levels are required to perform tasks that result in less overall clock time. In other words, maintainability is concerned with the *ease* and *economy* in the performance of maintenance. As such, an objective is to obtain the proper balance between elapsed time, labor time, and personnel skills at a minimum maintenance cost.

When considering measures of maintainability, it is not only important to address such factors as $\overline{M}ct$ and MDT, but it is also necessary to consider the labor-time element. Thus, some additional measures must be employed such as the following:

1. Maintenance manhours per system operating hour (MMH/OH).
2. Maintenance manhours per cycle of system operation (MMH/cycle).
3. Maintenance manhours per month (MMH/month).
4. Maintenance manhours per maintenance action (MMH/MA).

Any of these factors can be specified in terms of mean values. For example, $\overline{MMH}_c$ = mean corrective maintenance manhours, expressed as

$$\overline{MMH}_c = \frac{\sum (\lambda_i)(MMH_i)}{\sum \lambda_i} \tag{2.29}$$

where λ_i is the failure rate of the ith item (failures/hour), and MMH_i is the average maintenance manhours necessary to complete repair of the ith item.

Additionally, the values for mean preventive maintenance manhours and mean total maintenance manhours (to include preventive and corrective maintenance) can be calculated on a similar basis. These values can be predicted for each echelon or level of maintenance, and are employed in determining specific support requirements and associated costs.

C. MAINTENANCE FREQUENCY FACTORS

Section 2.1 covers the measures of reliability, with MTBF and λ being key factors. Based on the discussion thus far, it is obvious that reliability and maintainability are very closely related. The reliability factors, MTBF and λ, are the basis for determining the frequency of corrective maintenance. Maintainability deals with the characteristics in system design pertaining to minimizing the corrective maintenance requirements for the system when it assumes operational status later on. Thus, in this area, reliability and maintainability requirements for a given system must be compatible and mutually supportive.

In addition to the corrective maintenance aspect of system support, maintainability also deals with the characteristics of design which minimize (if not eliminate) preventive maintenance requirements for that system. Sometimes, preventive maintenance requirements are added with the objective of improving system reliability (e.g., reducing failures by specifying selected component replacements at designated times). However, the introduction of preventive maintenance can turn out to be quite costly if not carefully controlled. Further, the accomplishment of too much preventive maintenance (particularly for complex systems/products) often has a degrading effect on system reliability, as failures are frequently induced in the process. Hence, an objective of maintainability is to provide the proper balance between corrective maintenance and preventive maintenance at least overall cost.

1. Mean time between maintenance (MTBM). MTBM is the mean or average time between *all* maintenance actions (corrective and preventive) and can be calculated as

$$\text{MTBM} = \frac{1}{1/\text{MTBM}_u + 1/\text{MTBM}_s} \qquad (2.30)$$

where MTBM_u is the mean interval of unscheduled (corrective) maintenance and MTBM_s is the mean interval of scheduled (preventive) maintenance. The reciprocals of MTBM_u and MTBM_s constitute the maintenance rates in terms of maintenance actions per hour of system operation. MTBM_u should approximate MTBF, assuming that a combined failure rate is used which includes the consideration of primary inherent failures, dependent failures, manufacturing defects, operator and maintenance induced failures, and so on. The maintenance frequency factor, MTBM, is a major parameter in determining system availability and overall effectiveness.

2. Mean time between replacement (MTBR). MTBR, a factor of MTBM, refers to the mean time between item replacement and is a major parameter in determining spare part requirements. On many occasions, corrective and preventive maintenance actions are accomplished without generating the requirement for the replacement of a component part. In other instances, item replacements are required, which in turn necessitates the availability of a spare part and an inventory requirement. Additionally, higher levels of maintenance support (i.e., intermediate shop and depot levels) may also be required.

In essence, MTBR is a significant factor, applicable in both corrective and preventive maintenance activities involving item replacement, and is a key parameter in determining logistic support requirements. A maintainability objective in system design is to minimize MTBR where feasible.

D. MAINTENANCE COST FACTORS

For many systems/products, maintenance cost constitutes a major segment of total life-cycle cost. Further, experience has indicated that maintenance costs are significantly impacted by design decisions made throughout the early stages of system development. Thus, it is essential that total life-cycle cost be considered as a major design parameter, beginning with the definition of system requirements.

Of particular interest is the aspect of *economy* in the performance of maintenance actions. In other words, maintainability is directly concerned with the characteristics of system design that will ultimately result in the accomplishment of maintenance at minimum overall cost.

When considering maintenance cost, the following cost-related indices may be appropriate as criteria in system design:

1. Cost per maintenance action ($/MA).
2. Maintenance cost per system operating hour ($/OH).
3. Maintenance cost per month ($/month).
4. Maintenance cost per mission or mission segment ($/mission).
5. The ratio of maintenance cost to total life-cycle cost.

2.3. Supply Support Factors

Supply support includes the spare parts and the associated inventories necessary for the accomplishment of unscheduled and scheduled maintenance actions. At each maintenance level, one must determine the type of spare part (by manufacturing part number) and the quantity of items to be purchased and stocked. Also, it is necessary to know how often various items should be ordered and the number of items that should be procured in a given purchasing transaction.

Spare-part requirements are initially based on the system maintenance concept and are subsequently defined and justified throughout logistic support analysis (LSA). Essentially, spare-part quantities are a function of demand rates and include consideration of:

1. Spares and repair parts covering actual item replacements occurring as a result of corrective and preventive maintenance actions. Spares are major replacement items which are repairable, while repair parts are nonrepairable smaller components.

2. An additional stock level of spares to compensate for repairable items in the process of undergoing maintenance. If there is a backup (lengthy queue) of items in the intermediate maintenance shop or at the depot awaiting repair, these items obviously will not be available as recycled spares for subsequent maintenance actions; thus, the inventory is further depleted (beyond expectation), or a stock-out condition results. In addressing this problem, it becomes readily apparent that the test equipment capability,

personnel, and facilities directly impact the maintenance turnaround times and the quantity of additional spare items needed.

3. An additional stock level of spares and repair parts to compensate for the procurement lead times required for item acquisition. For instance, prediction data may indicate that 10 maintenance actions requiring the relacement of a certain item will occur within a 6-month period and it takes 9 months to acquire replacements from the supplier. One might ask—what additional repair parts will be necessary to cover the operational needs and yet compensate for the long supplier lead time? The added quantities will, of course, vary depending on whether the item is designated as repairable or will be discarded at failure.

4. An additional stock level of spares to compensate for the condemnation or scrapage of repairable items. Repairable items returned to the intermediate maintenance shop or depot are sometimes condemned (i.e., not repaired) because, through inspection, it is decided that the item was not economically feasible to repair. Condemnation will vary depending on equipment utilization, handling, environment, and organizational capability. An increase in the condemnation rate will generally result in an increase in spare-part requirements.

In reviewing the foregoing considerations, of particular significance is the determination of spares requirements as a result of item replacements in the performance of corrective maintenance. Major factors involved in this process are (1) the reliability of the item to be spared, (2) the quantity of items used, (3) the required probability that a spare will be available when needed, (4) the criticality of item application with regard to mission success, and (5) cost. Use of the reliability and probability factors are illustrated in the examples presented below.

A. PROBABILITY OF SUCCESS WITH SPARES AVAILABILITY
CONSIDERATIONS

Assume that a single component with a reliability of 0.8 (for time t) is used in a unique system application and that one backup spare component is purchased. Determine the probability of system success having a spare available in time t (given that failures occur randomly and are exponentially distributed).

This situation is analogous to the case of an operating component and a parallel component in standby (i.e., standby redundancy) discussed in Section 2.1. The applicable expression is stated as

$$P = e^{-\lambda t} + (\lambda t)e^{-\lambda t} \tag{2.31}$$

With a component reliability of 0.8, the value of λt is 0.223. Substituting this value into Equation (2.31) gives a probability of success of

$$P = e^{-0.223} + (0.223)e^{-0.223}$$
$$= 0.8 + (0.223)(0.8) = 0.9784$$

Assuming next that the component is supported with two backup spares (where all three components are interchangeable), the probability of success during time t is determined from

$$P = e^{-\lambda t} + (\lambda t)e^{-\lambda t} + \frac{(\lambda t)^2 e^{-\lambda t}}{2!}$$

or

$$P = e^{-\lambda t}\left[1 + \lambda t + \frac{(\lambda t)^2}{2!}\right] \tag{2.32}$$

With a component reliability of 0.8, and a value of λt of 0.223, the probability of success is

$$P = 0.8\left[1 + 0.223 + \frac{(0.223)^2}{(2)(1)}\right]$$
$$= 0.8(1.2479) = 0.9983$$

Thus, adding another spare component results in one additional term in the Poisson expression. If two spare components are added, two additional terms are added, and so forth.

The probability of success for a configuration consisting of two operating components, backed by two spares, with all components being interchangeable can be found from the expression

$$P = e^{-2\lambda t}\left[1 + 2\lambda t + \frac{(2\lambda t)^2}{2!}\right] \tag{2.33}$$

With a component reliability of 0.8 and $\lambda t = 0.223$,

$$P = e^{-0.446}\left[1 + 0.446 + \frac{(0.446)^2}{(2)(1)}\right]$$
$$P = 0.6402[1 + 0.446 + 0.0995] = 0.9894$$

These examples illustrate the computations used in determining system success with spare parts for three simple component configuration relationships. Various combinations of operating components and spares can be assumed, and the system success factors can be determined by using

$$1 = e^{-\lambda t} + (\lambda t)e^{-\lambda t} + \frac{(\lambda t)^2 e^{-\lambda t}}{2!} + \frac{(\lambda t)^3 e^{-\lambda t}}{3!} + \cdots + \frac{(\lambda t)^n e^{-\lambda t}}{n!} \tag{2.34}$$

Equation (2.34) can be simplified into a general Poisson expression

$$f(x) = \frac{(\lambda t)^x e^{-\lambda t}}{x!} \qquad (2.35)$$

The objective is to determine the probability of x failures occurring if an item is placed in operation for t hours, and each failure is corrected (through item replacement) as it occurs. With n items in the system, the number of failures in t hours will be $n\lambda t$, and the general Poisson expression becomes

$$f(x) = \frac{(n\lambda t)^x e^{-n\lambda t}}{x!} \qquad (2.36)$$

To facilitate calculations, a cumulative Poisson probability graph is presented in Figure 2-15 derived from Equation (2.36). The ordinate value can be viewed as a confidence factor. Several simple examples will be presented to illustrate the application of Figure 2-15.

B. PROBABILITY OF MISSION COMPLETION

Suppose that one needs to determine the probability that a system will complete a 30-hour mission without a failure when the system has a known mean life of 100 hours. Let

$\lambda = 1$ failure per 100 hours or 0.01 failure per hour

$t = 30$ hours

$n = 1$ system

$n\lambda t = (1)(0.01)(30) = 0.3$

Enter Figure 2-15 where $n\lambda t$ is 0.3. Proceed to the intersection where r equals zero and read the ordinate scale, indicating a value of approximately 0.73. Thus, the probability of the system completing a 30-hour mission is 0.73.

Assume that the system identified above is installed in an aircraft and that 10 aircraft are scheduled for a 15-hour mission. Determine the probability that at least 7 systems will operate for the duration of the mission without failure. Let

$$n\lambda t = (10)(0.01)(15) = 1.5$$

and

$$r = 3 \text{ failures or less (allowed)}$$

Enter Figure 2-15 where $n\lambda t$ equals 1.5. Proceed to the intersection where r equals 3, and read the ordinate scale indicating a value of approximately

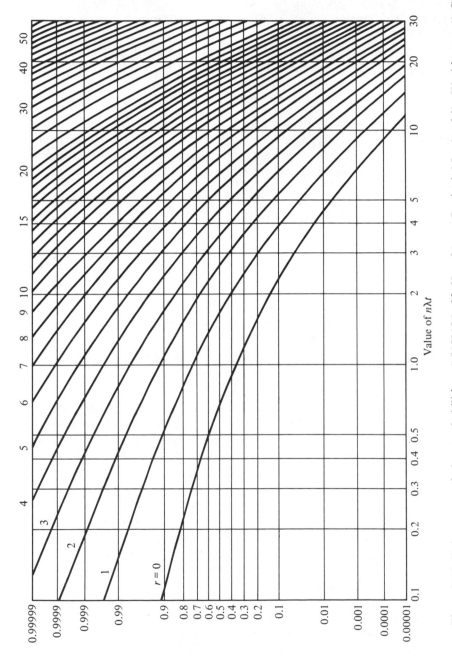

Figure 2-15. Poisson cumulative probabilities. (NAVAIR 00-65-502/NAVORD OD 41146, *Reliability Engineering Handbook,* U.S. Navy, Revised March 1968, Washington, D.C.)

0.92. Thus, there is a 92% confidence that at least 7 systems will operate successfully out of 10. If an 80% operational reliability is specified (i.e., 8 systems must operate without failure), the confidence factor decreases to about 79%.

Although the graph in Figure 2-15 provides a simplified solution, the use of Equation (2.34) is preferable for accurate results.

C. Spare-Part Quantity Determination

Spare-part quantity determination is a function of the probability of having a spare part available when required, the reliability of the item in question, the quantity of items used in the system, and so on. An expression, derived from the Poisson distribution, useful for spare-part-quantity determination is

$$P = \sum_{n=0}^{n=s} \left[\frac{(R)[-K(\ln R)^n]}{n!} \right] \tag{2.37}$$

where P = probability of having a spare of a particular item available when required

S = number of spare parts carried in stock

R = composite reliability (probability of survival); $R = e^{-n\lambda t}$

K = quantity of parts used of a particular type

$\ln R$ = natural logarithm of R

In determining spare-part quantities, one should consider the level of protection desired (safety factor). The protection level is the P value in Equation (2.37). This is the probability of having a spare available when required. The higher the protection level, the greater the quantity of spares required. This results in a higher cost for item procurement and inventory maintenance. The protection level, or safety factor, is a hedge against the risk of stock-out.

When determining spare-part quantities, one should consider system operational requirements (e.g., system effectiveness, availablility) and establish the appropriate level at each location where corrective maintenance is accomplished. Different levels of corrective maintenance may be appropriate for different items. For instance, spares required to support prime equipment components which are critical to the success of a mission may be based on one factor; high-value or high-cost items may be handled differently than low-cost items; and so on. In any event, an optimum balance between stock level and cost is required.

Figure 2-16 (sheets 1 and 2) presents a nomograph which simplifies the determination of spare-part quantities using Equation (2.37). The nomograph not only simplifies solutions for basic spare-part-availability questions, but provides information that can aid in the evaluation of alternative design

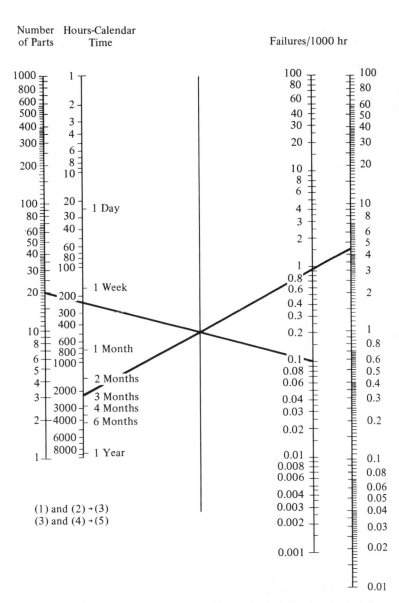

(1)	(4)	(3)	(2)	(5)
K	*T*	Index	λ	*KλT*

Number of Parts   Hours-Calendar Time   Failures/1000 hr

(1) and (2) → (3)
(3) and (4) → (5)

Figure 2-16A. Spare part requirement nomograph (sheet 1 of 2).

(5)   (7)   (6)

$K\lambda T$ S P

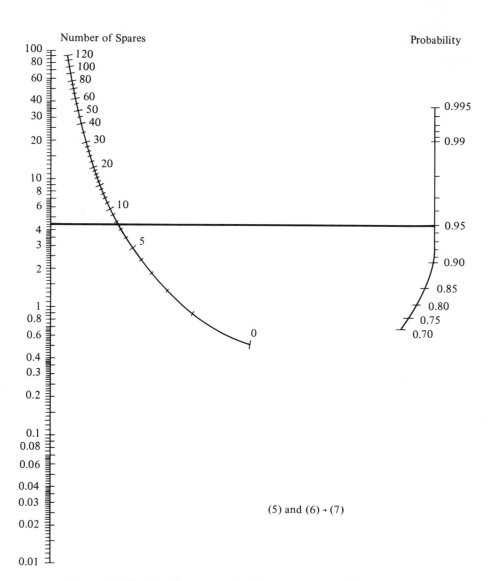

Number of Spares   Probability

(5) and (6) → (7)

Figure 2-16B. Spare part requirement nomograph (sheet 2 of 2). (NAVSHIPS 94324, *Maintainability Design Criteria Handbook for Designers of Shipboard Electronic Equipment*, U.S. Navy, Washington, D.C.)

approaches in terms of spares and in the determination of provisioning cycles. The following examples illustrate the use of the nomograph.[3]

Suppose that a piece of equipment contains 20 parts of a specific type with a failure rate (λ) of 0.1 failure per 1,000 hours of operation. The equipment operates 24 hours a day, and spares are procured and stocked at 3-month intervals. How many spares should be carried in inventory to ensure a 95% chance of having a spare part when required? Let

$$K = 20 \text{ parts}$$
$$\lambda = 0.1 \text{ failure per 1,000 hours}$$
$$T = 3 \text{ months}$$
$$K\lambda T = (20)(0.0001)(24)(30)(3) = 4.35$$
$$P = 95\%$$

Using the nomograph in Figure 2-16 as illustrated, approximately 8 spares are required.

As a second example, suppose that a particular part is used in three different equipments (A, B, C). Spares are procured every 180 days. The number of parts used, the part failure rate, and the equipment operating hours per day are given in Table 2-8.

Table 2-8. DATA FOR SPARES INVENTORY

Item	*K*	*Failures per 100 Hours* (λ)	*Operating Hours per Day* (T)
Equipment *A*	25	0.10	12
Equipment *B*	28	0.07	15
Equipment *C*	35	0.15	20

The number of spares that should be carried in inventory to ensure a 90% chance of having a spare available when required is calculated as follows:

1. Determine the product of K, λ, and T as

$$A = (25)(0.0001)(180)(12) = 5.40$$
$$B = (28)(0.00007)(180)(15) = 5.29$$
$$C = (35)(0.00015)(180)(20) = 18.90$$

---

[3]NAVSHIPS 94324, *Maintainability Design Criteria Handbook for Designers of Shipboard Electronic Equipment*, Naval Ship Systems Command, Department of the Navy, Washington, D.C., 1964.

2. Determine the sum of the $K\lambda T$ values as

$$\sum K\lambda T = 5.40 + 5.29 + 18.90 = 29.59$$

3. Using sheet 2 of the nomograph (Figure 2-16), construct a line from $K\lambda T$ value of 29.59 to the point where P is 0.90. The approximate number of spares required is 36.

D. INVENTORY CONSIDERATIONS

In progressing further, one needs to address not only the specific demand factors for spares, but to evaluate these factors in terms of the overall inventory requirements. Too much inventory may ideally respond to the demand for spares. However, this may be costly, with a great deal of capital tied up in the inventory. In addition, much waste could occur, particularly if system changes are implemented and certain components become obsolete. On the other hand, providing too little support results in the probability of causing the system to be inoperative due to stock-out, which also can be costly. In general, it is desirable to obtain an economic balance between the quantity of items in inventory at any given point in time, the frequency of purchase order transactions, and the quantity of items per purchase order.

Figure 2-17 presents a graphical portrayal of an inventory cycle. The illustration assumes a constant lead time and a constant item demand (e.g., failure rate). Stock depletions are represented by the sloping consumption

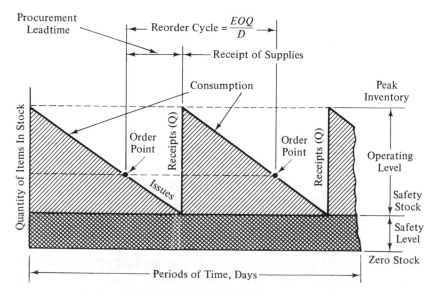

Figure 2-17. Theoretical inventory cycle.

line. When the stock is depleted to a designated level, additional items are ordered (represented at the order point) in enough time to allow for supply replenishment before a stock out condition occurs.[4] The terms identified in the figure are briefly defined as

1. *Operating level*—describes the quantity of material items required to support normal system operations in the interval between orders and the arrival of successive shipments of material.
2. *Safety stock*—additional stock required to compensate for unexpected demands, repair and recycle times, pipeline, procurement lead time, and unforeseen delays.
3. *Reorder cycle*—interval of time between successive orders.
4. *Procurement lead time*—the span of time from the date of order to receipt of the shipment in the inventory. This includes (a) administrative lead time from the date that a decision is made to initiate an order to the receipt of the order at the supplier; (b) production lead time or the time from receipt of the order by the supplier to completion of the manufacture of the item ordered; and (c) delivery lead time from completion of manufacture to receipt of the item in the inventory. Delivery lead time includes the pipeline.
5. *Pipeline*—the distance between the supplier and consumer, measured in days of supply. If a constant flow is assumed with a transit time of 30 days and the consumption rate is one item per day, then 30 items would be required in the pipeline at all times. An increase in the demand would require more in the pipeline.
6. *Order point (O.P.)*—the point in time when orders are initiated for additional quantities of spare/repair parts. This point is often tied to a given stock level (after the stock has been depleted to that level).

Figure 2-17 is a theoretical representation of an inventory cycle for a given item. Actually, demands are not always constant and quite often the reorder cycle changes with time. Figure 2-18 presents a situation that is more realistic.

Referring to Figure 2-17 (i.e., the theoretical inventory cycle), the ultimate goal is to have the correct amount and type of supplies available for the lowest total cost. Procurement costs vary with the quantity of orders placed. The economic inventory principle involves the optimization between the placing of many orders resulting in high material acquisition costs and the

---

[4]Inventory concepts may vary. A "fixed review time method" (when inventory is reviewed at fixed time intervals and depleted items are reordered in variable quantities) or a "fixed reorder point method" (standard orders are initiated when the inventory is depleted to a certain level) may be employed. However, the economic order principle should govern in most instances.

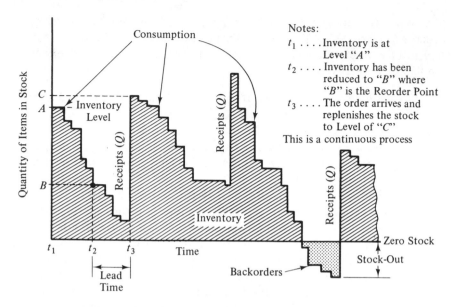

Figure 2-18. Representation of an actual inventory cycle.

placing of orders less frequently while maintaining a higher level of inventory, causing increasing inventory maintenance and carrying costs. In other words, ordering creates procurement cost while inventory creates carrying cost. The economic order principle equates the "cost to order" to the "cost to hold" and the point at which the combined costs are at a minimum indicates the desired size of order. Figure 2-19 graphically illustrates this concept.

Referring to the figure, the illustration forms the basis for the size of orders placed which is known as the "economic order quantity (EOQ)."[5] The total cost curve in Figure 2-19 is expressed as

$$\text{total cost} = \frac{C_h Q}{2} + \frac{C_p D}{Q} \qquad (2.38)$$

where C_p = average cost of ordering in dollars per order (includes cost of setup, processing orders, receiving, etc.)

C_h = cost of carrying an item in inventory (percent of the item price multiplied by the total acquisition price for the item)

D = annual item demand (this is assumed to be constant for the purposes of discussion)

Q = most economical quantity

---

[5] The EOQ concept presented is a simplified representation of the major consideration in establishing an inventory. However, there are many variations and additional material should be reviewed prior to making a decision on a specific application.

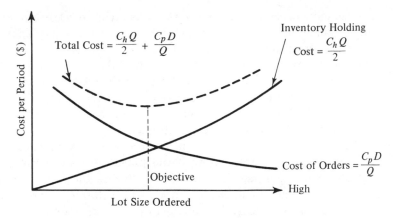

Figure 2-19. Economic inventory cost consideration.

Differentiating and solving for Q, which represents the quantity of units ordered, gives the following equation for EOQ:

$$Q^* = \text{EOQ} = \sqrt{\frac{2C_pD}{C_h}} \qquad (2.39)$$

where Equation (2.39) is the expression for determining the quantity of items per order, the number of purchase orders per year, N, can be determined from the equation

$$N = \frac{D}{\text{EOQ}} \qquad (2.40)$$

The EOQ model is generally applicable in instances where there are relatively large quantities of common spares and repair parts. However, it may be feasible to employ other methods of acquisition for major "high-value" items and for those items considered to be particularly critical to mission success.

High-value items are those components with a high unit acquisition cost, and should be purchased on an individual basis. The dollar value of these components is usually significant and may even exceed the total value of the hundreds of other spares and repair parts in the inventory. In other words, a relatively small number of items may represent a large percentage of the total inventory value. Because of this, it may be preferable to maintain a given quantity of these items in the inventory to compensate for repair and recycle times, pipeline and procurement lead times, and so on, and order new items on a one-for-one basis as failures occur and a spare is withdrawn from the inventory. Thus, where it may appear to be economically feasible to purchase many of these items in a given purchase transaction, only a small quantity of items are actually procured, because of the risks involved relative to tying up too much capital and the resultant high inventory maintenance cost.[6]

Another consideration in the spares acquisition process is that of "criticality." Some items are considered more critical than others in terms of impact on mission success. For instance, the lack of a $10 item may cause the system to be inoperative, while the lack of a $1,000 item might not cause a major problem. The criticality of an item is generally based on its function in the system and not necessarily its acquisition cost.

As a final point, the spares acquisition process may vary somewhat between items of a comparable nature if the usage rates are significantly different. Fast-moving items may be procured locally near the point of usage, such as the intermediate maintenance shop, while slower-moving items stocked at the depot, or a central repair facility, may be acquired from a remotely located supplier as the pipline and procurement lead times are not as critical.

2.4. Test and Support Equipment Factors

The general category of test and support equipment may include a wide spectrum of items, such as precision electronic test equipment, mechanical test equipment, ground handling equipment, special jigs and fixtures, maintenance stands, and the like. These items, in varying configurations and mixes, may be assigned to different maintenance locations and geographically dispersed throughout the country (or world). However, regardless of the nature and application, the objective is to provide the right item for the job intended, at the proper location, and in the quantity required.

Because of the likely diversification of the test and support equipment for any given system, it is difficult to specify quantitative measures that can be universally applied. Certain measures are appropriate for electronic test equipment, other measures are applicable to ground handling equipment, and so on. Further, the specific location and application of a given item of test equipment may also result in different measures. For instance, an item of electronic test equipment used in support of on-site organizational maintenance may have different requirements than a similar item of test equipment used for intermediate maintenance accomplished in a remote shop.

Although all of the test and support equipment requirements at each level of maintenance are considered to be important relative to successful system

---

[6]The classification of high-value items will vary with the program, and may be established at a certain dollar value (i.e., all components whose initial unit cost exceeds x dollars are considered as high-value items).

oper:.cion, the testers or test stations in the intermediate and depot maintenance facilities are of particular concern, since these items are likely to support a number of system elements at different consumer locations. That is, an intermediate maintenance facility may be assigned to provide the necessary corrective maintenance support for a large number of system elements dispersed throughout a wide geographical area. This means, of course, that a variety of items (all designated for intermediate-level maintenance) will arrive from different consumer sites at different times.

When determining the specific test equipment requirements for a shop, one must define (1) the type of items that will be returned to the shop for maintenance; (2) the test functions to be accomplished, including the performance parameters to be measured as well as the accuracies and tolerances required for each item; and (3) the anticipated frequency of test functions per unit of time. The type and frequency of item returns (i.e., shop arrivals) is based on the maintenance concept and system reliability data. The distribution of arrival times for a given item is often a negative exponential with the number of items arriving within a given time period following a Poisson distribution. As items arrive in the shop, they may be processed immediately or there may be a waiting line, or queue, depending on the availability of the test equipment and the personnel to perform the required maintenance functions.

When evaluating the test process itself, one should calculate the anticipated test equipment utilization requirements (i.e., the total amount of "on-station" time required per day, month, or year). This can be estimated by considering the repair time distributions for the various items arriving in the shop. However, the ultimate elapsed times may be influenced significantly depending on whether manual, semiautomatic, or automatic test methods are employed.

Given the test equipment utilization needs (from the standpoint of total test station time required for processing shop arrivals), it is necessary to determine the anticipated reliability and maintainability of the test equipment configuration being considered for the application. Thus, one must consider the MTBM and MDT values for the test equipment itself. Obviously, the test equipment configuration should be more reliable than the system component being tested. Also, in instances where the complexity of the test equipment is high, the logistic resources required for the support of the test equipment may be extensive (e.g., the frequent requirement to calibrate an item of test equipment against a secondary or primary standard in a "cleanroom" environment). In essence, there is a requirement to determine the time that the test equipment will be available to perform its intended function.

The final determination of the requirements for test equipment in a maintenance facility is accomplished through an analysis of various alternative combinations of arrival rates, queue length, test station process times, and/or quantity of test stations. Basically, one is dealing with a single-channel or multichannel queueing situation using queueing techniques. As the maintenance configuration becomes more complex, involving many variables (some of which are probabilistic in nature), then Monte Carlo analysis may be appropriate. In any event, there may be a number of feasible servicing alternatives, and a preferred approach is sought.

2.5. Organizational Factors

The measures associated with a maintenance organization are basically the same as those factors which are typical for any organization. Of particular interest relative to logistic support are:

1. The direct maintenance labor time for each personnel category, or skill level, expended in the performance of system maintenance activities. Labor time may be broken down to cover both unscheduled and scheduled and maintenance individually. Labor time may be expressed in

    a. Maintenance manhours per system operating hour (MMH/OH).
    b. Maintenance manhours per mission cycle (or segment of a mission).
    c. Maintenance manhours per month (MMH/month).
    d. Maintenance manhours per maintenance action (MMH/MA).

2. The indirect labor time required to support system maintenance activities (i.e., overhead factor).
3. The personnel attrition rate or turnover rate (in percent).
4. The personnel training rate or the worker-days of formal training per year of system operation and support.
5. The number of maintenance work orders processed per unit of time (e.g., week, month, or year), and the average time required for work order processing.
6. The average administrative delay time, or the average time from when an item is initially received for maintenance to the point when active maintenance on that item actually begins.

When addressing the total spectrum of logistics (and the design for supportability), the organizational element is critical to the effective and successful life-cycle support of a system. The right personnel quantities and skills must be available when required, and the individuals assigned to the job must be properly trained and motivated. As in any organization, it is important to establish measures dealing with organizational effectiveness and productivity.

2.6. Facility Factors

Facilities are required to support activities pertaining to the accomplishment of active maintenance tasks, providing warehousing functions for spares and repair parts, and providing housing for related administrative functions. Although the specific quantitative measures associated with facilities may vary significantly from one system to the next, the following factors are considered to be relevant in most instances.

1. Item process time or turnaround time (TAT): that is, the elapsed time necessary to process an item for maintenance, returning it to full operational status.
2. Facility utilization: for example, the ratio of the time utilized to the time available for use, percent utilization in terms of space occupancy, and so on.
3. Energy utilization in the performance of maintenance: for example, unit consumption of energy per maintenance action, cost of energy consumption per increment of time or per maintenance action, and so on.
4. Total facility cost for system operation and support: for example, total cost per month, cost per maintenance action, and so on.

2.7. Transportation and Handling Factors

Transportation requirements include the movement of human and material resources between the source(s) of supply and the various locations where maintenance activities are accomplished. More specifically, personnel and materials are often dispatched from a remote maintenance facility to a consumer location to provide needed on-site maintenance support. Further, equipment items requiring extensive repair are shipped from the consumer to either an intermediate maintenance shop or to the manufacturer's plant, depending on the extent of the repair required. In essence, transportation plays a key role in the area of logistic support.

When evaluating the effectiveness of transportation, one must deal with such measures as

1. Transportation capacity or capability: for example, transportation modes (rail, air, highway, waterway), volume of goods transported, quantity of items transported, ton-miles per year transported, quantity of car loads or truck loads, and so on.
2. Transportation time: for example, short-haul time, long-haul time, mean transportation time, and so on. This factor is, of course, signifi-

cant, particularly as it applies to the delivery of personnel, spare parts, and related resources to support maintenance activities.

3. Transportation cost: for example, cost per shipment, cost of transportation per carrier per mile, cost of packing and handling, transportation and handling cost per year, and so on.

Transportation and handling factors are significant with regard to the design of a system for transportability or mobility. Transportation requirements must be defined and the system (and its elements) must be designed such that the required transportation and handling activities can be accomplished both effectively and efficiently. The factors identified here, particularly transportation time and cost, are required input parameters in performing logistic support and life-cycle cost analyses.

2.8. Availability Factors

The term "availability" is often used as a measure of system readiness (i.e., the degree, percent, or probability that a system will be ready or available when required for use). Availability may be expressed differently, depending on the system and its mission. Three commonly used figures of merit (FOMs) are described below.

A. INHERENT AVAILABILITY (A_i)

Inherent availability is the probability that a system or equipment, when used under stated conditions in an *ideal* support environment (i.e., readily available tools, spares, maintenance personnel, etc.), will operate satisfactorily at any point in time as required. It excludes preventive or scheduled maintenance actions, logistics delay time, and administrative delay time, and is expressed as

$$A_i = \frac{\text{MTBF}}{\text{MTBF} + \bar{\text{M}}\text{ct}} \qquad (2.41)$$

where MTBF is the mean time between failure and $\bar{\text{M}}$ct is the mean corrective maintenance time, as described in Sections 2.1 and 2.2.

B. ACHIEVED AVAILABILITY (A_a)

Achieved availability is the probability that a system or equipment, when used under stated conditions in an *ideal* support environment (i.e., readily available tools, spares, personnel, etc.), will operate satisfactorily at any point in time. This definition is similar to the definition for A_i except that preventive (i.e., scheduled) maintenance is included. It excludes logistics delay time and administrative delay time and is expressed by

$$A_a = \frac{\text{MTBM}}{\text{MTBM} + \bar{\text{M}}} \tag{2.42}$$

where MTBM is the mean time between maintenance and $\bar{\text{M}}$ is the mean active maintenance time. MTBM and $\bar{\text{M}}$ are a function of corrective (unscheduled) and preventive (scheduled) maintenance actions and times.

C. OPERATIONAL AVAILABILITY (A_o)

Operational availability is the probability that a system or equipment, when used under stated conditions in an *actual* operational environment, will operate satisfactorily when called upon. It is expressed as

$$A_o = \frac{\text{MTBM}}{\text{MTBM} + \text{MDT}} \tag{2.43}$$

where MDT is the mean maintenance downtime.

If one is to impose an availability figure of merit as a design requirement for a given equipment supplier, and the supplier has no control over the operational environment in which that equipment is to function, then A_a or A_i might be appropriate figures of merit against which the supplier's equipment can be properly assessed. On the other hand, if one is to assess a system or an equipment in a realistic operational environment, then A_o is a preferred figure of merit to employ for assessment purposes. Further, the term "availability" may be applied at any time in the overall mission profile representing a point estimate, or may be more appropriately related to a specific segment of the mission where the requirements are different from other segments. Thus, one must define precisely what is meant by "availability" and how it is to be applied.

2.9. Economic Factors

Throughout the system life cycle there are many decisions that pertain to the evaluation of alternative system operational use profiles or mission scenarios, alternative design configurations, alternative production schemes, alternative maintenance concepts and logistic support policies, and so on. Such decisions should not only be based on performance and effectiveness criteria but should be justified in terms of economic factors as well. Anticipated revenues and costs (as applicable) must be considered in the selection of a preferred approach.

Of major concern here is the aspect of cost. Cost, as used in this text, means life-cycle cost.[7] As defined in Chapter 1, life-cycle cost includes the costs associated with all system activities pertaining to research and development, design, test and evaluation, production, construction, product distribution, system operation, sustaining maintenance and logistic support, and system retirement and disposal. Life-cycle cost is of particular significance in the definition of logistic support requirements, since the costs associated with system support are increasing at an alarming rate and often exceed the costs of system acquisition.

In developing life-cycle cost figures, one of the first steps is to construct a cost breakdown structure (CBS), as illustrated in Figure 2-20. The CBS links objectives and activities with resources, and constitutes a logical subdivision of cost by functional activity area, major element of a system, and/or one or more discrete classes of common or like items. The CBS, together with its design and its application, are discussed more thoroughly in Appendix A.

The next step is to estimate costs, by category in the CBS, for each year in the system life cycle. Cost estimates must consider the effects of inflation, learning curves, and any other factors that are likely to cause changes in cost, upward or downward. Cost estimates are derived from a combination of accounting records (historical data), project cost projections, supplier proposals, and predictions. When cost data are not available, cost estimates are often based on analogous and/or parametric estimating methods. Figure 2-21 and 2-22 illustrate typical linear and nonlinear cost estimating relationships (respectively), and Figure 2-23 presents some sample cost distributions.

Individual cost factors, estimated for each year in the life cycle in terms of the actual anticipated cost for that year (i.e., inflated cost), are totaled and projected in the context of a cost profile illustrated in Figure 2-24. This profile reflects future life-cycle budgetary requirements for the system.

In the evaluation of alternatives, each alternative configuration is represented by a different cost profile, since cost-generating activities will vary from one instance to the next, reliability and maintainability factors will be different, and the specific logistic support requirements will be unique for each situation. Figure 2-25 reflects the cost profiles for three potential system configurations being considered for a single application.

The comparison of various possible courses of action requires that the costs associated with the alternatives in question be related on an equivalent basis (i.e., the point in time when the decision is to be made, which is generally considered as the *present time* or *now*). Thus, the costs for each year in the life cycle (for each profile being evaluated) are discounted to the present value.

---

[7]Two references that deal with life cycle cost in more detail are (a) Blanchard, B. S., *Design and Manage to Life Cycle Cost*, M/A Press, International Scholarly Book Services, Inc., Forest Grove, Oreg., 1978; and (b) Seldon, M. R., *Life Cycle Costing: A Better Method of Government Procurement*, Westview Press, Inc., Boulder, Colo., 1979.

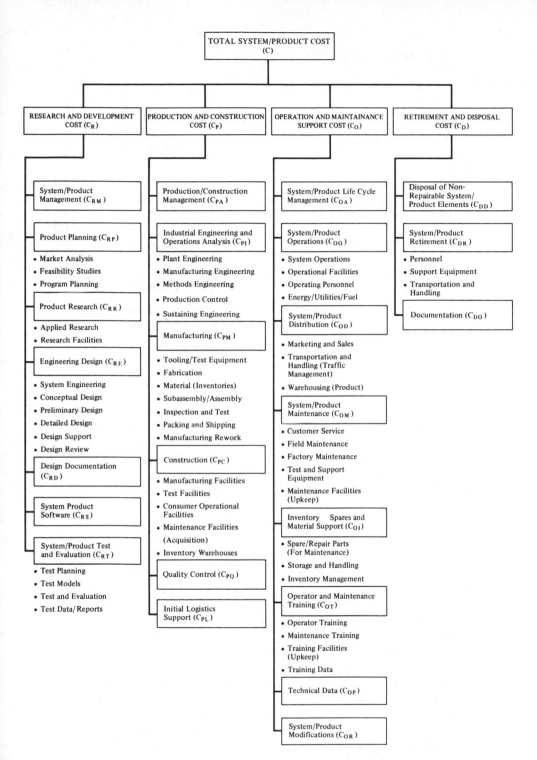

Figure 2-20. Cost breakdown structure (example).

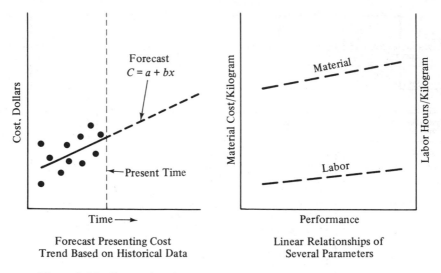

Forecast Presenting Cost
Trend Based on Historical Data

Linear Relationships of
Several Parameters

Figure 2-21. Cost estimating relationships—simple linear functions.

   The aspect of discounting refers to the application of a selected rate of interest to measure the differences in importance or preference between dollars at the present time and anticipated dollars in the future. Discounting allows for the evaluation of the time-phased profiles of cost streams for various alternative configurations as if they occurred at one point in time (the only fair method of evaluation if one is to make a decision today) rather than spaced over the life of the system.

   In every investment, one should recognize the fact that a dollar today is worth more than a dollar tomorrow because of the interest cost that is related to expenditures which occur over time; thus, a financial transaction (cash in-flow or cost) projected for tomorrow has a present value less than its undiscounted dollar value. Transactions that accrue in the future cannot be compared directly with investments made at the present because of this time value of money. Discounting is a technique for converting various cash flows/ costs occurring over time to equivalent amounts at a common point in time to facilitate a valid comparison of alternative investments.

   For the purposes of illustration, assume that costs are determined for a system with a life cycle of 5 years. Although costs actually occur continually or at discrete points throughout each year, they are usually treated either at the beginning or at the end of the applicable time period. In this instance, the costs are determined at the end of each year throughout the life cycle. The object is to relate these costs in "today's" value, since this is the point in time when decisions related to equipment design and logistic support are made. Figure 2-26 presents a simple illustration of the system life cycle, and the costs for each year must be conveyed in terms of the present value (decision point).

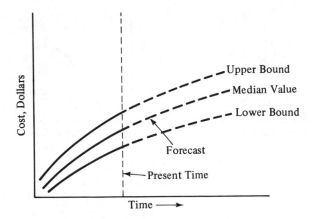

Forecast Using Delphi Estimates
for Cost Projections

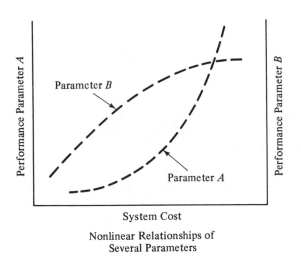

System Cost

Nonlinear Relationships of
Several Parameters

Figure 2-22. Cost estimating relationships—simple
nonlinear functions.

For the first year, costs are estimated for each applicable item and are
represented at point A. The question is: What is the value of that total cost
at point A in terms of the decision point? This can be determined from the
following single-payment present-value expression:[8]

---

[8]Thuesen, H. G., Fabrycky, W. J., and Thuesen, G. J., *Engineering Economy*, 5th ed.,
Prentice-Hall, Inc., Englewood Cliffs, N.J., 1977. This reference presents an in-depth coverage of present value, future value, equal-payment series, interest tables, and related
material.

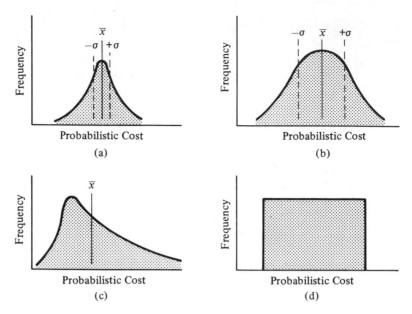

Figure 2-23. Sample cost distributions.

$$P = F\left[\frac{n}{(1 + i)^n}\right]$$ (2.44)

where P = present value or present principal sum
F = future sum at some interest period hence
i = annual interest rate
n = interest period

Assuming an interest rate of 10%, the present-value cost at point A is

$$P = 1,000\left[\frac{1}{(1 + 0.1)}\right] = \$909.09$$

For point B, this value becomes

$$P = 3,500\left[\frac{1}{(1 + 0.1)^2}\right] = \$2,892.40$$

Next, consider the present value of the costs at point A and point B combined. This is calculated from the expression

$$P = F_a\left[\frac{1}{(1 + i)}\right] + F_b\left[\frac{1}{(1 + i)^2}\right]$$ (2.45)

Assuming the undiscounted estimates of $1,000 and $3,500 at points A and

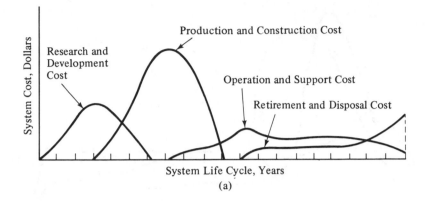

System Cost, Dollars

Research and
Development
Cost

Production and Construction Cost

Operation and Support Cost

Retirement and Disposal Cost

System Life Cycle, Years

(a)

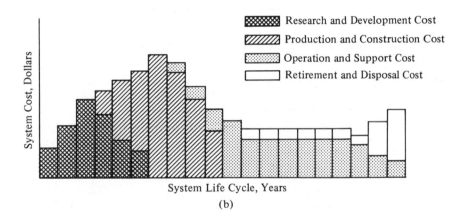

System Cost, Dollars

Research and Development Cost

Production and Construction Cost

Operation and Support Cost

Retirement and Disposal Cost

System Life Cycle, Years

(b)

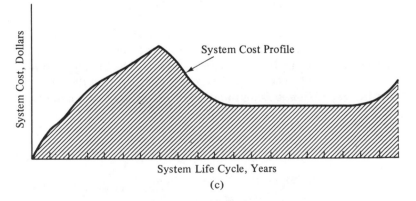

System Cost, Dollars

System Cost Profile

System Life Cycle, Years

(c)

Figure 2-24. Development of a cost profile.

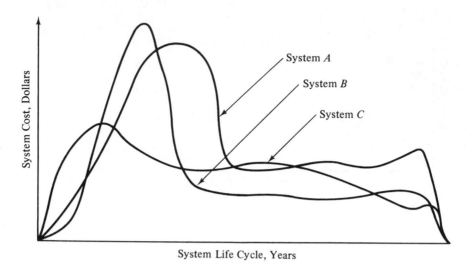

Figure 2-25. Life cycle cost profiles of alternatives.

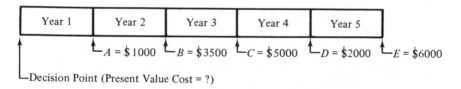

Figure 2-26. System life cycle costs.

B, respectively, the present value is

$$P = 1,000\left[\frac{1}{(1 + 0.1)}\right] + 3,500\left[\frac{1}{(1 + 0.1)^2}\right] = \$3,801.49$$

This continues until the costs for each year in the system life cycle are discounted to the present value and totaled. The total present-value cost for the system represented in Figure 2-26 is $12,649.74 (note that the undiscounted total value is $17,500). When costs are different for each year in the life cycle, the present-value expression is a continuation of Equations (2.44) and (2.45), or

$$P = F_a\left[\frac{1}{(1 + i)}\right] + F_b\left[\frac{1}{(1 + i)^2}\right] + F_c\left[\frac{1}{(1 + i)^3}\right] + \cdots$$
$$+ F_n\left[\frac{1}{(1 + i)^n}\right] \tag{2.46}$$

Present-value cost calculations can be simplified by using standard interest tables and multiplying the future sum by the appropriate factor. Table 2-9 presents an abbreviated example of available present-value factors.

As an example of the application of discounting in evaluating alternatives, suppose that a manufacturing firm is considering the possibility of introducing a new product into the market which is expected to meet sales projections for at least 10 years. The firm must invest in capital equipment in order to manu-

Table 2-9. PRESENT-VALUE FACTORS (TYPICAL)

n \ i	2%	4%	6%	8%	10%	15%	20%	25%
1	0.9804	0.9615	0.9434	0.9259	0.9091	0.8696	0.8333	0.8000
2	0.9612	0.9246	0.8900	0.8573	0.8264	0.7561	0.6944	0.6400
3	0.9423	0.8890	0.8396	0.7938	0.7513	0.6575	0.5787	0.5120
4	0.9238	0.8548	0.7921	0.7350	0.6830	0.5718	0.4823	0.4096
5	0.9057	0.8219	0.7473	0.6806	0.6209	0.4972	0.4019	0.3277
6	0.8880	0.7903	0.7050	0.6302	0.5645	0.4323	0.3349	0.2621
7	0.8706	0.7599	0.6651	0.5835	0.5130	0.3759	0.2791	0.2097
8	0.8535	0.7307	0.6274	0.5403	0.4665	0.3269	0.2326	0.1678
9	0.8368	0.7026	0.5919	0.5002	0.4241	0.2843	0.1938	0.1342
10	0.8203	0.6756	0.5584	0.4632	0.3855	0.2472	0.1615	0.1074
11	0.8043	0.6496	0.5268	0.4289	0.3505	0.2149	0.1346	0.0859
12	0.7885	0.6246	0.4970	0.3971	0.3186	0.1869	0.1122	0.0687
13	0.7730	0.6006	0.4688	0.3677	0.2897	0.1625	0.0935	0.0550
14	0.7579	0.5775	0.4423	0.3405	0.2633	0.1413	0.0779	0.0440
15	0.7430	0.5553	0.4173	0.3152	0.2394	0.1229	0.0649	0.0352
16	0.7284	0.5339	0.3936	0.2919	0.2176	0.1069	0.0541	0.0281
17	0.7142	0.5134	0.3714	0.2703	0.1978	0.0929	0.0451	0.0225
18	0.7002	0.4936	0.3503	0.2502	0.1799	0.0808	0.0376	0.0180
19	0.6864	0.4746	0.3305	0.2317	0.1635	0.0703	0.0313	0.0144
20	0.6730	0.4564	0.3118	0.2145	0.1486	0.0611	0.0261	0.0115
25	0.6095	0.3751	0.2330	0.1460	0.0923	0.0304	0.0105	0.0038
30	0.5521	0.3083	0.1741	0.0994	0.0573	0.0151	0.0042	0.0012
40	0.4529	0.2083	0.0972	0.0460	0.0221	0.0037	0.0007	0.0001
50	0.3715	0.1407	0.0543	0.0213	0.0085	0.0009	0.0001	....
100	0.1380	0.0198	0.0029	0.0005	0.0001	....	....	....

facture the product. Based on a survey of potential sources, there are two equipment alternatives considered to be feasible.

Table 2-10 gives the projected cash flow for the two equipment alternatives (both revenues and costs are given). A 6-year life cycle and an interest rate of 10% are assumed. There is an initial investment of $15,000 for equipment A and $20,000 for equipment B. Benefits (in terms of anticipated net

Table 2-10. NET-PRESENT-VALUE COMPARISON

Equipment A

| Year | Cash Flow | | Discount | Present Value | |
n	Benefits	Costs	Factor (10%)	Benefits	Costs
0		$15,000	0.0000		$15,000.00
1		6,000	0.9091		5,454.60
2	$ 5,000	3,000	0.8264	$ 4,132.00	2,479.20
3	12,000		0.7513	9,015.60	
4	16,500		0.6830	11,269.50	
5	25,800		0.6209	16,019.22	
6	23,000		0.5645	12,983.50	
Total	$82,300	$24,000		$53,419.82	$22,933.80

Equipment B

| Year | Cash Flow | | Discount | Present Value | |
n	Benefits	Costs	Factor (10%)	Benefits	Costs
0		$20,000	0.0000		$20,000.00
1		12,000	0.9091		10,909.20
2	$ 4,000	6,000	0.8264	$ 3,305.60	4,958.40
3	13,000	5,000	0.7513	9,766.90	3,756.50
4	17,000	3,000	0.6830	11,611.00	2,049.00
5	22,000		0.6209	13,569.90	
6	20,000		0.5645	11,290.00	
Total	$76,000	$46,000		$49,633.30	$41,673.10

revenues) and costs are shown in the table together with the interest factors from Table 2-9. The net present value (NPV) for equipment A is $30,486 and the NPV for equipment B is $7,960. Thus equipment A is preferred.

Prior to making making a final choice, the analyst should perform a break-even analysis and establish the payback points for each project.

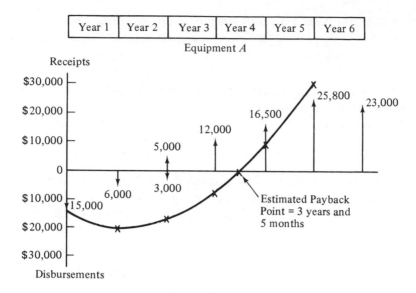

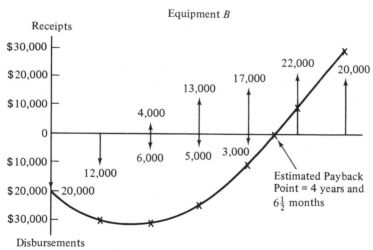

Figure 2-27. Cash flow and payback comparisons.

Although other factors may affect the ultimate decision, the project exhibiting an early payback is usually desirable when considering risk and uncertainty. Figure 2-27 illustrates cash flows and payback points, and equipment *A* retains its preferred status.

The discussion thus far has dealt with the conversion of anticipated future revenues and costs to the present value. This is necessary for the evaluation of proposals in terms of the *present* time. However, one may wish to relate money transactions to some future point in time, assuming this point to be at a time when a major investment decision will be made. In such instances, the single-payment present-value equation (2.44) can be transposed to

$$F = P[(1 + i)^n] \qquad (2.47)$$

This equation can be used to determine the results of various investments. For instance, assume that $6,000 is invested today in some venture and the annual interest rate is 8%. Then the compound amount at the end of year 2 is

$$F = 6,000[(1 + 0.08)^2] = \$6,998.40$$

With the application of present-value and future-value concepts, the analyst can relate these to the life cycle and convert revenues and costs to any designated decision point. Figure 2-28 illustrates this, where the anticipated decision point is at the end of year 2. Referring to the figure, the discounted value of the cost stream at 10% is

$$
\begin{aligned}
P_{\text{(decision point)}} = {} & 8,000 + 2,000(1.100) + 1,000(1.210) \\
& + 12,000(0.9091) + 18,000(0.8265) \\
& + 22,000(0.7513) = \$53,724.80
\end{aligned}
$$

In summary, revenues and costs may be treated differently depending on the problem at hand. Money has time value and discounting is appropriate in the direct comparison of alternative cost profiles. Discounting is employed to relate all revenues and costs to a specific decision point, whether now or in the future.[9]

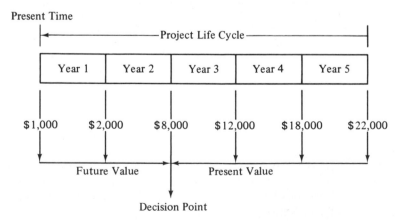

Figure 2-28. Present value/future value cost projection.

---

[9]If the analyst wishes to evaluate a preferred money profile on the basis of future *budget* requirements, then he or she may wish to convert the discounted values back to the inflated yearly values.

2.10. Effectiveness Factors

The aspect of effectiveness introduced in Chapter 1 can be quantified in terms of one or more figures of merit (FOMs), depending on the specific mission or system characteristics that one wishes to specify and measure. Effectiveness must consider

1. *System performance and physical parameters*—capacity, delivery rate, range, accuracy, volume, speed, weight, and so on.
2. *System operational and support factors*—availability, dependability, capability, operational readiness, reliability, maintainability, manability, supportability, transportability, and so on.
3. *Total life-cycle cost*—research and development cost, production/ construction cost, operation and maintenance cost, retirement and disposal cost, and so on.

Establishing a relationship between a performance or operational parameter and cost may constitute a desirable cost-effectiveness FOM. Other relationships may be equally as important. Some example FOMs are

$$\text{effectiveness FOM} = \frac{\text{availability}}{\text{life-cycle cost}} \tag{2.48}$$

or

$$\text{effectiveness FOM} = \frac{\text{reliability}}{\text{life-cycle cost}} \tag{2.49}$$

or

$$\text{effectiveness FOM} = \frac{\text{system capacity}}{\text{range}} \tag{2.50}$$

or

$$\text{effectiveness FOM} = \frac{\text{life-cycle cost}}{\text{facility space}} \quad \text{or other} \tag{2.51}$$

Figure 2-29 illustrates a relationship between reliability (MTBF) and total life-cycle cost, where the objective is to design a system to meet a specified set of values (MTBF and a budget limitation) and yet be cost-effective. Through allocations, predictions, assessments, and so on, system design characteristics are evaluated in terms of reliability and cost. Design changes (as required) are recommended to the extent that the system configuration is represented at or near the minimum-cost point on the curve in Figure 2-29.

The use of effectiveness FOMs is particularly appropriate in the evaluation of two or more alternatives when decisions involving design and/or logistic support are necessary. Each alternative is evaluated in a consistent

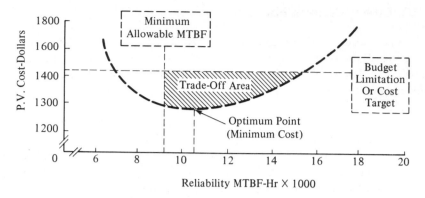

Figure 2-29. Reliability versus cost.

manner employing the same criteria for evaluation. In situations where the risks are high and available data for prediction are inadequate, one may wish to employ the three-level estimate approach using a pessimistic value, optimistic value, and expected value for performance, operational, and/or cost factors as appropriate. Using this approach, the cost-effectiveness relationship for the evaluation of two alternatives assumes the situation illustrated in Figure 2-30.

Referring to the figure, two alternatives are being evaluated on a comparable basis, and it appears that alternative *B* is the most cost-effective in the end. Prior to arriving at a final decision, however, one must address both the aspect of cost effectiveness (in terms of some quantitative FOM) and the point in time where alternative *B* becomes more cost-effective than

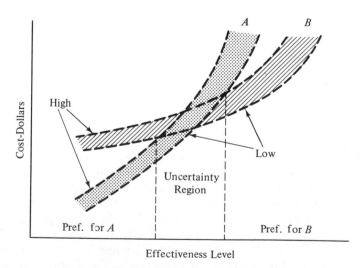

Figure 2-30. Range of estimates for two alternatives.

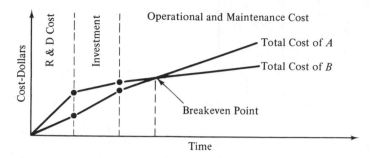

Figure 2-31. Breakeven analysis.

alternative *A*. Thus, a break-even analysis is required to determine this point in time. Figure 2-31 illustrates an approach to a break-even analysis where the cumulative costs for two programs (alternative *A* and alternative *B*) are estimated and projected.

Is the break-even point realistic in terms of expected system life or in view of possible obsolescence? The answer to this question will, of course, vary depending on the system and its intended mission. In the illustration, alternative *B* may be more cost-effective in the long run, but the advantages may be unrealistic in terms of time. This is an area that must be addressed in any analysis where two or more alternatives are being evaluated.

2.11. Summary

Figure 2-32 presents a basic equipment flow (the blocks shown may or may not represent a separate physical location and will vary depending on the type of system). Development is accomplished and the results are translated into production/construction and the distribution or delivery of an operational system. Logistic support in the design process (block 1) is primarily reflected through reliability, maintainability, and economic factors.

In production and/or construction, raw material and component parts (block 2) are transported to the plant (block 3), inspected, assembled, tested, and a finished product is delivered for operational use (block 5). Test and support equipment, spare/repair parts and inventory control, technical data, facilities, and personnel are required to support production/construction and distribution functions.

When operational (block 5), the system in performing its mission requires operators, trained personnel, transportation and handling equipment, data, and facilities. These elements of logistic support are necessary for successful mission fulfillment.

As the equipment progresses through its life cycle, corrective (unsched-

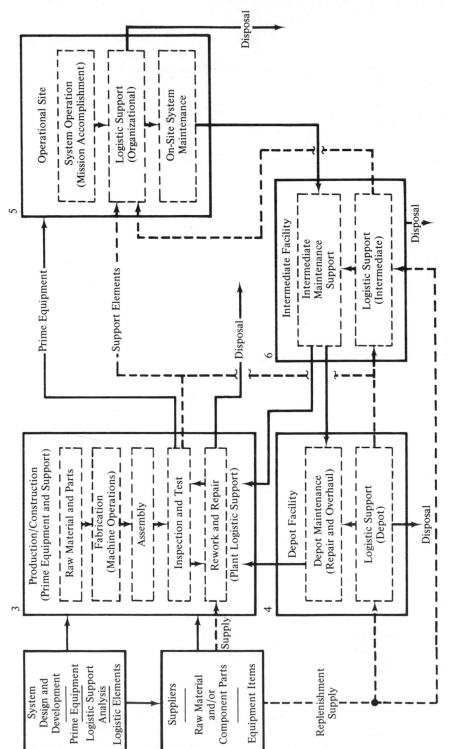

Figure 2-32. Operational/maintenance flow.

uled) and preventive (scheduled) maintenance actions are necessary to restore and/or retain the equipment in full operational status. Thus, Figure 2-32 presents the maintenance flow, including on-site or organizational maintenance (block 5), intermediate maintenance (block 6), and depot or plant support (blocks 3-4). Test and support equipment, spare/repair parts, maintenance personnel and training, data, and facilities are required to accomplish the maintenance functions at each level.

When dealing with total logistic support, the entire flow process must be treated as an entity. Each block represented in the figure impacts on another. The treatment of any single function must include consideration of the effects on other functions. For instance, a system is required to meet a particular operational effectiveness goal (e.g., availability of 90%). Considering that the system will fail at some point in time, a spares inventory is necessary at the organizational level (block 5) to ensure that the right spare item is available when needed. Assuming that the faulty item is a repairable, one has to determine the spares required at the intermediate level (block 6) or depot level (block 4) to support the necessary repair actions. Also, it is necessary to determine the test and support equipment required to accomplish the fault isolation and checkout to the equipment indenture level desired. The goal is to develop an overall optimum logistic support capability by evaluating alternative configurations, including various mixes of the logistic support elements at each level.

Accomplishment of this goal requires an understanding of the various logistics support measures presented in this chapter. These measures are closely interrelated, and each area must be addressed in the context of the system as an entity (i.e., the activities represented in Figure 2-32).

QUESTIONS AND PROBLEMS

1. Refer to Figure 2-1. What is the probability of success for a system if the system MTBF is 600 hours and the mission operating time is 420 hours? (Assume exponential distribution.)

2. A system consists of four subassemblies connected in series. The individual subassembly reliabilities are as follows:

   —Subassembly $A = 0.98$
   —Subassembly $B = 0.85$
   —Subassembly $C = 0.90$
   —Subassembly $D = 0.88$

   Determine the overall system reliability.

3. A system consists of three subsystems in parallel (assume operating redundancy). The individual subsystem reliabilities are as follows:

—Subsystem $A = 0.98$
—Subsystem $B = 0.85$
—Subsystem $C = 0.88$

Determine the overall system reliability.

4. Refer to Figure 2.8(c). Determine the overall network reliability if the individual reliabilities of the subsystems are as follows:

—Subsystem $A = 0.95$ —Subsystem $D = 0.94$
—Subsystem $B = 0.97$ —Subsystem $E = 0.90$
—Subsystem $C = 0.92$ —Subsystem $F = 0.88$

5. A system consists of five subsystems with the following MTBF's:

—Subsystem A: MTBF $= 10,540$ hours
—Subsystem B: MTBF $= 16,220$ hours
—Subsystem C: MTBF $= 9,500$ hours
—Subsystem D: MTBF $= 12,100$ hours
—Subsystem E: MTBF $= 3,600$ hours

The five subsystems are connected in series. Determine the probability of survival for an operating period of 1,000 hours.

6. The following corrective maintenance task times were observed:

Task Time (Min)	Frequency	Task Time (Min)	Frequency
41	2	37	4
39	3	25	10
47	2	35	5
35	5	31	7
23	13	13	3
27	10	11	2
33	6	15	8
17	12	29	8
19	12	21	14

(a) What is the range of observations?
(b) Using a class interval width of 4, determine the number of class intervals. Plot the data and construct a curve. What type of distribution is indicated by the curve?
(c) What is the geometric mean of the repair times?
(d) What is the standard deviation of the sample data?
(e) What is the M_{max} value?
(f) What is the $\bar{M}ct$?

7. The following corrective-maintenance task times were observed:

Task Time (Min)	Frequency	Task Time (Min)	Frequency
35	2	25	12
17	6	19	10
12	2	21	12
15	4	23	13
37	1	29	8
27	10	13	3
33	3	9	1
31	6	—	—

   (a) What is the range of observations?
   (b) Assuming 7 classes with a class interval width of 4, plot the data and construct a curve. What type of distribution is indicated by the curve?
   (c) What is the mean repair time?
   (d) What is the standard deviation of the sample data?
   (e) The system is required to meet a mean repair time of 25 minutes at a stated confidence level of 95%. Does the data reveal that the specification requirements will be met? Why?

8. Is the statistical distribution important in the prediction of specific reliability and maintainability factors? Why?

9. Assuming that a single component with a reliability of 0.85 is used in a unique application in the system and that one backup spare component is purchased, determine the probability of success by having a spare available in time, t, when required.

10. Assuming that the component in Problem 9 is supported with two backup spares, determine the probability of success by having two spares available when needed. Determine the probability of success for a configuration consisting of two operating components backed by two spares (assume that the component reliability is 0.875).

11. There are 10 systems located at a site scheduled to perform a 20-hour mission. The system has an expected MTBF of 100 hours. What is the probability that at least 8 of these systems will operate for the duration of the mission without failure?

12. An equipment contains 30 parts of the same type. The part has a predicted mean failure frequency of 10,000 hours. The equipment operates 24 hours a day and spares are provisioned at 90-day intervals. How many spares should be carried in the inventory to ensure a 95% probability of having a spare available when required?

13. Determine the economic order quantity of an item for spares inventory replenishment, where
    (a) The cost per unit is $100.
    (b) The cost of preparing for a shipment and sending a truck to the warehouse is $25.
    (c) The estimated cost of holding the inventory, including capital tied up, is 25% of the inventory value.
    (d) The annual demand is 200 units. Assume that the cost per order and the inventory carrying charge are fixed.

14. Refer to Figure 2-18. What happens to the EOQ when the demand increases? What happens when there are outstanding backorders? What factors are included in procurement lead time?

15. Assume that the average system maintenance cost is $5,000 per year for the next 10 years. What is the present value of the maintenance cost stream? The interest rate is 10%.

16. What is the present value of the cost stream illustrated below using an 8% discount rate?

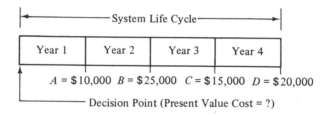

17. Two alternatives are being evaluated in terms of present cost in millions of dollars. Which one would you select? Why? Assume a 9% constant interest rate.

Design *A*

-R & D-				-Production-				-Operation and Maintenance-								
1	2	3	4	5	6	7	8	9	10	11	12	13	14	15	16	17
$ 0.5	0.9	1.2	1.3	5	7	9	8	8	1.5	1.5	1.5	1.6	1.7	1.7	1.8	1.9

Design *B*

-R & D-				-Production-				-Operation and Maintenance-								
1	2	3	4	5	6	7	8	9	10	11	12	13	14	15	16	17
$ 0.3	0.6	0.8	1.1	4	5	7	6	6	3	3	4	4	4	4	5	5

18. Compare the two design alternatives below in terms of equivalent costs at the designated decision point. Which alternative would you select? Assume a 10% constant interest rate.

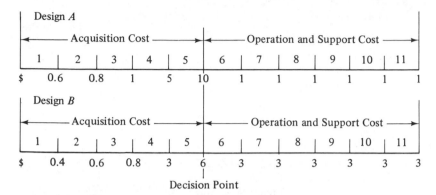

Design *A*

Decision Point

19. What is a break-even analysis? Why is it important?

20. Two different projects are identified by the cost streams illustrated below. Using a 10% discount rate, determine which project is preferred? At what point in time does the preferred project assume a favorable position? Illustrate by accomplishing a break-even analysis.

Project *A*

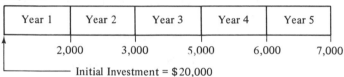

2,000   3,000   5,000   6,000   7,000

Initial Investment = $20,000

Project *B*

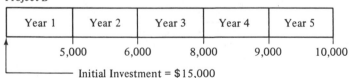

5,000   6,000   8,000   9,000   10,000

Initial Investment = $15,000

21. What would be the likely impact on LCC if:
(a) The system MTBF is decreased?
(b) The $\bar{M}ct$ is increased?
(c) The MMH/OH is increased?
(d) System utilization is increased?
(e) The fault isolation capability in the system were inadequate?
(f) The transportation time between the organizational and intermediate levels of maintenance increased?
(g) The turnaround time at the intermediate maintenance shop is decreased?
(h) The reliability of the test and support equipment at the intermediate maintenance shop is decreased?

22. Calculate as many of the following parameters as you can with the given information:

Determine:

A_i MTBM
A_a MTBF
A_o $\bar{\text{M}}$
$\bar{\text{M}}$ct   MTTR$_g$
M_{max}

Given:

$\lambda = 0.004$
Total operation time = 10,000 hours
Mean downtime = 50 hours
Total number of maintenance actions = 50
Mean preventive maintenance time = 6 hours
Mean logistics plus administrative time = 30 hours

23. Select a system of your choice and construct a flowchart identifying basic operational and maintenance functions similar to that presented in Figure 2-32. Identify areas where you believe that logistic support has an impact (be specific). What type of impact?

24. Given alternative *a* through *g*, which one would you select? Why?

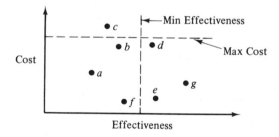

SYSTEM/EQUIPMENT OPERATIONAL REQUIREMENTS

With an understanding of the basic definitions and terminology presented thus far, one should be prepared to deal directly with the applications of logistics to the system life cycle. Chapters 3 through 10 cover various facets of the life cycle with the included material presented in a logical (evolutionary) order of development.

The life cycle commences with the identification of a need as illustrated in Figure 3-1. One might start by asking the following questions: What is the problem that we wish to solve? What is currently available or what must be developed in order to solve the problem? What is the type and extent of logistic support required?

There are many appropriate questions of this nature which must be addressed. As we answer some of these questions, pieces begin to fit together and a system need evolves. Once a system need is identified, it is necessary to "project" that need in terms of anticipated operational requirements. The identification of operational requirements, represented by block 1 of Figure 3-1, forms the basis for the development of the maintenance concept (block 2) and supporting logistic resources.

The operational concept as defined herein includes the following information:

3

1. *Mission definition*—identification of the prime mission of the system and alternate or secondary missions. What is the system to accomplish? How will the system accomplish its objectives? The mission may be defined through one or a set of scenarios.
2. *Performance and physical parameters*—definition of the operating characteristics or functions of the system (e.g., size, weight, range, accuracy, bits, capacity, transmit, receive, etc.). What are the critical system performance parameters?
3. *Operational deployment*—identification of the quantity of systems and the expected geographical location to include mobility requirements. What equipments are located where and when are they required? At what point in time does the system become fully operational?
4. *Operational life cycle (horizon)*—anticipated time that the system will be in operational use.
5. *Utilization requirements*—anticipated usage of the system and its elements (e.g., hours of operation per day, percentage of total capacity, operational cycles per month, facility loading, etc.).
6. *Effectiveness factors*—system requirements specified as figures of

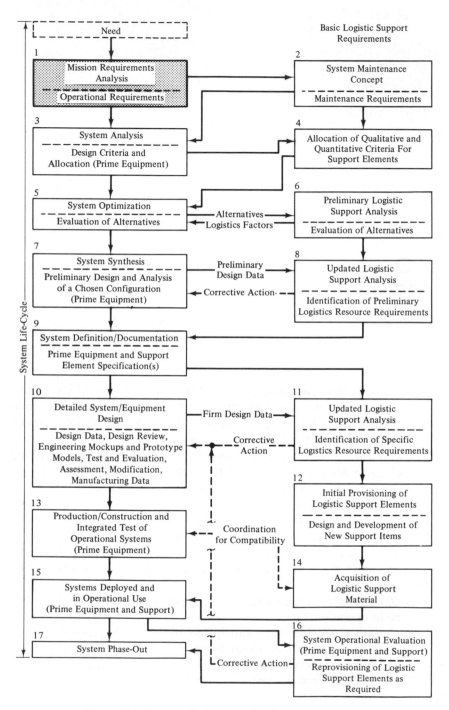

Figure 3-1. System design and development process.

merit for cost/system effectiveness, operational readiness, availability, dependability, MTBM, MTBR, MTBF, MDT, M̄ct, MMH/OH, $/OH, and so on.

7. *Environment*—definition of the environment in which the system is expected to operate (e.g., temperature, humidity, arctic, tropic, mountainous or flat terrain, airborne, ground, shipboard, etc.). This includes consideration of transportation and storage modes. What will the system be subjected to, and for how long?

Further discussion of system operational requirements is best covered through the presentation of two sample illustrations. The first illustration is a communication system with ground and airborne applications. The second deals with commercial airline requirements as related to a specific metropolitan area. These illustrations are discussed only to the depth necessary to show the relationship with the various elements of logistic support.

3.1. Illustration 1—Communication System

A new radio communication system with an increased range capability and improved reliability is required to replace several existing systems that are currently deployed in multiple quantities throughout the world. The system must accomplish three basic missions.

1. *Mission Scenario 1*—The system is to be installed in low-light aircraft (10,000 feet altitude or less) in quantities of one per aircraft. The system shall enable communication with ground vehicles dispersed throughout mountainous and flat terrain, and with a centralized area communication facility. It is anticipated that each aircraft will fly 15 missions per month with an average mission duration of 2 hours. A typical mission profile is illustrated in Figure 3-2. The communication system utilization requirement is 110%

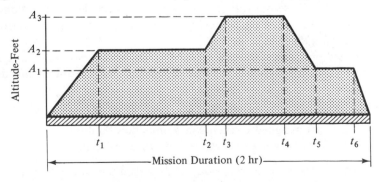

Figure 3-2. Mission profile.

(1.1 hours of system operation for every hour of aircraft operation, which includes air time plus some ground time). The system must be operationally available 99.5% of the time and have a reliability MTBF of not less than 2,000 hours.

2. *Mission Scenario 2*—The system is to be installed in ground vehicular equipment (e.g., car, light truck, or equivalent) in quantities of one per vehicle. The system shall enable communication with other vehicles at a range of 200 miles in relatively flat terrain, overhead aircraft at an altitude of 10,000 feet or less, and a centralized area communication facility. Sixty-five percent of the vehicles will be in operational use at any given point in time and the system shall be utilized 100% of the time for those vehicles which are operational. The system must have a reliability MTBF of at least 1,800 hours and a $\overline{M}ct$ of 1 hours or less.

3. *Mission Scenario 3*—The system is to be installed in 20 area communication facilities located throughout the world with 5 operational systems assigned to each facility. The system shall enable communication with aircraft flying at an altitude of 10,000 feet or less and within a radius of 500 miles from the facility, and with ground vehicles at a range of 300 miles in relatively flat terrain. Four of the systems are utilized 24 hours a day while the remaining system is a backup and used an average of 6 hours per day. Each operational system shall have a reliability MTBF of at least 2,500 hours and a $\overline{M}ct$ of 30 minutes or less. Each communication facility shall be located at an airport.

In the interest of minimizing the total cost of support (e.g., test and support equipment, spares, personnel, etc.), the transmitter–receiver, which is a major element of the system, shall be a common design for the vehicular, airborne, and ground applications. The antenna configuration may be peculiar in each instance.

Operational prime equipment shall be introduced into the inventory commencing 4 years from this date, and a maximum complement is acquired by 8 years. The maximum complement must be sustained for 10 years, after which a gradual phase-out will occur through attrition. The last equipment is expected to phase out of the inventory in 25 years. The program schedule is illustrated in Figure 3-3.

As stated previously, the new system will replace several different systems currently located throughout the world. Specifically, the requirements dictate the need for

—20 centralized communication facilities
—11 aircraft assigned to each communication facility
—55 vehicles assigned to each communication facility

Based on the three mission scenarios just defined, there is a total requirement for 1,420 prime equipments deployed in a series of communication networks (the total system) as illustrated in Figure 3-4.

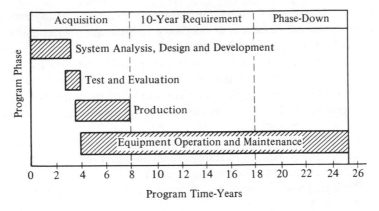

Figure 3-3. Program schedule.

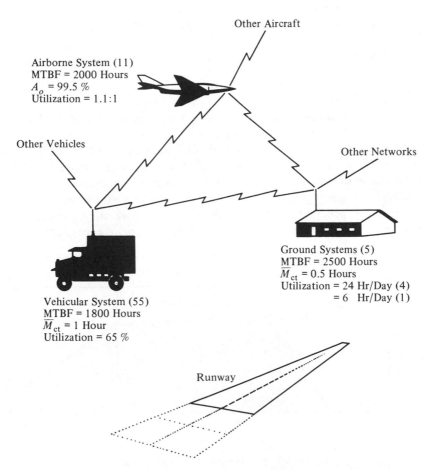

Other Aircraft

Airborne System (11)
MTBF = 2000 Hours
A_o = 99.5 %
Utilization = 1.1:1

Other Vehicles

Other Networks

Ground Systems (5)
$\underline{MTBF}$ = 2500 Hours
$\overline{M}_{ct}$ = 0.5 Hours
Utilization = 24 Hr/Day (4)
        = 6   Hr/Day (1)

Vehicular System (55)
$\underline{MTBF}$ = 1800 Hours
$\overline{M}_{ct}$ = 1 Hour
Utilization = 65 %

Runway

Figure 3-4. Illustration of a typical communication network.

A good definition of the planned system operational deployment (even if assumptions must be made) is necessary to determine what elements of logistic support are required and the location where the requirement will exist. For example, we know that 1,420 prime equipments are required and will be deployed to certain locations (designated by the need) as they are produced. We need to know the quantities deployed by designated location, time of deployment, distances, and operational environment to determine

1. Test and support equipment (to include transportation and handling requirements) needed to transport, install, and check out the systems as they arrive at the operational site(s).
2. Personnel and training requirements for operating and maintaining the system.
3. Spare-part types and quantities, inventory requirements, and so on, for maintaining the system.
4. Technical data, including system installation and operating instructions.
5. Facilities for equipment processing, installation, and operation.

The logistic support requirements are identified with the outflow of equipment indicated by blocks 1, 2, 3, and 5 of Figure 2-32. The depth and timing of logistic support is dependent on system production and the delivery rate specified by the program schedule (Figure 3-3).

In support of the program schedule and the basic need, it is necessary to develop an equipment inventory profile as shown in Figure 3-5. This provides an indication of the total quantity of prime equipments in the user's inventory during any given year in the life cycle. The front end of the profile represents the production rate, which of course may vary considerably, depending on the type and complexity of equipment, the capacity of the

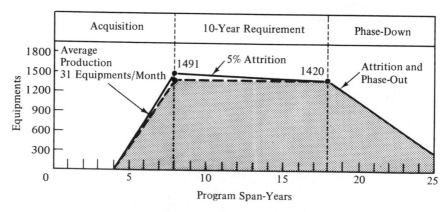

Figure 3-5. Equipment inventory profile.

production facility, and the cost of production. The total quantity of prime equipments produced is 1,491, which assumes (1) that 5% of the equipments will be condemned during the 10-year full-complement period due to loss or damage beyond economical repair; and (2) that production is accomplished on a one-time basis (to avoid production startup and shutdown costs). In other words, assuming that production is continuous, 1,491 equipments must be produced to cover attrition and yet maintain the operational requirement of 1,420 systems through the 10-year period. After the 10-year period, the quantity of systems is reduced by attrition and/or phaseout due to obsolescence until the inventory is completely depleted.

When predicting logistics requirements for system maintenance (e.g., the inflow of equipment items illustrated in Figure 2-32), one must initially determine the demand for maintenance. Given the demand, it is necessary to develop the system maintenance concept as described in Chapter 4. The demand for system maintenance is derived through an analysis of the inventory profile, the location of equipment, system utilization, equipment reliability, and so on.

The profile in Figure 3-5 indicates the total number of equipments in the inventory at any given time (i.e., 1,420 per year for the 10-year requirement). Operational deployment data will indicate the specific location of the equipment, and utilization factors will provide information on the hours of system operation. Although utilization will actually vary from one operational site to the next, the mission requirements described previously are used for planning purposes.

The intent is to determine the total hours of system operation for each year in the inventory profile (Figure 3-5). Considering each year of the 10-year full-complement period, we can calculate the total hours as

$$\text{total hours/year} = \text{(quantity of equipments)} \\ \times \text{(yearly hours of usage per equipment)} \quad (3.1)$$

or

$$\text{(20 communication facilities)} \times \text{(4 equipments)} \\ \times \text{(24 hours per day)} \times (360) = 691,200$$

and

$$\text{(20 communication facilities)} \times \text{(1 equipment)} \\ \times \text{(6 hours per day)} \times (360) = 43,200$$

and

$$\text{(220 airborne equipments)} \times \text{(30 hours per month)} \\ \times \text{(1.1 utilization)} \times (12) = 87,120$$

and

(1100 vehicular equipments) $\times$ (65%)
$$\times \text{ (24 hours per day)} \times (360) = \underline{6{,}177{,}600}$$
and

$$\text{total hours/year} = 6{,}999{,}120$$

Thus, the total usage for all prime equipments each year of the 10-year period is 6,999,120 hours. Usage during the introduction and phase-out periods is determined by the same method except that the quantity of systems is reduced. Using the required reliability MTBF factor specified for each mission (i.e., airborne, vehicular, and ground), one can predict the average number of corrective maintenance actions expected as a result of system failure. For instance,

$$\text{maintenance actions for vehicular systems} = \frac{\text{total vehicular hours}}{\text{MTBF}} \qquad (3.2)$$

or

$$\text{maintenance actions} = \frac{6{,}177{,}600}{1{,}800} = 3{,}432/\text{year}$$

For each centralized communication facility location where support is concentrated (55 vehicles per area communication facility), the expected quantity of maintenance actions due to failure is

$$\text{maintenance actions} = \frac{308{,}880}{1{,}800} = 171/\text{year/location}$$

By employing Poisson factors discussed earlier, one can predict the quantity of spare/repair parts. Through an analysis of each maintenance action, one can determine MDT, $\overline{M}ct$, MMH/OH, and associated logistic support resources.

Definition of the operational requirements for the radio communication system (e.g., deployment, utilization, effectiveness factors, etc.) provides the basis for determining the maintenance concept (refer to Chapter 4) and the identification of specific reliability, maintainability, and logistics quantitative factors. These data, in turn, are employed as input factors for system design and supporting analyses (refer to Chapter 5 and 6). As system development progresses, the communication system operational requirements are further refined (on an iterative basis). The presentation of an operational concept at the inception of a program is mandatory for the establishment of a baseline for all subsequent program actions.

3.2. Illustration 2—Commercial Airline Requirement

Three commercial airline companies are proposing to serve a large metropolitan area 8 years hence. As future growth is expected, additional airline companies may become involved at a later time. For planning purposes, the combined anticipated passenger handling requirement follows the projection in Figure 3-6.

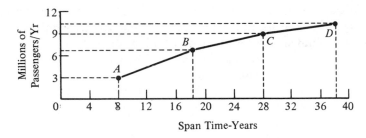

Figure 3-6. Projected passenger handling requirement.

The combined airline requirements are

A. Anticipated flight arrivals/departures (see Figure 3-6):

Time Period	Anticipated Flights per Day			
	Point A	Point B	Point C	Point D
6:00 a.m. to 11:00 a.m.	33	65	95	105
11:00 a.m. to 4:00 p.m.	17	43	50	55
4:00 p.m. to 9:00 p.m.	33	60	90	100
9:00 p.m. to 6:00 a.m.	3	10	15	18
Total	86	178	250	278

The flight arrivals are evenly spaced in the time periods indicated. It is assumed that 100 passengers constitute an average flight load.

B. The aircraft operational availability is 95%. In other words, 95% of all flights must be fully operational when scheduled (discounting aborts due to weather). Allowable factors for scheduled maintenance and passenger loading are

Function	Frequency	Downtime
Through service	Each through flight	30 minutes
Turnaround service	Each turnaround	1 hour
Termination check	Each terminal flight	6 hours
Service check	15 Days	9 hours

Periodic and main base checkouts will be accomplished elsewhere.

C. Allowable unscheduled maintenance in the area shall be limited to the organizational level and will include the removal and replacement of line replaceable items, tire changes, and engine replacements as required. The specific maintenance downtime (MDT) limits are

    Engine change   6 hours
    Tire change   1 hour
    Other items   1 hour

D. The metropolitan area must provide the necessary ground facilities to support the following types of aircraft (fully loaded): B–707, B–727, B–737, B–747, DC–10, L–1011, and V/STOL. In addition, provisions must be made for cargo handling and storage.

The airline companies have identified a need to provide air transportation service for a metropolitan area. From the airline standpoint, the metropolitan area must provide the necessary logistics resources (facilities, test and support equipment, personnel, etc.) to support this service. This involves selecting a site for an air transportation facility; accomplishing the design and construction of the facility; acquiring the test and support equipment, spare/repair parts, personnel and training, and data to support airline operations; and maintaining the total capability on a sustaining basis throughout the planning period.

Because of the size of the program and the growth characteristics projected in Figure 3-6, a three-phased construction effort is planned. The program schedule is presented in Figure 3-7.

The initial step is to select a location for the air transportation facility. The selection process considers available land, terrain, geology, wind effects, distance from the metropolitan area, access via highway and/or public transportation, noise and ecology requirements, and cost. Once a site has been established, the facility design and construction is accomplished. The facility must include runways, holding area, flight control equipment, airline terminal, control tower, operations building, hangars, maintenance docks, fuel docks, cargo handling and storage capability, utilities, and all the required support directly associated with passenger needs and comfort. Construction is accomplished in three phases, consistent with passenger handling growth and the schedule in Figure 3-7.

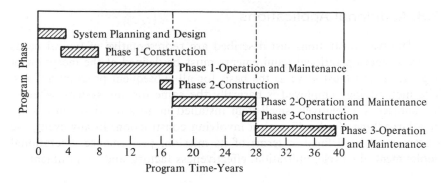

Figure 3-7. Program schedule.

The ultimate design configuration of the air transportation facility is based directly on the operational requirements—anticipated airline flight arrivals/departures, passenger loading, aircraft turnaround times, and maintenance and servicing requirements. For instance, at a point 18 years hence (Figure 3-6, point *B*), the anticipated average number of flights is 65 per day between the hours of 6:00 A.M. and 11:00 A.M. The number of through flights is 30 and the gate time for each is 30 minutes (to accomplish servicing and passenger loading), and the number of turnarounds is 35 with a gate time of 1 hour each. The total gate time required (considering no delays and assuming one gate for each aircraft arrival/departure) is 50 hours during the 6:00 A.M. to 11:00 A.M. time period; thus, at least 10 gates are required in the passenger terminal to satisfy the load. This, in turn, influences the size of the passenger waiting lobby and the number of airline personnel agents required. Further, the servicing and ground handling of the aircraft requires certain consumables (fuel, oil, lubricants), spare/repair parts, test and support equipment (towing vehicle, fuel truck, etc.), and technical data (operating and maintenance instructions). The possibility of unscheduled maintenance dictates the need for trained maintenance personnel, spare/repair parts, data, and a backup maintenance dock or hangar.

One can go on indefinitely identifying requirements to support the basic need of the metropolitan area and the commercial airline companies. It readily becomes obvious that logistic support plays a major role. There are logistic requirements associated with the aircraft, air transportation facility, and the transportation media between the air transportation facility and the metropolitan area. The commercial airline illustration presented herein merely touches on a small segment of the problem. The problem should be addressed from a total *systems approach* considering the functions associated with all facets of the operation. This would better emphasize the magnitude of the logistics involved.

3.3. Additional Applications

The two illustrations just described are representative of typical needs where system operational requirements must be defined at the inception of a program and must serve as the basis for all subsequent program actions. The methodology employed is basically the same for any system, whether the subject is a relatively small item installed in an aircraft or on a ship, or a large "one-of-a-kind" project involving construction. In any event, the system must be defined in terms of its mission, performance, operational deployment, life cycle, utilization, effectiveness factors, and environment.

QUESTIONS AND PROBLEMS

1. Why is the definition of system operational requirements important? What is included?

2. Select a system of your choice and develop an operational use plan. Include all of the factors that you consider necessary.

3. How do the following factors affect logistic support: operational deployment? system utilization? environment?

4. Referring to Figure 3-4, assume that we wish to determine the effectiveness of a communication network of one airplane, one vehicle, and one centralized area communication facility. Set up an expression for effectiveness.

5. If system utilization is increased, what is the impact on logistic support?

6. What is the impact on logistic support if the operational life cycle (horizon) is extended without producing additional equipments?

7. Why is the definition of the mission profile(s) important?

8. Referring to Figure 3-4, assume that equipment utilization is reduced from 65% to 50%. How is logistic support affected?

9. Referring to Figure 3-4, assume that the airborne equipment MTBF is reduced from 2,000 hours to 1,500 hours. How is logistic support affected?

10. Referring to Figure 3-5, if the equipment attrition is assumed to be 10% (average rate over the 10-year period when 1,420 equipments are required), how does this change in rate influence production?

11. What is the required availability for the facility communication system described in Mission 3 of Illustration 1? What is the allowable downtime for the aircraft communication system? What assumptions (if any) are required?

12. What operational requirements need to be specified to determine system life-cycle cost?

DEVELOPMENT OF MAINTENANCE
CONCEPT

The maintenance concept delineates maintenance support levels, repair policies, organizational responsibilities for maintenance, effectiveness measures (e.g., maintenance time and cost constraints, supply responsiveness factors, facility utilization requirements, etc.), maintenance environment(s), and is a principal factor in determining logistic support requirements. The concept serves several purposes.[1]

1. It provides the basis for the establishment of supportability requirements in system/equipment design. It also provides design criteria for major elements of logistic support (e.g., test and support equipment, large facility, etc.). For instance, if the repair policy dictates that no external test and support equipment is allowed at the operational site (organizational level), then the prime equipment design must incorporate some provision for built-in self-test.

2. It provides the basis for the establishment of requirements for total logistic support. The maintenance concept, supplemented by the logistic support analysis, leads to the identification of maintenance

---

[1]Additional references covering the maintenance concept in detail include (a) Blanchard, B. and Fabrycky, W., *Systems Engineering and Analysis*, Prentice-Hall, Inc., Englewood Cliffs, N.J., 1981; and (b) Blanchard, B. and Lowery, E., *Maintainability-Principles and Practices*, McGraw-Hill Book Company, New York, 1969.

4

tasks, task frequencies and times, personnel quantities and skill levels, test and support equipment, spare/repair parts, facilities, and other resources.

3. It provides a basis for detailing the maintenance plan and impacts upon the supply concept, training concept, supplier/customer services, phased logistic support, transportation and handling criteria, and production data needs.

Fulfillment of these purposes in an effective and economical manner requires that the maintenance concept be developed initially in conjunction with the definition of operational requirements at the inception of a program, and updated as the program develops. In any event, the maintenance concept must be defined prior to the start of system functional analysis and equipment design. The relative timing of concept definition in the system life cycle is illustrated in Figure 3-1 (block 2). Development of the maintenance concept at this stage will tend to ensure that all functions of design and support are integrated with each other and *track* the *same* concept. For instance, test and support equipment should accomplish functions that are compatible to the maintenance tasks accomplished at a given level, assigned personnel skills should be compatible with the complexity of the maintenance tasks performed, maintenance procedures should be oriented only to those tasks accomplished, and so on. If development of the maintenance concept is not considered at this stage, individual components of the system may reflect different design approaches (lack of standardization), and the various elements of support may be incompatible. This results in a costly situation.

Development of the maintenance concept evolves from the definition of operational requirements. For example, the radio communication system discussed in Chapter 3 (Figure 3-1) is deployed as shown in Figure 4-1.

The figure illustrates the quantity of systems deployed, the levels of maintenance, and the effectiveness factors (e.g., MTBF, $\overline{M}ct$, TAT, and

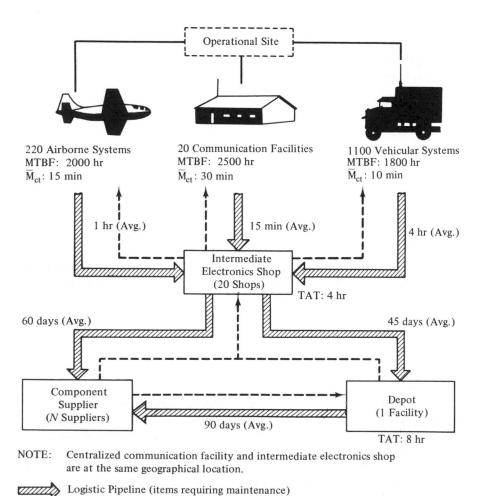

220 Airborne Systems
MTBF: 2000 hr
$\overline{M}_{ct}$: 15 min

20 Communication Facilities
MTBF: 2500 hr
$\overline{M}_{ct}$: 30 min

1100 Vehicular Systems
MTBF: 1800 hr
$\overline{M}_{ct}$: 10 min

1 hr (Avg.)   15 min (Avg.)   4 hr (Avg.)

Intermediate
Electronics Shop
(20 Shops)

TAT: 4 hr

60 days (Avg.)   45 days (Avg.)

Component
Supplier
(N Suppliers)

Depot
(1 Facility)

90 days (Avg.)

TAT: 8 hr

NOTE: Centralized communication facility and intermediate electronics shop
         are at the same geographical location.

⬜⬜⬜⇒   Logistic Pipeline (items requiring maintenance)

- - -►   Replenishment Supply (spare/repair parts)

Figure 4-1. Operational/maintenance concept.

logistics pipeline times). These factors are specified as design criteria for the prime equipment and its associated logistic support. It is realized that the times will vary depending on the specific geographical area of deployment. However, an average value is assumed and specified as a goal.

4.1. Levels of Maintenance

Maintenance may be classified as "on-equipment" maintenance or "off-equipment" maintenance, in terms of geographical location or type of facilities, on the basis of functions to be performed, and/or in terms of a combination of factors. The levels here are presented in the context of "organizational," "intermediate," and "depot" for the purposes of future reference and discussion. One must define the levels that are appropriate for the system in question, and these levels must be identified at this stage in the system life cycle.

A. ORGANIZATIONAL MAINTENANCE

Organizational maintenance is performed at the operational site (e.g., airplane, vehicle, or communication facility in Figure 4-1). Generally, it includes tasks performed by the using organization on its own equipment. Organizational-level personnel are usually involved with the operation and use of equipment, and have minimum time available for detail system maintenance. Maintenance at this level normally is limited to periodic checks of equipment performance, visual inspections, cleaning of equipment, some servicing, external adjustments, and the removal and replacement of some components. Personnel assigned to this level generally do not repair the removed components, but forward them to the intermediate level. From the maintenance standpoint, the least skilled personnel are assigned to this function. The design of equipment must take this fact into consideration (e.g., design for simplicity).

B. INTERMEDIATE MAINTENANCE

Intermediate maintenance tasks are performed by mobile, semimobile, and/or fixed specialized organizations and installations. At this level, end items may be repaired by the removal and replacement of major modules, assemblies, or piece parts. Scheduled maintenance requiring equipment disassembly may also be accomplished. Available maintenance personnel are usually more skilled and better equipped than those at the organizational level and are responsible for performing more detail maintenance.

Mobile or semimobile units are often assigned to provide close support to deployed operational equipments. These units may constitute vans, trucks or portable shelters containing some test and support equipment and spares. The mission is to provide on-site maintenance (beyond that accomplished by organizational-level personnel) to facilitate the return of the system to its full operational status on an expedited basis. A mobile unit may be used to support more than one operational site. A good example is the maintenance vehicle that is deployed from the airport hangar to an airplane parked at a commercial airline terminal gate and needing extended maintenance.

Fixed installations (permanent shops) are generally established to support both the organizational-level tasks and the mobile or semimobile units. Maintenance tasks that cannot be performed by the lower levels, due to limited personnel skills and test equipment, are performed here. High personnel skills, additional test and support equipment, more spares, and better facilities often enable equipment repair to the module and piece part level. Fixed shops are usually located within specified geographical areas. The intermediate electronics shop supporting the radio communication system illustrated in Figure 4-1 is an example. Rapid maintenance turnaround times are not as imperative here as at the lower levels of maintenance.

C. DEPOT MAINTENANCE

The depot level consitutes the highest type of maintenance, and supports the accomplishment of tasks above and beyond the capabilities available at the intermediate level. Physically, the depot may be a specialized repair facility supporting a number of systems/equipments in the inventory or may be the equipment manufacturer's plant. Depot facilities are fixed and mobility is not a problem. Complex and bulky equipment, large quantities of spares, environmental control provisions, and so on, can be provided if required. The high volume potential in depot facilities fosters the use of assembly-line techniques, which, in turn, permits the use of relatively unskilled labor for a large portion of the workload with a concentration of highly skilled specialists in such certain key areas as fault diagnosis and quality control.

The depot level of maintenance includes the complete overhauling, rebuilding, and calibration of equipment as well as the performance of highly complex maintenance actions. In addition, the depot provides an inventory supply capability. The depot facilities are generally remotely located to support specific geographical area needs or designated product lines. The three levels of maintenance discussed above are summarized in Table 4-1.

4.2. Repair Policies

Within the constraints of the concept illustrated in Figure 4-1, there are a number of possible repair policies. A repair policy specifies the anticipated extent to which repair of an equipment item will be accomplished (if at all). One or more policies may be stated as part of the initial mainte-

Table 4-1. MAJOR LEVELS OF MAINTENANCE

Criteria	Organizational Maintenance	Intermediate Maintenance			Depot Maintenance
		Mobile or semimobile units	Fixed units		
Done where?	At the operational site or wherever the prime equipment is located	Truck, van, portable shelter, or equivalent	Fixed field shop		Depot facility
					Specialized repair activity, or manufacturer's plant
Done by whom?	System/equipment operating personnel (low maint. skills)	Personnel assigned to mobile, semimobile, or fixed units (intermediate maintenance skills)			Depot facility personnel or manufacturer's production personnel (mix of intermediate fabrications skills and high maintenance skills)
On whose equipment?	Using organization's equipment	Equipment owned by using organization			
Type of work accomplished?	Visual inspection Operational checkout Minor servicing External adjustments Removal and replacement of some components	Detailed inspection and system checkout Major servicing Major equipment repair and modifications Complicated adjustments Limited calibration Overload from organizational level of maintenance			Complicated factory adjustments Complex equipments repairs and modifications Overhaul and rebuild Detailed calibration Supply support Overload from intermediate level of maintenance

nance concept. Each policy is evaluated in terms of impact on equipment design and logistic support, criteria are established, and equipment design progresses within the bounds of the repair policy selected. A typical repair policy is illustrated in Figure 4-2.

The repair policy may dictate that an item should be designed to be nonrepairable, partially repairable, or fully repairable.

A. NONREPAIRABLE ITEM

A nonrepairable item, generally modular in construction with a relatively low replacement cost, is one that is discarded when a failure occurs. No repair is accomplished and the item is replaced by a spare. The residue is then dispositioned as a throwaway or reclaimed for other usages. Referring to Figure 4-2, the policy may indicate that either Unit *A*, Unit *B*, or Unit *C* are discarded at the organizational level when the applicable item fails. No intermediate-level maintenance activity is required except for supplying a spare unit.

If this policy is selected, system design criteria should be established to promote a positive built-in unit self-test capability (high self-test thoroughness) to ensure that a failure has actually been confirmed prior to discarding the applicable unit. Otherwise when a failure is suspected, there is a good possibility of inadvertently discarding a good unit. This is costly!

The system should be designed such that the units are easily removable (plug-in). Since the unit is to be discarded at failure, the outside package can be hermetically sealed to improve reliability and add protection against humidity and corrosion. Further, there is no need for internal accessibility, test points, plug-in assemblies, modularization, and so on, which may result in a lighter-weight unit and a lower total production cost.

Logistic support requirements are minimal. Spare units must be stocked at each intermediate-level facility. No lower-level spares are required. Test and support equipment is necessary to initially check out units as they enter the inventory. No maintenance test equipment is required. Low personnel skills will suffice since maintenance is limited to a *remove and replace* function. Maintenance procedures are considerably simplified since there is no need to include coverage of unit maintenance. The objective is to weigh the cost of spares and unit disposal against the requirements for logistic support if the unit were repairable instead of being nonrepairable.

B. PARTIALLY REPAIRABLE SYSTEM

A partially repairable system may assume various forms. Referring to Figure 4-2, the policy illustrated indicates that unit repair is accomplished when a failure occurs. Unit repair constitutes the removal and replacement of assemblies, and the assemblies are repaired through the removal and replacement of circuit boards (CB's) and/or piece parts. Circuit boards are discarded at failure.

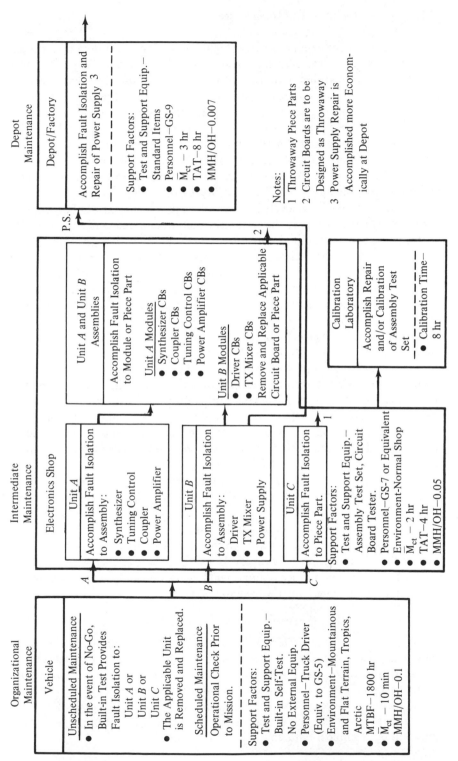

Figure 4-2. System maintenance concept flow (repair policy).

Organizational Maintenance

Vehicle

Unscheduled Maintenance
- In the event of No-Go, Built-in Test Provides Fault Isolation to:
  Unit A or
  Unit B or
  Unit C
- The Applicable Unit is Removed and Replaced.

Scheduled Maintenance
Operational Check Prior to Mission.

Support Factors:
- Test and Support Equip.—Built-in Self-Test. No External Equip.
- Personnel—Truck Driver (Equiv. to GS-5)
- Environment—Mountainous and Flat Terrain, Tropics, Arctic
- MTBF—1800 hr
- $\bar{M}_{ct}$ — 10 min
- MMH/OH—0.1

Intermediate Maintenance

Electronics Shop

Unit A
Accomplish Fault Isolation to Assembly:
- Synthesizer
- Tuning Control
- Coupler
- Power Amplifier

Unit B
Accomplish Fault Isolation to Assembly:
- Driver
- TX Mixer
- Power Supply

Unit C
Accomplish Fault Isolation to Piece Part.

Support Factors:
- Test and Support Equip.—Assembly Test Set, Circuit Board Tester.
- Personnel—GS-7 or Equivalent
- Environment—Normal Shop
- $\bar{M}_{ct}$ — 2 hr
- TAT—4 hr
- MMH/OH—0.05

Unit A and Unit B Assemblies
Accomplish Fault Isolation to Module or Piece Part

Unit A Modules
- Synthesizer CBs
- Coupler CBs
- Tuning Control CBs
- Power Amplifier CBs

Unit B Modules
- Driver CBs
- TX Mixer CBs
Remove and Replace Applicable Circuit Board or Piece Part

Calibration Laboratory
Accomplish Repair and/or Calibration of Assembly Test Set
- Calibration Time—8 hr

Depot Maintenance

Depot/Factory

Accomplish Fault Isolation and Repair of Power Supply 3

Support Factors:
- Test and Support Equip.—Standard Items
- Personnel—GS-9
- $\bar{M}_{ct}$ — 3 hr
- TAT—8 hr
- MMH/OH—0.007

Notes:
1 Throwaway Piece Parts
2 Circuit Boards are to be Designed as Throwaway
3 Power Supply Repair is Accomplished more Economically at Depot

P.S.

The selection of a repair policy is highly dependent on system operational requirements. For example, the system operational availability (A_0) may dictate a mean downtime requirement of such short duration that it can be met only providing for quick repair capability at the organizational level. Since the personnel skills and available equipment at the organizational level are limited, a need exists to design the equipment for easy and positive failure identification. Also, a requirement has been identified for the rapid removal and replacement of the applicable item once a failure has been confirmed. Thus, design criteria should cover built-in self-test features, modularization (plug-in units), and accessibility to the unit level.

At the intermediate level, a different requirement exists. The activity here is designed to support the organizational maintenance needs necessary to meet system operational mission objectives. Referring to Figure 4-2, internal test provisions (either an extension of the system built-in self-test or a set of separate test points) are necessary to enable fault isolation to the circuit board level. The circuit boards should be readily accessible and easily removable from the various assemblies. The circuit boards should be designed such that it becomes economical for discard at failure.

Alternative policies may dictate that units are repairable and assemblies are nonrepairable; or units are repairable, the synthesizer and driver assemblies are repairable, and the other assemblies are nonrepairable; or any combination of similar factors. The repair policy establishes goals for equipment design in terms of what is repairable and what is not, and the level of maintenance at which repair is accomplished. The support policy must consider *all* applicable levels of maintenance since a decision at one level impacts on the other levels, and must support system operational requirements.

Logistic support needs can be identified on a preliminary basis for each repair policy. For the policy conveyed in Figure 4-2, spare units, assemblies, and circuit boards are stocked at the intermediate electronics shop. No external test and support equipment is required at the organizational level; however, an assembly test set and circuit board tester are required at the intermediate shop. Personnel skill levels are specified together with effectiveness factors. These and other requirements are evaluated in terms of defining an optimal repair policy for the system.

C. FULLY REPAIRABLE SYSTEM

A fully repairable system promotes a level of maintenance beyond the repair policy illustrated in Figure 4-2. In other words, individual circuit boards within the Unit A and Unit B assemblies are deemed repairable. In this instance, specific design criteria must cover the circuit board down to the piece-part level. This policy reflects the greatest amount of logistic support in terms of test and support equipment, spare/repair parts, personnel and training, technical data coverage, and facilities.

As an aid in establishing and evaluating the various possible repair policies, the following questions may be employed as a guide to ensure complete coverage.

1. Are the anticipated scheduled and unscheduled maintenance functions defined for each maintenance level?
2. Are the applicable operational and supportability effectiveness factors identified for each maintenance level (e.g., A_0, MTBM, MTBR, MTBF, $\overline{M}$ct, $\overline{M}$pt, MMH/OH, TAT, logistics supply times)?
3. Do the applicable effectiveness factors support system operational requirements? Are they compatible from one maintenance level to the next?
4. What are the basic constraints and estimated requirements for test and support equipment?
5. What are the estimated personnel types and skill levels for each maintenance level?
6. What facility requirements are anticipated?
7. What are the anticipated maintenance environmental requirements associated with each level (e.g., transportation, storage, working conditions)?

A complete and comprehensive answer to these questions may not be possible at this stage in the system life cycle. However, it is necessary to identify these requirements on a preliminary basis in order to arrive at a preferred repair policy approach which is required as an input to the system/equipment design process.

4.3. Maintenance Concept Development

When developing the maintenance concept, one must analyze the system/equipment operational requirements and identify repair policies that will support these requirements. It is quite possible that there will be as many policy variations as one can imagine. The intent is to narrow the field down to one or two logical approaches.

At this stage in the system life cycle not too much is known about the equipment; thus, one might assume the options of *nonrepairable, partially repairable,* and *fully repairable,* as just described. Each option, which reflects the characteristics of equipment design and support, is evaluated in terms of an appropriate effectiveness figure of merit and life-cycle cost. Data input factors are based on experience obtained from similar systems as projected into the operational concept for the new system. The policy selected will be based on the relative merits of each when compared on an equivalent basis. If two policies are considered to be relatively effective, then the maintenance concept will include consideration of the two policies until detailed data

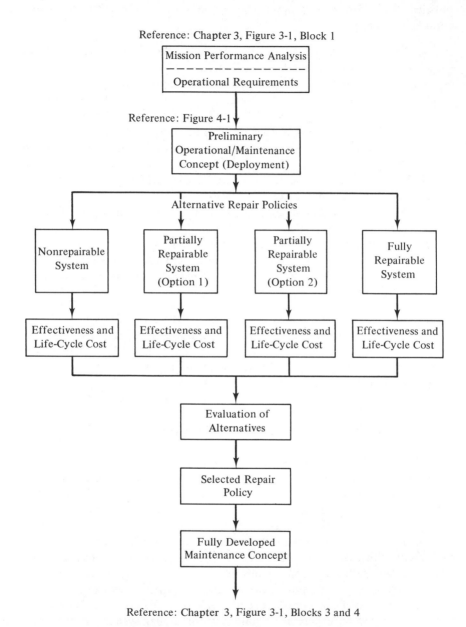

Figure 4-3. Maintenance concept development and optimization.

are available to enable the accomplishment of a more in-depth comparative analysis (i.e., logistic support analysis). The basic trade-off evaluation approach is illustrated in Figure 4-3.

Development of the maintenance concept is one of the most important steps in the system life cycle. It is from the maintenance concept that initial design requirements and support criteria evolve. Concept development must be relatively complete (covering all applicable levels of maintenance) to ensure that all significant alternative repair policies are adequately considered. Concept development is further supplemented by the logistic support analysis discussed in Chapter 6.

QUESTIONS AND PROBLEMS

1. When in the system life cycle should the maintenance concept be developed? Why?

2. What information should the maintenance concept convey?

3. How do system operational requirements influence the maintenance concept (be specific)?

4. How does the maintenance concept impact system/equipment design?

5. When evaluating alternative repair policies, what measures would you use? Why?

6. Develop a maintenance concept flow for a commercial airliner (refer to Figure 4-2.)

7. Select a system of your choice and develop a maintenance concept flow. Identify alternative repair policies where appropriate.

8. Develop a maintenance concept flow for a major home appliance.

9. Referring to Figure 4-1, what is the impact of the logistics pipeline times and facility turnaround times on total logistic support? What impact does the $\bar{M}ct$ value of 15 minutes for the airborne system have on the maintenance concept?

10. Reliability and maintainability quantitative factors defined as part of the maintenance concept serve what purpose?

11. What factors would be considered in determining which maintenance functions should be accomplished at the organization level, at the intermediate level, and at the depot level?

12. Personnel skill levels are higher at the organizational level that at other levels of maintenance. True or false? Why?

13. Maintenance concept development is pertinent to what type of system?

14. Referring to Figure 4-1, what factors must be considered in determining spare/repair part requirements at the intermediate electronics shop?

15. Referring to Figure 4-1, if the shop TAT is increased to 10 hours, how does this increase impact logistic support?

16. When developing the maintenance concept, all applicable echelons of maintenance must be considered on an integrated basis. Why?

FUNCTIONAL ANALYSIS
AND ALLOCATION

The translation of system operational and maintenance factors into specific qualitative and quantitative system design requirements is accomplished through a logical functional analysis and allocation process. Basically, the process provides

1. The identification and sequencing of operational and maintenance functions necessary to achieve the system requirements defined in Chapters 3 and 4.
2. The definition of performance parameters, operational effectiveness, and supportability factors associated with each function. This includes the consideration of system boundaries, constraints, and anticipated use conditions.
3. The identification of performance, operational, and supportability factors with a top-level physical description of the system or an equipment packaging scheme, and the allocation of requirements as appropriate to effect design.

These steps are accomplished early in the system/equipment life cycle and are represented by blocks 3 and 4 of Figure 3-1. As such, the functional analysis serves as the starting point for equipment design.

5

5.1. System Functional Analysis

The initial step constitutes the formulation of a functional description of the system and all facets of system development and operation. Functions are identified, and functional flow diagrams are developed for the primary purpose of structuring system requirements in functional terms. The functional approach assures

1. That all facets of system development, operation, and support are covered. This includes design, production/construction, test, deployment, transportation, training, operation, and maintenance as illustrated by the steps depicted in Figure 2-32.
2. That all elements of the system (e.g., prime equipment, test and support equipment, facilities, personnel, data, software, etc.) are fully recognized and defined.
3. That a means of relating equipment packaging concepts and support requirements to given functions is provided. This identifies the relationship between the "need" and the "resources required" to support that need.

The initial step in the functional analysis constitutes the formulation of a functional description of the system and all facets of system development and operation. Functions are identified, and functional flow diagrams are developed for the primary purpose of structuring system requirements in functional terms. Functions represent those top-level performance characteristics and/or actions that must be accounted for. Functions may be classified as independent functions or dependent functions and are presented in a series format, a parallel format, or a combination of both.

A. Functional Flow Diagrams

The translation of system operational and maintenance concepts into specific qualitative and quantitative design requirements commences with the identification of the major functions that the system is to perform followed by the development of functional flow diagrams. Functional flow diagrams are employed as a mechanism for portraying system design requirements in a pictorial manner, illustrating series–parallel relationships, the heirarchy of system functions, functional interfaces, and so on. Functional flow diagrams are designated as top level, first level, second level, and so on. The top level shows gross operational functions. The first-level and second-level diagrams represent progressive expansions of the individual functions of the preceding level. Functional flow diagrams are prepared down to the level necessary to establish the needs (hardware, software, facilities, personnel, data) of the system. Functions identified on each diagram are numbered in a manner that preserves the continuity of functions and provides traceability throughout the system to the function origin. The indenture numbering of functions by level is illustrated in Figure 5-1.

The functions identified should not be limited to only those necessary for operation of the system, but must consider the possible impact of maintenance on system design. Maintenance requirements (evolving from the maintenance concept) should be addressed to preclude the possibility of developing a technically feasible system from an operational viewpoint, without first determining whether or not the system can be effectively and economically supported throughout its planned life cycle. Experience has indicated that the costs associated with system maintenance and support often far exceed the cost of system acquisition. The objective is to attain the proper balance of performance, effectiveness, support, and economic factors.

The benefits associated with the generation of functional flows are many. First, the process enables the engineer to approach design from a logical and systematic standpoint. The proper sequences and design relationships are readily established. Second, the preparation of functional flows forces the integration of the numerous interfaces that exist in system development and operation. Both internal and external interface problems are quickly identified at an early stage in the life cycle. Sometimes these benefits are difficult to visualize unless one has actually had some experience in functional analysis. However, it has been shown that many design problems which occur later

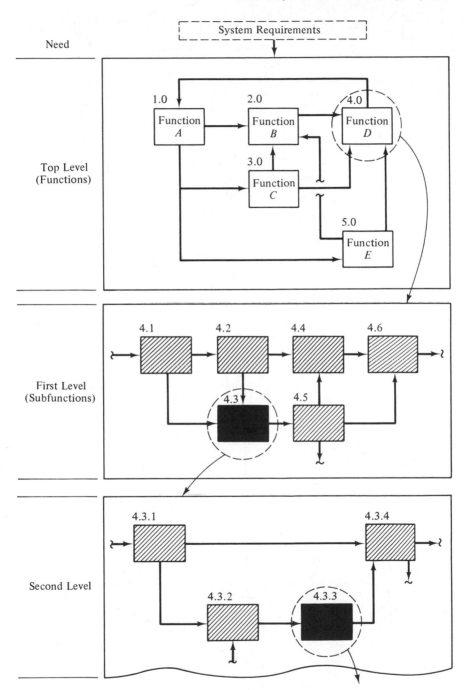

Figure 5-1. System functional indenture levels.

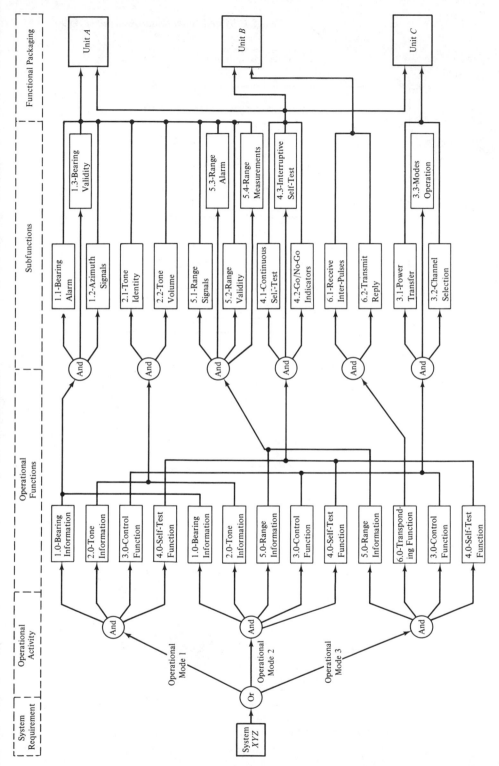

Figure 5-2. System XYZ operational functional-flow diagram.

120

in the life cycle could have been avoided had this approach been followed initially.

B. OPERATIONAL FUNCTIONS

The functional description represents an overall portrayal of the functions that are necessary to describe total system activities. Gross operational activities are defined in terms of mission activities (i.e., the system operational requirements described in Chapter 3). This may constitute a description of the various modes of system operation and utilization. For instance, typical gross operating functions might be (1) "prepared aircraft for flight," (2) "fly aircraft from point *A* to point *B*," and (3) "recycle aircraft for the next flight." In the case of a communications system, typical operation functions might include (1) "develop a communications system for an urban area of a given geographical size and population," (2) "produce and install a communications network," and (3) "accomplish the communication of certain designated information throughout the urban area for 7 days per week, 6 hours per day." System functions necessary to support the identified modes of operation are then described. Ultimately, the functional description is completed to the level where initial physical packaging concepts are visualized.[1]

Figure 5-2 represents a typical system operational functional flow diagram. The system covered will henceforth be noted as System *XYZ*.

Referring to Figure 5-2, the major operational functions of System *XYZ* are described, and the respective blocks are numerically identified for reference purposes. Each major function, in turn, is then analyzed and expanded through the identification of subfunctions as indicated in Figure 5-3.

Reference: Figure 5-2

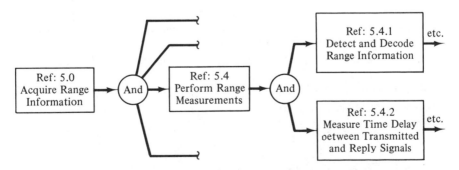

Figure 5-3. Range information functional-flow diagram.

---

[1]It should be noted that equipment design is by no means formulated at this time. A gross-level configuration is developed for the purpose of allocating requirements. This configuration which serves as a starting point may be verified or may change as a result of subsequent analyses.

Considering the desirability of packaging equipment by function (consistent with system size and weight constraints), the packaging scheme for System *XYZ* results in three basic units (Units *A*, *B*, and *C*). The operational functions incorporated in each of the three units are indicated in Figure 5-2. Developing the design concept further, an analysis of the functions contained within each unit will lead to the identification of major assemblies. Given a broad functional packaging scheme, it is then possible to allocate performance parameters and operational effectiveness factors to the unit level and possibly the assembly level. This allocation serves as the basis for subsequent detail design.

C. MAINTENANCE FUNCTIONS

Once operational functions are defined, the system description leads to the development of gross maintenance functions. For example, there are specified performance requirements (signal level, tolerances, accuracies, unit dimension, etc.) for each operational function. A check of the applicable function will indicate either a go or a no-go decision. A go decision leads to a check of the next operational function. A no-go indication (constituting a symptom of malfunction) provides a starting point for the development of detailed maintenance functional flows and logic troubleshooting diagrams. A gross-level maintenance functional flow is illustrated in Figure 5-4.

Maintenance functions identified at this point will reflect consideration for the effectiveness and supportability factors specified at the system level as well as available logistic resources. In some instances, it may be possible to expand top level functional flows in a manner similar to the example presented in Figure 5-3. In most cases, however, only an estimate of first-level maintenance functions can be made, since the availability of preliminary engineering data is limited. Maintenance functional flows can and should also be prepared for preventive maintenance, transportation and handling functions, support equipment corrective maintenance, servicing, inspections, and so on. In any event, the maintenance functional flow diagrams that are developed are used to update the system maintenance concept (discussed in Chapter 4) in terms of functions by level and a preliminary equipment packaging scheme. The maintenance concept/functional flow development process is iterative, and is continued throughout the early system definition process.

5.2. Allocation of Requirements[2]

The preceding discussion covered the first step in the process of translating system operational and maintenance activities into specific system

---

[2]Allocation refers to the distribution, allotment, or apportionment of top-level requirements to lower indenture levels of the system.

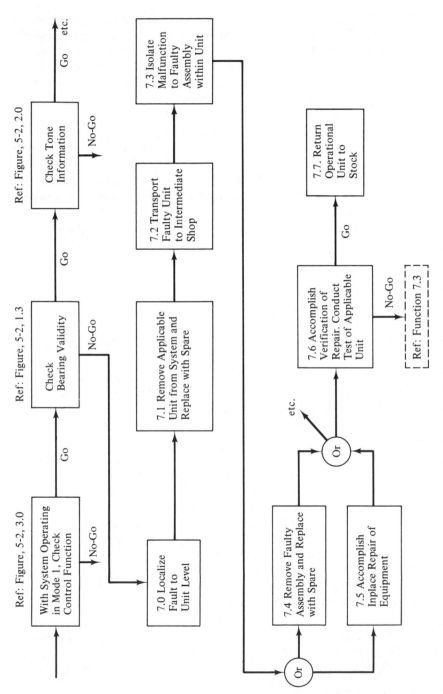

Figure 5-4. Maintenance functional-flow diagram.

123

design criteria.[3] The functional analysis provides a description of major system functions and defines a preliminary equipment packaging concept. The next step involves the allocation of system top level factors to the various subelements of the system. For instance, a reliability MTBF of 450 hours specified for System *XYZ* in Figure 5-2 should be allocated to Units *A*, *B*, and *C*. The MTBF value assigned at the unit level is employed as a design goal for that unit. The same is true for maintainability factors, supportability characteristics, performance parameters, cost goals, and so on. The individual factors for the three units, when combined, must support the overall system requirement.

Relative to logistic support, it is necessary to establish appropriate criteria that, when imposed on prime equipment design, will produce a system that can be supported in an optimum manner. This is the point in the system life cycle where design is flexible and supportability characteristics can be included at a minimum cost to the program.

A. RELIABILITY ALLOCATION[4]

After an acceptable reliability factor (e.g., probability of survival) or failure rate has been established for the system, it must be allocated among the various subsystems, units, assemblies, and so on. The allocation commences with the generation of a reliability block diagram. The block diagram is a further extension of the functional flow diagrams presented in Figures 5-2 and 5-3. The intent is to develop a reasonable approximation of those elements or items that must function for successful operation of the system. To the extent practicable, the diagram should be structured so that each block represents a functional entity that is relatively independent of neighboring blocks.

In the development of a block diagram, items that are predominantly electronic in function are noted as electronic elements and items that are basically mechanical are identified accordingly. Item redundancy contemplated at this stage of system planning should be illustrated along with any planned provisions for alternative operating mode capability.

Figure 5-5 is a simplified reliability block diagram and the progressive expansion of such from the system level down as design detail becomes known. Generally, levels I and II are available through conceptual design activity, while levels III and on are defined in preliminary system design.

Referring to the figure, the reliability requirement for the system (e.g.,

---

[3]A group of characteristics provided as input to the design process (e.g., factors that dictate system or equipment design).

[4]An in-depth coverage of reliability allocation is not intended nor is it practical within the confines of this text. The review of additional text material is recommended for students desiring comprehensive coverage of the subject matter.

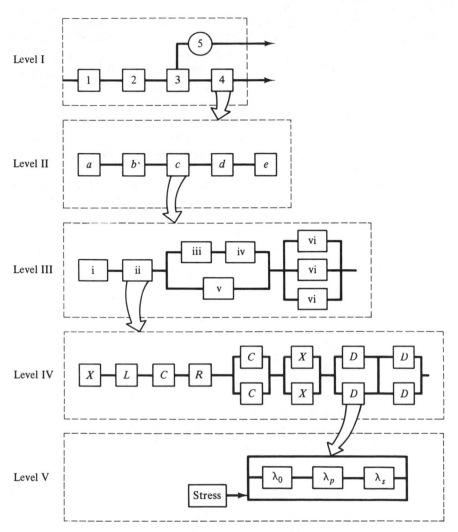

Figure 5-5. Reliability block diagram approach ("N" levels). (NAVAIR 00-65-502/NAVORD OD 41146, *Reliability Engineering Handbook*, U.S. Navy, Revised March 1968, Washington, D.C.)

λ, R, MTBF) is specified for the entire network identified in level I, and an individual requirement is specified for each individual block in the network. For instance, the reliability of block 3, Function X, may be expressed as a probability of survival of 0.95 for a 4-hour period of operation at level I. Similar requirements are specified for blocks 1, 2, 4, and 5. These, when combined, will indicate the system reliability, which in turn is evaluated in terms of the overall requirement.

Block diagrams are generated to cover each of the major functions identified in Figure 5-2. Success criteria (go/no-go parameters) are established and failure rates (λ) are estimated for each block, the combining of which provides an overall factor for a series of blocks constituting a function or subfunction. Depending on the function, one or more or these diagrams can be related to a physical entity such as Unit *A* in Figure 5-2 or an assembly of Unit *A*. The failure-rate information provided at the unit/assembly level represents a reliability design goal. This, in turn, represents the anticipated frequency of corrective maintenance that is employed in the determination of logistic resource requirements.

The approach used in determining failure rates may vary depending on the maturity of system definition. Failure rates may be derived from direct field and/or test experience covering like items, reliability prediction reports covering items that are similar in nature, and/or engineering estimates based on judgement. In some instances weighting factors are used to compensate for system complexity and environmental stresses.

When accomplishing reliability allocation, the following steps are considered appropriate.

1. Evaluate the system functional flow diagram(s) and identify areas where design is known and failure-rate information is available or can be readily assessed. Assign the appropriate factors and determine their contribution to the top-level system reliability requirement. The difference constitutes the portion of the reliability requirement which can be allocated to the other areas.
2. Identify the areas which are new and where design information is not available. Assign complexity weighting factors to each functional block. Complexity factors may be based on an estimate of the number and relationship of parts, the equipment duty cycle, whether an item will be subjected to temperature extremes, etc. That portion of the system reliability requirement which is not already allocated to the areas of known design is allocated using the assigned weighting factors.

The end result should constitute a series of lower-level values which can be combined to represent the system reliability requirement initially specified (i.e., MTBF of 450 hours for System *XYZ*). The combining of these values is facilitated through the application of a reliability mathematical model.

A reliability mathematical model is developed to relate individual "block" reliability to the reliabilities of its constituent blocks or elements. The procedure simply consists of determining a mathematical expression that represents the probability of survival for a small portion of the proposed configuration. Multiple applications of this process will eventually reduce the original complex system to an equivalent serial configuration. It is then possible to represent the system with a single probability statement. Some of the mathematical relationships used in this instance were described in Section 2.1.

When allocating a system level requirement (i.e., MTBF of 450 hours), one should construct a simplified functional breakdown as illustrated in Figure 5-6. The diagram must reflect series–parallel relationships.

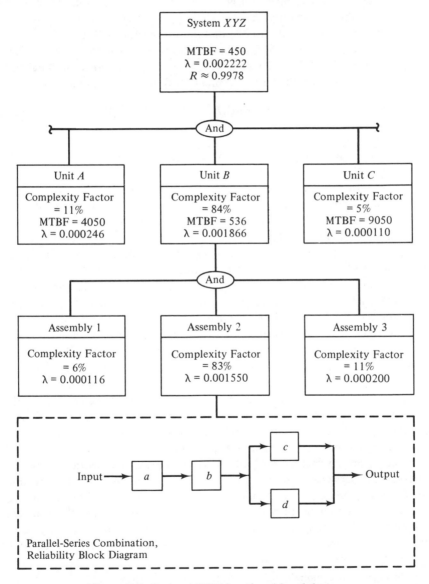

Figure 5-6. System *XYZ* functional breakdown.

Initially, failure rates are identified for items of known design and are deducted from the overall system requirement. A complexity factor may be established for each of the remaining items.[5] The complexity factors are used to apportion failure rates to the next lowest level and on down. As a check, failure rates at the assembly level are totaled to obtain the unit failure rate, and unit failure rates support the system failure rate (note that Units A, B, and C represent a series operation). The MTBF is usually assumed to be the reciprocal of the failure rate, and the reliability (R) of the system or unit may be determined from Equation (2.5) or the nomograph in Figure 2-3.

Referring to Figure 5-6, a reliability block diagram showing the functional relationship of four elements (a, b, c, and d) illustrates the "makeup" of Assembly 2. The mathematical expression for the four elements is

$$R_{\text{assy. 2}} = (R_a)(R_b)[R_c + R_d - (R_c)(R_d)] \tag{5.1}$$

Using the general relationships in Equation (2.5), reliability factors and failure rates can be determined. In this instance, the total failure rate for Assembly 2 should not exceed 0.00155.

Review of the equipment breakdown configuration illustrated in Figure 5-6 indicates a top-level system requirement supported by factors established at the unit level and on down. Unless otherwise specified, the requirements at the unit level may be altered or traded off as long as the combined unit level requirements support the system objective. In other words, the failure rate of Unit B may be higher and the failure rate of Unit A may be lower than indicated without affecting the requirement of 0.002222 and so on! The techniques of trading off different parameters to meet an overall requirement are discussed further in Chapter 6.

The reliability factors established for the various items identified in Figure 5-6 serve as design criteria. For instance, the engineer responsible for Unit B shall design Unit B such that the failure rate (λ) shall not exceed 0.001866. As design progresses, reliability predictions are accomplished and the predicted value is compared against the requirement of 0.001866. If the predicted value does not meet the requirement (i.e., higher failure rate or lower MTBF), then the design configuration must be reviewed for reliability improvement and design changes are implemented as appropriate.

The allocated factors not only provide the designer with a reliability criterion, but serve as an indicator of the frequency of corrective maintenance due to anticipated equipment failure. Assume that System XYZ is projected into an operational posture similar to the one described for the vehicular communication system in Chapter 3, and that the total system operating time per year is 60,000 hours for a 10-year period. The expected quantity of

---

[5]In Figure 5-6, complexity factors are assumed for all items.

system maintenance actions due to failure is

$$\text{expected maintenance actions} = \frac{\text{total operating hours per year}}{\text{MTBF}} \quad (5.2)$$

or

$$\text{expected maintenance actions} = \frac{60,000}{450} = 133/\text{year}$$

Assuming that each of the units is operating or energized on a full-time basis when the system is operational, then the quantity of expected maintenance actions for each unit can be determined from Equation (5.2). The results are 15 maintenance actions per year for Unit A, 112 maintenance actions per year for Unit B, and 6 maintenance actions per year for Unit C. The frequency of maintenance is a necessary input in the determination of logistic resource requirements (material and cost) for a system or equipment.

B. MAINTAINABILITY ALLOCATION

The process of translating system maintainability requirements (e.g., MTBM, $\bar{M}$ct, $\bar{M}$pt, MMH/OH) into lower-level design criteria is accomplished through maintainability allocation.[6] The allocation requires the development of a simplified functional breakdown as illustrated in Figure 5-6. The functional breakdown is based on the maintenance concept, functional analysis data, and a description of the basic repair policy—whether a system is to be repaired through the replacement of a unit, an assembly, or a part.

For the purpose of illustration, it is assumed that System XYZ must be designed to meet an inherent availability requirement of 0.9989, a MTBF of 450, and a MMH/OH (for corrective maintenance) of 0.2 and a need exists to allocate $\bar{M}$ct and MMH/OH to the assembly level.[7] The $\bar{M}$ct equation is

$$\bar{M}\text{ct} = \frac{\text{MTBF}(1 - A_i)}{A_i} \quad (5.3)$$

or

$$\bar{M}\text{ct} = \frac{450(1 - 0.9989)}{0.9989} = 0.5$$

Thus, the system's $\bar{M}$ct requirement is 0.5 hour, and this requirement must be allocated to Units A, B, C, and the assemblies within each unit. The

---

[6]Maintainability allocation is also discussed in Blanchard, B., and Lowery, E., *Maintainability—Principles and Practices*, McGraw-Hill Book Company, New York, 1969.

[7]MTBM and $\bar{M}$pt may be allocated on a comparable basis as MTBF and $\bar{M}$ct, respectively.

allocation process is facilitated through the use of a format similar to that illustrated in Table 5-1.

Referring to Table 5-1, each item type and the quantity (Q) of items per system are indicated. Allocated reliability factors are specified in column 3, and the degree to which the failure rate of each unit contributes to the overall failure rate (represented by C_f) is entered in column 4. The average corrective maintenance time for each unit is estimated and entered in column 6. These times are ultimately based on the inherent characteristics of equipment design, which are not known at this point in the system life cycle. Thus, corrective maintenance times are initially derived using a complexity factor which is indicated by the failure rate. As a goal, the item that contributes the highest percentage to the anticipated total failures (Unit B in this instance) should require a low $\overline{M}$ct, and those with low contributions may require a higher $\overline{M}$ct. On certain occasions, however, the design costs associated with obtaining a low $\overline{M}$ct for a complex item may lead to a modified approach which is feasible as long as the end result ($\overline{M}$ct at the system level) falls within the quantitative requirement.[8]

The estimated value of C_t for each unit is entered in column 7, and the sum of the contributions for all units can be used to determine the overall system's $\overline{M}$ct as

$$\overline{M}\text{ct} = \frac{\sum C_t}{\sum C_f} = \frac{1.077}{2.222} = 0.485 \qquad (5.4)$$

In Table 5-1, the calculated $\overline{M}$ct for the system is within the requirement of 0.5 hour. The $\overline{M}$ct values for the units provide corrective maintenance downtime criteria for design, and the values are included in equipment design specifications.

Once allocation is accomplished at the unit level, the resultant $\overline{M}$ct values can be allocated to the next lower equipment indenture item. For instance, the 0.4-hour $\overline{M}$ct value for Unit B can be allocated to Assemblies 1, 2, and 3, and the procedure for allocation is the same as employed in Equation (5.4). An example of allocated values for the assemblies of Unit B is included in Table 5-2.

The $\overline{M}$ct value covers the aspect of *elapsed* or *clock* time for restoration actions. Sometimes this factor, when combined with a reliability requirement, is sufficient to establish the necessary maintainability characteristics in design. On other occasions, specifying $\overline{M}$ct by itself is not adequate since there may be a number of design approaches which will meet the $\overline{M}$ct requirement but

---

[8]Note that, in any event, the maintainability parameters are dependent upon the reliability parameters. Also, it will frequently occur that reliability allocations are incompatible with maintainability allocations (or vice versa). Hence, a close feedback relationship between these activities is mandatory.

Table 5-1. SYSTEM XYZ ALLOCATION

1 Item	*2* Quantity of Items per System (Q)	*3* Failure Rate $(\lambda) \times 1000\ hr$	*4* Contribution of Total Failures $C_f = (Q)(\lambda)$	*5* Percent Contribution $C_p = C_f/\sum C_f \times 100$	*6* Average Corrective Maint. Time $\bar{M}ct\ (hr)$	*7* Contribution of Total Corrective Maint. Time $C_t = (C_f)(\bar{M}ct)$
1. Unit A	1	0.246	0.246	11%	0.9	0.221
2. Unit B	1	1.866	1.866	84%	0.4	0.746
3. Unit C	1	0.110	0.110	5%	1.0	0.110
Total			$\sum C_f = 2.222$	100%		$\sum C_t = 1.077$

$\bar{M}ct$ for System $XYZ = \dfrac{\sum C_t}{\sum C_f} = \dfrac{1.077}{2.222} = 0.485$ Hour (Requirement: 0.5 Hour)

Table 5-2. UNIT B ALLOCATION

1	2	3	4	5	6	7
Assembly 1	1	0.116	0.116	6%	0.5	0.058
Assembly 2	1	1.550	1.550	83%	0.4	0.620
Assembly 3	1	0.200	0.200	11%	0.3	0.060
Total			1.866	100%		0.738

$$\overline{\text{M}}\text{ct for Unit } B = \frac{\sum C_t}{\sum C_f} = \frac{0.738}{1.866} = 0.395 \text{ Hour (Requirement: 0.4 Hour)}$$

not necessarily in a cost-effective manner. Meeting a $\overline{\text{M}}$ct requirement may result in an increase in the skill levels of personnel accomplishing maintenance actions, increasing the quantity of personnel for given maintenance functions, and/or incorporating automation for manual operations. In each instance there are costs involved; thus, one may wish to specify additional constraints such as the skill level of personnel at each maintenance level and the maintenance manhours per operating hour (MMH/OH) for significant equipment items. In other words, a requirement may dictate that an item be designed such that it can be repaired within a specified elapsed time with a given quantity of personnel possessing skills of a certain level. This will influence design in terms of accessibility, packaging schemes, handling requirements, diagnostic provisions, and so on, and is perhaps more meaningful in terms of designing for logistic support.

The factor MMH/OH is a function of task complexity and the frequency of maintenance. The system-level requirement is allocated on the basis of system operating hours, the anticipated quantity of maintenance actions, and an estimate of the number of manhours per maintenance action. Experience data are used where possible.

Following the completion of quantitative allocations for each indenture level of equipment, all values are included in the functional breakdown illustrated in Figure 5-7. The illustration provides an overview of major system design requirements.

C. ALLOCATION OF LOGISTICS FACTORS

In addition to reliability and maintainability parameters and their impact on design, one must also consider other factors that are critical to successful system operation. These factors, some of which were introduced in Sections 2.3 through 2.7, deal with supply support, test and support equipment, personnel and maintenance organization, facilities, and transportation.

As mentioned earlier, *all* elements of the system must be addressed to include the various activities depicted in Figure 2-32. Thus, it may be neces-

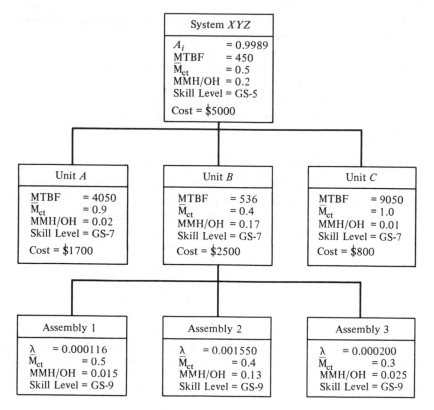

Figure 5-7. System XYZ functional requirements.

sary to establish some additional design criteria covering the various elements of logistic support. A few examples are noted below.

1. Test equipment utilization in the intermediate maintenance shop shall be at least 80%.
2. Self-test thoroughness for the system (using the built-in test capability) shall be 95% or better.
3. Personnel skill levels at the organizational level of maintenance shall be equivalent to grade x or below.
4. The maintenance facility at the intermediate level shall be designed for a minimum of 75% utilization.
5. The transportation time between the location where organizational maintenance is accomplished and the intermediate maintenance shop shall not exceed 48 hours.
6. The turnaround time in the intermediate maintenance shop shall be 5 days (or less), and 15 days (or less) in the depot maintenance facility.

7. The probability of spares availability at the organizational level of maintenance shall be at least 90%.

In essence, in defining system operational requirements and the maintenance concept (described in Chapters 3 and 4), system supportability factors must be determined along with performance parameters. These factors, established at the system level, may be allocated to the extent necessary to influence design activities.

D. ALLOCATION OF ECONOMIC FACTORS

Using an approach similar to that described in previous sections, cost factors may be allocated as appropriate to system needs. If the ultimate product is to be cost-effective, it may be desirable to assign cost targets for various equipment items. For instance, an objective might be to design System XYZ such that the unit system cost is $5,000, based on a production quantity of 300 and an operational life of 10 years. Unit cost constitutes total life-cycle cost (to include research and development, production, and operation and maintenance cost) divided by the quantity of systems. This cost factor, specified at the top level, can be apportioned to lower equipment indenture levels as cost targets for design. Cost targets combined with reliability (or equivalent) requirements may create a boundary situation for design as illustrated in Figure 2-29. In other words, one can *design to a cost*.

5.3. Design Criteria

With the identification of operational and maintenance functions and the accomplishment of requirements allocation, it is possible to generate detail design criteria. Such criteria constitute specific requirements in the areas of equipment packaging/modularization, standardization, interchangeability, mounting provisions, degree of self-test features and the placement of test points, extent of automation versus manual provisions, repair versus discard levels, safety features, labeling, and so on. These criteria may be stated qualitatively or quantitatively, and are employed as guidelines for the design engineer. Qualitative criteria must support the quantitative goals developed through allocation. The criteria thus established have a direct impact on system/equipment design, which, in turn, affects logistic support.

In regard to the development of design criteria, a few examples are provided for illustrative purposes:

1. Through evaluating the combination of requirements covering reliability and cost, it is often possible to determine whether an item should be designed for *repair at failure* or for *discard at failure*. If the reliability of an

item is high enough (e.g., one anticipated failure in 50,000 hours of system operation) and the unit cost is low enough (e.g., $100), it may not be economically feasible to establish a repair capability with the associated logistic support to enable repair of that item when failure occurs. Thus, the item is discarded at failure and there is no need to incorporate provisions for accessibility, test points, modular packaging, and so on, within that item. This, of course, has a significant impact on spare parts, test equipment, personnel training, and maintenance data requirements. Although many decisions of this type will be based on further analysis (refer to the discussion on trade-offs in Chapter 6), it is often possible to establish general criteria which specify that items with a reliability exceeding a given value and a unit cost less than a specific amount will be designed for discard at failure. Experience data from similar systems already in the operational inventory are used in establishing such criteria.

2. Referring to Unit B of System XYZ in Figure 5-7, the allocated $\overline{M}ct$ of 0.4 hour means that in the event of malfunction, the maintenance technician must be able to complete the corrective maintenance cycle (refer to Figure 2-9) in 24 minutes. Based on experience data for like equipment, about 60 % of the total corrective maintenance time (on the average) involves malfunction localization and isolation. Assuming that this percentage is valid for System XYZ, an estimate of allowable localization and isolation time for Unit B would be 14 minutes. Complying with the 14-minute goal would necessitate the availability of a few readily accessible test points or readout devices to allow positive fault isolation to any one of the three assemblies of Unit B. The exact quantity and placement of test points depends on the degree of functional packaging, and a preliminary indication of such can be determined through an analysis of maintenance functional-flow diagrams. The type of test and support equipment required will be based on the results.

Of the remaining 10 minutes in the maintenance cycle, the technician must accomplish the disassembly, repair, and checkout functions (or removal and replacement functions). This infers that each of the three assemblies of Unit B must be directly accessible and must not require the removal of another assembly to gain access. In addition, each assembly should be modular with plug-in and/or quick-release features, and should be interchangeable with like spares so as to minimize alignment and adjustment requirements after item installation. These and other similar considerations are necessary to meet the $\overline{M}ct$ objective.

3. The allocated skill level and maintenance manhour requirements (refer to Figure 5-7) indicate the personnel resources that will be available for the accomplishment of future system maintenance. The type and complexity of tasks which an individual with a given skill is able to perform are defined based on past experience. The specification of skill level and MMH/OH requirements dictates that equipment design shall be constrained to the

extent that anticipated maintenance tasks can be adequately and effectively accomplished within the prescribed limits. This infers that equipment design should consider the incorporation of simple readout devices, the proper layout of equipment front panels, automation of complex operating functions, standardization of components, labeling, and other provisions that will facilitate the ease and simplicity in the accomplishment of maintenance functions. The proper consideration of these provisions is facilitated through the application of good human engineering principles.

The established design criteria must be consistent with system operational requirements, the maintenance concept, and the factors defined through allocation. Such criteria provide initial guidelines to the design engineer. Through the early phases of system development, design progress is monitored in terms of compliance with these guidelines. This monitoring process is accomplished through day-to-day design liaison activity, reliability and maintainability predictions, logistic support analyses, and periodic design reviews.

4. An allocated cost target (i.e., design to a cost) will influence reliability, maintainability, supportability, and other characteristics of design. It may appear to be too costly (from the standpoint of design labor, production material, etc.) to incorporate certain provisions in the design; however, by not doing so, the subsequent operational and maintenance costs may be high. The allocation of criteria for design should be assessed on a continuing basis in terms of total life-cycle cost and not just one element of cost.

QUESTIONS AND PROBLEMS

1. A functional analysis serves what purpose?
2. Can a functional analysis be accomplished on any system or equipment item?
3. Select a task or function of your choice and develop operational and maintenance functional flow diagrams to the second level.
4. Expand the second-level functional flow diagrams in Problem 3 to the third level.
5. What is the purpose of allocation?
6. How does the allocation process affect logistic support?
7. What are the steps involved in a reliability allocation? What are the steps involved in a maintainability allocation?
8. In your own words, define "failure rate." How are failure rates determined?
9. Select a system of your choice and assign top-level requirements. Accomplish a reliability allocation to the second indenture level. Accomplish a maintainability allocation to the same level. Allocate supportability factors as appropriate.

10. What is meant by "design criteria"? How are criteria developed? How are criteria applied to the design process?

11. From the allocations in Problem 9, develop design criteria for the system.

12. Referring to Figure 5-7, System XYZ has the following requirements: MTBF = 650, $\bar{M}ct$ = 0.6, MMH/OH = 0.7, and unit cost = $10,000. Allocate these requirements to Units *A*, *B*, *C*, and to Assemblies 1, 2, and 3 of Unit *B*.

13. In the following figure, allocate the quantitative factors to the unit level as indicated.

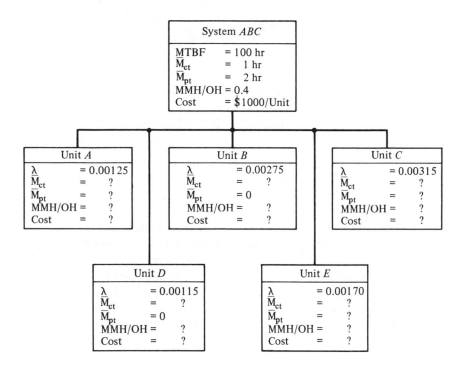

LOGISTIC SUPPORT ANALYSIS

Logistic support analysis (LSA) constitutes the integration and application of various analytical techiques to solve different types of problems of varying magnitudes.[1] LSA, in its application, is a *process* employed on an iterative basis throughout system design and development. The depth of application is appropriately tailored to the problem at hand.[2]

LSA, which is an inherent part of the overall system engineering effort, addresses itself to the evaluation of a given or proposed configuration in terms of (1) its direct impact on total logistic support for each proposed configuration, and (2) the feedback effects of logistic support on the configuration itself. As a result of these feedback effects, changes are made to improve the initial configuration. As illustrated in Figure 6-1, LSA forces the early consideration and ultimate compatibility of the prime equipment and its associated logistic support through an iterative process of analysis.

---

[1]Analytical techniques may include one or a combination of reliability analysis and prediction, cost-effectiveness modeling, maintenance analysis, logistics modeling, simulation, linear/dynamic programming, and so on. The application in this text relates to the usage of these techniques in defining and optimizing (to the extent possible) logistic support resource requirements for a given system. Some of the quantitative factors involved are covered in Chapter 2.

[2]Tailoring refers to the application of the proper level of anlaysis for the problem. Too much analysis or too little analysis can be costly. In addition, the analysis must be timely.

6

The LSA process is depicted in Figure in 6-2 and can be applied in varying degrees to a wide spectrum of problems. This application can be accomplished in a number of ways.

1. LSA aids in the evaluation of system operational requirements specified in the initial phases of a program (refer to Chapter 3). Given the choice of several alternative approaches relative to anticipated mission accomplishment, equipment deployment, utilization, and so on, the approach reflecting the most cost-effective solution should be apecified. LSA facilitates the evaluation of alternatives.

2. LSA aids in the evaluation of alternative repair policies allowable within the constraints dictated by the maintenance concept and the allocated criteria defined in Chapters 4 and 5, respectively. For example, LSA supports the determination of the repair policy to be established which is consistent with the maintenance concept and which will most favorably affect the system/equipment design in terms of supportability.

3. LSA aids in the evaluation of specific characteristics in the equipment design (e.g., inherent reliability and maintainability features). This includes alternative packaging schemes, test approaches, accessibility features, transportation and handling provisions, and so on. Logistic

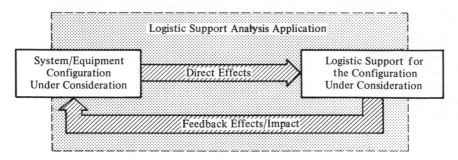

Figure 6-1. Prime equipment-logistic support interface relationship.

support resource requirements are estimated for each alternative being considered and a preferred approach is selected.[3] This, in turn, directly affects the final design.

4. LSA aids in the evaluation of two or more off-the-shelf equipment items being considered for a single application. Assuming that new design is not appropriate (due to cost, production lead time, etc.), which item, when installed as part of the system, will reflect the least overall logistics burden? LSA facilitates the evaluation effort which in turn impacts the type of procurement (e.g., single buy, multiyear buy if a number of systems are involved) as well as the type contract.

5. LSA aids (through reliability and maintainability analysis and predictions, maintenance analysis, cost-effectiveness modeling) in the determination of specific logistic support resource requirements based on a fixed or assumed design configuration. Once that design data are available, it is possible to determine the type and quantity of test and support equipment, spare/repair parts, personnel quantities and skills, training requirements, technical data, facilities, and transportation and handling requirements.

6. LSA aids (through application of operations analysis and logistics modeling with the appropriate input field data) in the measurement and evaluation of the overall effectiveness of the prime equipment and its associated support. Problem areas readily become apparent and LSA can assist in the evaluation of alternatives for corrective action, including inprovements in the uses and applications of support resources.

LSA, as applied to the overall system life cycle is represented by blocks 6, 8, and 11 in Figure 6-3. Basically, LSA serves as a tool employed in the

---

[3]The term *preferred* does not necessarily imply *optimal* as the operational requirements and maintenance concept may not permit true optimization. *Preferred* does imply the best among a number of alternatives within the given constraints.

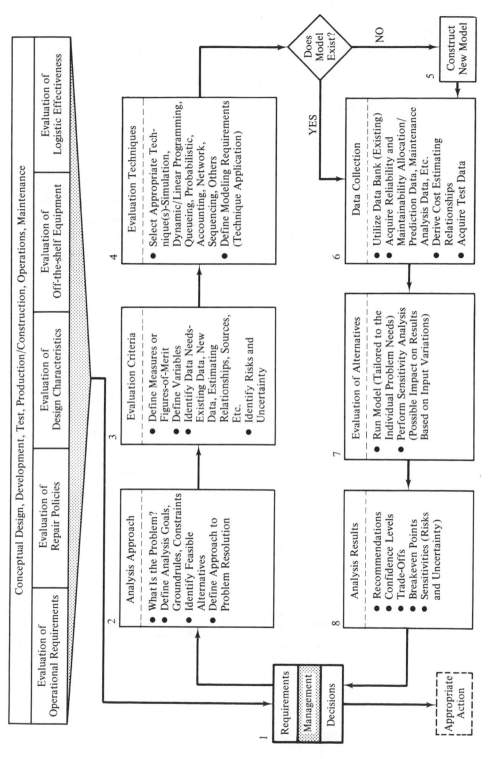

Figure 6-2. Logistic support analysis approach.

141

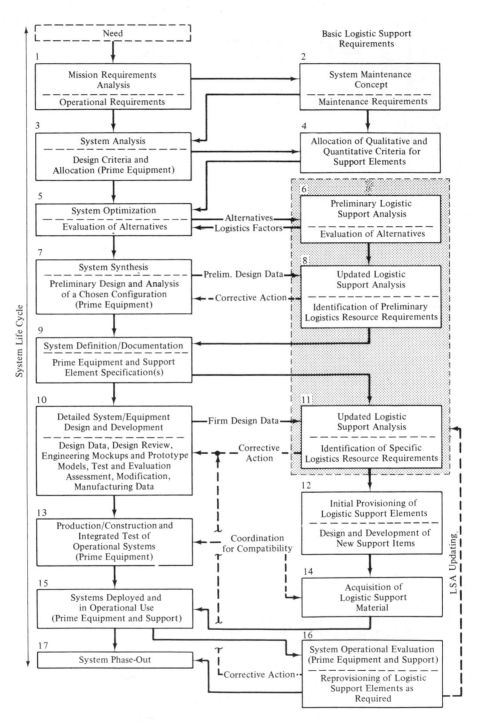

Figure 6-3. System development process.

evaluation of alternatives, the results of which lead to a preferred system prime equipment and support configuration in terms of a best mix of logistics resources. Through LSA, it is appropriate to evaluate both the total system as well as different aspects of the system on an independent basis. For instance: alternative design configurations may be evaluated in terms of fixed operational requirements and a known maintenance concept; different repair policies may be evaluated in terms of a fixed design configuration; and so on! Through numerous iterations of this type (supported by a responsive corrective action process), the overall system prime equipment and support configuration should approach an optimal state.

During the early conceptual stage of a new system development, LSA is accomplished at a gross level (using rough estimates for input data) since the various elements of the system are not adequately defined. As design progresses or in the event of an off-the-shelf item, the analysis assumes a more refined approach since firm design data and/or engineering models are available. Detailed predictions, maintenance analyses, and test results constitute input data into the LSA process. In any event, LSA is appropriate in all phases of system design and development, and the proper application of LSA is essential if the system produced is to be cost-effective and the logistic support is to be adequately planned.

6.1. Analysis Approach

The LSA process commences with the identification of a need for analysis supported by the necessary management action to initiate the steps required in fulfilling analysis objectives. The basic steps in a typical analysis are illustrated in Figure 6-2, although the extent of effort and depth of coverage will vary depending on the problem situation.

Early in the system life cycle (see Figure 6-3, block 6), the objective is to design a system to meet the requirements identified through functional analysis and allocation (discussed in Chapter 5). There may be a number of alternative approaches in accomplishing this objective, each of which represents a configuration which can be evaluated in terms of some measure of effectiveness, total life-cycle cost, or equivalent figure of merit. The intent is to select the best approach by conducting a series of individual evaluations where each evaluation stems from a specific problem definition.

A. DEFINITION OF PROBLEM

The initial step involves the clarification of objectives, defining the issues of concern, and limiting the problem such that it can be studied in an efficient and timely manner. In many instances, the nature of the problem appears to be obvious, whereas the precise definition of the problem may be the most difficult part of the entire process. Unless the problem is clearly and precisely defined, it is doubtful whether an analysis of any type will be meaningful.

B. IDENTIFICATION OF FEASIBLE ALTERNATIVES

The next step is to identify possible alternative solutions to the problem. All possible candidates must be initially considered, and yet the more alternatives that are considered, the more complex the analysis process becomes. Thus, it is desirable to list *all* possible candidates to ensure against inadvertent omissions, and then eliminate those candidates which are clearly unattractive, leaving only a few for evaluation. Those few candidates are then analyzed with the intent of selecting a preferred approach.

C. SELECTION OF EVALUATION CRITERIA

The criteria employed in the evaluation process may vary considerably depending on the stated problem and the level and complexity of the analysis. For instance, at the system level, parameters of primary importance include cost effectiveness, system effectiveness, logistics effectiveness, life-cycle cost, operational availability, performance, and so on. At the detail level, the order of parameters will be different, as illustrated in Figure 6-4.

The parameters selected as evaluation criteria should relate directly to the problem statement. For instance, the problem may be to design a system that will perform a certain mission with a specific degree of effectiveness at minimum life-cycle cost. There may be several possible alternative design approaches, each of which is evaluated in terms of system effectiveness and life-cycle cost. On the other hand, the problem may entail the selection of the best among several alternative off-the-shelf equipment items using support-ability characteristics in design as criteria (e.g., accessibility, standardization of components, diagnostic aids, etc.). In this instance, there are a number of evaluation factors.

In the event that a number of parameters are involved, each parameter should be reviewed from the standpoint of relevancy or degree of importance. The degree of importance may be realized by applying parameter weighting factors (the most important items receiving the heaviest weighting). The application of weighting factors will depend on the evaluation technique employed.

D. APPLICATION OF ANALYTICAL TECHNIQUES

The next step involves the analytical phase. This entails the selection and combining of various analytical techniques in the form of a model or a series of models.[4]

---

[4]There are many types of models to include physical models, abstract models, symbolic models, mathematical models, and so on. Model, as defined here, refers primarily to a mathematical (or analytical) model.

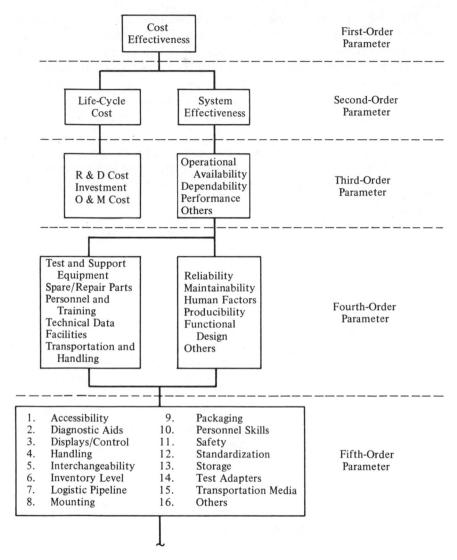

Figure 6-4. Order of evaluation parameters.

A model is a simplified representation of the real world which abstracts the features of the situation relative to the problem being analyzed. It is a tool employed by the analyst to assess the likely consequences of various alternative courses of action being examined. The model must be adapted to the problem at hand and the output must be oriented to the selected evaluation criteria. The model, in itself, is not the decision maker, but is a tool which provides the necessary data in a timely manner in support of the decision-making process.

The model may be quite simple or very complex, highly mathematical or not at all mathematical, computerized or manually implemented, and so on. The extensiveness of the model will depend on the nature of the problem relative to the quantity of variables, input parameter relationships, number of alternatives being evaluated, and the complexity of operation. The ultimate objective in the selection or development of a model is simplicity and usefulness. The model utilized should incorporate the following features.

1. The model should represent the dynamics of the system being evaluated in a way that is simple enough to understand and manipulate, and yet close enough to the operating reality to yield successful results.
2. The model should highlight those factors that are most relevant to the problem at hand, and suppress (with discretion) those that are not as important.
3. The model should be comprehensive by including *all* relevant factors and reliable in terms of repeatability of results.
4. Model design should be simple enough to allow for timely implementation in problem solving. Unless the tool can be utilized in a timely and efficient manner by the analyst or the manager, it is of little value. If the model is large and highly complex, it may be appropriate to develop a series of models where the output of one can be tied to the input of another. Also, it may be desirable to evaluate a specific element of the system independently from other elements.
5. Model design should incorporate provisions for easy modification and/or expansion to permit the evaluation of additional factors as required. Successful model development often includes a series of trials before the overall objective is met. Initial attempts may suggest information gaps which are not immediately apparent and consequently may suggest beneficial changes.

The use of mathematical models offers significant benefits.

1. In terms of system application, a number of considerations exist— operational considerations, design considerations, production/construction considerations, testing considerations, and logistic support considerations. There are many interrelated elements that must be integrated as a system and not treated on an individual basis. The model makes it possible to deal with the problem as an entity and allows consideration of all major variables of the problem on a simultaneous basis. Quite often the model will uncover relations between the various aspects of a problem which are not apparent in the verbal description.

2. The mathematical model enables a comparison of *many* possible solutions and aids in selecting the best among them rapidly and efficiently.
3. The mathematical model often explains situations that have been left unexplained in the past by indicating cause-and-effect relationships.
4. The mathematical model readily indicates the type of data that should be collected to deal with the problem in a quantitative manner.
5. The model facilitates the prediction of future events, such as effectiveness factors, reliability and maintainability parameters, logistics requirements, and so on. In addition, the model aids in identifying areas of risk and uncertainty.

When analyzing a problem in terms of selecting a mathematical model for evaluation purposes, it is desirable to first investigate the tools that are currently available.[5] If a model already exists and is proven, then it may be feasible to adopt that model. However, extreme care must be exercised to relate the right technique with the problem being addressed and to apply it to the depth necessary to provide the sensitivity required in arriving at a solution. Improper application may not provide the results desired and may be costly.

On the other hand, it might be necessary to construct a new model. In accomplishing such, one should generate a comprehensive list of system/ equipment parameters that will describe the situation being simulated. Next, it is necessary to develop a matrix showing parameter relationships, each parameter being analyzed with respect to every other parameter to determine the magnitude of relationship.[6] Model input/output factors and parameter feedback relationships must be established. The model is constructed by combining the various factors and then testing for validity. Testing is difficult to do since the problems addressed primarily deal with actions in the future which are impossible to verify. However, it may be possible to select a known system or equipment item which has been in the inventory for a number of years and exercise the model using established parameters. Data and relationships are known and can be compared with historical experience. In any event, the analyst might attempt to answer the following questions.[7]

---

[5] A representative sample of some currently available models and their application is included in Appendix C.

[6] An illustration of parameter relationships is indicated through the mathematical expressions included in Appendices A and B.

[7] Modeling and modeling applications are discussed further in (a) Blanchard, B. S., and Fabrycky, W. J., *Systems Engineering and Analysis*, Prentice-Hall, Inc., Englewood Cliffs, N. J., 1981; (b) Fabrycky, W. J., Ghare, P. M., and Torgersen, P. E., *Industrial Operations Research*, Prentice-Hall, Inc., Englewood Cliffs, N. J., 1972; (c) Fisher, G. H., *Cost Considerations in System Analysis*, American Elsevier Publishing Co. Inc., New York, 1971; and (d) other literature dealing with management science and operations research methods.

1. Can the model describe known facts and situations sufficiently well?
2. When major input parameters are varied, do the results remain consistent and are they realistic?
3. Relative to system application, is the model sensitive to changes in operational requirements, production/construction, and logistic support?
4. Can cause-and-effect relationships be established?

Model development is an art and not a science, and is often an experimental process. Sometimes the analyst requires several iterations prior to accomplishing his objectives of providing a satisfactory analytical tool.

E. DATA GENERATION AND APPLICATION

One of the most important steps in the analysis process is to assemble the appropriate input data. The right type of data must be collected in a timely manner and must be presented in the proper format. Specific data requirements are identified from the evaluation criteria and from the input requirements of the model used for evaluation purposes.

When evaluating a typical system or equipment item, it is necessary to consider operational requirements, the maintenance concept, design features, production/construction plans, anticipated logistic support, and so on. For instance, if the analyst wishes to compare alternative design approaches, each proposed configuration must be projected in terms of a planned operational posture. In addition, an assumed maintenance concept and an estimate of anticipated logistic support requirements are necessary in order to accomplish the evaluation on a life-cycle basis. On the other hand, the analyst may wish to evaluate alternative system operational concepts. This requires an assumed maintenance concept, design configuration, and logistic support policy. In other words, the analysis (particularly at an early phase in the life cycle) is an iterative process involving the evaluation of different element of the system in terms of the whole, keeping certain features constant while varying others, and so on. The objective is to accomplish the analysis keeping in mind the interface relationship between logistic support and the prime system/equipment configuration depicted in Figure 6-1.

Fulfilling this overall objective requires a variety of data, the depth and scope of which depends on the type of evaluation being performed and the program phase during which the evaluation is accomplished. In the early phases of system development, available data are limited; thus, the analyst must depend on the use of various estimating relationships, projections based on past experience covering similar type systems, and intuition. As the system design progresses, improved data (analyses and predictions) are available and used as an input to the evaluation. Ultimately, when hardware is available and in the field, test and field data are available for assessment purposes; thus, the analyst starts with a rough estimation and works toward a valid assessment through the system life cycle. The sources of data may be summarized in the following categories.

1. Current data banks, which provide historical information (field data) on existing systems/equipments in operational use and similar in configuration and function to the item being developed. Often, it is feasible to use such data and apply complexity factors to compensate for differences in technology, configuration, environment, and the time frame.

2. Estimating relationships, which relate one parameter in terms of another, provide rules of thumb or simple analogies from which specific factors are derived. For instance, in the cost area various cost categories are related to cost generating or explanatory variables (e.g., dollars per pound of weight, dollars per mile, dollars per part). Quite often, these explanatory variables represent characteristics of performance, physical configuration, logistics policy, and/or operational concept. Given one parameter, the analyst can estimate the second parameter. Estimating relationships are covered further in Appendix A.

These relationships are developed by collecting accumulated data on similar systems and correlating various individual factors to the appropriate characteristics of the new system. Forecasting techniques are used to facilitate the development process. (e.g., use of Delphi estimates, multiple-regression techniques, etc.).

3. Advance system planning, preliminary system specifications, functional analyses, allocations, reliability and maintainability predictions, maintenance analyses, and related project reports provide much of the required input data when equipment design information is first available.

4. Engineering test data and field data on equipments in the operational inventory are of course the best sources of data for actual assessment purposes. Such data are usually employed when the LSA is applied in evaluating the impact of modifications on prime equipment and/or the elements of logistic support.

The analyst relies on one or a combination of the sources listed above. The data utilized should be as accurate as possible, represent the operational situation, reflect current system conditions, and be used in sufficient quantity to provide a significant sample size covering the various system parameters being studied.

F. ANALYSIS RESULTS

As described earlier, LSA constitutes the integration and application of different analytical techniques applied to a variety of problem situations. In addition, LSA is developed on a progressive basis and the output data will vary from application to application. However, to provide the reader with some idea as to the type of information derived through LSA, a listing of typical output data elements is presented in Figure 6-5.

Referring to Figure 6-5, it is noted that LSA, as a product, contains a summary of the necessary data to define total logistic support requirements. This includes reliability and maintainability factors, and the cost data necessary to evaluate effectiveness of the support configuration for a given system or equipment. This is not to say that LSA is all-encompassing as it does not include technical manuals, facility plans, training plans, and so on, but it does indicate the requirements for such.

The methods employed in developing the data output reflected in Figure 6-5 are illustrated in the typical problem summaries discussed in Section 6.2 and supported by the information presented in Appendices A, B, and C.

1. Appendix A includes a discussion of cost breakdown structure, cost categories, cost estimating, discounting, learning curves, and cost factors used in the LSA for life-cycle cost measures.
2. Appendix B covers maintenance analysis data (e.g., maintenance tasks, task times and frequencies, reliability and maintainability factors, etc.). The factors described in Chapter 2 and listed in Figure 6-5 (other than cost elements) are derived from maintenance analysis data as part of the LSA process.
3. Appendix C includes a brief summary of experience related to typical uses of mathematical models in the evaluation of logistic support and related elements of a system.

The information presented in this chapter and in Appendices A and B has been applied in a number of instances as discussed. The LSA output is a composite of these elements.

G. SENSITIVITY ANALYSIS

In performance of a given analysis, there may be a few key parameters about which the analyst is very uncertain (due to inadequate data, pushing the state of the art, etc.). The question is: How sensitive are the results of analysis variations to these uncertain parameters? The analyst might wish to run the model using a baseline system configuration, and then rerun the model varying different key input parameters to determine the affect on the results. Variation is accomplished by applying different multiple factors to the input parameter being tested. For instance, the analyst may wish to investigate

1. Variation of MTBF as a function of total life-cycle cost and spare/repair part requirements. Since MTBF is the basis for the corrective maintenance frequency and is obtained through reliability allocation

1. Maintenance Echelons

2. Maintenance Tasks/Echelon
- Task Sequences
- Task Time
- Task Frequency

3. Test and Support Equipment
- Quantity and Type/Echelon
- Utilization Rate
- Utility Requirements
- R & D Cost
- Investment Cost
- O & M Cost

4. Spare/Repair Parts
- Repair Levels
- Nonrepairable or -
  Consumable Items-Quantity and Type
- Repairable Items-Quantity and Type
- Replacement Frequency
- Inventory Level
- Safety Stock Level
- Condemnation Rate
- Hi-Value Items
- Provisioning Cycle
- Pipeline Time
- Wearout Rate
- Shelf Life
- Spares Availability
- Order Cost
- Inventory Holding Cost
- Material Cost

5. Personnel and Training
- Personnel Quantity, Rating and
  Skill Level Requirements/Echelon
- Attrition Rate
- Learning Curve
- Personnel Effectiveness
- Personnel Cost-Direct Cost and
  Overhead
- Initial Training Requirements-
  Personnel Quantity and Type
- Replenishment Training Requirements-
  Personnel Quantity and Type
- Training Courses
- Training Data
- Training Equipment
- Personnel Training Cost
- Training Data and Equipment Costs

6. Technical Data
- Technical Manual Requirements
- Logistics Provisioning Data
- Data Collection System Requirements
- Initial Data Cost
- Change Data Cost

7. Transportation and Handling
- Equipment Requirements—Quantity,
  Type, Location
- Packaging (Containers) and Shipping
- Equipment Cost (R & D, Investment, O & M)
- Transportation Cost

8. Modifications

9. Facilities
- Operational, Maintenance and
  Training Facility Requirements
- Facility Utilization
- Space Requirements—Layout
- Storage Requirements
- Utility Requirements (Electrical
  Power, Light, Heat, Water)
- Capital Equipment
- Tooling and Special Handling
  Equipment
- Environmental Requirements (Shielding,
  Clean Room, etc.)
- Facilities Cost (R & D, Investment,
  O & M)

10. Additional Factors
- Availability (A_o, A_a, A_i)
- MTBM, MTBF, λ, R, MTBR
- Cost/System Effectiveness
- MDT, M_{ct}, $\bar{M}_{pt}$, M_{ct}, M_{pt}, MTTR$_G$,
  M_{max}, $\bar{M}$, Confidence Level
- MMH/OH, MMH/MO, MMH/YR
- Turnaround Time (TAT)
- Self-Test Thoroughness
- Maintenance Actions/Year
- Dependability
- Life-Cycle Cost (R & D, Investment,
  O & M)
- Cost/MA, Cost/OH
- Escalation Factor
- Discount Rate
- Prime Equipment Utilization
- Failure Modes, Effects, Criticality

Figure 6-5. Logistic Support Analysis (LSA) Data output summary.

and/or prediction, it might be worthwhile to test the effect of MTBF on life-cycle cost. For example, MTBF multiple factors of 0.5 and 1.5 are selected and the model is run once for each factor. The results indicate the range in total cost on the basis of possible input data variation(s).

2. Variation of system utilization or operating time as a function of the quantity of maintenance actions, test and support equipment utilization, and facility usage.
3. Variation of MDT as a function of total maintenance cost.
4. Variation of spares availability in terms of inventory levels.
5. Variation of direct maintenance manhours as a function of personnel and organization costs.
6. Variation of condemnation rate as a function of spare/repair part cost.

There are many system parameters that may be tested in a like manner, and the results are used to support decisions pertaining to the selection of a preferred approach and in identifying areas of risk and uncertainty.

When evaluating alternatives, the sensitivity analysis may create a situation similar to that presented in Figure 2-30 or it may affect the breakeven point illustrated in Figure 2-31. In any event, the analyst will be able to readily determine whether or not to probe further for better input data or to select an alternative that is less risky.

H. CONTINGENCY ANALYSIS

Closely related with the sensitivity analysis is the contingency analysis, which involves the investigation of decisions in terms of relevant changes in the initial criteria. For example, suppose that the analyst believes there is a good probability that the number of operational site locations for the communication system discussed in Chapter 3 (see Figure 3-4) will be reduced to one-half of that indicated because of a change in operational requirements. How will this change affect the maintenance concept and the logistic support requirements for the system? Experience tells us that one probable area of impact is the repair policy decision. The reduction in operational sites may shift the policy from *repair at the intermediate level* to *repair at depot*. This, in turn, has an impact on test and support equipment requirements, personnel and training, facility needs, and so on.

As new systems are being developed, there is always the possibility that the basic requirements will change. To the extent possible, the analyst must anticipate such changes, apply the LSA appropriately, and alert management as to the impact of the change on the prime equipment and its associated logistic support.

I. RISK AND UNCERTAINTY

The process of evaluation leads to decisions having significant impact on the future. Inherent in this process are the aspects of risk and uncertainty since the future is, of course, unknown. With this in mind, it becomes extremely important to have a good understanding of the underlying concepts associated with the nature of risk and uncertainty.[8] As the intent in any evaluation process is to minimize risk and uncertainty, the approach employed must properly address the following basic areas (not to be considered as being all inclusive).

1. Selection of evaluation criteria. The selection of evaluation criteria defined in Section 6.1 C is one of the most formidable areas of concern in the analysis. The problem is the greatest for large-scale systems when comparisons are made between alternatives which satisfy a given requirement but by different means (e.g., ship versus airplane). In such instances, evaluation criteria should cover system performance characteristics, effectiveness factors, political, economical, cultural, and ethical considerations. Some of these features are impossible to quantify realistically and are conveniently left out of the analysis. In addition, those factors that are quantifiable are often combined into a single criterion that creates an *apple–orange* mixing effect introducing bias into the analysis.

For smaller–scale systems, the problem of criteria selection is considerably reduced although not completely eliminated. Many of the large-scale system interaction effects drop out in the evaluation process. Nevertheless, there are still features of the system that cannot be quantified and the analysis of a multiple mix of criteria (in lieu of a single combined criterion factor) continues to be appropriate.

In order to minimize the introduction of risk and uncertainty in the analysis, the evaluation criteria must be selected judiciously to capture as many of the relevant system characteristics as possible. Inappropriate mixing must be avoided. Those features that cannot be quantitatively expressed must be identified and all assumptions must be defined.

2. Weighting of evaluation factors. Assuming that a number of individual criterion factors are to be employed in the evaluation process, the significance of each of these factors is often determined through the establish-

---

[8]For simplicity purposes, the terms *risk* and *uncertainty* are often used jointly. Actually, risk implies the availability of discrete data in the form of a probability distribution around a certain parameter. Uncertainty implies a situation that may be probabilistic in nature, but one that is not supported by discrete data. Certain factors may be measurable in terms of risk or may be stated under conditions of uncertainty. It is not intended to elaborate further within the confines of this text.

ment of relative weighting values. These values will vary depending on problem definition and the system operational requirements. For example, a system whose overall mission is repetitive in nature (commercial airliner) will be evaluated differently than a system whose mission is not repetitive (e.g., space booster). In addition, a system that is produced in relatively large quantities is reviewed from a different standpoint than a one-of-a-kind item. Should performance be weighted highter than reliability? Reliability higher than maintainability? Supportability higher than cost?

When considering the aspect of weighting, there are a number of known techniques currently in use.[9] A common approach is to assign weights to all evaluation factors, determine the degree of compatibility of the system configuration being evaluated with each of the various evaluation factors and assign a score, multiply the weighting factors by the appropriate scores, and add the adjusted scores for each option. The one with the best adjusted score is selected.

In applying this and other similar methods, one can introduce a high degree of bias through:

a. The inclusion of extraneous evaluation factors which may favor one alternative over another.
b. The improper assignment of weighting values.
c. The presence of central tendency, proximity, and similarity errors in the scoring process.[10]

Successful employment of this approach requires particular thoroughness in the design of the rating instrument and in the establishment of scoring criteria. This approach sometimes is time consuming and costly to implement, but is nevertheless worthwhile when many criteria are to be used in the evaluation process.

3. The use of ratios as means of evaluation scoring. When evaluating alternative systems in terms of ratios (e.g., system effectiveness/total cost or total cost/system effectiveness, cost–benefit ratio, etc.), the alternatives are generally ranked in accordance with their ratios and the one with the best

---

[9]The *Delphi technique* is one commonly known method. Expert opinion (from a group of experienced personnel) is systematically solicited, compiled, and reviewed with quantified value criteria being established. Through numerous iterations constituting additional opinion solicitations, the criteria become more and more refined and bias (introduced through improper weighting factors) is reduced.

[10]*Central tendency error* results from the scorer's reluctance to use extreme scale scores in the rating. *Proximity error* (sometimes referred to as *ordering effect*) results from the influence that surrounding items on the list have on the factor being scored. *Similarity error* results from the scoring of an item in terms of some other nonrelated item which is preferred by the scorer. Personal preferences tend to influence the scores.

ratio is selected. This approach is considered valid in the absence of rationing. However, where budget limitations are imposed, the ranking is limited to those projects that meet the budget objectives. Preferred alternatives having a better ratio may be eliminated if the cost aspect of the ratio exceeds the allocated budget.

The process of selection using the ratio criteria, although seemingly appropriate in many applications, sometimes tends to ignore the actual magnitude of the values in the numerator and denominator of the ratio. When considering the risks and uncertainty associated with a given decision, the magnitude of what is being risked has a definite bearing on the degree of acceptability of that risk. The use of ratios for measurement purposes tends to preclude an adequate evaluation of the risks which are to be assumed for a given decision.

4. The selection of an operational horizon. In the evaluation of alternative systems, one must consider two basic areas.

    a. The individual initial availability dates of alternative systems.
    b. The projected operational life of each alternative system.

In actuality, different systems have different horizons (operational life). Some become obsolete sooner than others (resulting from technical obsolescence, wear-out, or change in mission requirements). With different horizons, systems are not directly comparable; thus, it is desirable that a common horizon be established for each system being considered in the evaluation process.

5. Data input. The sources of data available to the analyst are briefly described in Section 6.1E. From these sources, the analyst must identify operator and maintenance tasks, reliability and maintainability values, logistics factors, cost factors, and the like. Many of these data elements are represented by a discrete quantitative value or a range of values with a probability distribution. The values and the probability distributions assumed have a significant impact on the analysis results, the extent of which is readily verified through a sensitivity analysis.

The accuracy and completeness of input data depend not only on the sources of data available, but on the personal experience and motivations of the analyst in doing a good job. Risk and uncertainty are introduced through errors in data interpretation and extrapolation, errors in estimating relationships, application of the wrong techniques, and making unrealistic or invalid assumptions.

Since many current data collection systems are inadequate from the standpoint of providing realistic historical information, the analyst usually must depend on estimating relationships, allocations and/or predictions requiring much interpretation and an understanding of the underlying assumptions supporting the techniques employed. Thus, unless the analyst possesses the right background and training (e.g., some understanding of system operations and maintenance, mission requirements, correlation of allocation/prediction results with operational experience), the entire analysis effort may turn out to be a waste of time and money.

The importance of good valid input data cannot be overemphasized. Having a model available is of little value unless the data input is adequate.

J. VALIDITY OF THE ANALYSIS

As a final check on the analysis, a number of questions may be posed as to the validity of the stated assumptions, model parameter relationships, inclusions/exclusions, and stated conclusions. Figure 6-6 presents a checklist that may be employed by the analyst or the manager as an aid in assessing the final output results.

6.2. Typical Analysis Applications (Summary Description)

As a means of simply illustrating the process discussed in the preceding paragraphs, five examples of typical problem applications involving the Logistic Support Analysis have been selected. The topics discussion are

1. Cost-effectiveness analysis, involving the evaluation of two alternative systems using reliability and life-cycle cost as decision criteria.
2. Level of repair analysis comparing the options of designing an item for discard at failure, repair at the intermediate level of maintenance, or repair at the depot/supplier facility.
3. Optimum system/equipment packing design using the *branch-and-bound* technique for seeking a feasible solution among a large number of alternatives.
4. Evaluation of three alternative test and support equipment configurations in terms of performance, operability, effectiveness, design characteristics, logistic support, schedule, cost, and so on. Weighting factors are employed in the scoring process.
5. Reliability and maintainability trade-off evaluation (variation of MTBF and $\bar{M}$ct in terms of a given inherent availability).

There are numerous examples of a related nature. However, it is hoped that the student will acquire the insight desired through a careful in-depth review of what is presented herein. Through such a review, many additional

A. Assumptions

1. Are all assumptions adequately identified?
2. Do any of the specified assumptions treat quantitative uncertainties as facts?
3. Do any of the specified assumptions treat qualitative uncertainties as facts?
4. Are major assumptions reasonable?

B. Alternatives

1. Are current capabilities adequately considered among alternatives?
2. Are mixtures of systems considered among the alternatives?
3. Are any feasible and significant alternatives omitted?

C. Documentation

1. Is the study adequately documented?
2. Are the facts stated correctly?
3. Are the facts stated with proper qualification?
4. Are all applicable reference sources listed?

D. Model Relationships

1. Does the model adequately address the problem?
2. Are cost and effectiveness parameters linked logically?
3. Does the model allow for a timely response?
4. Does the model provide valid (comprehensive) and reliable (repeatable) results?
5. Has a sensitivity analysis been performed?

E. Effectiveness Parameters

1. Are the measures of effectiveness identified?
2. Is the effectiveness measure appropriate to the mission function? Are logistic support requirements adequately defined? Are operational and maintenance concepts adequately defined?
3. Do the effectiveness measures employed ignore some objectives and concentrate on others?
4. Are performance measures mistaken for effectiveness measures?
5. Does the effectiveness of a future system take into account the time dimension?
6. Are expected and average values used correctly to measure effectiveness?
7. If quantitative measures of effectiveness are unattainable, is a qualitative comparison feasible?
8. Is the effectiveness measure sensitive to changes in assumptions?

9. In the event that two or more effectiveness measures are appropriate, are the measures properly weighted (the relative weighting in terms of significance or level of importance of each applicable criterion factor employed)?

F. Cost

1. Are cost categories adequately defined?
2. Are cost estimates relevant?
3. Are incremental and marginal costs considered?
4. Are variable and fixed costs separately identifiable?
5. Are escalation factors specified and employed?
6. Are learning curves specified and employed?
7. Is the discount rate specified and employed?
8. Are all costs elements considered? Conceptual/Feasibility Studies; Design and Development; Evaluation Test; Production/Construction; Installation and Checkout; Personnel and Training; Technical Data; Facility Construction and Maintenance; Spare/Repair Parts; Test and Support Equipment; Inventory Maintenance; Transportation and Handling; Program Management?
9. Are the cost aspects of all alternatives treated in a consistent and comparable manner?
10. Are the cost estimates (cost estimating relationships) reasonably accurate? Are areas of risk and uncertainty identified?
11. Is cost amortization employed? If so, how?
12. Has the sensitivity of cost estimates been properly addressed through a sensitivity analysis?

G. Conclusions and Recommendations

1. Are the conclusions and recommendations logically derived from the material contained in the study?
2. Have all the significant ramifications been considered in arriving at the conclusions and recommendations presented?
3. Are the conclusions and recommendations really feasible in light of political, cultural, policy or other considerations?
4. Do the conclusions and recommendations indicate bias?
5. Are the conclusions and recommendations based on external considerations?
6. Are the conclusions and recommendations based on insignificant differences?

Figure 6-6. Analysis checklist (typical).

questions should arise encouraging the student to pursue the subject matter further.

A. Cost-Effectiveness Analysis (Example 1)

This example illustrates a cost-effectiveness evaluation where logistic support is a major input factor. The example as presented emphasizes the total systems approach.

1. Definition of the problem. A ground vehicle currently in the development phase requires the incorporation of a radio communication equipment. A decision is needed as to the type of equipment deemed most feasible from the standpoint of performance, reliability, and life-cycle cost. Budget limitations suggest that the equipment unit cost (based on life-cycle cost) should not exceed $20,000.

2. Analysis approach

a. The accomplishment of a cost-effectiveness evaluation requires further expansion of the problem definition. A description of system operational requirements (discussed in Chapter 3) and the maintenance concept (Chapter 4) are essential. In addition, one needs to know the program schedule.

The communication equipment is to be installed in a light vehicle. The equipment shall enable communication with other vehicles at a range of 200 miles, overhead aircraft at an altitude of 10,000 feet or less, and a centralized area communication facility. The system must have a reliability MTBF of 450 hours, a $\overline{\text{M}}$ct of 30 minutes, and a MMH/OH requirement of 0.2. The operational and maintenance concepts and program time frame are illustrated in Figure 6-7.

b. Review of all possible supplier sources indicates that there are two (2) design configurations that appear (based on preliminary design data) to meet the specified requirements. Each is evaluated on an equivalent basis in terms of reliability MTBF and total life-cycle cost.

c. The next step is to identify data needs and to structure the analytical model for use in the evaluation process. For each configuration the analyst needs

—A reliability allocation or prediction providing estimated component failure rates and a system MTBF.[11] The system MTBF must be 450 hours or greater.

---

[11]Sources covering reliability prediction include (a) Lloyd, D. K. and Lipow, M., *Reliability: Management, Methods, and Mathematics*, 2nd ed., TRW Systems and Energy, Redondo Beach, Calif., 1977; and (b) NAVAIR 01–1A–31,–32,–33 (3 Volumes), *Reliability Engineering Handbook*, Department of the Navy, Washington, D.C., July 1977.

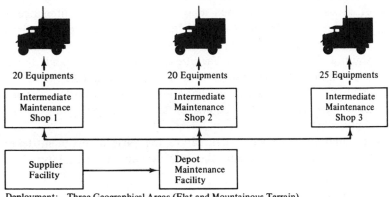

20 Equipments   20 Equipments   25 Equipments

| Intermediate Maintenance Shop 1 | Intermediate Maintenance Shop 2 | Intermediate Maintenance Shop 3 |

| Supplier Facility | Depot Maintenance Facility |

Deployment: Three Geographical Areas (Flat and Mountainous Terrain)
Utilization: Four (4) hr/day Throughout Year (Average)

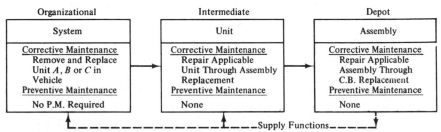

Organizational	Intermediate	Depot
System	Unit	Assembly
Corrective Maintenance Remove and Replace Unit *A, B* or *C* in Vehicle Preventive Maintenance No P.M. Required	Corrective Maintenance Repair Applicable Unit Through Assembly Replacement Preventive Maintenance None	Corrective Maintenance Repair Applicable Assembly Through C.B. Replacement Preventive Maintenance None

Supply Functions

The Illustrated Maintenance Concept should be expanded to include such factors as $\overline{M}_{ct}$, TAT, MMH/OH, Pipeline, etc., for each level. Refer to Chapter 3, Figure 3-5.

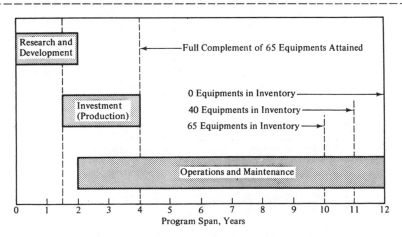

Research and Development

Full Complement of 65 Equipments Attained

0 Equipments in Inventory

Investment (Production)

40 Equipments in Inventory

65 Equipments in Inventory

Operations and Maintenance

Program Span, Years

Figure 6-7. Basic system concepts.

—A maintainability allocation or prediction providing $\bar{M}ct$ and MMH/ OH factors for the equipment and its components.[12]

—A gross-level maintenance analysis describing maintenance tasks, task times and frequencies, and basic logistic support requirements (test and support equipment, spare/repair parts, personnel and training, technical data, facilities, transportation and handling). The maintenance analysis is discussed in Appendix B.

—A life-cycle cost analysis involving a definition of cost categories plus input cost factors. The details of a cost analysis are presented in Appendix A.

—An analytical model structured on the basis of problem definition, the evaluation criteria, and the data available to the analyst.

3. Analysis results. The problem is to select the best among two alternatives on the basis of reliability and life-cycle cost. A comparison of reliability and life-cycle cost data for each of the two configurations is illustrated in Figure 6-8.

In this instance, configuration A is the preferred alternative with the highest reliability and lowest life-cycle cost.

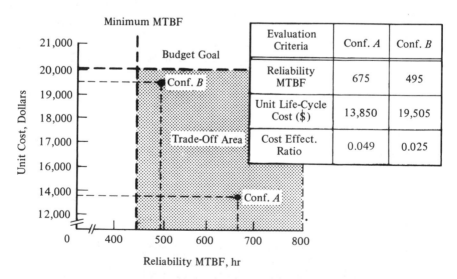

Evaluation Criteria	Conf. A	Conf. B
Reliability MTBF	675	495
Unit Life-Cycle Cost ($)	13,850	19,505
Cost Effect. Ratio	0.049	0.025

Figure 6-8. Reliability versus unit cost.

[12]Maintainability prediction is covered in (a) Blanchard, B. S. and Lowery, E. E., *Maintainability-Principles and Practices*, McGraw-Hill Book Company, New York, 1969; and (b) MIL-HDBK-472, Military Handbook, *Maintainability Prediction*, Department of Defense, Washington, D.C.

Table 6-1. LIFE-CYCLE COST ANALYSIS BREAKDOWN

Cost Category (Refer to Figure A-1, Appendix A)	Configuration A		Configuration B	
	P.V. Cost	*% of Total*	*P.V. Cost*	*% of Total*
1. Research and development (C_R)	$70,219	7.8	$53,246	4.2
(a) Program management (C_{RM})	9,374	1.1	9,252	0.8
(b) Advanced R and D (C_{RR})	4,152	0.5	4,150	0.4
(c) Engineering design (C_{RE})	41,400	4.5	24,581	1.9
(d) Equipment development and test (C_{RT})	12,176	1.4	12,153	0.9
(e) Engineering data (C_{RD})	3,117	0.3	3,110	0.2
2. Investment (C_I)	407,814	45.3	330,885	26.1
(a) Manufacturing (C_{IM})	333,994	37.1	262,504	20.8
(b) Construction (C_{IC})	45,553	5.1	43,227	3.4
(c) Initial logistic support (C_{IL})	28,267	3.1	25,154	1.9
3. Operations and maintenance (C_O)	422,217	46.9	883,629	69.7
(a) Operations (C_{OO})	37,811	4.2	39,301	3.1
(b) Maintenance (C_{OM})	384,406	42.7	844,328	66.6
• Maintenance personnel and support (C_{OMM})	210,659	23.4	407,219	32.2
• Spare/repair parts (C_{OMX})	103,520	11.5	228,926	18.1
• Test and support equipment maintenance (C_{OMS})	47,713	5.3	131,747	10.4
• Transportation and handling (C_{OMT})	14,404	1.6	51,838	4.1
• Maintenance training (C_{OMP})	1,808	0.2	2,125	Neg.
• Maintenance facilities (C_{OMF})	900	0.1	1,021	Neg.
• Technical data (C_{OMD})	5,402	0.6	21,452	1.7
(c) System/equipment modifications (C_{ON})	....	....	....	....
(d) System phase-out and disposal (C_{OP})	....	....	....	....
GRAND TOTAL*	$900,250	100%	$1,267,760	100%

*The cost values presented are hypothetical but realistically derived. A 10% discount factor was used in determining present-value costs.

A breakdown of life-cycle cost is presented in Table 6-1. Note that the acquisition cost (R & D and Investment) is higher for configuration *A* ($478,033 versus $384,131). This is due partially to a better design using more reliable components. Although the initial cost is higher, the overall life-cycle cost is lower due to a reduction in maintenance actions resulting in lower O&M costs. These characteristics in equipment design have a tremendous affect on life-cycle cost.

Category	Program Year												Total
	1	2	3	4	5	6	7	8	9	10	11	12	
Research and Development	32,119	38,100	—	—	—	—	—	—	—	—	—	—	70,219
Investment	—	94,110	156,852	156,852	—	—	—	—	—	—	—	—	407,814
Operations and Maintenance	—	—	12,180	32,480	60,492	57,472	53,480	50,484	50,470	50,494	37,480	17,185	422,217
Total	32,119	132,210	169,032	189,332	60,492	57,472	53,480	50,484	50,470	50,494	37,480	17,185	$900,250

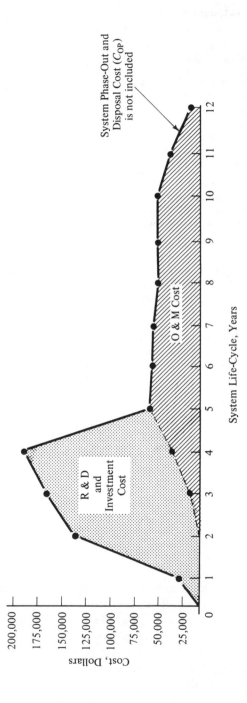

Figure 6-9. Cost profile for configuration *A*.

162

Figure 6-9 projects the life-cycle cost in the form of a profile. The anticipated cost for each year is indicated. These figures can be directly applied for budgeting purposes (when undiscounted).

As stated earlier, configuration *A* is preferred on the basis of total life-cycle cost. Prior to a final decision, however, the analyst should perform a breakeven analysis to determine the point in time that configuration *A* becomes more effective than configuration *B*. Figure 6-10 illustrates the payback point that is 6 years and 5 months, or a little more than a year after the equipment is introduced into the operational inventory. This point is early enough in the life cycle to support the decision. On the other hand, if the payback point were much further out in time, the decision might be questioned.

Referring to Table 6-1, the analyst can readily pick out the *high contributors* (those which contribute more than 10% of the total cost). These are the areas where a more refined analysis is required and greater emphasis is needed in providing valid input data. For instance, maintenance personnel and support cost (C_{OMM}) and spare/repair parts cost (C_{OMX}) contribute 23.4% and 11.5%, respectively, of the total cost for configuration *A*. This leads the analyst to reevaluate the design in terms of impact on personnel support and spares; the prediction methods used in determining maintenance frequencies and inventory requirements; the analytical model to ensure that the proper parameter relationships are established; and cost factors such as personnel labor cost, spares material costs, inventory holding cost; and so on. If the analyst wishes to determine the sensitivity of these areas to input variations, he may perform a sensitivity analysis. In this instance, it is

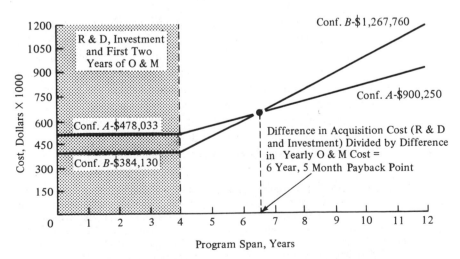

Figure 6-10. Investment payback (breakeven analysis).

appropriate to vary MTBF as a function of maintenance personnel and support cost (C_{OMM}) and spare/repair parts cost (C_{OMX}). Figure 6-11 presents the results.

The analyst or decision maker should review the break-even analysis in Figure 6-10 and determine how far out in time he or she is willing to go and remain with configuration *A*. Assuming that the selected maximum payback point is 7 years, the difference in alternatives is equivalent to approximately \$65,000 (the present value difference between the two configurations at the 7-year point). This indicates the range of input variations allowed. For instance, if the design configuration *A* changes or if the reliability prediction is in error resulting in a MTBF as low as 450 hours (the specified system requirement), the maintenance personnel and support cost (C_{OMM}) will increase to approximately \$324,000, an increase of about \$113,340 above the baseline value. Thus, although the system reliability is within the specified requirements, the cost increase due to the input MTBF variation causes a decision shift in favor of configuration *B*. The analyst must assess the sensitivity of significant input parameters and determine their impact on the ultimate decision.

B. Level of Repair Analysis (Example 2)[13]

In defining the detailed maintenance concept and establishing criteria for equipment design, it is necessary to determine whether items should be repaired at the intermediate echelon, repaired at the depot/supplier facility, or discarded in the event of failure. This example evaluates these alternatives through a level of repair analysis.

1. Definition of the problem. A computer subsystem will be distributed in quantities of 65 throughout three major geographical areas. The subsystem will be utilized to support both scientific and management functions within various industrial firms and government agencies. Although the actual system utilization will vary from one consumer organization to the next, an average utilization of 4 hours per day (for a 360-day year) is assumed.

The computer subsystem is currently in the early development stage, should be in production in 18 months, and will be operational in 2 years. The full complement of 65 computer subsystems is expected to be in use in

---

[13]It should be noted that some repair-level decisions are based on noneconomic screening criteria such as safety, technical feasibility, policy, security, contractual provisions, and so on. This analysis addresses repair-level decisions based on economic criteria. Two good documents covering level of repair analysis are (a) MIL-STD-1390A, Military Standard, "Level of Repair," Department of the Navy, Washington, D.C., 1974; and (b) AFLCM/AFSCM 800-4, U.S. Air Force Manual, *Optimum Repair-Level Analysis*, Department of the Air Force, Washington, D. C., 1971.

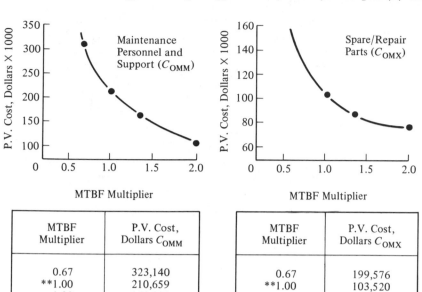

MTBF Multiplier	P.V. Cost, Dollars C_{OMM}
0.67	323,140
**1.00	210,659
1.33	162,325
2.00	112,565

MTBF Multiplier	P.V. Cost, Dollars C_{OMX}
0.67	199,576
**1.00	103,520
1.33	92,235
2.00	80,130

**Baseline Configuration *A*   **Baseline Configuration *A*

Figure 6-11. Sensitivity analysis.

4 years, and will be available through the eighth year of the program before subsystem phase-out commences. The life cycle, for the purposes of the analysis, is 10 years.

Based on early design data, the computer subsystem will be packaged in five major units, with a built-in test capability that will isolate faults to the unit level. Faulty units will be removed and replaced at the organizational level (i.e., consumer's facility), and sent to the intermediate maintenance shop for repair. Unit repair will be accomplished through assembly replacement, and assemblies will be either repaired or discarded. There is a total of 15 assemblies being considered, and the requirement is to justify the assembly repair or discard decision on the basis of life-cycle cost criteria. The operational requirements, maintenance concept, and program plan are illustrated in Figure 6-12.

2. Analysis approach and results. The stated problem definition pertains primarily to the analysis of 15 major assemblies of the given comput/ r subsystem configuration to determine whether the assemblies should ᴊe repaired or discarded when failures occur. In other words, the various assemblies will be individually evaluated in terms of (a) assembly repair at the

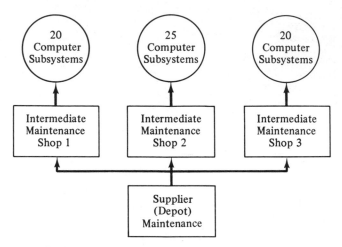

Distribution: Three major geographical areas
Utilization: Four hours/day throughout year average

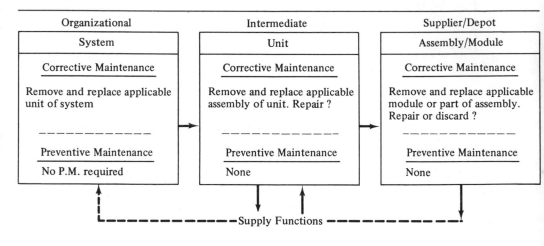

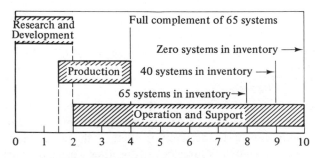

Figure 6-12. Basic subsystem concepts.

intermediate level of maintenance, (b) assembly repair at the supplier or depot level of maintenance, and (c) disposing of the assembly. Life-cycle costs, as applicable to the assembly level, shall be developed and employed in the alternative selection process. Total overall computer sybsystem costs have been determined at a higher level, and are not included in this case study.

Given the information in the problem statement, the next step is to develop a cost-breakdown structure (CBS) and to establish evaluation criteria. The CBS employed in this analysis and specific cost categories are similar to the structure presented in Appendix A. Not all cost categories in the CBS are applicable in this case; however, the structure is used as a starting point, and those categories that are applicable are identified accordingly.

The evaluation criteria include consideration of all costs in each applicable category of the CBS, but the emphasis is on operation and support (O&S) costs as a function of acquisition cost. Thus, the research and development cost and the production cost are presented as one element, while various segments of O&S costs are identified individually. Table 6-2 presents evaluation criteria, cost data, and a brief description and justification supporting each category. The information shown in the figure covers only one of the 15 assemblies, but is typical for each case.

In determining these costs, the analyst must follow an approach similar to that conveyed in the process illustrated in Figure 6-2 and discussed in Example 1. That is: operational requirements and a basic maintenance concept must be defined; a program plan must be established; an inventory profile must be identified; a CBS must be established; reliability, maintainability, and logistic support factors must be identified; cost-estimating relationships must be developed; and so on.

The next step is to employ the same criteria presented in Table 6-2 to determine the recommended repair-level decision for each of the other 14 assemblies (i.e., assemblies 2 through 15). Although acquisition costs, reliability and maintainability factors, and certain logistics requirements are different for each assembly, many of the cost-estimating relationships are the same. The objective is to be *consistent* in analysis approach and in the use of input cost factors to the maximum extent possible and where appropriate. The summary results for all 15 assemblies are presented in Table 6-3.

Referring to the table, note that the decision for Assembly A-1 favors repair at the intermediate level; the decision for Assembly A-2 is repair at the supplier or depot level; the decision for Assembly A-3 is not to accomplish repair at all but to discard the assembly when a failure occurs; and so on. The table reflects recommended policies for each individual assembly. In addition, the overall policy decision, when addressing all 15 assemblies as an integral package, favors repair at the supplier.

Prior to arriving at a final conclusion, the analyst should reevaluate each situation where the decision is close. Referring to Table 6-2, it is clearly

Table 6-2. REPAIR VERSUS DISCARD EVALUATION (ASSEMBLY A-1)*

Evaluation Criteria	Repair at Intermediate Cost ($)	Repair at Supplier Cost ($)	Discard at Failure Cost ($)	Description and Justification
1. Estimated acquisition costs for Assembly A-1 (to include R&D cost and production cost)	550/assy. or 35,750	550/assy. or 35,750	475/assy. or 30,875	Acquisition cost includes all applicable costs in categories C_R, C_{PI}, C_{PM}, and C_{PQ} allocated to each Assembly A-1, based on a requirement of 65 systems. Assembly design and production are simplified in the discard area.
2. Unscheduled maintenance cost (C_{OLA})	6,480	8,100	Not applicable	Based on the 8-year useful system life, 65 systems, a utilization of 4 hours/day, a failure rate (λ) of 0.00045 for Assembly A-1, and a $\overline{\text{M}}ct$ of 2 hours, the expected number of maintenance actions is 270. When repair is accomplished, two technicians are required on a full-time basis. The labor rates are $12/hour for intermediate maintenance and $15/hour for supplier maintenance.
3. Supply support—spare assemblies (C_{PLS} and C_{OLS})	3,300	4,950	128,250	For intermediate maintenance 6 spare assemblies are required to compensate for transportation time, the maintenance queue, TAT, etc. For supplier/depot maintenance, 9 spare assemblies are required. 100% spares are required in the discard case.
4. Supply support—spare modules or parts for assembly repair (C_{PLS} and C_{OLS})	6,750	6,750	Not applicable	Assume $25 for materials per repair action.

Item				Description
5. Supply support—inventory management (C_{PLS} and C_{OLS})	2,010	2,340	25,650	Assume 20% of the inventory value (spare assemblies, modules, and parts).
6. Test and support equipment (C_{PLT} and C_{OLE})	5,001	1,667	Not applicable	Special test equipment is required in the repair case. The acquisition and support cost is $25,000 per installation. The allocation for Assembly A-1 per installation is $1,667. No special test equipment is required in the discard case.
7. Transportation and handling (C_{OLH})	Not applicable	2,975	Not applicable	Transportation costs at the intermediate level are negligible. For supplier maintenance, assume 340 one-way trips at $175/100 pounds. One assembly weighs 5 pounds.
8. Maintenance training (C_{OLT})	260	90	Not applicable	Delta training cost to cover maintenance of the assembly is based on the following: Intermediate—26 students, 2 hours each, $200/student week; Supplier—9 students, 2 hours each, $200/student week.
9. Maintenance facilities (C_{OLMI})	594	810	Not applicable	From experience, a cost-estimating relationship of $0.55 per direct maintenance manhour is assumed for the intermediate level, and $0.75 is assumed for the supplier level.
10. Technical data (C_{OLD})	1,250	1,250	Not applicable	Assume 5 pages for diagrams and text covering assembly repair at $250/page.
11. Disposal (C_{DIS})	270	270	2,700	Assume $10/assembly and $1/module or part as the cost of disposal
Total estimated cost	61,665	64,952	187,475	

*The cost breakdown structure (CBS) used as a basis for the data presented herein is included in Blanchard, B. S., *Design and Manage to Life Cycle Cost*, M/A Press, International Scholarly Book Services, Inc., Forest Grove, Oreg., 1978.

Table 6-3. SUMMARY OF REPAIR-LEVEL COSTS

Assembly Number	Maintenance Status			Decision
	Repair at Intermediate Cost ($)	Repair at Supplier Cost ($)	Discard at Failure Cost ($)	
A-1	61,665	64,952	187,475	Repair—intermediate
A-2	58,149	51,341	122,611	Repair—supplier
A-3	85,115	81,544	73,932	Discard
A-4	85,778	78,972	65,072	Discard
A-5	66,679	61,724	95,108	Repair—supplier
A-6	65,101	72,988	89,216	Repair—intermediate
A-7	72,223	75,591	92,114	Repair—intermediate
A-8	89,348	78,204	76,222	Discard
A-9	78,762	71,444	89,875	Repair—supplier
A-10	63,915	67,805	97,212	Repair—intermediate
A-11	67,001	66,158	64,229	Discard
A-12	69,212	71,575	82,109	Repair—intermediate
A-13	77,101	65,555	83,219	Repair—supplier
A-14	59,299	62,515	62,005	Repair—intermediate
A-15	71,919	65,244	63,050	Discard
Policy cost	1,071,267	1,035,612	1,343,449	Repair—supplier

uneconomical to accept the discard decision; however, the two repair alternatives are relatively close. Based on the results of the various individual analyses, the analyst knows that repair-level decisions are highly dependent on the unit acquisition cost of each assembly and the total estimated number of replacements over the expected life cycle (i.e., maintenance actions based on assembly reliability). The trends are illustrated in Figure 6-13, where the decision tends to shift from discard to repair at the intermediate level as the unit acquisition cost increases and the number of replacements increases (or the reliability decreases).[14] In instances where the individual analysis result lies close to the crossover lines in the figure, the analyst may wish to review the input data, the assumptions, and accomplish a sensitivity analysis involving the high-cost contributors. The purpose is to assess the risk involved and verify the decision. This is the situation for Assembly A-1, where the decision is close relative to repair at the intermediate level versus repair at the supplier's facility.

After reviewing the individual analyses of the 15 assemblies to ensure that the best possible decision is reached, the results in Table 6-3 are updated

---

[14]The curves projected in Figure 6-13 are characteristic for this particular life-cycle cost analysis and will vary with changes in operational requirements, system utilization, the maintenance concept, production requirements, and so on.

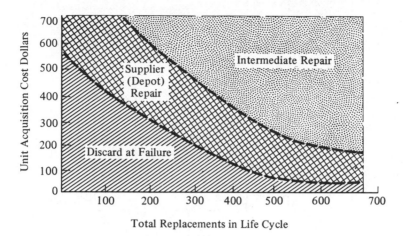

Figure 6-13. Economic screening criteria.

as required. Assuming that the decisions remain basically as indicated, the analyst may proceed in either of two ways. First, the decisions in Table 6-3 may be accepted without change, supporting a *mixed* policy with some assemblies being repaired at each level of maintenance and other assemblies being discarded at failure. With this approach, the analyst should review the interaction effects that could occur (i.e., the effects on spares, utilization of test and support equipment, maintenance personnel utilization, etc.). In essence, each assembly is evaluated individually based on certain assumptions; the results are reviewed in the context of the whole; and possible feedback effects are assessed to ensure that there is no significant impact on the decision.

A second approach is to select the overall "least-cost" policy for all 15 assemblies treated as an entity (i.e., assembly repair at the supplier or depot level of maintenance). In this case, all assemblies are designated as being repaired at the supplier's facility and each individual analysis is reviewed in terms of the criteria in Table 6-2 to determine the possible interaction effects associated with the single policy. The result may indicate some changes to the values in Table 6-3.

Finally, the output of the repair-level analysis must be reviewed to ensure compatibility with the initially specified system maintenance concept. The analysis data may either directly support and be an expansion of the maintenance concept, or the maintenance concept will require change as a consequence of the analysis. If the latter occurs, other facets of system design may be significantly impacted. The consequences of such maintenance concept changes must be thoroughly evaluated prior to arriving at a final repair-level decision. The overall process employed in level of repair analyses is illustrated in Figure 6-14.

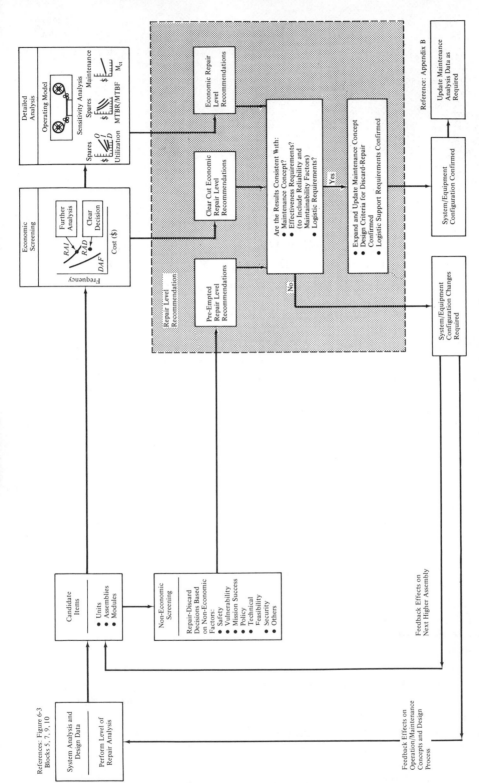

Figure 6-14. Level of repair analysis procedure.

C. Optimum System/Equipment Packaging Design (Example 3)

In the design of equipment, the engineer is faced with the task of packaging. The basic packaging criteria are identified through the functional analysis in Chapter 5. However, a more detailed approach is required to determine the optimum packaging configuration at a lower indenture level. This example, which relates closely with the level of repair analysis in Example 2, illustrates use of the branch-and-bound technique in design. Once again, logistic support is a major weighting factor in the decision process.

1. Definition of the problem. Unit B of the communication equipment defined in Example 1 constitutes 10 operational functions. How should these functions be packaged (10 removable assemblies, $9, 8, \ldots, 1$) to reflect a high reliability design at the lowest life-cycle cost? The task is to evaluate n alternative Unit B packaging concepts, where n is a large number.

2. Analysis approach

a. Initially, the analyst must assess the number of possible alternatives and construct a solution tree (decision tree). The solution tree will include many branches. The nodes correspond to partial solutions and the branches indicate how the solution was obtained from a previous partial solution. Figure 6-15 illustrates a particular branch of the solution tree.

   From the figure, the function assignment for a given modular package is noted. The total solution in this instance (indicated by the terminal nodes designated by the asterisk) constitutes five packages.

b. The analyst then must determine reliability and life-cycle cost figures of merit for each branch, and compare the results of various branch combinations in order to arrive at a feasible solution.

As there are many possible solution combinations, use of the branch and bound can be viewed as an intelligently structured search of groups of solutions from a tree of logical possibilities. In general, the tree of all possible solutions is repeatedly partitioned into smaller and smaller subsets, and a lower bound (for minimization) is determined for reliability and cost within each subset. After each partitioning, the subsets with a bound that exceeds the cost (or is less than the prescribed reliability bound) of a known feasible solution are excluded from all future partitions. The partitioning continues until a feasible solution is found such that its cost is no greater than the bound for any subset or its reliability is no less. The problem can be solved through the use of integer programming.

Function	Package Assignment
1. Function *A*	1
2. Function *B*	1
3. Function *C*	1
4. Function *D*	2
5. Function *E*	2
6. Function *F*	3
7. Function *G*	4
8. Function *H*	4
9. Function *I*	4
10. Function *J*	5

*The branch illustrated consists of five (5) removable assemblies or modular packages. There are other possible branch combinations ranging from all functions in a single package to 10 packages

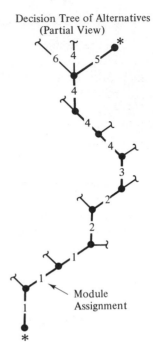

Decision Tree of Alternatives (Partial View)

Module Assignment

Figure 6-15. Branch and bound technique for optimum packaging.

3. Analysis results. This example, like the level of repair analysis, illustrates a technique that can be applied to the design process with the intent of influencing design for optimum logistic support. Through the use of reliability and life-cycle cost figures of merit as evaluation criteria, the impact of logistic support for each possible alternative becomes a major factor in the design process. As indicated, five packages are preferred here.

D. SELECTION OF TEST AND SUPPORT EQUIPMENT CONFIGURATION (EXAMPLE 4)

This example illustrates the selection of test and support equipment for the depot-level of maintenance. The evaluation criteria include a number of parameters, such as performance, effectiveness, design characteristics, schedule, and cost considerations. Through this means, both qualitative and quantitative logistic support considerations are covered in the evaluation process.

1. Definition of the problem. A system requires test and support equipment for maintenance functions at the depot. The operational requirements and the maintenance concept have been defined, and a preliminary maintenance analysis has identified items assigned to the depot, arrival rates, and loading factors. A specific configuration of test and support equipment must be selected to fulfill this requirement.

Based on a review of the market, three alternative configurations are being considered. Each configuration is in existence (supporting other systems in the inventory), and with some redesign could be made compatible with the new requirements. The design and development of new equipment is precluded on the basis of cost and need date.

2. Analysis approach

a. The analyst commences with developing a list of major evaluation parameters, as depicted in Table 6-4.

b. Quantitative weighting factors from 0 to 100 are assigned to each parameter in accordance with the degree of importance. The Delphi or some equivalent technique may be used to establish the weighting factors. The sum of all weighting factors is 100.

c. Each of the three alternative test and support equipment configurations is independently evaluated using special checklist criteria. Such criteria shall include desired logistic support qualitative and quantitative goals for the 11 evaluation parameters in Table 6-4. Using the criteria, base rating values from 0 to 10 are applied according to the degree of compatibility with the desired goals. If all goals are met, a rating of 10 is assigned.

d. The base rating values are multiplied by the weighting factors to obtain the score. The total score is then determined by adding the individual scores for each configuration. Since some redesign is required in each instance, a special derating factor is applied to compensate for risk and uncertainty. The resultant values are summarized in Table 6-4.

3. Analysis results.   Referring to the table, configuration B represents the preferred approach based on the highest total score (730 points). This configuration is recommended in terms of its inherent features relating to performance, operability, effectiveness, design characteristics, logistic support, and so on.

E. RELIABILITY–MAINTAINABILITY EVALUATION (EXAMPLE 5)

This example presents a trade-off evaluation of reliability and maintainability, given a specific inherent availability (A_i). The results impact logistics in terms of frequency of maintenance, maintenance downtime, and cost.

1. Definition of the problem.   There is a requirement to replace an existing equipment in the inventory (with a new item) for the purpose of improving operational effectiveness. The current need specifies that the equip-

Table 6-4. EVALUATION SUMMARY

Item	Evaluation Parameter	Weighting Factor	Conf. A		Conf. B		Conf. C	
			Base Rate	Score	Base Rate	Score	Base Rate	Score
1	PERFORMANCE—Compatibility, maintenance capability, maintenance load, method/mode of testing, versatility of testing	14	6	84	9	126	3	42
2	OPERABILITY—Simplicity of operation	4	10	40	7	28	4	16
3	EFFECTIVENESS—A_O, MTBM, $\overline{Mct}$, $\overline{Mpt}$, MMH/OH	12	5	60	8	96	7	84
4	DESIGN CHARACTERISTICS—Reliability maintainability, human factors, safety, transportability, producibility, interchangeability	9	8	72	6	54	3	27
5	DESIGN DATA—Design drawings, specifications, logistics provisioning data, technical manuals, reports	2	6	12	8	16	5	10
6	TEST AIDS—General test equipment, calibration standards, maintenance tapes	3	5	15	8	24	3	9
7	FACILITIES and UTILITIES—Space, weight, volume, environment, power, heat, water, air conditioning	5	7	35	8	40	4	20
8	SPARE/REPAIR PARTS—Part type and quantity, standard parts, procurement time	6	9	54	7	42	5	30
9	FLEXIBILITY/GROWTH POTENTIAL—Test accuracies, performance range, space, reconfiguration, design change acceptability	3	4	12	8	24	6	18
10	SCHEDULE—R and D, production	17	7	119	8	136	9	153
11	COST—Life-Cycle (R and D, investment, O & M)	25	10	250	9	225	5	125
Subtotal		100		753		811		534
Derating factor (development risk)				113 15%		81 10%		107 20%
Grand Total				640		730		427

ment must operate 8 hours per day, 360 days per year, for 10 years. The existing equipment meets an availability of 0.961, a MTBF of 125 hours, and a $\overline{M}$ct of 5 hours. The new system must meet an availability of 0.990, a MTBF greater than 300 hours, and a $\overline{M}$ct not to exceed 5.0 hours.

An anticipated quantity of 200 equipments is to be procured. Three different alternative design configurations are being considered to satisfy the requirement, and each configuration constitutes a modification of the existing equipment.

Figure 6-16 graphically shows the relationships between inherent availability (A_i), MTBF, and $\overline{M}$ct, and illustrates the allowable area for trade-off. The selected configuration must reflect the reliability and maintainability characteristics represented by the shaded area. Obviously, the existing design is not compatible with the new requirement.

Further, the figure indicates that three alternative design configurations are being considered. Each configuration meets the availability requirement, with configuration A having the highest estimated reliability MTBF and configuration C reflecting the best maintainability characteristics with the lowest $\overline{M}$ct value. The objective is to select the best of the three configurations on the basis of cost.

When considering cost, there are costs associated with research and development (R&D) activity, investment or manufacturing costs, and operation and maintenance (O&M) costs. For instance, improving reliability and/or maintainability characteristics in design will result in an increase in R&D and investment (manufacturing) cost. In addition, experience has indicated that such improvements will result in lower O&M cost, particularly in the areas of maintenance personnel and support cost and the cost of spare/repair parts. Thus, initially the analyst looks only at these categories. If the

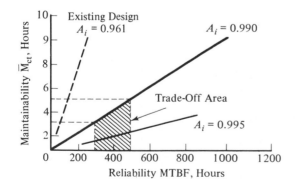

Conf.	A_i	MTBF	$\overline{M}_{ct}$
Existing	0.961	125	5.0
Alt. A	0.991	450	4.0
Alt. B	0.990	375	3.5
Alt. C	0.991	320	2.8

Other systems are eligible for consideration as long as the effectiveness parameters fall within the trade-off areas

Figure 6-16. Reliability-maintainability trade-off.

Table 6-5. COST SUMMARY (PARTIAL COSTS)

Category	Conf. A	Conf. B	Conf. C	Remarks
R and D cost ●Reliability design ●Maintainability design	$ 17,120 2,109	$ 15,227 4,898	$ 12,110 7,115	High Reliability Parts, Packaging, Accessibility
Investment cost manufacturing (200 Systems)	$3,422,400	$3,258,400	$3,022,200	$17,112/Equipment A; $16,292/Equipment B; $15,111/Equipment C
O & M cost ●Maintenance personnel and support ●Spare/Repair parts	$1,280,000 342,240	$1,536,000 325,840	$1,800,000 302,220	12,800 Maint. Action/Equipment A; 15,360 Maint. Action/Equipment B; 18,000 Maint. Action/Equipment C; 10% of manufacturing cost for spares
Total Cost	$5,063,869	$5,140,365	$5,143,645	

final decision is close, it may be appropriate to investigate other categories. A summary of partial cost data is presented in Table 6-5.

Referring to the table, the delta costs associated with the three alternative equipment configurations are included for R&D and investment. Maintenance personnel and support costs, included as part of O&M cost, are based on estimated operating time for the 200 equipments throughout the required 10-year period of use (i.e., 200 equipments operating 8 hours per day, 360 days per year, for 10 years) and the reliability MTBF factor. Assuming that the average cost per maintenance action is $100, maintenance personnel and support costs are determined by multiplying this factor by the estimated quantity of maintenance actions, which is determined from total operating time divided by the MTBF value.

2. Analysis results. Configuration *A* satisfies the system availability, reliability, and maintenance requirements with the least life-cycle cost.

6.3. Summary of Analysis Results

The examples presented in Section 6.2 represent a very small sample of the type of problems facing the designer during the early stages of system development. In addition, the problems as defined are addressed individually. Although these examples are realistic, quite often we are required to evaluate many different facets of a system on a relatively concurrent basis. For instance, for a given design configuration it may be feasible to accomplish a system availability analysis, a shop turnaround-time analysis, a level of repair analysis, and a spares inventory policy evaluation as part of verifying design adequacy in terms of compliance with system requirements. We may also wish to determine the impact of one system parameter on another or the interaction effects between two elements of logistic support. In accomplishing such, problem resolution may require the utilization of a number of different models combined in such a manner to provide a variety of output factors.[15]

The analysis of a system (to include the prime equipment and its associated elements of logistic support) is sometimes fairly complex; however, this process can be simplified by applying the right techniques and developing the proper analytical tools. The combining of techniques to facilitate the analysis task can be accomplished by following the steps in Section 6.1 (i.e., defining the problem, identifying feasible alternatives, selecting evaluation criteria, etc.). The output may appear as illustrated in Figure 6-17.

Referring to the figure, the analyst may wish to develop a series of individual models as illustrated. Each model may be used separately to solve

---

[15]Appendix C provides some examples of experience in this area.

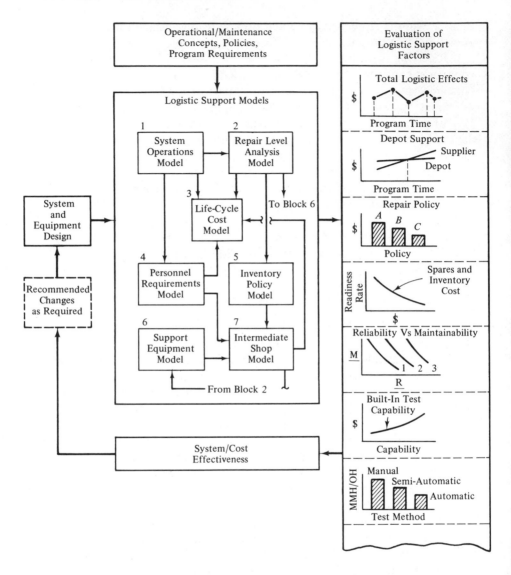

Figure 6-17. Application of support models.

a specific detailed problem, or the models may be combined to solve a higher level problem. The models may be used to varying degrees depending on the depth of analysis required. In any event, the overall analytical task must be approached in an organized methodical manner and applied judiciously to prove the results desired.

QUESTIONS AND PROBLEMS

1. What is logistic support analysis?
2. When is LSA accomplished in the system life cycle?
3. What precautions are involved in applying LSA?
4. What is a model? List the basic characteristics.
5. What is a sensitivity analysis? What are the benefits of a sensitivity analysis?
6. What are the basic outputs of LSA? What input data are required for accomplishing LSA?
7. What factors should influence the formulation of a cost-breakdown structure?
8. What management benefits can be derived from LSA?
9. How does LSA affect system/equipment design?
10. How does LSA affect the provisioning and acquisition of logistic support elements for operational use?
11. What steps would you perform in accomplishing a life-cycle cost analysis of two or more alternatives?
12. The maintenance disposition of failed items is influenced by a number of factors. List three factors.
13. Of what value is a break-even analysis?
14. Does LSA affect the system maintenance concept? If so, how?
15. What is the purpose of a functional analysis as it relates to the maintenance analysis?
16. What is the first step in the LSA process?
17. In accomplishing an analysis, how would you assess the aspect of risk?
18. Develop a life-cycle cost model on a system of your choice. Identify model input/output factors, develop the model, and evaluate the results (be prepared to present the model in class).
19. How are cost factors determined for an input to a life-cycle cost model?
20. What is the purpose of discounting? What effect does discounting have on the results of an analysis?
21. What is a cost-estimating relationship? Give some examples.
22. What is meant by "design to a cost"? What aspect of cost is considered?
23. How do learning curves affect life-cycle cost analyses? What factors influence learning curves?
24. Referring to Figure 6-13, the repair–discard screening criteria presented are applicable to all systems. True or false? Why?
25. Referring to Table 6-1, what do the figures presented tell you? How do these figures relate to equipment design? What action(s) would you take, if any?
26. Referring to Table 6-2, if the unit acquisition cost of Assembly A-1 is one-half of the value indicated, how would the decision be affected?

27. If, in Table 6-2, the reliability of Assembly A-1 is four times the value indicated, what would be the results of the evaluation? What would be the results if the reliability of Assembly A-1 is one-tenth (0.1) of the value indicated?

28. Select a system of your choice and identify a particular component or element of that system. Assume that the component selected has failed, and develop a maintenance task analysis covering troubleshooting, repair, and functional checkout.

29. What is the purpose of the maintenance analysis? Name some benefits (be specific).

30. A maintenance analysis is always accomplished on every repairable component of a system. True or false? Why?

31. Based on the information provided below, compute the life-cycle cost in terms of present value using a 10% discount factor for System *XYZ*. Indicate the total value at the start of the program (decision point) and plot the cost stream or profile.

    System *XYZ* is installed in an aircraft which will be deployed at five operational bases. Each base will have a maximum force level of 12 aircraft with the bases being activated in series (e.g., Base 1 at the end of year 3, base 2 in year 5, etc.). The total number of System *XYZ*'s in operation are:

Year Number									
1	2	3	4	5	6	7	8	9	10
0	0	0	10	20	40	60	55	35	25

System *XYZ* is a newly designed configuration packaged in three units (Unit *A*, Unit *B*, and Unit *C*) with the following specified requirements for each of the units.

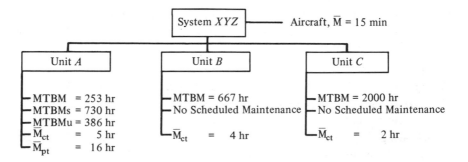

The average System *XYZ* utilization is 4 hours per day and Units *A*, *B*, and *C* are operating 100% of the time when System *XYZ* is on. One of the aircraft crew members will be assigned to operate several different systems throughout flight and it is assumed that 10% of his time is allocated to System *XYZ*.

Relative to the maintenance concept, System *XYZ* incorporates a built-in self-test that enables rapid system checkout and fault isolation to the unit level. No external support equipment is required at the aircraft. In the event of a no-go condition, fault isolation is accomplished to the unit and the applicable unit is removed, replaced with a spare, and sent to the intermediate-level maintenance shop (located at the operational base) for corrective maintenance. Unit repair is accomplished through module replacement with the modules being discarded at failure. Scheduled (preventive) maintenance is accomplished on Unit *A* in the intermediate shop every 6 months. No depot maintenance is required; however, the depot does provide backup supply and support functions as required.

The requirements for System *XYZ* dictate the following program profile. For each corrective maintenance action involving Unit *A*, Unit *B*, or Unit *C*, two technicians are required on a full-time basis. One technician is low-skilled, at $9.00/hour, and one technician is high-skilled, at $11.00/hour. Direct and indirect costs are included in these rates. For each preventive maintenance action, one high-skilled technician at $11.00/hour is required on a full-time basis.

System operator personnel costs are $12.00/hour.

Facility costs are based on a burden rate of $0.20/direct maintenance manhour associated with the prime equipment.

Maintenance data costs are assumed to be $20/maintenance action.

Assume that there is a "design-to-unit-flyaway-cost" requirement of $15,000 maximum. Has this requirement been met? Assume that there is a "design-to-LCC" requirement of $40,000 maximum. Has this requirement been met?

In solving Problem 31, be sure to state all assumptions in a clear and concise manner.

32. Operational and maintenance facility requirements are based on what factors?

33. Personnel requirements for the operation and maintenance of a system are based on what factors?

34. Personnel training requirements are based on what factors?

LOGISTICS IN SYSTEM DESIGN

System or product design is basically accomplished through the systems engineering process. Systems engineering constitutes the application of scientific and engineering efforts to (1) transform an operational need into a description of system performance parameters and a preferred system configuration through the use of an iterative process of functional analysis, synthesis, optimization, definition, design, test and evaluation; (2) integrate related technical parameters and assure compatability of all physical, functional, and program interfaces in a manner that optimizes the total system definition and design; and (3) integrate reliability, maintainability, logistic support, human factors, safety, security, structural integrity, producibility, and other related specialties into the total engineering effort. The systems engineering process, in its evolving of functional detail and design requirements, has as its goal the achievement of the proper balance among operational (e.g., performance, effectiveness), economic, and logistics factors. The process employs a sequential and iterative methodology to reach cost-effective solutions, and the information developed through this process is used to plan and integrate the engineering effort for the system as a whole.

The process of design evolution is illustrated in Figure 1-1, and is tailored to meet a specific need. Actually, regardless of the system type and size, design commences with the identification of a need and the establishment of requirements, constraints, and design criteria. Based on the results, func-

7

tional analyses and allocations are generated to apportion the appropriate system-level requirements down to the subsystem, unit, and lower indenture levels of the system. Trade-off studies and system optimization are performed to evaluate the various alternative approaches that are considered feasible in meeting the identified need, with the output reflecting a preferred system configuration. This configuration is then defined through the system specification(s).

The steps just described represent *conceptual design* and *preliminary system design*, and are reflected by blocks 1 through 9, Figure 1-1. This portion of the system design process may be repetitive and iterative in nature until the ultimate output constitutes a system configuration that will not only meet performance requirements, but one that can be operated and supported in an effective and efficient manner throughout its planned life cycle.

Given a preferred configuration (described in the system specification), *detail design and development* commences with the generation of lower-level supporting specifications, detail analyses and trade-offs, functional equipment layouts, and formal design documentation. The output is reviewed on the basis of compliance with the initially established requirements, and corrective action is implemented where appropriate. The system configuration represented on paper and approved through a series of formal design reviews is then converted into an engineering model or prototype system that can be used for test and evaluation. Test and evaluation at this stage is accomplished to the extent possible to verify that the system requirements have been met prior to entering into the production and/or construction phase.

This process, leading from the identification of a need through the development of a physical model of the system (including prime mission equipment, elements of logistic support, software, personnel, and data), is addressed in this chapter. Emphasis is placed on detail design and development as reflected in blocks 10 through 12, Figure 1-1.

7.1. Conceptual Design

Conceptual design constitutes the starting point for a design project, and includes a feasibility study directed toward defining a set of useful solutions to the problem being addressed. The output represents a technical baseline for a proposed system, a definition of system operational requirements, the system maintenance concept, and a preliminary systems analysis. System operational requirements and the maintenance concept were described in Chapters 3 and 4. All subsequent design activities should be based on the information provided therein.

7.2. Preliminary System Design

Preliminary system design (sometimes referred to as advance development) starts with the baseline configuration for the system identified in conceptual design and proceeds toward translating the established system-level requirements into detailed qualitative and quantitative design characteristics. Preliminary design, illustrated by blocks 3 through 9 of Figure 1-1, includes the process of functional analysis and allocation, the accomplishment of trade-off studies and optimization, initial logistic support analyses, system synthesis, and configuration definition in the form of a system specification and supporting specifications as required. Chapters 5 and 6 cover activities included in this phase.

7.3. Detail Design and Development

The detail design phase begins with the concept and configuration derived through preliminary system design; that is, a configuration with performance, effectiveness, logistic support, cost, and other requirements has been described in the system specification. An overall system design configuration has been established, and now it is necessary to convert that configuration to the definition and subsequent realization of hardware, software, and items of support. The process from here on includes:

1. The description of subsystems, units, assemblies, and lower-level components and parts of the prime mission equipment and the elements of logistic support (e.g., test and support equipment, facilities, personnel and training, technical data, spare/repair parts).
2. The preparation of design documentation (e.g., specifications, analysis results, trade-off study reports, predictions, detailed drawings), describing *all* elements of the system.
3. The definition and development of computer software (as applicable).
4. The development of an engineering model, a service test model, and/or a prototype model of the system and its elements for test and evaluation to verify design adequacy.
5. The test and evaluation of the system model that has been developed.
6. The redesign and retest of the system, or an element of the system, as necessary to correct any deficiencies noted through initial system testing.

While the preliminary design stage established the top system-level configuration, now it is necessary to define subsystems, units, assemblies, and on down to the part level. This definition process results in the identification of specific characteristics which have a considerable impact on logistic support. For instance,

1. Equipment packaging significally influences:

   a. Maintenance time and frequency throughout the life cycle.
   b. Type of transportation and handling equipment.
   c. Capability of test and support equipment (scope and depth of operational checkout and maintenance diagnostic provisions).
   d. Type and quantity of spare/repair parts.
   e. Extent of coverage in maintenance procedures.
   f. Facility space for storage of spare/repair parts.

2. Item standardization affects:

   a. Type and quantity of test and support equipment.
   b. Type and quantity of spare/repair parts.
   c. Procurement source and the time for acquisition of spare/repair parts (supply pipeline).
   d. Personnel quantities and training requirements.
   e. Extent of coverage in maintenance procedures.
   f. Facility space for storage of spare/repair parts.

3. Component selection affects:

    a. Maintenance time and frequency throughout the life cycle.
    b. Quantity and capability of test and support equipment.
    c. Type and quantity of spare/repair parts.
    d. Facility space for storage of spare/repair parts.
    e. Extent of coverage in maintenance procedures.
    f. Personnel training requirements.

Because these and many other design features have such an impact on the support of a system (e.g., accessibility, mounting methods, size, weight, cost, safety provisions, standardization, etc.), it is imperative that logistics be considered and properly addressed throughout the design process. The most effective way of ensuring that this is accomplished is through a closely intergrated program effort involving those activities which deal most directly with the design for supportability. Reliability, maintainability, and human factors are considered as being significant in this area. A major objective of reliability is to provide features in the design necessary to sustain system operation and minimize equipment failure. However, knowing that systems will fail at some point in time, maintainability design provisions are incorporated to allow for accomplishment of the necessary maintenance support in a specified period of time with a minimum expenditure of total logistics resources. The field of human factors deals with the human–machine interface, and is critical in the design from the standpoint of simplifying operator and maintenance task accomplishment and reducing personnel errors. Humankind's physical actions and the consequences of decision making in the performance of operational and maintenance tasks have a major impact on logistic support. These functions are integrated in the design process to produce an effective product output at lower life-cycle cost (i.e., cost of ownership).

A. APPLICATION OF DESIGN CRITERIA

To facilitate the design task, appropriate criteria are developed to provide specific guidelines covering areas such as accessibility, packaging, mobility, transportability, human factors, standardization, and many others. These criteria are directed toward incorporating the necessary characteristics compatible with the system goals for optimum logistic support.

Design criteria can be classified as *general* or *specific*. Within the overall guidelines established through functional analysis and allocation (refer to Chapter 5), there may be a number of options available to the designer. It is important that supportability considerations be inherent in the decision process. To ensure that this is accomplished, illustrated qualitative and quantitative data, checklists, and related material are made available. Figures 7-1 through 7-4 represent examples of general criteria. These and other

<u>M</u> Criteria

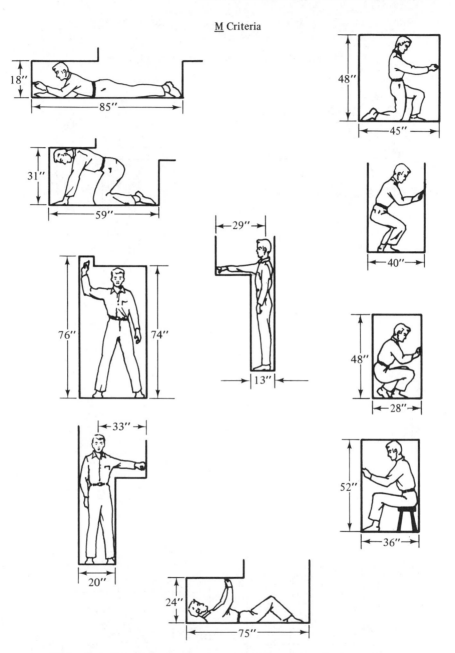

Figure 7-1. Limiting clearances required for various body positions. (NAVSHIPS 94324, *Maintainability Design Criteria Handbook for Designers of Shipboard Electronic Equipment*, U.S., Navy Washington, D.C.)

M Criteria
(Accessibility)

Minimum Openings For Using Common Hand Tools

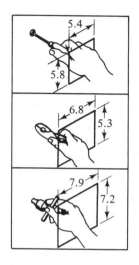
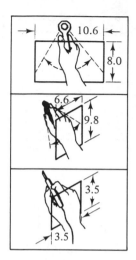

M Criteria
(Accessibility)

Space Required For Using Common Hand Tools

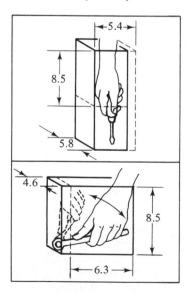
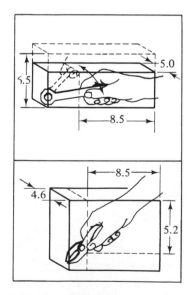

Figure 7-2. General criteria (accessibility). (NAVSHIPS 94324, *Maintainability Design Criteria Handbook for Designers of Shipboard Electronic Equipment*, U.S. Navy, Washington, D.C.)

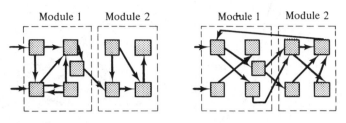

Good   Bad

Module 1   Module 2   Module 1   Module 2

Design for Functional Unitization that Corresponds to Modularization

M Criteria
(Standardization and Interchangeability)

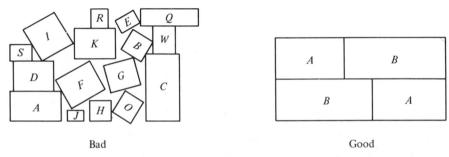

Bad   Good

Figure 7-3. General criteria. (AMCP 706-134, *Engineering Design Handbook—Maintainability Guide for Design*, U.S. Army, Washington, D.C.)

examples are supported by documentation covering the results of studies, engineering experiments, and field tests.[1]

As a supplement to the general criteria approach, appropriate checklists may be developed which serve to remind the designer of areas of particular

---

[1]Four references are (a) NAVSHIPS 94324, *Maintainability Design Criteria Handbook for Designers of Shipboard Electronic Equipment*, Naval Ship Systems Command, Washington, D.C.; (b) AMCP 706-134, *Engineering Design Handbook—Maintainability Guide for Design*, U.S. Army Material Command, AMCRD-TV, Washington, D.C.; (c) ASD-TR-61-424, *Guide to Integrated System Design for Maintainability*, U.S. Air Force, Behavioral Sciences Laboratory, WPAFB, Ohio; and (d) MIL-STD-1472, Military Standard, "Human Engineering Design Criteria for Systems, Equipment, and Facilities," Department of Defense, Washington, D.C. The documents listed include a wide variety of criteria. It is recommended that these and other documents be reviewed and that items applicable to the type of equipment being designed be extracted and combined (as necessary) into an appropriate set of guidelines for the designer. Presenting the designer with four rather comprehensive documents will not produce effective results.

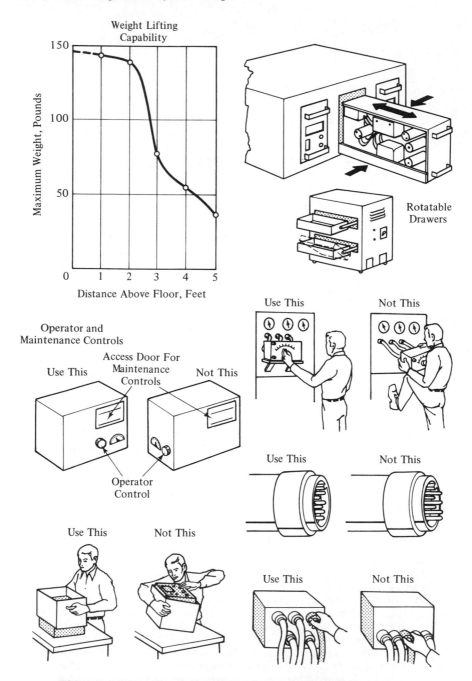

Figure 7-4. General criteria. (DH 1-3, *Design Handbook Personnel Subsystems*, AFSC, U.S. Air Force, Washington, D.C.)

concern. An example is presented in Figure 7-5. Referring to the figure, the designer may quickly review the appropriate factors, determine applicability, and assess the extent to which a design reflects consideration of these factors. If the designer desires to investigate further the meaning of certain checklist items, he or she may call on a specialist for an interpretation or refer to a more in-depth coverage as presented in Appendix D.[2]

On the other hand, as design progresses, the designer may be faced with certain problems which require specific guidance. Data, consistent with overall system design objectives for logistic support and compatible with the general criteria referenced above, may be developed in response to a particular need. Quite often, several alternative approaches may be feasible, and in such instances, the designer formalizes the decision through the accomplishment of trade-off studies.

B. ANALYSIS AND TRADE-OFF STUDIES

Throughout the design process, analyses and trade-off studies are accomplished in the evaluation of alternatives. Early in design, these trade-off evaluations are conducted at a relatively high level, as discussed in the previous chapters. As design progresses, evaluations are accomplished at a lower level in the system hierarchy. For instance, it may be necessary to:

1. Determine alternative methods for mounting components in an assembly or on a designated surface.
2. Determine whether it is desirable to use a light indicator or a meter on a front operator panel to provide certain information.
3. Determine whether it is more feasible to design a repairable assembly internally within the organization or to purchase a comparable item from an outside supplier.
4. Determine the feasibility of repairing a given subassembly when a failure occurs or discarding it (this constitutes an extension of the level-of-repair analysis described in Sections 4.2 and 6.2B).
5. Determine whether to use standard components in a given application or to use new nonstandard components with higher reliability.
6. Determine alternative inventory stock levels for a given spare-part consumption.
7. Determine whether new test equipment should be developed or whether existing items should be used.

The concepts and techniques employed in the evaluation of alternative design approaches are the same here as described in Chapter 6 (refer to Figure

---

[2]The design review questions presented in Appendix D directly support the checklist items included in Figure 7-5. These questions are intended to highlight the characteristics in design that are considered desirable.

System Design Review Checklist

General

1. System Operational Requirements Defined

2. Effectiveness Factors Established

3. System Maintenance Concept Defined

4. Functional Analysis and Allocation Accomplished

5. Logistic Support Analysis Accomplished

6. Logistic Support Operation Plan Complete

Logistic Support Elements

Requirements Known and Optimized for

1. Test and Support Equipment

2. Supply Support (Spare/Repair Parts)

3. Personnel and Training

4. Technical Data (Procedures)

5. Facilities and Storage

6. Transportation and Handling

Design Features

Does the Design Reflect Adequate Consideration Toward

1. Selection of Parts

2. Standardization

3. Test Provisions

4. Packaging and Mounting

5. Interchangeability

6. Accessibility

7. Handling

8. Fasteners

9. Panel Displays and Controls

10. Adjustments and Alignments

11. Cables and Connectors

12. Servicing and Lubrication

13. Calibration

14. Environment

15. Storage

16. Transportability

17. Producibility

18. Safety

19. Reliability

When reviewing design (layouts, drawings, part lists, engineering reports), this checklist may prove beneficial in covering various program functions and design features applicable to logistic support. The items listed are supported with more detailed criteria in Appendix D. The response to each item listed should be YES.

Figure 7-5. Sample design review checklist.

6-2). However, one must ensure that the depth of application is tailored to the problem at hand.

C. DESIGN FOR RELIABILITY

Reliability design includes the tasks that are necessary in the design process to ensure that the resultant product configuration meets system operational requirements (i.e., system/equipment MTBM or MTBF). The scope of coverage in this text includes those actions which are considered to have the greatest impact on logistic support.[3]

1. Reliability allocation. Reliability allocation is one of the first steps in the design process. Once an acceptable reliability or failure rate has been established for the system, it must be allocated among the various subsystems, units, assemblies, and so on. This provides criteria for the designer, and establishes an initial frame of reference for logistic support in terms of anticipated maintenance rates. Reliability allocation was discussed rather thoroughly in Section 5.2A.

2. Reliability models. Throughout the design process, reliability models are used to aid in the evaluation of alternatives and to accomplish the various types of analyses. There are series models, parallel models, partial redundancy models, and standby redundancy models employed to evaluate different equipment design options. These models depend on valid input failure-rate information and the appropriate failure-rate distribution. As discussed in Chapter 2, the *exponential distribution* is commonly used when item failure rates are relatively constant, the *Weibull distribution* is continuous and can be used for increasing and decreasing failure rates, and the *Poisson distribution* is used to determine multiple failures. The output from these models aids in assessing equipment stress conditions and in the accomplishment of predictions, and the results are used as an input to the logistic support models discussed in Appendix C.

3. Selection of component parts. The reliability of an equipment is a function of the component parts, part applications, stresses, and tolerances

---

[3]The author appreciates the fact that the subject of reliability is rather comprehensive and cannot be adequately treated within the confines of this text. It is hoped that students will realize the impact that reliability has on total logistic support, and will further supplement their knowledge through review of additional material. Three references are (a) Bazovsky, I., *Reliability Theory and Practice*, Prentice-Hall, Inc., Englewood Cliffs, N.J., 1961; (b) Calabro, S. R., *Reliability Principles and Practices*, McGraw-Hill Book Company, New York, 1962; and (c) Kapur, K. C. and Lamberson, L. R., *Reliability in Engineering Design*, John Wiley & Sons, Inc., New York, 1977.

intrinsic in the basic design. Consequently, a fundamental approach in attaining a high level of reliability is to select and apply those components and materials of known reliabilities and capable of meeting system requirements. Major emphasis in the design for reliability should consider

a. The selection of standardized components and materials.
b. The evaluation of all components and materials prior to design acceptance. This includes studying the effects, stresses, tolerances, and other characteristics of the component in its intended application. A tolerance evaluation or worst-case analysis can support this task.
c. The utilization of only those component parts capable of meeting reliability objectives.

The effect of standardization on logistic support is significant. First, the standard component has a known reliability that is often better than that of a nonstandard item incorporated to perform an equivalent function. The failure rate and the requirement for spares can be realistically determined. Second, with standardization, the quantity of different component types in the supply system is reduced. This results in lower provisioning (procurement) and inventory maintenance cost. Alternative supplier sources can be established, cataloging changes are reduced, and spares storage requirements are minimized. Third, the test requirements are standard, which in turn causes a reduction in the variety of test equipment and a reduction in procedures (maintenance documentation) and personnel training; thus, the incorporation of standardization in equipment design has a very beneficial effect on logistic support.

4. Failure mode and effects analysis (FMEA).[4] The FMEA is an analysis performed during early design to determine the manner in which the most probable failure modes would be likely to affect the operation of the end item. This analysis constitutes a systematic approach to consider how an item can fail. Component modes of failure are listed together with their effects on the next higher assembly and on the system as a whole. Methods of failure determination are also evaluated, together with failure frequencies. The analysis serves to point out critical failure areas (as related to system mission requirements), and guide the designer in terms of areas needing special emphasis and possible modification for design improvement.

As part of maintainability design, the FMEA is used to generate logic troubleshooting flow diagrams which are discussed in Chapter 5 (refer to the maintenance functional flow in Figure 5-4) and in Appendix B covering the

---

[4]The FMEA, sometimes known as the "failure modes, effects, and criticality analysis (FMECA)," is closely related to the hazard analysis usually accomplished as a safety program task. Refer to Hammer, W., *Handbook of System and Product Safety*, Prentice-Hall, Inc., Englewood Cliffs, N.J., 1972.

maintenance analysis. Where reliability evaluates the component failure in terms of system impact (working from the bottom up), maintainability commences with a symptom of failure at the system level and evaluates the equipment in terms of the time, tasks, and resources required for repair (working from the top down). Maintenance personnel needs, troubleshooting routines, test and support equipment requirements, and so on, are determined. Equipment design characteristics are then evaluated in terms of supportability. Major problem areas in the design are readily identified and brought to the attention of the designer.

It is evident that the FMEA is a significant contributor in determining logistic support requirements for the front end of the corrective maintenance cycle (see Figure 2-9). In addition, the resultant logic troubleshooting flows provide test parameters and checkout procedures for the maintenance manuals used throughout the life cycle when equipment is deployed in the field.

5. *Critical-useful-life-analysis.* A critical-useful-life item is one which, because of its short life, is incapable of satisfying the functional requirements imposed by its application unless corrective or preventive maintenance is performed. During the design phase, critical items are listed along with their expected life in terms of calendar time, operating cycles, or equipment operating hours. This listing specifies the requirement for maintenance, personnel support, and spare/repair parts. In the interest of equipment design for supportability, all critical items should be eliminated if at all possible.

6. *Reliability prediction.* As engineering data become available, reliability prediction is accomplished as a check on design in terms of the system requirement and the factors specified through allocation. The predicted values of MTBM, MTBF, or failure rate (λ) are compared against the requirement, and areas of incompatibility are evaluated for possible design improvement.

Prediction is accomplished at different times in the equipment design process and will vary somewhat depending on the type of data available. Basic prediction techniques are summarized as follows:

a. Prediction may be based on the analysis of similar equipment. This technique should only be used when the lack of data prohibits the use of more sophisticated techniques. The prediction uses MTBF values for similar equipments of similar degrees of complexity performing similar functions and having similar reliability characteristics. The reliability of the new equipment is assumed to be equal to that of the equipment which is most comparable in terms of performance and complexity. Part quantity and type, stresses, and environmental factors are not considered. This technique is easy to perform, but not very accurate.

b. Prediction may be based on an estimate of *active element groups* (AEG). The AEG is the smallest functional building block that controls or converts energy. An AEG includes one active element (e.g., relay, transistor, pump, machine) and a number of passive elements. By estimating the number of AEGs and using a complexity chart, one can predict MTBF.

c. Prediction may be accomplished from an equipment parts count. There are a variety of methods used that differ somewhat due to data source, the number of part-type categories, and assumed stress levels. Basically, a design parts list is used and parts are classified in certain designated categories. Failure rates are assigned and combined to provide a predicted MTBF at the system level. A representative approach is illustrated in Table 7-1.

Table 7-1. RELIABILITY PREDICTION DATA SUMMARY

Component Part	λ/Part (%/ 1000 Hours)	Quantity of Parts	(λ/Part) (Quantity)
Part A	0.161	10	1.610
Part B	0.102	130	13.260
Part C	0.021	72	1.512
Part D	0.084	91	7.644
Part E	0.452	53	23.956
Part F	0.191	3	0.573
Part G	0.022	20	0.440
Failure Rate (λ) = 48.995%/1000 Hours $\quad$ MTBF $= \dfrac{1000}{0.48995} = 2041$ Hours		$\sum = 48.995\%$	

Data Source: MIL-HDBK-217, *Military Standardization Handbook, Reliability and Failure Rate Data For Electronic Equipment.*

d. Prediction may be based on a stress analysis. When detailed equipment design is relatively firm, the reliability prediction becomes more sophisticated. Part types and quantities are determined, failure rates are applied, and stress ratios and environmental factors are considered. The interaction effects between components are addressed. This approach is peculiar and varies somewhat with each particular equipment design. Computer methods are often used to facilitate the prediction process.

The figures derived through reliability prediction constitute a direct input to maintainability prediction data, logistic support analysis, and the determination of specific support requirements (e.g., test and support equipment, spare/repair parts, etc.). Reliability basically determines the frequency of maintenance and the quantity of maintenance actions anticipated throughout the life cycle; thus, it is imperative that reliability prediction results be as accurate as possible.

7. Effects of storage, shelf life, packaging, transportation, and handling.
Another critical design task is to determine the reliability degradation (if
any) on the equipment due to storage, packing, transportation, and handling.
The equipment is subjected to these environments when initially shipped
from the factory to the operational site, stored as spares, returned to the depot
or supplier for maintenance, and so on. Sometimes, these environments
include extreme conditions of rain, sand, salt spray, and high and low temperatures. In the event of degradation, either additional design provisions
are needed to compensate for the reduction in reliability or an increase in
the quantity of maintenance actions will result. In either case, the impact on
logistic support is evident.

Reliability design—summary. Throughout the design process, the tasks
defined above are accomplished on a progressive basis by qualified reliability
personnel serving as part of the design team. The results of these tasks are
extremely beneficial to the designer and are necessary for an early assessment
of total logistic support.

D. DESIGN FOR MAINTAINABILITY

Maintainability design includes those functions in the design process
necessary to ensure that the ultimate product configuration is compatible
with the top system-level objectives from the standpoint of the allocated
MTBM, MDT, $\bar{M}$ct, $\bar{M}$pt, MMH/OH, cost/maintenance action, and related
factors. Maintainability is concerned with maintenance times, supportability
factors in design, and projected maintenance cost over the life cycle (refer
to Section 2.2).

Because of its objectives, maintainability is perhaps the largest contributor in the design relative to addressing logistic support from an optimum
viewpoint. Much of logistic support stems from maintenance, and maintenance is a result of design. Maintainability is concerned with influencing
design such that maintenance is optimized and life-cycle cost is minimized.
The scope of coverage in the following paragraphs includes those activities
that are considered to have the greatest impact on logistic support.[5]

1. Maintainability allocation. Maintainability allocation is accomplished along with reliability allocation as one of the first steps in the design

---

[5]The subject of maintainability is rather comprehensive and the student should refer to
additional material to gain full appreciation of its scope. Three (3) sources are (a) Cunning-
ham, C. E. and Cox, W., *Applied Maintainability Engineering*, John Wiley & Sons, Inc.,
New York, 1972; (b) Blanchard, B. S. and Lowery, E. E., *Maintainability—Principles and
Practices*, McGraw-Hill Book Company, New York, 1969; and (c) Goldman, A. and
Slattery, T., *Maintainability—A Major Element of System Effectiveness*, John Wiley & Sons,
Inc., New York, 1967.

Table 7-2. MAINTAINABILITY PREDICTION WORKSHEET

Item: Assembly 4/Part Number: 12345/Sheet No: 4

Part Category	λ	N	$(N)(\lambda)$	Maintenance Times (Hours)							$(N)(\lambda)(\mathrm{Mct}_i)$
				Loc	Iso	Acc	Ali	Che	Int	Mct_i	
Part A	0.161	2	0.322	0.02	0.08	0.14	0.01	0.01	0.11	0.370	0.119
Part B	0.102	4	0.408	0.01	0.05	0.12	0.01	0.02	0.12	0.330	0.134
Part C	0.021	5	0.105	0.03	0.04	0.11	—	0.01	0.14	0.330	0.034
Part D	0.084	1	0.084	0.01	0.03	0.10	0.02	0.03	0.11	0.300	0.025
Part E	0.452	9	4.060	0.02	0.04	0.13	0.02	0.03	0.08	0.320	1.299
Part F	0.191	8	1.520	0.01	0.02	0.11	0.01	0.02	0.07	0.240	0.364
Part G	0.022	7	0.154	0.02	0.05	0.15	—	0.05	0.15	0.420	0.064
Total			6.653							Total	2.039

N = Quantity of Parts   Iso = Isolation   Che = Check-out
λ = Failure Rate   Acc = Access   Int = Interchange
Loc = Localization   Ali = Alignment Mct_i = Maintenance Cycle Time
For determination of $\overline{\mathrm{MMHc}}$, enter manhours for maintenance times.

process. Requirements at the system level, stated both qualitatively and quantitatively, are allocated among the various subsystems, units, and assemblies to provide guidelines for the designer. Maintainability allocation is discussed rather thoroughly in Section 5.2B.

2. *Maintainability prediction.* Maintainability prediction commences early in the design. The predicted values of MTBM, $\overline{M}ct$, $\overline{M}pt$, MMH/OH, $\overline{MMH}_c$, and so on, are compared with the allocated factors for compatibility with system requirements. The prediction is a design tool used to identify possible problem areas where redesign might be required to meet system requirements.

Several prediction techniques are available and their particular application will vary somewhat depending on the definition of the design (supported by engineering data) at the time. These are summarized as follows:

a. Prediction of corrective maintenance time may be accomplished using a system functional-level breakdown and determining maintenance tasks and associated times in progressing from one function to another. The functional breakdown is an expansion of the illustration in Figure 5-6, and covers subsystems, units, assemblies, and parts. Maintainability characteristics such as localization, isolation, accessibility, repair, and checkout as incorporated in the design are evaluated and identified with one of the functional levels. Times applicable to each part (assuming that every part will fail at some point) are combined to provide factors for the next higher level. A sample data format for an assembly is presented in Table 7-2.

Similar data prepared on each assembly in the system are combined as illustrated in Table 7-3, and the factors are computed to arrive at the predicted $\overline{M}ct$ or $\overline{MMH}_c$, whichever is desired.

Table 7-3. MAINTAINABILITY PREDICTION DATA SUMMARY

Work Sheet No.	Item Designation	Work Sheet Factors	
		$\Sigma\,(N)(\lambda)$	$\Sigma\,(N)(\lambda)(\text{Mct}_i)$
1	Assembly 1	7.776	3.021
2	Assembly 2	5.328	1.928
3	Assembly 3	8.411	2.891
4	Assembly 4	6.653	2.039
5	Assembly 5	5.112	2.576
13	Assembly 13	4.798	3.112
Grand Total		86.476	33.118

$$\overline{M}ct = \frac{\Sigma\,(N)(\lambda)(\text{Mct}_i)}{\Sigma\,(N)(\lambda)} = \frac{33.118}{86.486} = 0.382 \text{ Hours}$$

Maintenance tasks and task times are estimated from experience data obtained on similar systems in the field. Failure rates are derived from reliability predictions.

b. Prediction of preventive maintenance time may be accomplished using a method similar to the corrective maintenance approach previously summarized. Preventive maintenance tasks are estimated along with frequency and task times. An example is presented in Table 7-4.

Table 7-4. PREVENTIVE MAINTENANCE DATA SUMMARY

Description of Preventive Maintenance Task	Task Frequency $(fpt_i)(N)$	Task Time (Mpt_i)	Product $(fpt_i)(N)(Mpt_i)$
1. Lubricate	0.115	5.511	0.060
2. Calibrate	0.542	4.234	0.220
31. Service	0.321	3.315	0.106
Grand Total	13.260		31.115

$$\overline{M}pt = \frac{\Sigma\,(fpt_i)(N)(Mpt_i)}{\Sigma\,(fpt_i)(N)} = \frac{31.115}{13.260} = 2.346 \text{ Hours}$$

c. Prediction of corrective maintenance time may be accomplished using a checklist developed from experience on similar systems. The checklist provides scoring criteria for desired maintainability characteristics in the design. A random sample of parts reflected in the new equipment is identified and the characteristics of design as related to each part are evaluated against the checklist criteria. Scores are noted and a predicted $\overline{M}ct$ is derived using a regression equation which supports the checklist.[6]

The figures derived through maintainability prediction are a direct input to the logistic support analysis (particularly the life-cycle cost and maintenance analyses), and form the basis for determining logistic resource requirements for a given design configuration.

3. Logistic support analysis (LSA). As discussed in Chapter 6, the LSA at this phase in the system life cycle accomplishes several major purposes.

a. It provides a systematic check on equipment design for supportability (e.g., reliability, maintainability, and human factors). Areas of poor design that contribute to a high maintenance frequency, lengthy maintenance times, extensive support requirements, and/or excessive cost readily become evident.

---

[6]This procedure is discussed further in Blanchard, B. S. and Lowery, E. E., *Maintainability—Principles and Practices*, McGraw-Hill Book Company, New York, 1969, chap. 10.

b. It provides a basis for the determination of all logistic support requirements to include maintenance functions and tasks, test and support equipment, spare/repair parts, personnel and training, transportation and handling equipment, technical data, and facilities. These requirements are then provisioned for follow-on system support.

LSA is an activity that is extremely important in the maintainability design effort. The analysis provides a systematic evaluation of a proposed design configuration. The evaluation considers size, weight, mobility, packaging, test provisions, standardization, accessibility, and other related maintainability characteristics as incorporated in the design. The evaluation is accomplished through a review of design specifications, layouts and drawings, part and material lists, and other information obtained through consulation with the designer. The results include the data elements presented in Figure 6-5 and discussed further in Appendices A and B.

The procedural approach for development of LSA as it relates to the design process is illustrated in Figure 7-6. Reliability, maintainability, and human factors design data are generated from engineering data, and the results are compiled as part of LSA.[7] LSA is reviewed from the standpoint of equipment design for supportability and the associated logistic support requirements for the system. Problem areas are brought to the attention of the designer, and design changes are initiated as appropriate. LSA is updated on a continuing basis as design matures and serves as a design assessment tool.

The effectiveness of LSA in the design process is dependent on its responsiveness to certain needs. The designer requires support, and needs it immediately. If the support is not available, the design proceeds according to schedule, and the results may not be beneficial to logistic support. Incorporating changes after the fact are costly and may be impractical.

LSA as described in this text should be viewed in a conceptual manner, and its application must be appropriately tailored to the problem at hand. The generation of large volumes of data is not practical in this instance nor are the results timely. On the other hand, LSA can be effectively applied by judiciously selecting specific analysis segments combined with the use of appropriate computerized methods.

4. Related analyses. In support of the prediction and LSA tasks, maintainability design often includes the accomplishment of special studies

---

[7]The generation of other data elements (e.g., value engineering, producibility, performance) is not precluded by the author's reference to reliability, maintainability, and human factors only. The author's selection is based on an opinion relative to the major design factors affecting logistic support.

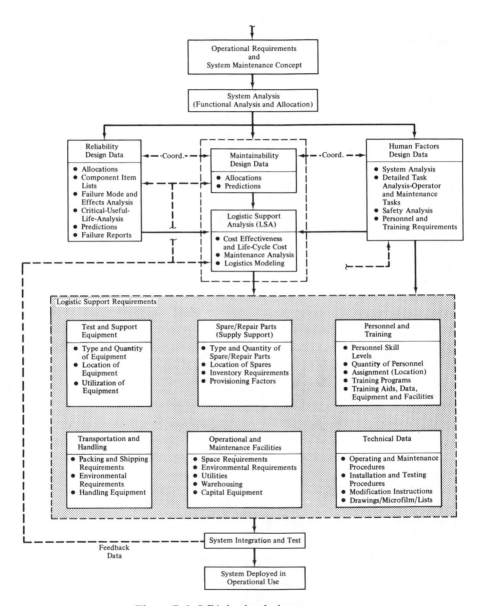

Figure 7-6. LSA in the design process.

related to test provisions (e.g., test point data, test routines, etc.), functional packaging, calibration requirements, and the like. These studies are generated on an "as required" basis.

Maintainability design—summary. Throughout the equipment design phase, the tasks described above are accomplished on an iterative basis by qualified maintainability and logistics personnel. The results are a necessary input to the designer if the ultimate product is to be supported in an effective manner.

E. DESIGN FOR HUMAN FACTORS

Until fairly recently, human factors in the design has received little priority in relation to performance, schedule, cost, and even reliability and maintainability. However, it has been realized that for the system design to be complete, one also needs to address the human element and the interface(s) between the human being and the machine. Optimum hardware (and software) design alone will not guarantee effective results. Consideration must be given to anthropometric factors (e.g., human physical dimensions), human sensory factors (e.g., sight, hearing, feel), human physiological factors (e.g., reaction to environment), psychological factors (e.g., need, expectation, attitude, motivation), and their interrelationships. Human factors in design deal with these considerations, and the results affect not only system operation (i.e., the operator) but the human being in the performance of maintenance and support activities. Human physical and psychic behavior is a major consideration in determining operational and maintenance functions, personnel and training requirements, procedural data requirements, and facilities.

The gross-level operational and maintenance functions of the system (defined through the functional analysis described in Chapter 5) should be allocated between human being and equipment so as to utilize the capabilities of each in the most efficient manner possible. It is obvious that human beings and equipment are not directly comparable. Equipment, when operating, performs in a consistent manner but is relatively inflexible. Human beings, on the other hand, are flexible but do not always perform in a consistent manner.

The human factors effort in the design process is directed toward providing an optimum human–equipment interface. Where manual functions are performed (requiring information handling, communications, decision making, and coordination), it is necessary to ensure that personnel performance and labor utilization are maximized, and that personnel attrition and training costs are held to a minimum. Further, the personnel errors in the operation and maintenance of equipment must be eliminated if possible.

The inclusion of features in the design that are simple to understand, facilitate task accomplishment, and result in clear-cut decisions is necessary.

The relationship between human factors and logistic support is rather pronounced since personnel and training requirements constitute a large factor in the support picture, and these requirements are a direct result of human factor considerations in the design. In addition, the aspect of human factors is very closely allied and integrated with reliability and maintainability, and in some areas an overlap exists.[8]

1. Human factors analysis. Throughout system design, a human factors analysis is performed as an integral part of the overall system analysis effort. The human factors analysis constitutes a composite of individual program activities directed toward (a) the initial establishment of human factors requirements for system design, (b) the evaluation of system design to ensure that an optimum interface exists between the human being and other elements of the system, and (c) the assessment of personnel quantity and skill-level requirements for a given system design configuration The analysis effort employs a number of the analytical techniques and is closely related to the reliability analysis, maintainability analysis, logistic support analysis, and life-cycle cost analysis.

The human factors analysis begins with conceptual design when functions are identified and trade-off studies are accomplished to determine whether these functions are to be performed manually using human resources, automatically with equipment, or by a combination thereof (refer to Chapters 3, 4, and 5). Given the requirements for human resources, one must then ensure that these resources are utilized as efficiently as possible. Thus, the analysis continues through an iterative process of evaluation, system modifications for improvement, reevaluation, and so on. In support of this latter phase of the overall analysis process, there are a number of methods and techniques that can be employed for evaluation purposes. These include the generation of operational sequence diagrams, the accomplishment of detail task analyses, the performance of an error analysis and a safety analysis, the preparation of duty and task worksheets, and so on.

a. *Operational sequence diagrams.* As part of the human factors analysis activity, one of the major tasks is the evaluation of the flow of information from the point in time when the operator first becomes involved with the

---

[8]Human factors requirements and criteria are defined in a number of references. Three (3) sources are (a) Meister, D., *Human Factors: Theory and Practice*, John Wiley & Sons, Inc., New York, 1971; (b) McCormick, E. J., *Human Factors in Engineering and Design*, 4th ed., McGraw-Hill Book Company, New York, 1976; and (c) MIL-STD-1472B, Military Standard, "Human Engineering Design Criteria for Military Systems, Equipment, and Facilities," Department of Defense, Washington, D.C., 1974.

system to completion of the mission. Information flow in this instance pertains to human decisions, human control activities, and the transmission of data.

There are a number of different techniques that can be employed to show information flow. The use of operational sequence diagrams is one.[9] Operational sequence diagrams are decision-action flow devices that integrate operational functions and equipment design. More specifically, these diagrams project different sequences of operation showing:

1. Manual operations.
2. Automatic operations.
3. Operator decision points.
4. Operator control actuations or movements.
5. Transmitted information.
6. Received information using indicator displays, meter readouts, and so on.

Operational sequence diagrams are similar to industrial engineering work-flow process charts and time-line analyses, and are used to evaluate decision–action sequences and human–machine interfaces. The evaluation of operator control panel layouts and workspace design configurations are good examples of where these diagrams may be profitably used.

b. *Detail task analysis.* This facet of analysis involves a systematic study of the human behavior characteristics associated with the completion of a system task(s). It provides data basic to human engineering design and to the determination of personnel types and skill-level requirements. Tasks may be classified as being discrete or continuous. Further, there are operator tasks and maintenance tasks. Thus, one may wish to divide the analysis effort into the "Detail Operator Task Analysis" and the "Detail Maintenance Task Analysis." The portion of the analysis covering maintenance tasks may evolve directly from a combination of the maintainability analysis and logistic support analysis.

In accomplishing a task analysis, there are varying degrees of emphasis and types of formats used. However, the following general steps apply in most instances:

1. Identify system operator and maintenance functions and establish a hierarchy of these functions in terms of job operations, duties, tasks, subtasks, and task elements.
2. Identify those functions (or duties, tasks, etc.) that are controlled

---

[9] Operational sequence diagrams are discussed further and illustrated in DeGreene, K. B., *Systems Psychology*, McGraw-Hill Book Company, New York, 1970, chap. 8.

by the human being and those functions that are automated and controlled by the equipment.

3. For each function involving the human element, determine the specific information necessary for operator and/or maintenance personnel decisions. Such decisions may lead to the actuation of a control, the monitoring of a system condition, or the equivalent. Information required for decision making may be presented in the form of a visual display or an audio signal of some type.

4. For each action, determine the adequacy of the information fed back to the human being as a result of control activations, operational and maintenance sequences, and so on.

5. Determine the impact of the environmental and personnel factors and constraints on the human activities identified.

6. Determine the time requirements, frequency of occurrence, accuracy requirements, and criticality of each action (or series of actions) accomplished by the human being.

7. Determine the human skill-level requirements for all operator and maintenance personnel actions.

A task analysis is generated to ensure that each stimulus is tied to a response, and that each response is directly related to a stimulus. Further, individual human motions are analyzed on the basis of dexterity, mental and motor skill requirements, stress and strain characteristics of the human being performing the task, and so on. The purpose is (1) to identify those areas of system design where potential human–machine problems exist, and (2) to identify the necessary personnel skill-level requirements for operating and maintaining the system in the future.

c. *Error analysis.* One of the major objectives in system design is to minimize (if not eliminate) the possibility of introducing human error in the performance of system operating functions and in the accomplishment of maintenance tasks. Errors may occur as a result of a combination of factors such as:

1. Failure to comply with system operating and maintenance procedures.
2. Failure to obtain and/or consider the proper input data for decision-making purposes.
3. Failure to read displays or operate controls properly.
4. Failure to monitor and respond to system changes.

An error analysis may be accomplished in conjunction with the detail task analysis, using a fault-tree approach or a failure mode and effects analysis. Given the requirement for human manipulation in the accomplishment of a task, one must address the question "What else can happen?" or "How might a fault be introduced in the system?" After recognizing, verifying, and classifying failures, one must determine the effects of these failures on the overall system and on the mission to be fulfilled. Verifying a failure at the operator level and determining its effects(s) at the system level is a prime objective of the reliability FMEA. In this instance, the primary source of failure is the human being.

d. *Safety analysis.* Human factors are closely aligned with system safety, particularly when personnel safety is involved.[10] Hence, a safety analysis is often accomplished in conjunction with or as part of the detailed task analysis. Possible hazard areas are noted and classified. Critical items are brought to the attention of the designer for corrective action. Items of a less hazardous nature may be covered through the inclusion of a warning notice in the operating or maintenance procedures. Product safety is of particular significance when dealing with the legalities of consumerism, the establishment of warranties, and the burden of risk or liability assigned to the equipment producer. In any event, the human factors engineer should be consulted when safety is a question.

2. Personnel and training requirements. Personnel skill levels and quantities are identified by evaluating the complexity and frequency of tasks in the detailed task analysis. Job proficiency levels are established for each location where prime equipment is operated and where maintenance support is performed. These requirements are compared against the personnel goals initially specified for the system. In addition, these factors are compared with the maintenance analysis data (described in Appendix B) for compatibility. Areas of difference are corrected through an update of the maintenance analysis data.

Given the requirements for personnel as dictated by the system design, one must determine the personnel resources that actually will be assigned to operate and maintain the system in the field. The difference in skills between the specified requirements and the personnel that will be assigned is the basis for a formalized training program (i.e., that effort required to upgrade personnel to the desired proficiency level). Training needs are defined in terms of program content, duration of training, training data and training equipment requirements.

Human factors engineers are interested in the personnel and training requirements to ensure that these requirements are realistic for the system. If

---

[10]For additional coverage in system safety, refer to Hammer, W., *Product Safety Management and Engineering,* Prentice-Hall, Inc., Englewood Cliffs, N.J., 1980; and Rodgers, W. P., *Introduction to System Safety Engineering*, John Wiley & Sons, Inc., New York, 1971.

skill level requirements are high and a large amount of training is anticipated, then the equipment design should be reevaluated to see if changes can be made to simplify the situation. In addition, the need for high personnel skills significantly limits the market in terms of finding qualified people.

Human factors—summary. The ultimate result of this effort, accomplished during the design process, not only is directed toward assessing the human–equipment interface, but forms the basis for the personnel and training element of total logistic support.

F. SUPPLIER DESIGN ACTIVITIES

When equipment is defined, the design engineer is faced with a "make-or-buy" decision (whether to design and produce an item internally within his organization or to contract for the item with an outside supplier). Initially, the designer makes a survey of all qualified suppliers, and then evaluates each in terms of capability of meeting schedule requirements, cost, manufacturing facilities, availability of an adequate labor force, and management integrity. Supplier capabilities are compared with internal resources. If the decision is to "buy," supplier specifications and work statements are prepared. These will vary somewhat depending on whether new design and development is required or whether the item is procured as off-the-shelf. If new design is to be accomplished, the supplier requirements will specify appropriate input criteria and the need for predictions and analyses, design reviews, and so on.[11] If the item is procured as off-the-shelf where design and development is not necessary, the supplier requirements will constitute a definition of basic operational, performance, and supportability features and will reference the supplier's initial specification covering the item in question.

Whether the item is newly designed or off the shelf, the procurement specification should include performance characteristics, reliability and maintainability factors (both qualitative and quantitative), human factors, and related requirements. Reliability and maintainability parameters, including supportability considerations, are derived from the functional analysis and allocation data defined in Chapter 5. The allocated factors for the item in question are identified and specified as for any other significant component of the system.

When the appropriate specifications and work statements are prepared, each potential supplier is invited to submit a technical and management/cost proposal. The individual proposals are evaluated, leading to the ultimate selection of the best source. Such an evaluation may entail a visit to the

---

[11]Activities and tasks necessary for the evaluation of design progress in terms of meeting basic system/equipment requirements are specified.

supplier's facility, and an evaluation of the supplier's equipment if an off-the-shelf item is being considered.

The designer may call on the reliability/maintainability/human factors engineer to assist in the evaluation and selection process. For newly designed equipment, it is necessary to ensure that appropriate supportability characteristics are incorporated in the design. When evaluating two or more off-the-shelf items, the evaluation should lead to the selection of the item which is most feasible from the standpoint of total logistic support, even though the best alternative may not incorporate all the desired features.

The evaluation of available off-the-shelf equipment may take the form of the "Selection of Test and Support Equipment" problem defined in Section 6.2. A checklist is developed and weighting factors are established for selected evaluation parameters. Each alternative is reviewed and scored against the checklist criteria. The checklist criteria may include the parameters listed in Table 6-4 or may constitute any combination of selected parameters from the design review checklist in Appendix D.

G. Utilization of Design Aids

During the early stages of the design process, the design engineer is confronted with the task of defining equipment layout and packaging schemes, unit size and weight, access points, and the like. This function is often quite difficult when relying on two-dimensional layout drawings as all assemblies, subassemblies, and so on, are not shown in their true perspective. As an aid to the designer, three-dimensional scale models or mock-ups are sometimes developed to provide a realistic simulation of a proposed final equipment configuration at an early point in the program prior to the development of formal design data or actual prototype hardware.

Models or mock-ups can be developed to any desired scale and to varying degrees of detail depending on the level of emphasis required. Mock-ups may be constructed of heavy cardboard, wood, metal, or a combination of materials. Mock-ups can be developed on a relatively inexpensive basis and in a short period of time when employing the right materials and personnel services (industrial design, human factors, and/or model–shop personnel are usually well oriented to this area and should be utilized to the greatest extent possible). The uses and values of a mock-up are numerous.

1. It provides the design engineer with the opportunity of experimenting with different facility layouts, packaging schemes, panel displays, etc., prior to the preparation of formal design data.
2. It provides the reliability/maintainability/human factors engineer with the opportunity to accomplish a more effective review of a proposed design configuration for the incorporation of supportability characteristics. Problem areas readily become evident.

3. It provides the maintainability/human factors engineer with a tool for use in the accomplishment of predictions and detailed task analyses. It is often possible to simulate operator and maintenance tasks to acquire task sequence and time data.
4. It provides the design engineer with an excellent tool for conveying the final design approach during a formal design review.
5. It serves as an excellent marketing tool.
6. It can be employed to facilitate the training of system operator and maintenance personnel.
7. It is utilized by production and industrial engineering personnel in developing fabrication and assembly procedures and in the design of factory tooling and associated test fixtures.
8. At a later stage in the system life cycle, it may serve as a tool for the verification of a modification kit design prior to the preparation of formal data and the development of kit hardware.

In general, the mock-up is extremely beneficial. It has been used effectively in facility design, aircraft design, and the design of smaller systems/equipments. Examples of several mock-ups that have actually been employed for the foregoing purposes are presented in Figures 7-7 and 7-8.

7.4. Design Review

Design is a progression from an abstract notion to something that has form and function, is fixed, and can be reproduced in designated quantities to satisfy a need. The designer produces a model that is used as a template for the replication of additional models. In the course of production, an error made in any one model will result in a single rejection. However, an error in the design, repeated in all subsequent models, may lead to a serious problem (e.g., complete recycling of all equipment for a major modification). Thus, the designer's responsibility is significantly large. The basic philosophy or evolution of design is illustrated in Figure 7-9.

Initially, a requirement or need is specified. From this point, design evolves through a series of phases (i.e., conceptual design, preliminary system design, detail design and development).[12] In each major phase of the design process, an evaluative function is accomplished to ensure that the design is correct at that point prior to proceeding with the next phase. The evaluative function includes both the informal day-to-day project coordination and data review, and the formal design review. A more detailed procedure illustrating the evaluative function is presented in Figure 7-10.

---

[12]The various phases of design may be labeled differently to suit individual preferences. However, regardless of the assigned nomenclature, the same basic steps exist.

Figure 7-7. Full scale aircraft mock-up showing structure and equipment installation (*top*) and aircraft crew capsule mating with fuselage (*bottom*). (*Courtesy* Rockwell International Corporation.)

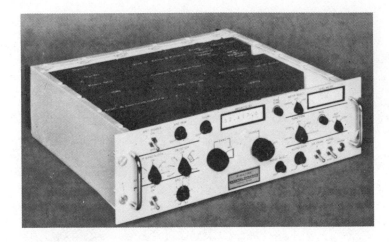

Figure 7-8. Equipment mock-ups (examples). (B. Blanchard and E. Lowery, *Maintainability—Principles and Practices*, McGraw-Hill Book Co., 1969.)

Referring to Figure 7-10, design information is released and reviewed for compliance with the basic system/equipment requirements (i.e., performance, reliability, maintainability, human factors). If the requirements are satisfied, the design is approved as is. If not, recommendations for corrective action are prepared and submitted to the designer for action. If no action is taken as a result of the day-to-day liaison activity, the recommendations

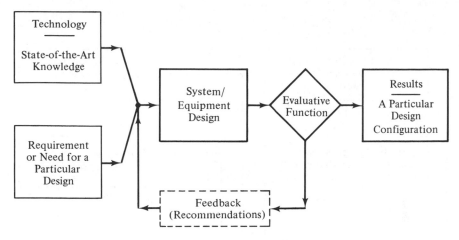

Figure 7-9. Evolution of design.

are presented and discussed as part of the next formal design review. The informal daily liaison activity is covered in the previous sections of this chapter. This section is directed toward the formal design review.

The formal design review constitutes a coordinated activity (including a meeting or series of meetings) directed to satisfy the interests of the design engineer, the technical discipline support areas (reliability, maintainability, human factors), logistics, manufacturing, industrial engineering, quality control, program management, and so on. The purpose of the design review is to formally and logically cover the proposed design from the "total system standpoint" in the most effective and economical manner through a combined integrated review effort. The formal design review serves a number of purposes.[13]

1. It provides a formalized check (audit) of the proposed system/equipment design with respect to contractual and specification requirements. Major problem areas are discussed and corrective action is taken.

2. It provides a common baseline for all project personnel. The design engineer is provided the opportunity to explain and justify his design approach, and representatives from the various supporting organizations (e.g., maintainability, logistic support) are provided the opportunity to hear the design engineer's problems. This serves as a tremendous communication media and creates a better understanding among design and support personnel.

---

[13]The purposes of a formal design review are also covered in Blanchard, B. S. and Lowery, E. E., *Maintainability—Principles and Practices*, McGraw-Hill Book Company, New York, 1969; and Blanchard, B. S. and Fabrycky, W. J., *Systems Engineering and Analysis*, Prentice-Hall, Inc., Englewood Cliffs, N.J., 1981.

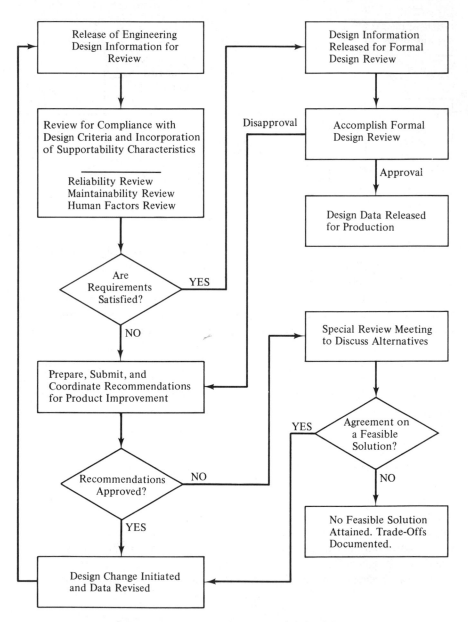

Figure 7-10. Design engineering data review.

3. It provides a means for solving interface problems, and promotes the assurance that all system elements will be compatible. For instance, major interface problems between engineering and manufacturing, relative to lack of producibility, are often not detected until after design data are released and production is underway. The results of major problems discovered at that time are quite costly. Another major problem (which seems to be a common occurrence) is the lack of compatibility between the different elements of logistic support with the prime equipment and the elements of logistic support with each other. Such problems are often undetected at an early point in time due to a wide variance of organizational interests and activity, the rush to get the hardware into production, the physical separation of members of the design team, or some other related reason. A formal design review is intended to prevent the occurrence of these problems.

4. It provides a formalized record of what design decisions were made and the reasons for making them. Analyses, predictions, and trade-off study reports are noted and are available to support design decisions. Compromises to reliability, maintainability, human factors, and logistic support are documented and included in the trade-off study reports.

5. It promotes a greater probability of mature design as well as the incorporation of the latest techniques (where appropriate). Group review may identify new ideas, possibly resulting in simplified processes and ultimate cost savings.

In summary, the formal design review, when appropriately scheduled and conducted in an effective manner, causes a reduction in the producer's risk relative to meeting contract and specification requirements, and often results in improvement of the producer's methods of operation.

A. Scheduling of Design Reviews

Design reviews are generally scheduled prior to each major evolutionary step in the design process. In some instances, this may entail a single review toward the end of each phase (i.e., conceptual, preliminary system design, detail design and development). For other projects, where a large system is involved and the amount of new design is extensive, a series of formal reviews may be conducted on designated elements of the system. This may be desirable to allow for the early processing of some items while concentrating on the more complex high risk items.[14]

---

[14]Items that are procured as off-the-shelf or items where the design is basic and proven may be processed expeditiously to suit both engineering and production schedules. Complex newly designed items (those pushing the state of the art) will require more indepth reviews followed by some modifications and possibly a second review before being released for production.

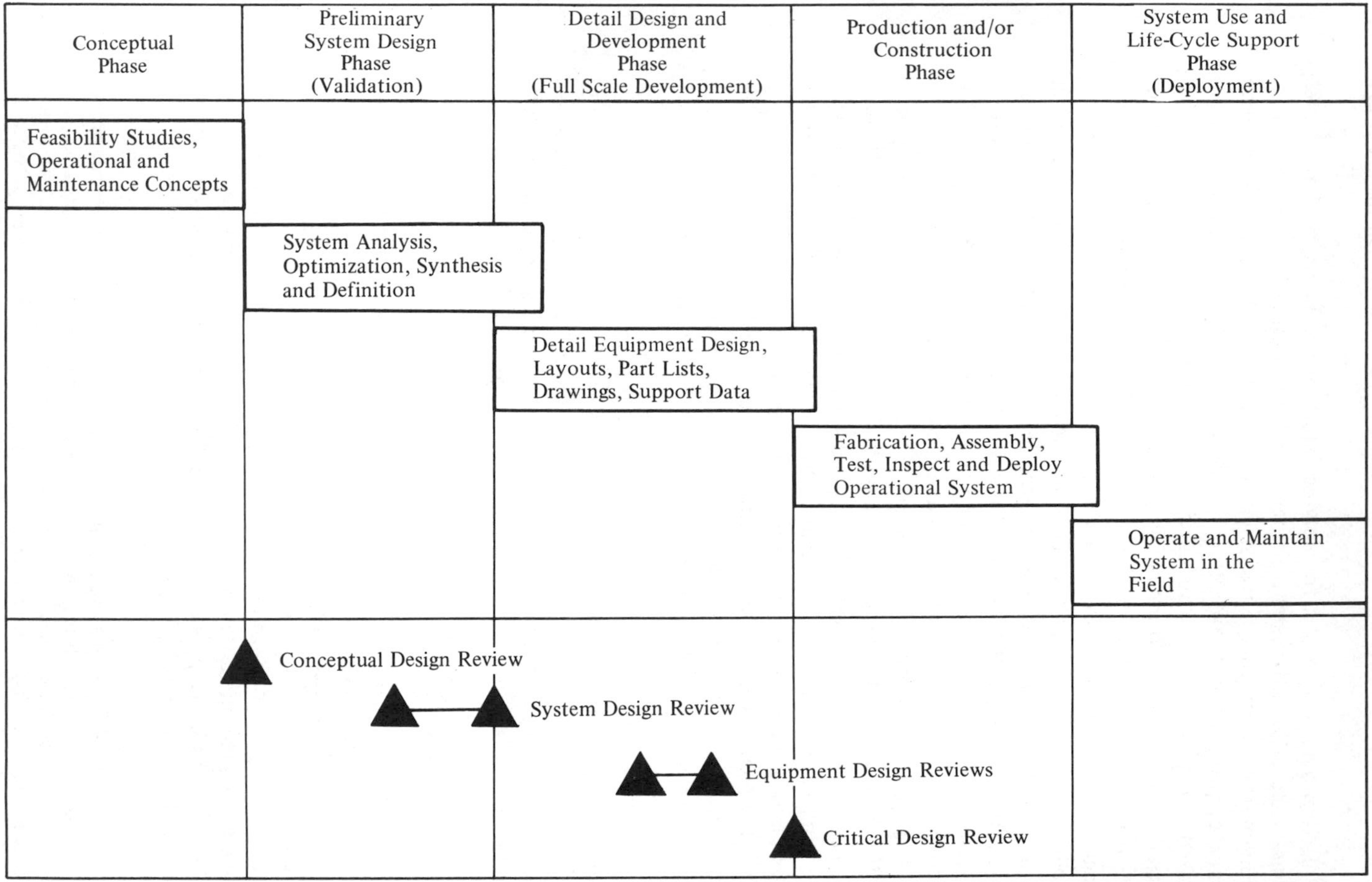

Conceptual Phase	Preliminary System Design Phase (Validation)	Detail Design and Development Phase (Full Scale Development)	Production and/or Construction Phase	System Use and Life-Cycle Support Phase (Deployment)
Feasibility Studies, Operational and Maintenance Concepts	System Analysis, Optimization, Synthesis and Definition	Detail Equipment Design, Layouts, Part Lists, Drawings, Support Data	Fabrication, Assembly, Test, Inspect and Deploy Operational System	Operate and Maintain System in the Field

Conceptual Design Review

System Design Review

Equipment Design Reviews

Critical Design Review

Figure 7-11. Design review schedule in relationship to program phases.

Althouth the quantity and type of design reviews scheduled may vary from program to program, four basic types are readily identifiable and common to most programs. They include the conceptual design review (i.e., system requirements review), the system design review, the equipment design review, and the critical design review. The time phasing of these reviews is illustrated in Figure 7-11. In the figure, the conceptual and preliminary system design phases may be considered "advanced development," and the detail design may be considered "full-scale development."

1. Conceptual design review. The conceptual design review may be scheduled during the early part of a program (preferable not more than 4 to 8 weeks after program start) when operational requirements and the maintenance concept have been defined. Feasibility studies justifying preliminary design concepts should be reviewed. Logistic support requirements at this point are generally included in the maintenance concept definition.

2. System design review. System design reviews are generally scheduled during the preliminary system design phase when preliminary system layouts and specifications have been prepared (prior to their formal release). These reviews are oriented to the overall system configuration in lieu of individual equipment items. Supporting data may include functional analyses and allocations, preliminary logistic support analyses, and trade-off study reports. There may be one or more formal reviews scheduled depending on the size of the system and the extent and complexity of the new design. The purpose of the review is to determine whether the design is compatible with all system requirements and whether the documentation supports the design.

3. Equipment design review. Equipment reviews are scheduled during the detail design and development phase when layouts, preliminary mechanical and electrical drawings, functional and logic diagrams, and component part lists are available. In addition, these reviews cover engineering breadboards (hardware), models or mockups, and prototypes. Supporting the design are reliability analyses (FMEA, critical item data, etc.) and predictions, maintainability analyses and predictions, human factors analyses (system analysis and detailed task analysis), and logistic support analyses. The design process at this point has identified specific design constraints, additional or new requirements, and major problem areas. Such reviews are conducted prior to proceeding with finalization of the detail design.

4. Critical design review. The critical design review is scheduled after detail design has been completed but prior to the release of firm design data to production. Such a review is conducted to verify the adequacy and producibility of the design. Design is essentially *frozen* at this point, and manufacturing methods, schedules, and costs are reevaluated for final approval.

The critical design review covers all design effort accomplished subsequent to the completion of the equipment review. This includes changes resulting from recommendations for corrective action stemming from the equipment design review. Data requirements include manufacturing drawings and material lists, a production management plan, final reliability and maintainability predictions, engineering test reports, a firm logistic support analysis (i.e., maintenance analysis), and a formal logistic support plan.

B. DESIGN REVIEW REQUIREMENTS

The success of a formal design review is dependent on the depth of planning, organization, and data preparation prior to the review itself. A tremendous amount of coordination is required relative to the establishment of:

1. The item(s) to be reviewed.
2. A selected date for the review.
3. The location or facility where the review is to be conducted.
4. An agenda for the review (including a definition of the basic objectives).
5. A design review board representing the organizational elements and disciplines affected by the review. Reliability, maintainability, human factors, and logistic support representation are included. Individual organization responsibilities should be identified. Depending on the type of review, the user and/or individual equipment suppliers may be included.
6. Equipment (hardware) and software requirements for the review. Engineering breadboards, prototypes, and/or mock-ups may be required to facilitate the review process.
7. Design data requirements for the review. This may include all applicable specifications, lists, drawings, predictions and analyses, logistics data, and special reports.
8. Funding requirements. Planning is necessary in identifying sources and a means for providing the funds for conducting the review.
9. Reporting requirements and the mechanism for accomplishing the necessary follow-up action(s) stemming from design review recommendations. Responsibilities and action item time limits must be established.

C. CONDUCTING THE DESIGN REVIEW

As indicated earlier, the design review involves a number of different discipline areas and covers a wide variety of design data and in some instances hardware and software. In order to fulfill its objective expeditiously (i.e., review the design to ensure that all system requirements are met in an optimum manner), the design review must be well organized and firmly controlled by the design review board chairman. Design review meetings should be brief and to the point and must not be allowed to drift away from the topics on the agenda. Attendance should be limited to those having a direct interest and who can contribute to the subject matter being presented. Specialists who participate should be authorized to speak and make decisions concerning their area of specialty. Finally, the design review must make provisions for the identification, recording, scheduling, and monitoring of corrective actions. Specific responsibility for follow-up action must be designated by the design review board chairman.

7.5. Summary

Experience has indicated that the costs associated with the various elements of logistics are increasing at an alarming rate. Further, based on an analysis of "cause-and-effect" relationships, we find that the bulk of these costs are generally the result of management and design decisions made during the early planning and design stages of a program. Hence, it becomes essential that logistics be properly addressed early in the system life cycle (particularly during the various phases of design) if the resultant product output is to be cost-effective.

The consideration of logistics in the early phases of the system life cycle is accomplished through the definition of operational requirements and the maintenance concept, the initial allocation of qualitative and quantitative logistics requirements, the design for supportability (e.g., reliability, maintainability, human factors, etc.), and the verification of logistics effectiveness through system test and evaluation. The measures of logistics are covered in Chapter 2, and may be employed as quantitative "design to" goals; the design for supportability basically involves the various activities described in Chapters 3 through 7; and the test and evaluation of the system in terms of overall effectiveness is covered in Chapter 8.

In essence, it is during these early phases of a program that the logistics capability for a system is conceived and developed. Although revisions and system modifications may be accomplished later, the impact will likely not be as great and the results may be costly.

QUESTIONS AND PROBLEMS

1. How is logistics considered in the design process?
2. How does reliability design affect logistic support?
3. How does maintainability design affect logistic support?
4. What is the relationship between human factors and logistic support?
5. How does LSA tie in with the design process?
6. How does FMEA relate to the maintenance analysis? How does FMEA influence design?
7. Why are design criteria developed?
8. Design is a team effort. True or false? Why?
9. How are supplier requirements identified and specified?
10. Identify a system or equipment item of your choice and develop a design review checklist for use in evaluating the item in terms of design for supportability.
11. How does standardization in equipment design affect logistic support?
12. Define "producibility."
13. What are some of the benefits of physical models or mock-ups?
14. What is the purpose of the evaluative function in design?
15. What benefits are provided by a formal design review?
16. Referring to Table 7-1, which item would you investigate for improvement? Why?
17. What is meant by "interchangeability"? How does it affect logistic support?
18. What are the objectives of logistic support in the design process?
19. What is the purpose of the detailed task analysis? What does it tell you? How does it relate to the maintenance analysis?
20. What are the input requirements for the conceptual design review?
21. Describe the "checks" and "balances" of the design process as you see them.
22. Select a system of your choice and accomplish a reliability prediction.
23. Select a system of your choice and accomplish a maintainability prediction.
24. Select an equipment item of your choice and accomplish a FMEA. Transform the FMEA into a logic troubleshooting flow diagram.
25. Select a system of your choice and perform a detailed task analysis (including provisions for safety analysis).
26. How does the critical-useful-life analysis affect logistic support?

TEST AND EVALUATION

Thus far, text material has included the specification of requirements, the establishment of design criteria, design and support activities, analyses and predictions, and design review. Through the accomplishment of these functions, the designer has been able to establish specific system objectives and later evaluate a given design configuration relative to compliance with these objectives. The evaluation function up to this point has been analytical in nature, providing a certain level of confidence that all qualitative and quantitative requirements have been met. Although the analytical approach fulfills a need, it has its limitations because it does not reflect actual experience with the applicable hardware. A more realistic evaluation of whether a system or equipment complies with the initially specified requirements is accomplished through the test and demonstration of the prime equipment hardware and its associated logistic support.

8.1. Categories of Test and Demonstration

A true test (that which is relevant from the standpoint of assessing logistic support) constitutes the evaluation of a system deployed in an operational environment and subjected to actual use conditions. For example, an equip-

8

ment designed for aircraft use should be tested onboard an aircraft flying in a typical operational profile. User personnel should accomplish operator and maintenance functions with the designated field test and support equipment, technical manual procedures, and so on. In such a situation, actual operational and maintenance experience in a realistic environment can be recorded and subsequently evaluated to reflect a true representation of the system design for supportability. A demonstraiion of this type can best be accomplished by the user during standard operations supported through the employment of normal resources (during the operational use phase).

Although idealistically it is desirable to wait until equipment is in operational use before accomplishing an evaluation of system effectiveness and logistic supportability, it is not practical from the standpoint of allowing for possible corrective action. In the event that the evaluation indicates noncompliance (i.e., the system as presently designed will not meet the operational requirements and fulfill its mission), corrective action should be initiated as early as possible in the system life cycle. Accomplishing corrective action after equipment is produced and fully deployed in the field can result in extensive modification programs which are costly. Thus, it is feasible to establish an overall test program which allows for the evauation of hardware and its support elements on an evolutionary basis. As is the case for the earlier design evaluation using analytical techniques, an evaluation of hardware is accomplished commencing with the development of the first engineering model and extending through the test of equipment deployed in the field. This evaluation process includes various types of demonstrations. For the purpose of discussion, tests and demonstrations are classified as follows.

A. TYPE 1 TESTING

During detail design and development, engineering models, service test models, breadboards, bench models, and so on, are built with the intent of verifying performance and physical design characteristics. These models operate functionally (electrically and mechanically) but do not by any means represent production equipment. Tests may involve equipment operational and logistic support actions which are directly comparable to tasks performed in an operational situation (e.g., measuring a performance parameter, accomplishing a remove–replace action, accomplishing a servicing requirement, etc.). Although these tests are not formal demonstrations in a true operational environment, information pertinent to logistic support characteristics can be derived and used as an input to the logistic support analysis (see Chapter 6). Such testing is performed in the producer/supplier's facility by engineering technicians using "jury-rigged" test equipment and engineering notes for test procedures. It is during this initial phase of testing that changes to the design can be incorporated on a minimum cost basis.

B. TYPE 2 TESTING

Formal tests and demonstrations are accomplished during the latter part of the detail design and development phase when preproduction prototype hardware is available. Prototype equipments are similar to production equipment (that which will be deployed for operational use) but are not necessarily fully qualified at this point in time.[1] A test program may constitute a series of individual tests, tailored to the need, to include

1. *Environmental qualification*—temperature cycling, shock and vibration, humidity, wind, salt spray, dust and sand, acoustic noise, explosion proofing, and electromagnetic interference. These factors are oriented to what the equipment will be subjected to during operation, maintenance, and during transportation and handling functions.
2. *Reliability qualification*—tests accomplished on one or more equip-

---

[1]Qualified equipment refers to a production configuration which has been verified through the successful *completion* of environmental qualification tests (e.g., temperature cycling, shock, vibration), reliability qualification, maintainability demonstration, and compatibility tests. Type 2 testing primarily refers to that activity associated with the qualification of a system.

ments to determine the true MTBF and MTBM. The results are compared with the initially specified requirement, and are used to update the logistic support analysis and provisioning factors specified for the acquisition of logistic support.

3. *Maintainability demonstration*—tests accomplished on one or more equipments to determine the values for $\bar{M}$, $\bar{M}ct$, $\bar{M}pt$, $\tilde{M}ct$, $\tilde{M}pt$, M_{max}, and MMH/OH. In addition, maintenance tasks, task times and sequences, prime equipment-test equipment interfaces, maintenance personnel quantities and skills, maintenance procedures, and maintenance facilities are verified to varying degrees. The elements of logistic support are initially evaluated on an individual basis.

4. *Support equipment compatibility tests*—tests often accomplished to verify the compatibility between the prime equipment, test and support equipment, and transportation and handling equipment.

5. *Personnel test and evaluation*—tests often accomplished to verify the relationships between man and equipment, the personnel skill levels required, and training needs. Both operator and maintenance tasks are evaluated.

6. *Technical data verification*—the verification of operational and maintenance procedures.

The ideal situation is to plan and schedule these individual tests such that they can be accomplished on an integrated basis as *one* overall test. The intent is to provide the proper emphasis, consistent with the need, and eliminate redundancy and excessive cost. Proper test planning is essential.

Another aspect of testing in this category includes *production sampling tests* when multiple quantities of an equipment item are produced. The above defined tests basically qualify the system; that is, the equipment hardware configuration meets the requirements for production and operational use. However, once an item is initially qualified, some assurance must be provided that all subsequent replicas of that item are equally qualified; thus, in a multiple quantity situation, samples are selected from the production line and tested.[2]

Production sampling tests may cover certain critical performance characteristics, reliability, or any other designated parameter which may significantly vary from one serial-numbered item to the next, or may vary as a result of a production process. Samples may be selected on the basis of a percentage of the total equipments produced or may tie in with x number of equipments in a given calendar time period. This depends on the peculiarities of the system and the complexities of the production process. From

---

[2]These tests are in addition to the normal performance tests that are accomplished on every equipment after fabrication and assembly prior to delivery.

production sampling tests, one can measure system growth (or degradation) throughout the production/construction phase.

Type 2 tests are generally performed in the producer/supplier's facility by personnel at that facility. Test and support equipment, designated for operational use, and preliminary technical manuals are employed where possible. User personnel often observe and/or participate in the testing activities. Equipment changes as a result of corrective action are handled through a formalized engineering change procedure.

C. TYPE 3 TESTING

Formal tests and demonstrations, conducted after initial system qualification and prior to the completion of production, are accomplished at a designated field test site by user personnel.[3] Operational test and support equipment, operational spares, and formal operator and maintenance procedures are used. Testing is generally continuous, accomplished over an extended period of time, and covers the evaluation of a number of equipments (of the same type) scheduled through a series of simulated operational exercises.

This is the first time that all elements of the system (i.e., prime equipment, software, and the elements of logistic support) are operated and evaluated on an integrated basis. The compatibility of the prime equipment with logistic support is verified as well as the compatibility of the various elements of logistic support with each other. Turnaround times and logistics supply times, stock levels, personnel effectiveness factors, and other related operational and logistic parameters are measured. In essence, system performance (based on certain use conditions) and operational readiness characteristics (i. e., operational availability, dependability, system effectiveness, etc.) can be determined to a certain extent.[4]

D. TYPE 4 TESTING

During the operational use phase, formal tests are sometimes conducted to gain further insight in a specific area. It may be desirable to vary the mission profile or the system utilization rate to determine the impact on total system effectiveness, or it might be feasible to evaluate several alternative support policies to see whether system operational availability can be improved. Even though the system is designed and deployed in the field, this is actually the first time that we really know its true capability. Hopefully, the system will accomplish its objective in an efficient manner; however,

---

[3]The test site may constitute a ship at sea, an aircraft or space vehicle in flight, a facility in the artic or located in the middle of the desert, or a mobile land vehicle traveling between two points.

[4]Type 3 testing does not represent a complete operational situation; however, tests can be designed to provide a close approximation.

there is still the possibility that improvements can be realized by varying basic operational and maintenance support policies.

Type 4 testing is accomplished at one or more operational sites (in a realistic environment) by user operator and maintenance personnel, and supported through the normal logistics capability. The elements of logistic support as designated through predictions and analyses, earlier testing, and so on, are evaluated in the context of the total system.

Although there are variations from program to program, the basic types of testing are oriented to the program phases as illustrated in Figure 8-1.

8.2. Test Planning

Test planning actually commences early in the conceptual phase when basic system operational requirements are initially established. If a system requirement is to be specified, there must be a way to evaluate the system later to ensure that the requirement has been met; hence, testing considerations are intuitive at an early point in time.

Throughout the various stages of system development, a number of individual equipment tests may be specified. Often there is a tendency to design a test to measure one system characteristic, design another test to measure a different parameter, and so on. Before long, the amount of testing specified may be overwhelming and prove to be quite costly. Test requirements must be considered on an integrated basis. Where possible, individual tests are reviewed in terms of resource requirements and output results, and are scheduled in such a manner so as to gain the maximum benefit possible. For instance, maintainability data can be obtained from reliability tests resulting in a possible reduction in the amount of maintainability testing required. Support equipment compatibility data and personnel data can be obtained from both reliability and maintainability testing; thus, it might be feasible to schedule reliability qualification testing first, maintainability demonstration second, and so on. In some instances, the combining of tests may be feasible as long as the proper characteristics are measured and the data output is compatible with the initial testing objectives.

For each system program, an integrated test planning document is prepared during the preliminary system design phase but not later than 60 days prior to the start of test preparation for Type 1 testing. Test planning should include

1. The definition and schedule of all test requirements (Types 1, 2, 3, and 4). Anticipated test output (in terms of what the test is to accomplish) is defined for each individual test, and integrated where possible.
2. The definition of organization, administration, and control respon-

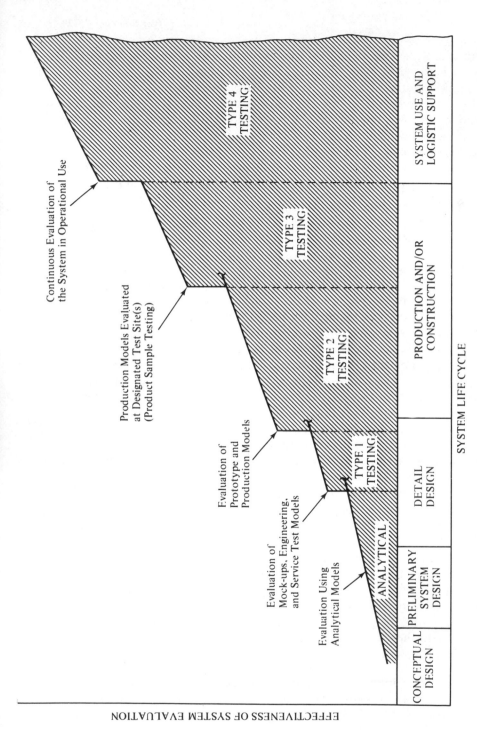

Figure 8-1. Stages of system evaluation during the life cycle.

sibilities (organization functions, organizational interfaces, monitoring of test activities, cost control, and reporting).
3. The definition of test conditions and logistic resource requirements (test environment, facilities, test and support equipment, spare/repair parts, test personnel, and test procedures).
4. A description of the test preparation phase for each type of testing (selection of specific test method, training of test personnel, acquisition of logistic resource requirements, and preparation of facilities).
5. A description of the formal test phase (test procedures, and test data collection, reduction, and analysis methods).
6. A description of conditions and provisions for a retest phase (methods for conducting additional testing as required due to a reject situation).
7. The identification of test documentation (test reporting requirements).
8. A projection of anticipated test funding requirements (i.e., total cost).

The basic test plan serves as a valuable reference throughout system design, development, and production. It indicates what is to be accomplished, the requirements for testing, a schedule for the processing of equipment and material for test support, data collection and reporting methods, and so on. It is an integrating device for a number of individual tests in each of the four categories, and a change in any single test requirement will affect the total plan.

8.3. Test Preparation Phase

After initial test planning (which defines the requirements for test) and prior to the start of formal testing, a period of time is set aside for test preparation. During this period, the proper test conditions must be established to ensure effective results. Although there is some variance depending on the type of test, these conditions or prerequisites include the selection of the item to be tested, establishment of test proceudres, selection and training of test personnel, preparation of facilities, and the acquistion of support equipment and spare/repair parts.

A. Selection of Test Model

The equipment configuration used in the test must be representative of the operational item to the maximum extent possible. For Type 1 tests, engineering models are used which are not often directly comparable with operational equipment; however, most subsequent testing will be accomplished at such a time that equipments representing the final configuration are available.

A prerequisite task involves selecting the test model by serial number, defining the configuration in terms of incorporated versus unincorporated engineering changes (if any), and ensuring that it is available at the time needed.

B. LOGISTIC SUPPORT ANALYSIS

LSA, as described in Chapter 6, provides a data base in defining the maintenance concept and logistic support requirements for the operational system. LSA should, where applicable, identify the appropriate logistic requirements for the test program, particualry for Type 2, 3, and 4 testing.

C. TEST ENVIRONMENT

If the system or equipment is to be operated in the artic or tropics, on mountainous or flat terrain, on land or on shipboard, outside or in a shelter, and so on, the appropriate conditions should be identified and simulated in the test as closely as possible. For Types 1 and 2 testing, this may be partially accomplished, particularly for smaller equipments, through the use of special environmental facilities and test chambers. In Types 3 and 4 testing, these conditions can be controlled through proper test site selection.

D. TEST FACILITIES AND RESOURCES

The necessary test facilities, test chambers, capital equipment, environmental controls, special instrumentation, and associated resources (e.g., heat, water, air conditioning, gas, telephone, power, lighting, etc.) must be identified and scheduled. In many instances, new design and construction is required which directly affects the scheduling and duration of the test preparation phase. A detailed description of the test facility and the facility layout should be included in test planning documentation and in the final test report.

E. TEST PERSONNEL AND TRAINING

Test personnel in this instance include those individuals who will actually operate and maintain the equipment during the test (not the instrumentation technicians, data recorders, or test management personnel). These individuals should possess backgrounds and skill levels similar to the personnel who will normally be assigned to the system when in operational field use. The various tasks being demonstrated through test should be accomplished in a realistic manner. A more highly trained individual from the producer's organization who has virtually lived with the equipment through design and development will obviously influence the results of test in a different manner than an individual with lesser skills. Recommended personnel quantities and skill levels are derived from LSA (i.e., maintenance analysis described in Appendix B).

In regard to personnel selection and acquisition, three basic possibilities exist.

1. The selection of consumer or user personnel with the appropriate background and skill levels. Such personnel are assigned to the test site on a loan basis and are provided formalized training on the equipment being tested.

2. The selection of personnel from the producer's organization who have been assigned to programs not related to the equipment being tested. Such personnel are assigned to the test site on a loan basis, and are provided formalized training on the applicable equipment.

Although these personnel have not had direct experience on the actual equipment being tested, they are familiar with the producer's design, test, and production methods. Through association with similar equipments, their inherent ability may tend to influence test results by biasing operator and maintenance task proficiency and task times (i.e., higher proficiency and lower times for task accomplishment). This is particularly relevant when evaluating an equipment in terms of its design for supportability, and for Types 1 and 2 testing when the tests are conducted at the producer's facility.

On the other hand, these personnel are generally not familiar with the user's organization, operational methods, and environment. As a result, other factors (i.e., primarily those dealing with system interfaces and the elements of logistic support) may be biased in a different direction. This can be compensated for to a certain degree by providing formalized training covering user operations; however, full compensation requires actual experience or on-the-job training in the field.

3. The selection of personnel from the producer's organization who have been involved in the design and development of the equipment being tested. In this instance, the personnel assigned will be thoroughly familiar with the equipment, and the test results may be highly biased (to a greater extent than with producer personnel previously assigned to other programs) in the performance of specific operator and maintenance tasks. Task proficiencies are likely to be high and task times lower than what would be expected if the equipment where in operational use in the field. In addition, the nonfamiliarity with the user's operational methods and environment exists.

From the standpoint of approaching a realistic operational situation for test and demonstration, the preference in personnel selection involves items 1, 2, and 3 in that order. The realization of this preference is more likely as the equipment progresses through the various phases of testing.

In addition, the desired approach is more probable if the test is accomplished at a user operational test site. In any event, the test plan must specify the approach to be used. Potential individuals being considered for participation in the test should be identified by name. During the test preparation phase, these individuals are assigned to the test program and receive the necessary formalized training as prescribed. This training will vary somewhat depending on the background and skills of the personnel selected.

F. TEST PROCEDURES

Fulfillment of test objectives involves the accomplishment of both operator and maintenance tasks. Completion of these tasks should follow formal approved procedures which are generally in the form of technical manuals developed during the latter phases of detail equipment design. Following approved procedures is necessary to ensure that the equipment is operated and maintained in a proper manner. Deviation from approved procedures may result in the introduction of personnel induced failures, and will distort maintenance frequencies and task times as recorded in the test data. The identification of the procedures to be used in testing should be included in the test plan.

G. SUPPORT EQUIPMENT

The accomplishment of certain tasks within the specified system allocation requirements (e.g., $\bar{M}$ct, $\bar{M}$pt, MMH/OH) is often dependent on the type of support equipment used. Manually operated equipment will obviously have a different impact on maintenance times and maintenance manhours than automatic equipment. Hence, the proper type of support equipment as specified through the LSA is considered essential for effective testing.

Test and support equipment requirements are initially considered in the maintenance concept and in the establishment of design criteria for the prime equipment (see Chapter 5). During the latter phases of prime equipment detail design, the necessary support items are acquisitioned and should be available for Types 2, 3, and 4 testing. In the event that the proper type of support equipment is not available and alternative items are required, such items must be identified in the test plan. The use of alternative items generally results in distorted maintenance times and causes a change in maintenance test procedures. In such instances, the necessary maintenance procedural changes are noted and maintenance time adjustment factors are applied to the test data.

H. SUPPLY SUPPORT

The types of spare/repair parts needed at each level of maintenance are dependent on the maintenance concept and the results of the level of repair analysis, and are noted in LSA. For large-scale tests (i.e., Types 3 and 4 testing), spare/repair parts will generally be required for all levels since these tests primarily involve an evaluation of the system as an entity and its total logistic support capability. The complete maintenance cycle, supply support provisions (the type and quantity of spares specified at each level), supply times, turnaround times, and related factors are evaluated. In certain instances, the producer's facility may provide depot level support. Thus, it is important to establish a realistic supply system (or a close approximation) for the item being tested.

On smaller tests and demonstrations, the primary objective is to measure only active elements of the maintenance cycle or factors applicable to that portion of the system being tested. In such cases, the requirements for spares may not be as critical. For example, maintenance tasks involving troubleshooting, disassembly, remove and replace, reassembly, and system checkout are evaluated. If the maintenance sequence involves the replacement of a major repairable assembly, the newly installed assembly may be the same one that was removed. Maintenance times other than for actual removal and replacement are discounted, and repair actions associated with the assembly are not applicable. For testing of this type (i.e., Types 1 and 2), the quantity of spares required may be negligible with careful planning. Recorded test data cover only to active maintenance task elements.

The type and quantity of spare/repair parts and the procedures for spares inventory control throughout the test program should be specified in the test plan. Usage rates, reorder requirements, procurement lead times, and stock-out conditions during the test are recorded and included in the test report.

8.4. Formal Test and Demonstration

A. RELIABILITY TESTING

Reliability qualification tests are conducted to provide an evaluation of system development progress as well as the assurance that specified requirements have been met prior to proceeding to the next phase. Initially, a reliability MTBF (or MTBM) is established for the system, followed by allocation and the definition of design criteria. Equipment design is accomplished and reliability predictions are made to evaluate the design configuration (on an analytical basis) relative to compliance with system requirements. If the predictions indicate compliance, the design phases into the construction of prototype or preproduction equipment. The next step is to accomplish the necessary reliability tests prior to commencing with full-scale production.

Reliability qualification, an element of Type 2 testing, constitutes a verification that the MTBF achieved in equipment development meets the initially specified requirement.[5] Test conditions, procedures, and the methods of data analysis are preplanned on the basis of engineering requirements and statistical considerations. Statistical considerations pertain to the desired accuracy of the test results and the confidence limits assigned. One must establish the confidence (degree of trust or assurance in a given result) placed in the decisions made based on test results.

Engineering requirements relate to the duty cycles, environmental stress level, applications, and the performance values and their limits which define the basis for success or failure of the item being tested. A clear definition of what constitutes successful system operation is necessary. On the other hand, one must be able to recognize when a failure occurs.

To ensure that the testing will produce effective results, it is necessary to define the test objectives, establish specific test requirements, design the test, implement the test, and analyze the results. The reliability test approach generally involves selecting a designated quantity of equipments, operating the equipments under certain performance conditions over an extended period of time, and monitoring the equipments for failure.[6] Failures are noted as *events*, corrected through appropriate maintenance actions, and the applicable equipment(s) is returned to full operational status for continued testing. The total operating time for all systems in test is divided by the total number of failures to determine the demonstrated MTBF.

For a given system, one may specify that the reliability test shall cover as least *x* number of system operating hours. Often, this number constitutes a multiple of the specified MTBF (e.g., 10 times the MTBF of 400 hours or 4,000 hours of testing). This value is generally established by the user and is based on the confidence placed on the system relative to meeting the specified MTBF requirement.

If a single model is designated for test with a minimum of 4,000 test hours required, the length of the test program (assuming continuous testing) will obviously extend beyond 6 months. This may not be feasible in terms of the overall program schedule and the delivery of qualified equipment. On the other hand, the use of two or more models will result in a shorter test program. Sometimes the implementation of accelerated test conditions will

---

[5]In the event that a MTBF requirement has not been specified, the engineer may wish to conduct an investigative-type test to assess the reliability of a given item. This assessment is required for the prediction of logistic support requirements.

[6]Reliability test methods are varied and relatively complex. This text presents an extremely broad view of input/output factors and their relationship to logistic support. For a more in-depth presentation, refer to (a) MIL-STD-781C, Military Standard, "Reliability Design Qualification and Production Acceptance Tests: Exponential Distribution," Department of Defense, Washington, D.C., October 1977; and (b) Lloyd, D. K. and Lipow, M., *Reliability: Management, Methods, and Mathematics*, 2nd ed., Defense and Space Systems Group, TRW Systems and Energy, Redondo Beach, Calif., 1977.

result in an additional number of failures. These effects should be evaluated, and an optimum balance should be established between a smaller sample size and longer test times and a larger sample size and shorter test times.

Once the quantity of test models has been defined, the applicable models should be identified by serial number, inspected, and accepted in accordance with the same procedures to be followed for the acceptance of full-scale production equipment. Testing then commences by operating each system through a designed program duty cycle characteristic of what the equipment may experience in the field.[7]

The designed program cycle may constitute operating the equipment for awhile at high temperature while measuring performance, shutting the equipment off while lowering the temperature, operating the equipment while measuring performance, vibrating the equipment for a certain duration, raising the temperature and making performance measurements, and so on through a series of repeated cycles. An illustrated program test cycle is shown in Figure 8-2.

The cycle is continuous through the specified number of test hours designated for each equipment model. The total unit hours of test and unit hours per equipment will be monitored continuously. No single equipment should accumulate less time than the specified MTBF.

During equipment performance measurement, go/no-go decisions are made depending on whether the characteristics measured fall within the equipment specification requirements. If an out-of-tolerance situation exists, a failure is recorded (classified as an event) and the equipment is shut down

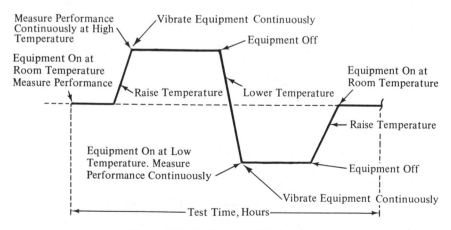

Figure 8-2. Program test duty cycle.

---

[7]The duty cycle or performance profile is the time-phased apportionment of modes of operation and functions to be performed during the on-time portion of the environmental test cycle. It is intended that the duty cycle be representative of field operations.

for corrective maintenance. After the completion of corrective maintenance, the system is once again operated through the test cycle.

When a failure occurs, the steps involved in corrective maintenance should follow formal maintenance and test procedures. Test and support equipment should be the same type as specified for maintenance support of the equipment in the field. If test equipment item part number "xxxx" is recommended for support of operational equipment, the same configuration should be used to support corrective maintenance actions during a formal test program. This is required to evaluate the supportability characteristics inherent in the prime equipment design as well as the compatibility between the prime equipment and the recommended test and support equipment. Maintenance task sequences and task times are monitored, and test data are analyzed and compared against equipment maintainability requirements. Logistic resource requirements are identified and LSA data are revised accordingly.

Reliability testing continues until an *accept–reject decision* is made. Accept–reject criteria will vary with the program, the equipment type, and the specified reliability requirement. However, one approach which is commonly employed is the sequential test plan illustrated in Figure 8-3.

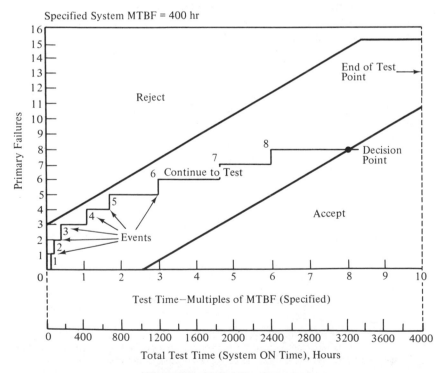

Figure 8-3. Reliability test plan.

Referring to the figure, total equipment operating time is indicated along the abscissa while failures (i.e., events) are noted on the ordinate. Testing commences and the time is recorded until the first failure occurs, which is event 1. All subsequent events are noted, and testing is continued until the data indicate either an excessive number of failures (when the line enters the reject region) or an allowable number of failures for the test time experienced (when the line enters the accept region). Testing is discontinued when one or the other occurs. Reliability growth during the test is illustrated in Figure 8-4.

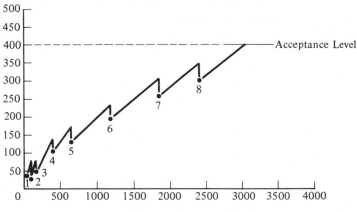

Total System Operating Hours

Event No.	Time of Occurrence (Hours of System Operation)	Calculated MTBF
1	42	42
2	78	39
3	152	51
4	420	105
5	657	131
6	1190	198
7	1810	259
8	2385	298
Decision	3200	400

Figure 8-4. Reliability growth during test.

A reject decision infers corrective action through either a design change or a manufacturing process change. An analysis of each event should determine the cause of failure, and trends may be established if more than one failure is traceable to the same cause. This may be referred to as a "pattern" failure and, in such cases, a change should be initiated to eliminate the occurrence of future failures of the same type.

If testing continues and no decision is reached at the designated *end of test* point (i. e., 4,000 test hours or 10 times the specified MTBF), the test is discontinued and a decision is made based on an analysis of test results. It may be feasible to accept the equipment if it is concluded that the necessary corrective action has been implemented to cover the majority of those failures experienced during test in such a way as to preclude future occurrence. On the other hand, additional testing may be recommended in order to provide greater assurance that the MTBF requirement will be met. This may involve an extended test period for the same equipment and/or the introduction of new models into the test program.

The sequential test plan allows for an early decision. Highly reliable equipment will be accepted with a minimum amount of required testing. If the equipment is unreliable, this will also be readily evident at an early point in time. In this respect, sequential testing is extremely beneficial. On the other hand, if the equipment inherent reliability is marginal, the amount of test time involved can be rather extensive and costly.

The reliability test plan (i. e., the accept–reject criteria as reflected by the lines and truncation point in the illustration presented in Figure 8-3) incorporates several statistical considerations. Built into the plan are decision risks.

1. *Producer's risk* (α)—the probability of rejecting equipment(s) when the measured MTBF is equal to the specified MTBF. In other words, this refers to the probability of rejecting an equipment when it really should be accepted, which constitutes a risk to the equipment manufacturer or producer (also known as a Type I error).

2. *User's or consumer's risk* (β)—the probability of accepting equipment(s) when the measured MTBF is less than the specified MTBF. This refers to the probability of accepting an equipment that actually should be rejected, which constitutes a risk to the consumer or user (also known as a Type II error). This is also defined as the probability of accepting equipment(s) when the true MTBF is equal to the minimum acceptable MTBF. The minimum acceptable MTBF is a value so selected that an associated and specified risk of accepting equipment of this value is tolerable. In other words, there may be some minimum value of MTBF that the user is willing to accept at a risk. The ratio of the specified MTBF to the minimum acceptable MTBF is referred to as the "discrimination ratio," which is quite often

used in reliability testing as a basis for equipment acceptance and the determination of test requirements.

The probability of making an incorrect decision on the basis of test results must be addressed in a manner similar to any hypothesis testing. An assumption is made and a test is accomplished to support (or disprove) that assumption. In other words, a null hypthesis (H_0) is established, which is a statement or conjecture about a parameter, such as "the true MTBF is equal to 100." The alternative hypothesis (H_1) is: "the MTBF is not equal to 100." When testing an equipment sample, the question arises as to whether to accept H_0. The desired result is to accept when the null hypothesis is true and reject when false, or to minimize the chances of making an incorrect decision. The relationship of risks in sample testing is illustrated below.

True State of Affairs	Accept H_0 and Reject H_1 (i.e., MTBF = 100)	Reject H_0 and Accept H_1 (i.e., MTBF ≠ 100)
H_0 is True (i.e., MTBF = 100)	High Probability, $1 - \alpha$ (i.e., 0.90)	Low Probability Error, α (i.e., 0.10)
H_0 is False and H_1 is True (i.e., MTBF ≠ 100)	Low Probability Error, β (i.e., 0.10)	High Probability, $1 - \beta$ (i.e., 0.90)

The consideration of risk in sample testing is addressed in a number of textbooks on statistics, and it is recommended that the student familiarize himself with the basic principles involved prior to accomplishing a reliability test. It is these principles that are inherent in the different test plans available for use.

When reliability qualification testing is completed, the measured MTBF may be determined by

$$\text{MTBF} = \frac{\text{total operation hours}}{\text{number of failures}} \qquad (8.1)$$

The resultant value represents the best estimate of the equipment mean life based on the quantity of equipments in the sample used in the test program. Since the value obtained is derived from a relatively small sample size, the true MTBF for the total population of equipments could lie either somewhat above or below this estimate. A range of values, within which it can be stated with a certain confidence (e.g., 90%, 95%) that the true MTBF value will fall, is established by placing upper and lower estimates about the test value. If the confidence level is 90%, there is a 10% chance of the MTBF being too low (user's risk—β), and there is also a 10% chance that the equipment MTBF is acceptable even though test data indicate a reject situation (producer's risk). Any desired degree of confidence may be chosen and the corresponding confidence limits may be derived from statistical tables.

As indicated earlier, reliability testing may be accomplished as part of qualification testing prior to commencing with full-scale production (which has been discussed) and during full-scale production on a sampling basis. In order to determine the effects of the production process on equipment reliability, it may be feasible to select a sample number of equipments from each production lot and test them in the same manner as described above. The sample may be based on a percentage of the total equipments spread over the entire production period, or a set number of equipment(s) selected during a given calendar time period (e.g., two equipments per month throughout the production phase). In any event, the selected equipments are tested and an assessed MTBF is derived from the test data. This value is compared against the specified MTBF and the measured value determined from earlier testing. Growth MTBF trends (or negative trends) may be determined by plotting the resultant values as testing progresses.

The results of reliability testing may be employed (judiciously) for logistic support purposes. The predicted equipment corrective maintenance frequency is based on the MTBF; thus, the measured value of MTBF is employed in the development of logistic support provisioning factors. Test results are certainly more accurate than the earlier allocations and predictions; hence, LSA data are updated to reflect more accurate estimates of maintenance frequency, spare/repair part demand rates, test and support equipment utilization rates, and so on.

On the other hand, it must be recognized that the MTBF value from reliability testing often reflects only equipment primary failures and not secondary failures, operator and maintenance induced faults, and the like.[8] Primary failures cause some of the maintenance actions in an operational situation, but certainly not all of them. In addition, when a design change is implemented to correct a situation which previously caused one or more of the failures during the test, these failures are often classified as *nonrelevant* and omitted from the MTBF calculation. Thus, the analyst must thoroughly evaluate the data and the basis for the MTBF calculation prior to arbitrarily using test results for logistics purposes.

B. MAINTAINABILITY DEMONSTRATION

Maintainability demonstration, as part of Type 2 testing, is conducted to verify that qualitative and quantitative maintainability requirements have been achieved. It also provides for the assessment of various logistic support

---

[8] Refer to Section 2.1 (Table 2-1) and Appendix B for a definition of the different factors that influence the corrective maintenance frequency.

factors related to and impacting maintainability parameters and item down-time (e.g., test and support equipment, spare/repair parts, technical data, personnel, maintenance policies).

Maintainability demonstration is usually accomplished during the latter part of the detail design and development phase, and should be conducted in an environment which simulates, as closely as practicable, the operational and maintenance environment planned for the item. The maintainability demonstration approach may vary considerably depending on system requirements and the test objectives.[9] However, two representative approaches are now briefly described to give the student an idea of the steps involved.

1. Demonstration method number 1. This method follows a sequential test plan approach which is similar to the reliability test described earlier. Two different sequential test plans are employed to demonstrate $\bar{M}ct$ and M_{max} (for corrective maintenance). An accept decision for the equipment under test is reached when that decision can be made for both test plans. The test plans assume that the underlying distribution of corrective maintenance task times is log-normal. The sequential test plan approach allows for a quick decision when the maintainability of the equipment under test is either far above or far below the specified values of $\bar{M}ct$ and M_{max}.

Testing is accomplished by simulating faults in the system and observing the task times and logistic resources required to correct the situation. Specifically:

a. A failure is induced in the equipment without the knowledge of the test team. The induced failure should not be evident in any respect other than that normally resulting from the simulated mode of failure. In other words, the technician(s) scheduled to perform the maintenance demonstration shall not be given any hints (through visual evidence) as to where the failure is induced.

b. The maintenance technician will be called upon to operationally check out the equipment. At some point in the checkout procedure, a symptom of malfunction is detected.

c. Once that a malfunction has been detected, the maintenance technician(s) will proceed to accomplish the necessary corrective maintenance

---

[9]As in the case of reliability testing described earlier, maintainability demonstration methods vary considerably and are too complex to allow for adequate coverage herein. The material in this text is presented to the depth necessary to provide a basic understanding of test methods, input/output factors, and their relationship to logistic support. For a more in-depth presentation, refer to (a) MIL-STD-471A, Military Standard, "Maintainability Verification, Demonstration, Evaluation," Department of Defense, Washington, D.C., March 1973; and (b) Blanchard, B. S. and Lowery, E. E., *Maintainability-Principles and Practices*, McGraw-Hill Book Company, New York, 1969.

tasks (i.e., fault localization, isolation, disassembly, remove and replace, repair, reassembly, adjustment and alignment, and system checkout). In the performance of each step, the technician should follow approved maintenance procedures and use the proper test and support equipment. The maintenance tasks performed must be consistent with the maintenance concept and the specified levels of maintenance appropriate to the demonstration. Replacement parts required to perform repair actions being demonstrated shall be compatible with the spare/repair parts recommended for operational support.

d. While the maintenance technician is performing the corrective tasks (commencing with the identification of a malfunction and continuing until the equipment has been returned to full operational status), a test recorder collects data on task sequences, areas of task difficulty, and task times. In addition, the adequacies and inadequacies of logistic support are noted. Was the right type of support provided? Were there test delays due to inadequacies? Was there an overabundance of certain items and a shortage of others? Did each specified element of logistic support do the job in a satisfactory manner? Were the test procedures adequate? These and related questions should be in the mind of the data recorder during the observation of a test.

This cycle is accomplished *n* times, where *n* is the selected sample size. For the sequential test, the number of demonstrations could possibly extend to 100 assuming that a *continue to test* decision prevails. Thus, in preparing for the test, a sample size of 100 demonstrations should be planned. The selected tasks should be representative and based on the expected percent contribution toward total maintenance requirements. Those items with high failure rates will fail more often and require more maintenance and logistic resources; hence, they should appear in the demonstration to a greater extent than items requiring less maintenance.

The task selection process is accomplished by proportionately distributing the 100 tasks among the major functional elements of the system. Assuming that three units compose the system, the 100 tasks may be allocated as illustrated in Table 8-1.

Referring to the table, the elements of the system and the associated failure rates (from reliability data) are listed. The percent contribution of each item to the total anticipated corrective maintenance (column 5) is computed as

$$\text{item percent contribution} = \frac{Q\lambda}{\sum Q\lambda} \times 100 \qquad (8.2)$$

This factor is used to allocate the tasks proportionately to each unit. In a similar manner, the 21 tasks within Unit *A* can be allocated to assemblies

Table 8-1. CORRECTIVE MAINTENANCE TASK ALLOCATION

(1) *Item*	(2) *Quantity* *of Items* *(Q)*	(3) *Failures/Item* *% 1000 Hours* *(λ)*	(4) *Total* *Failures* *(Q)(λ)*	(5) *%* *Contribution*	(6) *Allocated* *Maint. Tasks* *for* *Demonstration*
Unit *A*	1	0.48	0.48	21	21 Tasks
Unit *B*	1	1.71	1.71	76	76 Tasks
Unit *C*	1	0.06	0.06	3	3 Tasks
TOTAL			2.25	100%	100 Tasks

within that unit, and so on. When the allocation is completed, there may be one (1) task assigned to a particular assembly and the assembly may contain a number of components, the failure of which reflect different failure modes (e.g., no output, erratic output, low output, etc.). Through a random process, one of the components in the assembly will be selected as the item where the failure is to be induced, and the method by which the failure is induced is specified.

With the tasks identified and listed in a random order, the demonstration proceeds with the first task, then the second, third, and so on. The criteria for accept–reject decisions are illustrated in Figure 8-5. Task times (Mct_i) are measured and compared with the specified $\overline{M}ct$ and M_{max} values. When the demonstrated time exceeds the specified value, an event is noted along the ordinate of the graph and problem areas are described. Testing

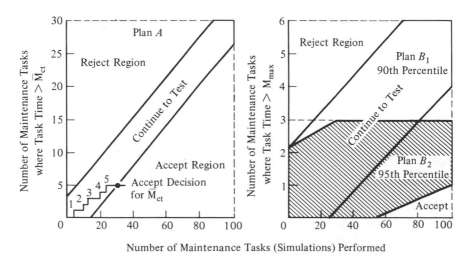

Figure 8-5. Graphical representation of $\overline{M}$ demonstration plans.

then continues until the event line either enters the reject region or the accept region.

An example of the demonstration test score sheet is illustrated in Table 8-2. The accept–reject numbers support the decison lines in Figure 8-5 (refer to the $\bar{M}$ct curve). In this instance, 29 tasks were completed before an accept decison was reached.

The sequential test requires that both the $\bar{M}$ct criteria and the M_{max} criteria be met before the equipment is fully acceptable. M_{max} may be based on either the 90th or 95th percentile depending on the specified system requirement and the test plan selected. If one test plan is completed with the event line crossing into the accept region, testing will continue until a decision is made in the other test plan.

Referring to Figure 8-5, the criteria for sequential testing specify that the minimum number of tasks possible for a quick decision for $\bar{M}$ct is 12 (Test Plan *A*). For M_{max} at the 90th percentile, the least number of tasks possible is 26 (Test Plan *B*$_1$) while the figure is 57 for the 95th percentile

Table 8-2. DEMONSTRATION SCORE SHEET

REQMT: $\bar{M}$ct $= 0.5$ HOURS $= 30$ Min　　　　　　　　　　　　　　　　Plan *A*

Maint. Task No.	*Task Time* Mct_i	*Cum No.* $Mct_i > \bar{M}ct$	*Accept When* $Cum \leq Than$	*Reject When* $Cum > Than$
1	12 Min.	0	. . . .	. . . .
2	6	0	. . . .	. . . .
3	18	0	. . . .	. . . .
4	32	1	. . . .	. . . .
5	19	1	. . . .	5
6	27	1	. . . .	6
7	108	2	. . . .	6
8	6	2	. . . .	6
9	14	2	. . . .	7
10	47	3	. . . .	7
11	28	3	. . . .	7
12	19	3	0	7
13	4	3	0	8
14	24	3	0	8
15	78	4	1	8
24	20	4	3	11
25	127	5	4	11
26	21	5	4	12
27	13	5	4	12
28	28	5	4	12
29	8	5	5	12

Accept for $\bar{M}$ct

(Test Plan B_2). Thus, if the maintainability of an item is exceptionally good, demonstrating the complete sample of 100 tasks may not be necessary, thus saving time and cost. On the other hand, if the maintainability of an item is marginal and a *continue to test* decision prevails, the test program may require the demonstration of all 100 tasks. If truncation is reached, the equipment is acceptable for $\bar{M}$ct if 29 or less tasks exceed the specified $\bar{M}$ct value. Comparable factors for M_{max} are 5 or less for the 90th percentile and 2 or less for the 95th percentile.

2. Demonstration method number 2. This method is applicable to the demonstration of $\bar{M}$ct, $\bar{M}$pt, and $\bar{M}$. The underlying distribution of maintenance times is not restricted (no prior assumptions), and the sample size constitutes 50 corrective maintenance tasks for $\bar{M}$ct and 50 preventive maintenance tasks for $\bar{M}$pt. $\bar{M}$ is determined analytically from the test results for $\bar{M}$ct and $\bar{M}$pt. $\bar{M}_{max}$ can also be determined if the underlying distribution is assumed to be log-normal. This method offers the advantage of a fixed sample size, which facilitates the estimation of test costs.

The method involves the selection and performance of maintenance tasks in a similar manner as described for Demonstration Method 1. Tasks are selected based on their anticipated contribution to the total maintenance picture, and each task is performed and evaluated in terms of maintenance times and required logistic resources. Illustration of this method is best accomplished through an example. It is assumed that a system is designed to meet the following requirements and must be demonstrated accordingly.

$$\bar{M} = 75 \text{ minutes}$$
$$\bar{M}\text{ct} = 65 \text{ minutes}$$
$$\bar{M}\text{pt} = 110 \text{ minutes}$$
$$\bar{M}_{max} = 120 \text{ minutes}$$
$$\text{Producer's risk } (\alpha) = 20\%$$

The test is accomplished and the data collected are presented in Table 8-3.

Table 8-3. MAINTENANCE TEST TIME DATA

Demonstration Task Number	*Observed Time* Mct_i	$\text{Mct}_i\text{-}\bar{M}\text{ct}$ $(\text{Mct}_i - 62)$	$(\text{Mct}_i - \bar{M}\text{ct})^2$
1	58	−4	16
2	72	+10	100
3	32	−30	900
50	48	−14	196
	3105		15,016

The determination of $\bar{M}$ct (upper confidence limit) is based on the expression

$$\text{upper limit} = \bar{M}\text{ct} + Z\frac{\sigma}{\sqrt{N_c}} \tag{8.3}$$

where $\bar{M}\text{ct} = \dfrac{\sum \text{Mct}_i}{N_c} = \dfrac{3{,}105}{50} = 62.1$ (assume 62)

$Z = 0.84$ (refer to Table 2-5)

$$\sigma = \sqrt{\frac{\sum_1^{N_c} (\text{Mct}_i - \bar{M}\text{ct})^2}{N_c - 1}} = \sqrt{\frac{15{,}016}{49}}$$

$\sigma = 17.5$

$N_c = $ corrective maintenance sample size $= 50$

$$\text{upper limit} = 62 + \frac{(0.84)(17.5)}{\sqrt{50}} = 64.07 \text{ minutes}$$

The computed $\bar{M}$ct statistic is compared to the corresponding accept–reject criteria, which is

accept if

$$\bar{M}\text{ct} + Z\frac{\sigma}{\sqrt{N_c}} \leq \bar{M}\text{ct}   \text{(specified)} \tag{8.4}$$

reject if

$$\bar{M}\text{ct} + Z\frac{\sigma}{\sqrt{N_c}} > \bar{M}\text{ct}   \text{(specified)} \tag{8.5}$$

Applying demonstration test data, it can be seen that 64.07 minutes (the upper value of $\bar{M}$ct derived by test) is less than the specified value of 65 minutes. Therefore, the system passes the $\bar{M}$ct test and is accepted.

For preventive maintenance the same approach is used. Fifty preventive maintenance tasks are demonstrated and task times (Mpt_i) are recorded. The sample mean preventive downtime is

$$\bar{M}\text{pt} = \frac{\sum \text{Mpt}_i}{N_p} \tag{8.6}$$

The accept–reject criteria is the same as stated in Equations (8.4) and (8.5) except that preventive maintenance factors are used. That is,

accept if

$$\bar{M}\text{pt} + Z\frac{\sigma}{\sqrt{N_p}} \leq 110 \text{ minutes} \tag{8.7}$$

reject if

$$\bar{M}pt + Z\frac{\sigma}{\sqrt{N_p}} > 110 \text{ minutes} \tag{8.8}$$

Given the test values for $\bar{M}ct$ and $\bar{M}pt$, the calculated mean maintenance time is

$$\bar{M} = \frac{(\lambda)(\bar{M}ct) + (fpt)(\bar{M}pt)}{\lambda + fpt} \tag{8.9}$$

where λ = corrective maintenance rate or the expected number of corrective maintenance tasks occurring in a designated period of time

fpt = preventive maintenance rate or the expected number of preventive maintenance tasks occurring in the same time period

Using test data, the resultant value of $\bar{M}$ should be equal to or less than 75 minutes. Finally, M_{max} is determined from

$$M_{max} = \text{antilog } [\log \bar{M}ct + Z\sigma_{\log M ct_i}] \tag{8.10}$$

The calculated value should be equal to or less than 120 minutes for acceptance. An example of calculation for M_{max} is presented in Chapter 2.

If all the demonstrated values are better than the specified values, following the criteria defined above, then the system is accepted. If not, some retest and/or redesign may be required depending on the seriousness of the problem.

C. ENVIRONMENTAL QUALIFICATION

Environment qualification, accomplished toward the end of the detail design and development phase, constitutes a series of tests covering temperature cycling, shock, vibration, sand and dust, salt spray, fungus, humidity, acoustic noise, explosion proofing, and so on. The intent is to simulate all of the environmental extremes that an equipment is likely to encounter when operational or in a transportation and handling mode. For instance, a system installed in an aircraft may be subjected to temperature extremes from $-65°$ to $+125°F$ ($-54°$ to $+52°$ C); thus, it is important to test the system in that range to see if it performs in accordance with specification requirements. Likewise, it is important to see if an equipment item can withstand rust and corrosion caused by saltwater spray if the equipment is to be installed on board a ship.

In the performance of certain tests, failures occur and maintenance repair actions are required. Data from these tests are analyzed and factors applicable to the logistic support of operational equipment are used as an input to LSA. However, care must be taken to ensure that the environmental conditions at the time that the data are recorded are relevant to a true operational situation. Environmental testing serves as another one of the many program activities where the results can be used to verify the degree of supportability in the design.

D. SYSTEM TEST AND EVALUATION

The reliability, maintainability, and environmental tests described above are generally accomplished on an independent basis, and the data obtained are in the form of bits and pieces of information. In most instances, it has not been possible up to this time to test the prime mission equipment and its associated support elements as an entity (i.e., the total system).

System test and evaluation, accomplished as Types 3 and 4 testing, provides the first real opportunity to look at the system as a whole. Prime equipment and all of the required elements of logistic support are delivered to an operational test site, integrated, and scheduled through a series of missions, during which operational, performance, and supportability characteristics are measured and evaluated. Through the accomplishment of successive missions over an extended period of time, the system can be measured in terms of its effectiveness, operational readiness, availability, dependability, etc. Reliability and maintainability can be evaluated on a more realistic basis than possible during Type 2 testing. The elements of logistic support can be assessed in terms of capability and adequacy. As an example, it is assumed that an aircraft system has been designed to accomplish three basic missions (e.g., mission profiles 1, 2, and 3). The three mission profiles and the performance requirements of the various individual components of the aircraft during each profile are defined as part of the operational requirements when the system was first conceived. In addition, the following factors are specified as requirements.

—Operational availability of the system   0.95
—Dependability of the system during the mission   0.85
—Maintenance labor-hours per system operating hour   1.5
—Turnaround times:

    a. Organizational maintenance   12 minutes
    b. Intermediate maintenance   2 hours
    c. Depot maintenance   80 hours

A test program may be designed to evaluate the system and measure these factors. A representative number of flights are scheduled over a designated period of time with specific flights assigned to each of the three missions. There must be enough flights scheduled to ensure that valid data are obtained. If the *Central Limit Theorem* applies for downtime distribution, then at least 50 flights should be scheduled for an adequate sample size. By virtue of the mission definition, the numerous functions and operational modes of the aircraft will be exericsed to varying degrees. A realistic operational situation should be simulated to the greatest extent possible. One or more aircraft may be assigned to the test program depending on the number of test flights scheduled and the time period allowed for testing. Figure 8-6 illustrates the basic test cycle.

As the test program progresses, the availability of the aircraft to commence with its assigned mission is measured. Assuming that the aircraft is available and takes off on schedule, the probability that the aircraft will complete its mission successfully becomes significant. When failures occur, it is then necessary to perform corrective maintenance at the organizational level within the prescribed time to get the aircraft back into an *operationally ready* state and meet the availability requirement. Organizational maintenance is supported by labor and material at the intermediate level, which in turn is supported by the depot level. The supply system, test and support equipment, personnel quantities and skill levels, facilities, and data at each level are evaluated to ensure responsiveness to the turnaround time, maintenance manhours, and operational availability requirements.

Data collection throughout the test program is somewhat extensive, and is based on the type and depth of information required from the test. Both system operational data and maintenance data are collected, and good and bad points are noted. Discrepancies are recorded and events are analyzed to determine cause and effect relationships. Failure trends are identified and should result in corrective action leading to a change in an operating procedure or a modification to the equipment.

When the required number of test flights has been completed, the recorded data are analyzed and the results are compared with the specified system requirements. These requirements not only include operational availability, dependability, maintenance manhours per operating hour, but also include such lower-level requirements as reliability MTBF and maintainability $\overline{M}$ct. The type of requirements specified will dictate the type of data recorded, which in turn is included in the basic test planning document.

Given an assemblage of test data, the analyst can determine operational availability from the expression

$$A_o = \frac{\text{MTBM}}{\text{MTBM} + \text{MDT}} \tag{8.11}$$

Assuming that the proper type of data has been collected, the following factors can be derived:

$$\lambda = \frac{\text{number of failures}}{\text{total system operating time}} \tag{8.12}$$

$$\text{MTBF} = \frac{1}{\lambda} = \text{MTBM}_u \tag{8.13}$$

$$\text{fpt} = \frac{\text{number of preventive maintenance actions}}{\text{total system operating time}} \tag{8.14}$$

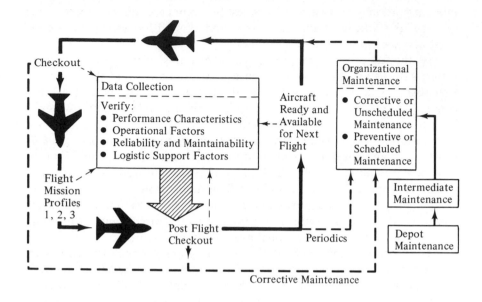

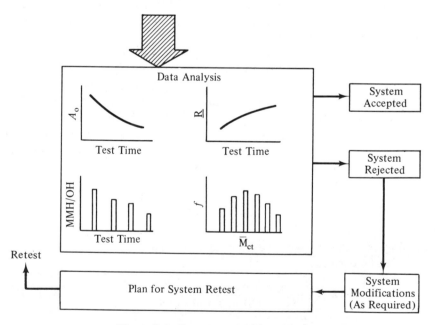

Figure 8-6. System test and evaluation.

$$\text{MTBM}_p = \frac{1}{\text{fpt}} \tag{8.15}$$

$$\text{MTBM} = \frac{1}{1/\text{MTBM}_c + 1/\text{MTBM}_p} \tag{8.16}$$

$$\text{MDT} = \overline{\text{M}} + \overline{\text{administrative time}} + \overline{\text{logistics time}} \tag{8.17}$$

$$\overline{\text{M}} = \frac{(\lambda)(\overline{\text{M}}\text{ct}) + (\text{fpt})(\overline{\text{M}}\text{pt})}{\lambda + \text{fpt}} \tag{8.18}$$

$$\overline{\text{M}}\text{pt} = \frac{\sum (\text{fpt}_i)(\text{Mpt}_i)}{\sum \text{fpt}_i} \tag{8.19}$$

$$\overline{\text{M}}\text{ct} = \frac{\sum (\lambda_i)(\text{Mct}_i)}{\sum \lambda_i} \tag{8.20}$$

$$\text{MMH/OH} = \frac{\text{maintenance labor-hours}}{\text{total system operating time}} \tag{8.21}$$

Other factors may be determined as deemed feasible. For instance, when evaluating the logistic support capability, the analyst may wish to know:

1. Turnaround times at the organizational, intermediate, and depot levels of maintenance.
2. Spare part supply times between the levels of maintenance. This includes the evaluation of a *nonoperationally ready* system due to a supply shortage or delay.
3. Spare/repair part stock levels and the demand rates for individual items.
4. Personnel effectiveness factors (organizational efficiency, assignment of the proper skill levels by function, adequacy of the prescribed formal training program, human error rates).
5. Adequacy of the operating and maintenance procedures (comprehensiveness and clarity).
6. Compatibility and utilization of test and support equipment. (Will it do the job and is it being effectively utilized?)
7. Adequacy of operational and maintenance facilities (proper environment, effective use of facilities, personnel facility interfaces, adequate storage for spares and test equipment).
8. Total cost effectiveness of logistic support capability.

Discrepant areas are recorded and reviewed in terms of possible corrective action. Corrective action may constitute a modification to the equipment, procedures, and/or element of logistic support. Depending on the seriousness of the problem, the system may be subjected to retest or the applicable modification may be incorporated into the operational system without requiring a retest.

8.5. Data Analysis and Corrective Action

Needless to say, the data analysis and corrective-action loop is a significant aspect of the program. Without it, all the testing in the world would not be of much value. If a system is to meet the operational requirements (which is the purpose of the system to begin with), it must be evaluated and areas of deficiency must be corrected; thus, the continuous feedback of data and a means by which corrective action is accomplished should be identified. In addition, the corrective-action loop must have teeth!

It is realized that corrective action may at times be rather costly. Unforeseen events often pop up. On the other hand, the lack of adequate consideration of logistic support in the design phase is predicable and will definitely become evident through testing. In this instance, neglecting to do what should have been done earlier in the program may cause no end of problems later. Costly modifications may be required (as a result of testing) which could have been avoided if the necessary steps had been taken.

The corrective-action loop is illustrated in Figure 8-7. Test data are analyzed and the results are compared with the system requirements. Areas of noncompliance are corrected and the system may be retested or not depending on the seriousness of the problem. The retest phase is designed to repeat certain tests because either the system, when initially tested, failed to meet all requirements by a significant margin, or the system met all requirements by a narrow margin. In the first instance, the following may occur.

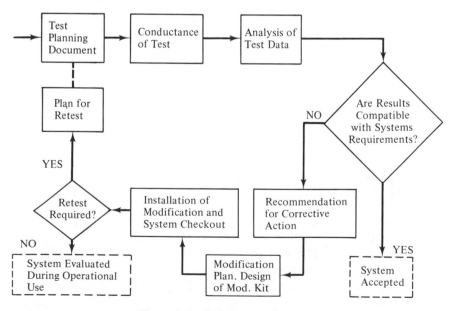

Figure 8-7. Corrective action loop.

1. Redesign of the prime equipment, or a change in supplier.
2. A major modification to a manufacturing or quality control process.
3. A change in the basic logistic support policy or a modification to a particular element of logistic support.

The system will be retested to verify that the incorporated change corrected the identified problem(s).

In the second case (i.e., requirements are met, but by a narrow margin), it may be desirable to gain more experience through formal testing in order to provide added confidence that system requirements will be met in the operational use phase.

When retesting is specified, a plan for the retest is required and should contain the same basic information included in the initial test planning document.

8.6. Test Reporting

The final effort in the test program constitutes the preparation of a test report. The final test report should reference the initial test planning document and should describe test conditions, test data, and the results of data analysis. These results may include appropriate recommendations for logistics provisioning and support actions as applicable to the operational use phase.

QUESTIONS AND PROBLEMS

1. How are system test requirements determined?
2. When is test planning accomplished?
3. What factors are considered in test planning?
4. What criteria are used in the selection of personnel for the demonstration of maintenance tasks? Define the criteria for the selection of test and support equipment.
5. How are the elements of logistic support evaluated through testing?
6. How is system reliability and maintainability growth determined through testing? Plot a typical curve showing growth during the various phases of equipment development.
7. What mechanism is provided for corrective action if the test results indicate noncompliance with a system requirement?
8. The conductance of testing in general is costly. However, it can prove to be more costly than necessary under certain circumstances. What are they?
9. How are test results fed into the logistic support process?

10. The output of reliability and maintainability testing serves to verify the capability and adequacy of logistic support. True or false? If true, how?

11. When planning a reliability test, what factors should be well defined prior to test start?

12. The maintenance concept and LSA are used to establish the requirements for test and demonstration. True or false? If true, how?

13. Under what conditions can a retest requirement be specified?

14. What are the benefits of sequential testing?

15. Are the four types of testing applicable to all systems and equipments? Why?

16. What is meant by "producer's risk"? "User's risk"? How do these values influence management decisions?

17. When selecting tasks for maintainability demonstration, how does the selection process result in a representative sample of what is to be expected in an operational situation?

18. Refer to Maintainability Demonstration Method 2 and determine whether the system will meet the $\bar{M}ct$ requirement if the assumed producer's risk is 5%.

19. How does the confidence factor in maintainability demonstration affect the accept–reject criteria?

20. Select a system of your choice and specify the appropriate operational, performance, and logistic support requirements. Assume that you have been appointed as test director and are responsible for demonstrating that all requirements have been met. Develop a test plan that you intend to implement.

21. The $\bar{M}ct$ requirement for an equipment item is 65 minutes and the established risk factor is 10%. A maintainability demonstration is accomplished and yields the following results for the 50 tasks demonstrated.

39	57	70	51	74	63	66	42	85	75
42	43	54	65	47	40	53	32	50	73
64	82	36	63	68	70	52	48	86	36
74	67	71	96	45	58	82	32	56	58
92	91	75	74	67	73	49	62	64	62

(Task times are in minutes.)

Did the equipment item pass the M demonstration?

22. The $\bar{M}$pt requirement for the equipment in Problem 21 is 100 minutes and the risk is the same. A maintainability demonstration is accomplished and yields the following results for the 50 tasks demonstrated.

150	120	133	92	89	115	122	69	172	161
144	133	121	101	114	112	181	78	112	91
82	131	122	159	135	108	95	67	118	103
78	93	144	152	136	86	113	102	65	115
113	101	94	129	148	118	102	106	117	115

(Task times are in minutes.)

Did the equipment item pass the M demonstration?

23. What is the calculated mean maintenance time for the equipment in Problems 21 and 22 if the equipment operation time is 1,000 hours?

24. Referring to the test plan in Figure 8-3, assume that six events occur in the first 600 hours. What is the test status and what would you do next?

25. Can the results of reliability testing be used directly in the determination of logistic support requirements? Why?

PRODUCTION AND/OR CONSTRUCTION

The earlier chapters dealt primarily with the design, development, test and evaluation of systems and equipment for consumer use. At this point, the design of the consumer product is considered *fixed*, and the next step involves the production (or construction) and the subsequent distribution of the product in the field.[1]

When dealing with production, one must consider the total flow of materials, commencing with the acquisition of raw materials from suppliers and extending to the delivery of the finished product to the ultimate user or consumer. The finished product may constitute (1) the prime mission-oriented equipment or segment of a system designated for field use, (2) a small consumable product designated for the commercial market, or (3) an element of logistic support designated for operational use (e.g., test and support equipment, an item of special handling equipment, spares for maintenance of the prime equipment, handbook or technical data package).

The production process and the follow-on activities of product distri-

---

[1] This does not mean that the proposed design configuration is optimal. However, the design has been validated to the extent necessary to ensure that the resultant product will fulfill all mission and operational requirements. Design changes from this point on will be limited primarily to the correction of problems related to producibility (or lack thereof).

9

bution, regardless of the type of product, involve procurement and the acquisition of materials, product inventories and inventory control, tooling and test equipment, transportation and handling provisions, facilities (manufacturing facilities and warehouses), personnel, and data. Thus, there is a facet of logistics applicable to the production of an item, and in many instances the elements of logistics required for production are directly comparable to those elements associated with the sustaining life-cycle support of large systems in the field being used by the consumer. In other words, we are actually dealing with two facets of logistics:

1. The production and distribution of elements of logistic support, identified by logistic support analysis (LSA), that are required in the field to support the system during consumer operation.
2. The aspects of support necessary in the production and distribution process itself relating to material acquisition, material flow, inventory control, packaging and shipping, transportation, warehousing, and so on.

The first facet of logistics is emphasized throughout this text, while the second aspect, the subject of *industrial logistics* or *business logistics*, is covered rather extensively in other literature.[2] Nevertheless, both facets must be dealt with in the transition of a product from a fixed design concept to a usable entity responsive to the fulfillment of mission requirements. The intent of this chapter is to briefly discuss production requirements, industrial engineering, production operations, and the logistic support involved in this phase of the system life cycle.

9.1. Production/Construction Requirements

Production requirements initially stem from system operational data developed during advanced planning and conceptual design (refer to Chapter 3), and subsequently are refined through the system design process.[3] The basic information desired includes a detail description of the item to be produced (i.e., a set of specifications), the quantity of items needed, the time of need and place of delivery, and the general environmental conditions associated with the transportation of the finished product from the production facility to the user's operational site.

Production requirements may vary considerably depending on the type of system, available capacity in the producer's plant and supporting resource needs, management decisions pertaining to "make or buy," and so on. These requirements may specify a multiple quantity of a single item, a multiple quantity of a number of items, and/or a single quantity of a wide variety of items. Further, when dealing with multiple quantities, production may be continuous or discontinuous, as illustrated in Figure 9-1, depending on specific monthly demand factors and associated cost.[4]

The production of multiple quantities of an item assumes a *flow-shop* pattern where the output variety is limited and each kind of output follows the same basic path and sequence of processing steps. Plant layout, inven-

---

[2]Throughout this text, logistics is addressed in the life-cycle context beginning with system design and continuing through system operational use and retirement. Industrial logistics primarily deals with the material flow and physical distribution of consumer products, and is primarily associated with production operations (i.e., only one facet of the overall life cycle). Four good references on industrial logistics and production are (a) Heskett, J. L., Glaskowsky, N. A., and Ivie, R. M., *Business Logistics*, 2nd ed., The Ronald Press Company, New York, 1973; (b) Bowersox, D. J., *Logistical Management*, Macmillan Publishing Co., Inc., New York, 1974; (c) Magee, J. F., *Industrial Logistics*, McGraw-Hill Book Company, New York, 1968; and (d) Fabrycky, W. J., Ghare, P. M., and Torgersen, P. E., *Industrial Operations Research*, Prentice-Hall, Inc., Englewood Cliffs, N.J., 1972.

[3]This is comparable to the marketing analysis and the forecasting of demand data referred to in the numerous textbooks on industrial logistics, production, and related areas.

[4]The demand must consider the prime equipments that are actually employed in accomplishment of the designated mission plus any spare equipments that are needed for backup (to cover maintenance and attrition).

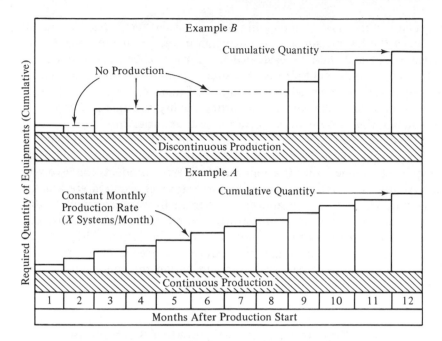

Figure 9-1. Continuous and discontinuous production runs.

tory stockpoints, test and inspection stations, and personnel functions are designed to handle a large volume (i.e., mass production). When production is continuous and at an approximate steady rate (Figure 9-1, example *A*), the associated logistics resources required are somewhat constant and production costs are relatively easy to determine. On the other hand, when production is discontinuous (to include production line startups and shutdowns, Figure 9-1, example *B*), the logistic support resources required are variable and are somewhat greater. Discontinuities result in personnel retraining and problems related to workmanship, quality level, and production realization rates. The probability of items being rejected through test and inspection is high, and the applicable items must be recycled through certain steps in the production process resulting in added resource requirements and possibly a shift in production schedules. These factors, combined with associated changes in material procurement practices, generally result in higher overall production costs.

Given a large quantity production requirement, there may be a number of approaches considered which will result in the same final output. It may be feasible to establish a faster buildup rate at the beginning of the production cycle or to vary the production rate at other times. In addition, there is the consideration of a single versus multiple production line capability, or different combinations of capability in the detailed functions of production (e.g., subassembly, final assembly, inspection and test, etc.). Each variation will impact the logistic support requirements in the production phase to a different extent and must be evaluated in terms of effectiveness and cost.

In contrast to the multiple-quantity situation discussed above, a requirement may constitute the production of a mix of items or the construction of a single item such as the commercial airline facility example in Chapter 3. This assumes a *job-shop* pattern where the output varies from item to item and the activity involves a mix of jobs following different paths through a program network. In the pure sense, no two jobs are exactly alike, and each job requires a unique setup. If a number of different products are involved (i.e., large product mix), the logistic support resources required are usually general purpose and can be adjusted rather easily to accommodate the variety of output. For the single construction project, the logistics resources will of course be peculiar to that particular product output. The ultimate objective in production planning is to produce the necessary items that will satisfy the need at the lowest total cost and within the constraints of the established system design configuration.

9.2. Industrial Engineering and Operations Analysis

Industrial engineering in this instance refers to a composite of activities responsible for the design and development of a production capability.[5] A production capability is a complex collection of elements (facilities, labor, equipment, and materials) combined and operated to provide a product or service. That is, the production capability is the process of transition from a fixed design configuration (defined by approved design drawings, layouts, material lists, procedures, etc.) to a finished deliverable product. The product may include prime equipment, test and support equipment, training equipment, spare/repair parts, or any other hardware item which is part of the system. Industrial engineering activities are concerned with the design and development of this capability, and may be subdivided into the following categories.

A. PLANT ENGINEERING

Based on the requirements for production, it is necessary to:
1. Determine the capacity and location of both production (e.g., fabrication, assembly, and test) and storage facilities.
2. Determine utility requirements (e.g., power, telephone, environmental controls, etc.).

---

[5]This definition is employed to establish a frame of reference for further discussion. It is not intended that the definition be aligned to any particular organization.

3. Determine capital equipment needs (e.g., machines, heavy equipment, etc.).
4. Accomplish a plant layout of utilities and capital equipment.
5. Design and incorporate material handling provisions.
6. Establish a maintenance capability for the corrective and preventive maintenance of facilities, utilities, and equipment.

Plant engineering involves the general design, development, construction, operation, and maintenance of production facilities.[6]

B. MANUFACTURING ENGINEERING

As discussed in earlier chapters, the consumer (or customer) specifies the need for a system. This need is defined in terms of functions and ultimately a design specification is prepared which forms the basis for equipment design and development. The output, constituting a combination of prototype hardware and various types of design data, must be converted into process specifications. Manufacturing engineering defines the production process through the process specification. Specific manufacturing engineering functions are to:

1. Assess the various elements of the system and assist in determining *make-or-buy* decisions (i.e., whether an item is to be produced within or purchased off-the-shelf on the outside).[7] This function must be accomplished early enough in the system design and development cycle to allow for proper production planning.
2. Select the material to be used in the fabrication of each *make* item.
3. Select the basic process for item fabrication. The process should consider the degree of neatness, accuracy, precision, thoroughness, and/or other characteristics which are required and are economically feasible. The process specification should include tolerances or upper and lower limits. Variability of materials and processes can be estimated from an empirical frequency distribution. Manufacturing engineering, in conjunction with quality control, establishes the necessary combinations to ensure that the production output is compatible with consumer requirements.

---

[6]Several references dealing with plant engineering and plant layout are (a) Apple, J. M., *Plant Layout and Materials Handling*, 2nd ed., The Ronald Press Company, New York, 1963; and Moore, J. M., *Plant Layout and Design*, Macmillan Publishing Co., Inc., New York, 1962.

[7]Generally, a make-or-buy committee is established with representation from design engineering, procurement, manufacturing engineering, logistics, and producer/consumer management. Decisions are made concerning the source of supply, and are based on item availability, expected production horizon period, schedule, cost, and related political implications.

4. Specify, in conjunction with methods engineering, the sequence of manufacturing operations. Develop flowcharts and identify functional sequences for manufacturing processes.

5. Identify human–machine operations. Apply human factors criteria in determining a manual task versus a function that can be automated (e.g., application of numerical control techniques). Decisions in this area must be considered with the results of methods engineering.

6. Select the appropriate tools, test equipment, and handling equipment required for each manufacturing operation. This includes machines, tools, jigs, and fixtures.

7. Design special tools, test equipment, jigs, and fixtures. Where feasible, the items of test and support equipment designated for operational use and for support of prime equipment in the field should be used to support manufacturing operations. For instance, if an assembled item requires a test prior to being processed to the next manufacturing station and that test is comparable to a test that is required in the field, the operational test equipment should be used rather than designing a new item specifically for production purposes. This tends to ensure compatibility in system testing, helps to verify the adequacy of operational test equipment, and reduces the cost of production.

C. METHODS ENGINEERING

The aspect of analyzing production operations in terms of effectiveness and cost is accomplished through methods engineering. Specifically, this includes the following functions.

1. Establish work methods, time, and cost standards. Select jobs that can be standardized, analyze the jobs in terms of elements, synthesize and evaluate alternative job approaches, select a preferred approach, establish cost and time standards for each job, and apply the established standards for all applicable manufacturing operations. Cost data generated in this area are used in life-cycle cost analyses.
2. Estimate part and manufacturing operation costs.
3. Determine job-skill requirements and estimate manufacturing personnel quantities and labor grades.
4. Design subassembly and assembly operations.
5. Analyze overall production operations in terms of cost and effectiveness and initiate changes for improvement where appropriate.

D. PRODUCTION CONTROL REQUIREMENTS

The remaining aspect of early production design is to establish the procedures and requirements necessary to maintain control of production operations. Primary production control functions are to

1. Determine the production lot quantities and batch sizes. How many equipment items should be produced in a given lot to maintain the proper control of processes, quality, change implementation, and so on?
2. Determine the economic inventory levels for materials and parts. Establish economic order quantities and procurement cycles.
3. Establish a system for work order processing and assignment.

As part of the industrial engineering function, one of the initial steps is to develop a process flowchart covering the overall production operation. This flow should be an expansion of the activity identified in block 3, Figure 2-32, and presented in the manner illustrated in Figure 9-2.

Referring to Figure 9-2, the intent is to show all the major functions required to produce the equipment. An expansion of each function can be accomplished through a work process analysis illustrated in Figure 9-3.[8] The functional flowchart and work process analysis approach is similar to the maintenance task analysis described in Appendix B for the prime equipment. That is, functions and tasks are identified, analyzed, and the results are employed to determine specific logistic support requirements for the field during the operational use phase. In this instance, functions and tasks are identified, evaluated, and the results lead to the identification of logistic support requirements in the production operation. In addition, the results are used to measure the effectiveness of production operations. The approach is similar although the functional descriptions are different.

When defining production requirements, the industrial engineering activity is charged with the responsibility of seeking an optimum solution. The functions of plant engineering, manufacturing engineering, methods engineering, and production control are accomplished and the results are considered in the decision-making process. The student, when analyzing the situation, might consider the production operation as a large system by itself and attempt to evaluate input-output requirements for different internal production configurations. In any event, designing a production capability will lead to many questions and numerous decisions must be made. For instance,

1. Where should the production facility be located? Should a new facility be acquired or should an existing facility be modified?
2. How many production lines should be established, and how many machines should be assigned to each line?
3. What is the optimum production rate and output on a month-to-month basis?

---

[8] The work process analysis is discussed further in McGarrah, R. E., *Production and Logistics Management*, John Wiley & Sons, Inc., New York, 1963.

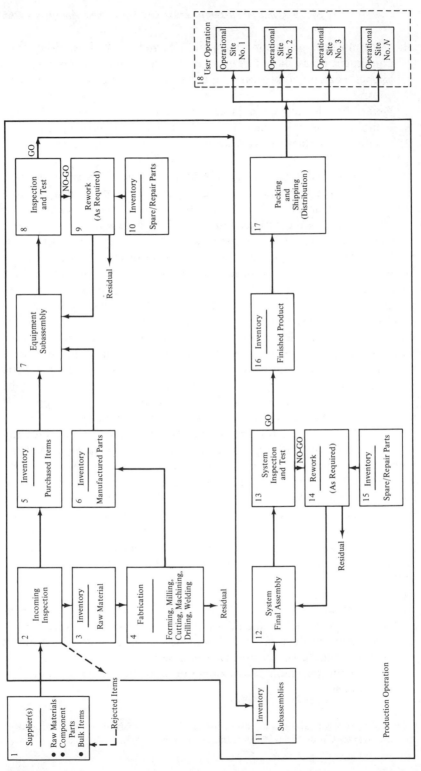

Figure 9-2. Production process flow.

Reference: Figure 9-2, Blocks 7, 8, 11

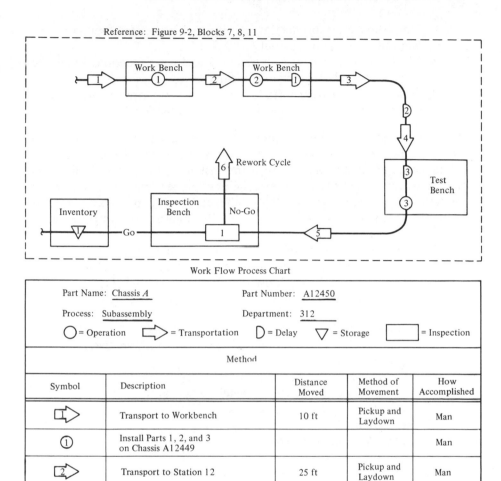

Work Flow Process Chart

Part Name: Chassis *A*			Part Number: A12450		

Process: Subassembly Department: 312

◯ = Operation   ⇨ = Transportation   D = Delay   ▽ = Storage   ▢ = Inspection

Method					
Symbol	Description		Distance Moved	Method of Movement	How Accomplished
⇨ 1	Transport to Workbench		10 ft	Pickup and Laydown	Man
①	Install Parts 1, 2, and 3 on Chassis A12449				Man
⇨ 2	Transport to Station 12		25 ft	Pickup and Laydown	Man
②	Install Parts 4, 5, and 6 on Chassis A12449				Man
D	On Workbench				
⇨ 3	Transport to Conveyor		10 ft	Pickup and Laydown	Man
D 2	On Conveyor				Power

Figure 9-3. Work process approach.

4. Where should maintenance and rework be accomplished?
5. What preventive maintenance should be accomplished on production facilities, utilities, and capital equipment?
6. Where should inventory stock points be located and what levels of inventory should be maintained?

7. How should the production facility and associated equipment be laid out for optimum output?
8. What functions should be automated and what functions should be accomplished through manual means?
9. What modes of transportation should be employed in the accomplishment of transportation and handling functions?

Answers to these and other questions require a rather in-depth operations analysis. There are numerous alternatives to consider and the input variable relationships are quite complex. In many instances, the analysis effort and the evaluation of alternatives require the development and use of analytical models. Requirements are identified, alternatives are proposed, and the industrial engineer must evaluate each feasible alternative and recommend a preferred solution.[9]

The operational analysis of a production capability is a separate subject in itself, and the student is advised to review additional literature in order to understand the scope and complexities involved.[10] Typical subject areas that can be addressed through the use of appropriate analytical techniques are

1. Economic evaluation of production operations.
2. Evaluation of single and multiple production alternatives.
3. Optimum equipment replacement.
4. Procurement quantities and inventory levels.
5. Evaluation of production sequencing.
6. Evaluation of waiting-line effects.
7. Evaluation of transportation options.
8. Optimum machine assignment.
9. Optimum quality control levels.
10. Evaluation of material purchasing alternatives.
11. Production project evaluation and control.

9.3. Quality Control[11]

The quality of a product is the degree to which it satisfies the wants of a specific consumer or user, or may be stated in terms of a measure of the

---

[9]The analysis of production operations is comparable to logistic support analysis (LSA), described in Chapter 6. That is, the steps include definition of the problem, identification of feasible alternatives, selection of evaluation criteria, and so on.

[10]A good source pertaining to analysis of production operations is Fabrycky, W. J., Ghare, P. M., and Torgersen, P. E., *Industrial Operations Research*, Prentice-Hall, Inc., Englewood Cliffs, N.J., 1972.

[11]The subjects of quality and quality control are rather extensive and far beyond the summary discussion presented herein. The student may wish to review the following four references for more in-depth coverage; (a) Juran, J. M. (ed., *Quality Control Handbook*,

degree to which it conforms to specification and workmanship standards. It can be expressed in terms of a given set of attributes required for that product to meet operational requirements. These attributes may include size, weight, shape, durability, hardness, performance, reliability, maintainability, supportability, attractiveness, and the like, and should be defined in measurable quantitative terms. Measurement accuracies and tolerances (upper and lower limits) should be defined for each attribute. Quality level is measured by the percentage defective in a given lot or population.

The purpose of quality control is to assure that these attributes are maintained throughout the production cycle. Quality control is a function of management relative to all procedures, inspections, examinations, and tests required during procurement, production, receipt, storage, and issue that are necessary to provide the user with an item of required quality.[12] Quality control is a production oriented operation designed for causing a process to manufacture a uniform product within specified limits of percent defective in accordance with the design requirements.

The conformance to good quality (the adherence of a product to specification requirements) is particularly significant for the following reasons.

1. It reduces item rejects and the recycling for repair rework, testing, and inspection. The reworking of an item requires additional manpower and machine usage and results in a high material waste. Good quality causes a reduction in production costs.

2. It reduces the probability of requiring an extensive amount of maintenance in the field shortly after an item is delivered for operational use. An item may pass a series of inspections in the production cycle and yet fail shortly after delivery due to one or more manufacturing defects. The added maintenance burden will result in a need for additional logistic support resources or cause those resources available to be depleted earlier than expected. Good quality causes a reduction in system operation and maintenance costs.

3. It reduces the probability of product liability suits, particularly if warranty provisions prevail. Manufacturing defects may cause accidents resulting in damage to equipment and facilities, and/or result in the death of personnel. Good quality reduces the risk to the producer.

4. It causes a favorable impact of future reprocurements and new sales.

2nd ed., McGraw-Hill Book Company, New York, 1962; (b) Feigenbaum, A. V., *Total Quality Control*, McGraw-Hill Book Company, New York, 1961; (c) Duncan, A. J., *Quality Control and Industrial Statistics*, 3rd ed., Richard D. Irwin, Inc., Homewood, Ill., 1965; and (d) Grant, E. L. and Leavenworth, R. S., *Statistical Quality Control*, 4th ed., McGraw-Hill Book Company, New York, 1972.

[12]Gluck, F., ed., Technical Report No. 5, *A Compendium of Authenticated Logistics Terms and Definitions*, School of Systems and Logistics, USAFIT, WPAFB, Ohio, 1970.

Items 1 and 2 both significantly impact logistic support (in the production facility and in the field, respectively). The initial engineering design may be suitable; however, unless the equipment is producible and the production process is adequate, the product output will not necessarily reflect what was initially intended. Without adequate standards and controls, each individual equipment item may turn out to be somewhat different, operational effectiveness may fall short of initial objectives, the reliability of equipment may degrade, etc. Good quality control is necessary to ensure that both prime equipment and logistic support objectives, defined through the design and development process, are realized.

The assurance of good quality is accomplished through (1) the establishment of quality tests, setting up quality standards and acceptance criteria, and interpreting quality data; and (2) the subsequent implementation of a sustaining quality control effort constituting a combination of tests and inspections. The development of quality standards and acceptance criteria is accomplished in conjuction with the activities of plant engineering, manufacturing engineering, methods engineering, and production control. Processes are analyzed and quality levels are established. A quality level is chosen by considering the probabilities of accepting bad quality products as good and of rejecting good quality products as bad. Selecting the proper level is dependent on the costs of inspection and the risks.[13] Once that quality levels are identified for the attributes to be measured, accuracies and tolerances must be specified and acceptance criteria are established. Tests and inspections are then planned at different times in the production cycle to ensure proper quality standards at the various stages of production (e.g., after fabrication, subassembly, and/or final assembly). These requirements are then included in the applicable process specifications developed as a manufacturing engineering output.

The second aspect of quality control involves the function of inspection and test. Inspection is the process of verifying the quality of an item with respect to some standard. Inspection serves several purposes. The first is to determine the quality of some portion of the items being turned out by a process. The problem is to determine whether to accept or reject a production lot on the basis of an analysis of the selected items. This is often referred to as *acceptance control*. The second purpose is to determine the condition of an operation or process in terms of its quality-producing performance. In this instance, the intent is *process control*. A given inspection may satisfy both purposes.

There are two different categories of inspection. The first is 100% *inspec-*

---

[13]The student would benefit at this point by a review of the basic principles of statistical quality control. The acceptance of bad products, a function of the established quality level, will directly impact logistic support.

tion or screening, and the second is *sampling inspection*. For critical components, 100% inspection is often desirable. This includes those instances where measurement accuracies and tolerances of an item are critical or when a given production process is suspect. Each and every item in the production lot is inspected against the process specification. In sampling inspection, a random sample of items is selected from a production lot (a statistical population), and each item in the sample is inspected in accordance with the requirements of the process specification. An accept decision constitutes the acceptance of the entire lot. The frequency of sampling and the sample size are dependent on the type of equipment, the length of the production run, the number of items produced per lot, and the risks involved.

As indicated earlier, the purpose of inspection and test is to ensure that a specified level of product quality is maintained *throughout* the production process. From the standpoint of logistic support, there are many system attributes considered significant which must be closely monitored and controlled. For instance:

1. The equipment reliability (MTBF), demonstrated during Type 2 testing, should be maintained for all production models. To assure that the required MTBF is attained, a sample number of equipments may be selected from each production lot and subjected to the reliability sequential test plan described in Section 8.4A. In some instances, a lower MTBF will be evident which means that reliability degradation is occurring through the production process. This will necessitate an adjustment to input quality standards (e.g., improve component acceptance criteria, tighten manufacturing processes, increase testing, etc.) in such a manner as to improve product reliability. On the other hand, the test results may indicate a higher MTBF which demonstrates equipment maturity and reliability growth.

2. Certain equipment performance parameters (i.e., range, accuracy, flow rate, etc.) are critical to success of the system mission in the field. Operational test and support equipment has been identified by LSA and developed to check the prime equipment in terms of these parameters. A test, accomplished during Type 2 testing, initially ensures the compatibility between the prime equipment and its associated test and support equipment. It is required that this compatibility be maintained for all production items; thus, it may be feasible to select certain equipments at random from different production lots and repeat the test.

3. One of the important aspects of maintainability and logistic support is *interchangeability*; that is, an item can be removed and a like item installed in its place without significantly affecting equipment performance operation. The replacement must be compatible in form, fit, and function. With the variations often occurring in production processes, it may be feasible to accomplish maintainability demonstrations on a select number of

equipments from each production lot to ensure that configuration control and interchangeability features are being maintained.

There are numerous examples and considerations which apply to quality control in the production operation. The measure of quality is a function of specified product standards and the established test and inspection requirements. It is not the intent nor is it necessarily feasible to seek quality perfection as the associated production and inspection costs may be prohibitive. On the other hand, poor quality is costly for the reasons stated above. An optimum quality level is defined at that point where all product operational and performance characteristics are attained and the total production cost is minimized. The relationship between levels of quality and cost is illustrated in Figure 9-4.[14] Quality is assessed by inspecting the product (to varying degrees) at one or more points in the production process. Accept–reject decisions are made and defects are recycled for corrective action. The object is to establish a production process with the necessary controls that will realize a tolerable defect rate.

9.4. Production Operations[15]

Implementation of the functions defined in the previous paragraphs results in the initial design of the production capability. Materials and services are acquired and actual production commences in accordance with the prescribed quantities and schedule. Production includes:

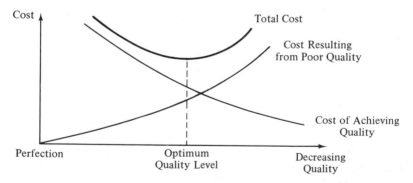

Figure 9-4. Relationship between levels of quality and cost.

[14]Fabrycky, W. J., Ghare, P. M., and Torgersen, P. E., *Industrial Operations Research*, Prentice-Hall, Inc., Englewood Cliffs, N.J., 1972.

[15]Two references that deal with production operations in a broad context are (a) Buffa, E. S., *Modern Production Management*, 5th ed., John Wiley & Sons, Inc., New York, 1977; and (b) Starr, M. K., *Operations Management*, Prentice-Hall, Inc., Englewood Cliffs, N.J., 1978.

1. Fabrication, assembly, inspection, and test of prime equipment.
2. Manufacture and test of small consumable products.
3. Fabrication, assembly, inspection, and test of logistic support hardware items designated for operational use in the field. This includes:

   a. Test and support equipment.
   b. Transportation and handling equipment.
   c. Spare/repair parts.
   d. Training equipment.

4. Assembly and inspection of software (e.g., computer program tapes) and operation and maintenance data for use in the field.
5. Provisioning and acquisition of off-the-shelf equipment, associated software, and data (that which is already available in some inventory and is acquired through procurement).

Conventionally, we think of production as being primarily associated with the manufacture of prime equipment only. Although the prime equipment is generally the most significant item, the various elements of logistic support must also be considered in the production process. In some instances, the same producer and physical facility are employed in the production of both prime equipment and logistic support items. In other cases, different production facilities are involved. In any event, the preproduction planning and design effort (i.e., plant engineering, manufacturing engineering, methods engineering, production control, and quality control) must address all elements of the system.

Throughout the production operation many varied activities take place. There are fabrication and assembly functions, inventory and material handling functions, test and inspection functions, and so on. These functions in themselves require work benches, tools and test equipment, handling provisions, material inventories, personnel, and data. So in reality, we are dealing with two aspects of logistics—the items of logistic support that are produced for field use (identified by LSA in Chapter 6) and the logistic support required to accomplish production.

When considering the production operation as a system in itself, we are dealing with the product that is required by the consumer (to include all four categories above such as prime equipment, spare/repair parts, software, etc.) and the processes, materials, and services necessary to manufacture the product. The combination constitutes the production capability discussed above and illustrated in Figure 9-2. At designated points in the production process, various facets of the operation are measured and evaluated to ensure that a proper level of effectiveness is being maintained. In the design of the production capability, input–output requirements are established for each major function. These requirements may constitute the assembly, inspection, or test of n gidgets per unit of calendar time; the fabrication of x parts per a given level of cost; the percentage of items reworked; the quantity of labor-hours expended per item subassembly; and so on. In addition, the items involved must exhibit a specified level of quality. The combining of these requirements results in a total production capability, and this capability must be assessed on a continuing basis to verify that consumer requirements are being met.

The measurement and evaluation occur through the application of inspection and test functions and work sampling techniques. Inspection and test provisions, including a combination of acceptance control and sampling inspections, verify that product performance and operational characteristics (i.e., proper level of product quality) are being maintained. Work sampling techniques are employed to evaluate production operations.

Work sampling is a method of analyzing and assessing the time (clock time and manhours) required for the performance of work tasks, and is accomplished through a series of random observations which are extended over the production period. These observations may be acquired: by establishing timekeeping procedures by job and analyzing the collected time data; observing jobs and monitoring task sequences and time with a stopwatch; taking motion pictures of a job and synchronizing camera speed and film frames with time; and/or by making recordings of certain data and relating the output to probability distributions that are representative of various machine and human activity functions. Each of the available techniques is advantageous in certain situations. For instance, in analyzing an organizational entity which is responsible for a number of functions within the overall production operation, the timekeeping procedure (measuring laborhours expended for a given level of work) may be preferable. When establishing a detailed time standard or measuring the time for mounting one part on another, monitoring and recording time with a stopwatch may be appropriate. On the other hand, in the assembly of an item, particularly if the item is large and the assembly procedure is relatively complex, the motion picture approach may be the most feasible. The use of motion pictures allows for the evaluation of task sequences, personnel actions and error rates, and task times. The selection of the technique (s) to be employed is obviously dependent on the type of data desired.

The evaluation of production operations is accomplished by using a combination of inspection and test results and work sampling data. The output data are compared with the initially established equipment quality requirements and manufacturing standards. Corrective action is initiated in areas of noncompliance (i.e., when the operation is not producing the desired results) or when changes can be incorporated to improve the effectiveness of production.

Figure 9-5 illustrates the basic production cycle and the feedback corrective action loop. That is, requirements are initially established, a produc-

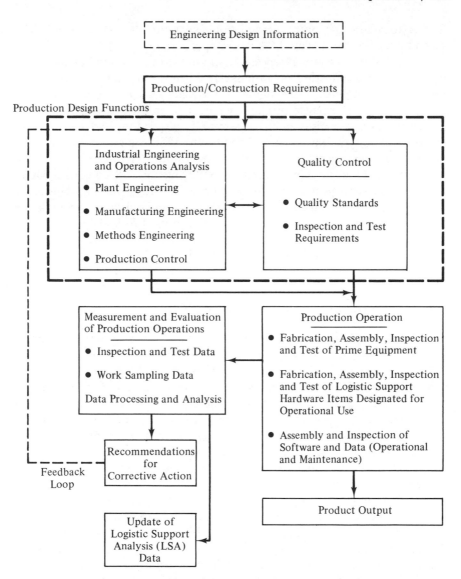

Figure 9-5. Basic production cycle.

tion capability is designed, production commences, the overall process is assessed on a continuing basis to ensure adequacy, and improvements are incorporated where appropriate.

Referring to Figure 9-5, it should be noted that measurement and evaluation data covering production operations serves several purposes. The first is to assess the overall production capability discussed earlier. The second purpose is to update LSA where appropriate.

Many of the assembly, inspection, and test procedures and quality standards used in production operations are identical to those proposed for operation and support of the system in the field during the operational use phase. In the performance of maintenance actions, throughout the system life cycle, there are disassembly, reassembly, inspection, and test requirements. Although the environmental conditions differ somewhat, the methods of task accomplishment are directly comparable in terms of task times, sequences, and logistic support needs. Monitoring and collecting data covering these functions provide results which are directly applicable. Thus, it is beneficial to identify and observe applicable functions and gain insight relative to future requirements. This information is then used to update LSA where appropriate. Results of LSA are evaluated (on a continuing basis) to assess the product in terms of design for supportability and producibility.

9.5. Configuration Change Control[16]

Quite often in the production process, changes are initiated to correct a deficiency and/or to improve the product. A change may result from the redesign of a prime equipment item, the revision of a production process, or a combination of both. In most instances, a change in one element of a system will have a direct impact on other elements. For instance, a change in the design configuration of prime equipment (e.g., change in size or weight, repackaging, added performance capability) will in all probability affect the design of test and support equipment, the type and quantity of spare/repair parts, technical data, facilities, the production process, and so on. A change in a production process may impact the reliability of the product, which, in turn, affects test and support equipment, spare/repair part requirements, and other elements of logistic support. Each change must be thoroughly evaluated in terms of its impact on other elements of the system prior to a decision on whether or not to incorporate the change. Figure 9-6 describes the basic steps in the change procedure. The incorporation of a change after production commences may be quite costly, particularly if the change is accomplished in the latter stages of the production cycle. The change will require the acquisition of additional materials and services, and a given amount of the already expended product input resources will have been wasted. For equipments which are produced in multiple quantities, the addi-

---

[16]By change control, the author is referring to the necessary management functions required to ensure that complete compatibility is maintained between *all* elements of a system whenever any single given element is changed for any reason.

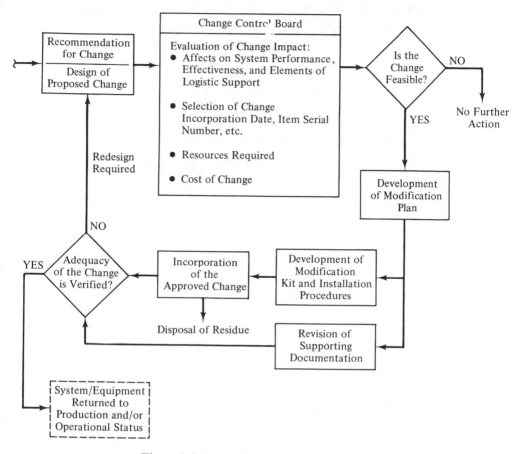

Figure 9-6. System/equipment change cycle.

tional resources and resultant waste may be multiplied on the basis of the number of equipments requiring the change. If the change is incorporated in certain equipments (i.e., equipment item serial numbers 24 and on) and not retrofited on earlier models (i.e., equipment items with serial numbers 1 through 23), then each of two configurations will require a different type of logistic support which is highly undesirable.

Past experience with a variety of systems has shown that configuration changes in the production phase are costly. With some systems, many different changes have been initiated at various points. Not always have the required changes been incorporated in all applicable production models, nor have the effects of each change on other elements of the system been considered. This has resulted in the delivery of prime equipment models of different configurations and elements of logistic support that are not compatible with the prime equipment. In such situations, system effectiveness is seriously compromised, the right type of system support is not available, and much waste occurs. The causes related to these occurrences may vary.

1. The system or equipment may enter into the production phase without first establishing a *fixed* design configuration. In other words, the design has not been formally reviewed, verified analytically, or demonstrated through test.
2. The original need and operational requirements for the system may change causing a necessary equipment change downstream.
3. The technical state of the art may be advanced through the introduction of a new design technique or process, and the producer decided to initiate a change as a result.
4. The supplier of certain items may decide to discontinue his source of supply and no other suppliers of the same item are available. Thus, redesign is often required.

There may be other reasons for incorporating changes in production; however, is most instances, these causes can be avoided through proper planning and progressing systematically through the steps of system design and development described in earlier chapters of this text. Changes to equipment hardware, software, and manufacturing operations must be controlled and held to a minimum.

If, on the other hand, changes are required for corrective-action purposes, then it is essential that change control be implemented. That is, the impact of each change on the total system and its various elements must be thoroughly evaluated. When a change is incorporated in any one item, all other affected elements of the system must be modified for compatibility. As an example, it is assumed that Unit *B* of System *XYZ* (refer to Figure 5-7) is modified to improve performance, and the system is to be produced in multiple quantities. The change involves the redesign of three assemblies, and the change is scheduled to be incorporated in system serial number 25 and on. A retrofit for serial numbers 1 through 24 is recommended.

First, the change will require some modification to the production processes (e.g., fabrication and subassembly methods) and material inventories to cover the future production of system serial numbers 25 and on. This, in turn, may affect manufacturing tools, jigs, fixtures, and so on. For the earlier models, modification kits and installation instructions must be developed. The systems are then pulled out of operation (assuming that the first 24 systems have been delivered to the user) while the change is implemented and verified. The change involves added production costs and operation costs in the field.

As a second consideration, the change will affect each element of logistic support to some extent. Reliability and the frequency of maintenance (anticipated number of maintenance actions) are affected, either upward or downward. Maintainability characteristics will change along with detailed maintenance tasks, task frequencies, and possibly the level of repair decisions made earlier. Test and support equipment must be modified to incorporate test provisions covering the added performance capability. Spare parts must be changed at the assembly level and below if the assemblies are designated repairable. Personnel training, training data, and operating and maintenance procedures for field use must be revised to reflect the change. Facilities may also require some modification.

Thus, what initially appears to be a simple system modification often has a tremendous impact on the prime equipment, the production capability, and logistic support. The incorporation of such a change must be identified with a specific equipment serial number. Each unit, assembly, and subassembly of that particular equipment must be marked in such a way as to be identified with that equipment. Spares with the same part number as items in the prime equipment must be treated in a like manner. A change incorporated in the system must be traceable through *all* affected elements (i.e., hardware, software, and data).

Configuration change control is particularly significant when the system undergoes a number of changes in the production phase. The results of the single change to System *XYZ* described above may be multiplied many times. Without the proper controls, there is no guarantee that the production output will provide effective results.

9.6. Transition from Production to User Operation

After the system, equipment, product, and/or associated elements of logistic support are produced (refer to block 16, Figure 9-2), the appropriate items are then distributed for consumer use. This distribution process may include a number of activities such as packaging, storing, warehousing, shipping or transporting, handling, item installation and checkout, and customer service. Further, this process may vary considerably depending on the type of item being distributed and the nature of the consumer and the market place. In the interests of simplicity, it seems appropriate to cover this facet of activity in two segments—the distribution of large-scale systems and equipment, and the distribution of small consumable products for the commercial markets.

A. DISTRIBUTION OF LARGE-SCALE SYSTEMS AND EQUIPMENT

The transition process from production/construction to full-scale operational use is critical since the prime equipment, software, and logistic support must be delivered on a concurrent basis and in a timely manner. The goal is to meet user requirements and provide an operational system ready to go at the required point in time.

The designated operational sites and activation dates are specified early in the program through the definition of operational requirements (refer to Chapter 3).[17] The transition from production to user operation is covered in the formal logistic support plan prepared prior to the start of the production phase (refer to Chapter 11). This plan supplements the operational requirements data and includes

1. The identification of operational sites, location, and activation date.
2. The identification of items to be delivered at each site, the time and route of delivery, and the mode of transportation used for delivery.
3. The requirements and procedure used to install equipment and make the system completely operational once that the appropriate items have been delivered. This may entail the establishment of a maintenance shop, installation and checkout of test and support equipment, initiation of a supply support capability, and so on.
4. The type and extent (in terms of time duration) of logistic support provided by the producer after the system activation date has passed and the system is considered fully operational. This may entail the immediate transfer of support responsibility from the producer to the user, or the provision of a sustaining support capability by the producer throughout the system life cycle.

The period of transition will vary in time depending on the system type and complexity. If the system is relatively simple to install, operate, and maintain, the transition may require only a few days before the user is able to assume full responsibility for system operation and support. On the other hand, if the system is large and complex, the transition may be much longer and accomplished on a gradual basis. An extensive amount of training may be required, producer field service engineers may be assigned to user site locations to assist in system operation, and the producer may provide an interim repair capability until such time that the user is fully qualified in all aspects of system support.[18] The objective is to accomplish transition at the proper

---

[17]The activation date is considered as the point in time when the applicable site has initially attained full operational status in accordance with user requirements. This date may be different for each site if two or more sites are involved.

[18]For some systems the producer will retain full support of the system or equipment throughout the life cycle under a leasing agreement or a repair/rework contract. The reference here pertains to the point in time until the ultimate support capability (whichever policy is followed) is attained.

time such that program risks are minimized.[19] Logistic support in this transitional stage addresses two basic areas.

1. The packing and shipping of the product from the producer's facility to the user's operational site, and the inspecting, installing, and checkout of the product at the site. The product may include prime equipment, support equipment, spare/repair parts, and so on. Logistics involves the consideration of

  a. Methods of packing and type of containers used for shipping.
  b. Mode of transportation used in shipment (e.g., cargo aircraft, truck, railroad, and/or ship).
  c. Test and support equipment, personnel, facilities, and technical data required for inspection, installation, and checkout of the product at the operational site. Hopefully, the logistic items assigned to support the prime equipment for the life cycle will be adequate to accomplish these functions.

2. The provision of a logistic support capability for the system at each operational site until full activation is attained (i.e., for the duration of the transition period). Although many of the elements of support are identical to those specified for the system life cycle, there are three basic considerations that should be dealt with in arriving at this interim capability.

  a. Depending on the type of equipment, established production and quality standards, and equipment maturity acquired through testing during production operations, there may be a greater number of corrective maintenance actions occurring immediately after equipment delivery than the estimated quantity derived from reliability predictions. Reliability predictions, which form the basis for the frequency of maintenance, often assume a constant failure rate. At this point in the equipment life, the failure rate may not be at the constant state. Figure 9-7 illustrates a typical failure-rate curve (introduced in Chapter 2, Figure 2-4). The frequency corrective maintenance is a function of primary failures (inherent reliability characteristics), dependent or secondary failures, manufacturing defects, operator and maintenance induced faults, and so on. The primary failure rate, the largest contributor to the corrective maintenance factor, is based on the value specified at point B in Figure 9-7. Equipment delivery may occur at point A before the equipment assumes a mature steady-state condition,

---

[19]In certain instances, it may be preferable to defer the transition of a support capability to the user until such time that the user is able to provide such a capability without causing a degrading effect on system operation. The proper time phasing of transitioning different aspects of the total logistic support capability (often referred to as *phased logistic support*) should be considered from a cost effectiveness basis and covered in the formal logistic support plan.

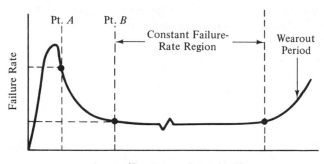

Figure 9-7. Reliability failure-rate curve.

and a greater quantity of initial failures will occur. Early logistic support must consider the possibility of realizing a burden beyond that which is initially planned.

b. When considering the introduction of a new system in the inventory, there is a period of time where formal training and equipment familiarization occurs. Until such time when user operator and maintenance personnel are thoroughly familiar with the system, there will be a certain number of operator induced faults and the system will not be fully utilized in an effective manner. In addition, the equipment may not be properly maintained, and it is quite probable that total maintenance and support requirements will exceed initial expectations.

c. If the system is large and complex in nature, the user may be able to successfully operate the system at the time of activation, but is unable to provide full logistic support at all echelons of maintenance. For instance, material procurement lead times may force the delay in establishing a necessary capability in the performance of certain maintenance functions; thus, an interim support capability of some sort must be maintained to ensure successful system operation.

Logistic support requirements for the initial *start-up* period, as determined by LSA, must address the considerations listed above. In some cases, however, the support policy may vary somewhat from that recommended for operational use (see Chapter 4). For instance: it may be feasible for a preestablished period of time to accomplish all depot-level maintenance at the producer's manufacturing facility in lieu of at user's depot installation; it may be desirable for the producer to train and locate experienced field service engineers at the operational sites and intermediate maintenance shops to facilitate user personnel training and to assist in the performance of system operating functions; or it may be feasible to provide only higher level spares (e.g., unit spares in lieu of both unit and assembly spares) at the intermediate shop for a limited period of time and repair the assemblies at the producer's facility until user personnel are adequately trained in the maintenance of assemblies. These and other policy diversions may occur to satisfy the needs during the transition from production/construction to user operation. However, the ultimate objective is to phase into full operational status defined by the maintenance concept and LSA.

B. DISTRIBUTION OF CONSUMABLE PRODUCTS FOR COMMERCIAL MARKETS

The distribution requirements pertaining to consumable items for the commercial markets are based on a completely different set of assumptions. A market analysis is usually accomplished at program inception to determine the size of the potential market, geographical location, and the market share for a given product. In general, we are dealing with a large number of individual consumers throughout the country (or world), and the marketplace may be subdivided into designated geographical territories, regions, districts, and the like. Further, there are larger numbers of end items with which to be concerned, product turnover is usually greater, and the potential for future sales becomes a driving force. The challenge is to provide the right product (in the proper quantities) at the place of need in a timely manner, and with a minimum expenditure of resources. The distribution of too many products, too few products, products to the wrong location, and so on, may be quite costly.

When dealing with the distribution of consumable products, one must be concerned with the activities conveyed by the network illustrated in Figure 9-8. Specifically, one must determine:

1. The quantity and distribution of potential consumers.
2. The number and location of potential retail outlets for the product.
3. The number, location, and size of product warehousing facilities. Should the facilities be completely automated, semiautomated, or operated through manual means?
4. The size and mix of product inventories at each location (i.e., retail outlet, warehouse, producer's manufacturing plant).
5. The requirements for product packaging, preservation, and storage.
6. The required mode, or modes, of transportation (i.e., aircraft, truck, railroad, and/or ship).

The response to these questions leads to the evaluation of many possible alternatives involving different mixes of consumer concentrations, retail outlets, product warehouses, transportation and handling modes, and so on. The application of simulation techniques, optimizing techniques, location models, inventory models, transportation models, and so on, is common in arriving at a preferred solution in an effective manner. In essence, one is

THE ELEMENTS OF INDUSTRIAL LOGISTICS

(Procurement, Material Flow, Inventories, Warehousing,
Packaging, Transportation, and Customer Service)

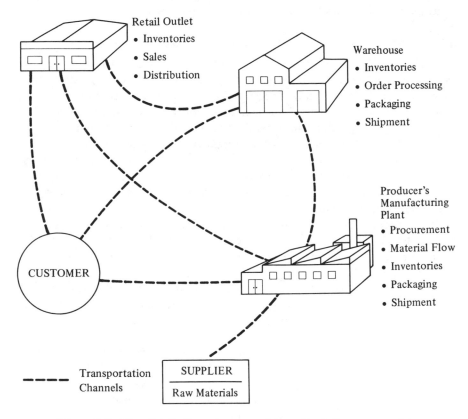

Figure 9-8. The distribution of consumable products for commercial markets.

dealing with a large network which involves many variables and is dynamic in nature.[20]

---

[20]As you are aware, the activity discussed herein and illustrated in Figure 9-8 is included within the broad spectrum of *industrial* (or *business*) *logistics* defined in Chapter 1 and referenced in the introduction of this chapter. Since this area of activity is rather broad and complex, and yet extremely important in the understanding of logistics overall, the reader is advised to review some of the reference material in Appendix F.

9.7. Summary

This chapter briefly deals with (1) the production and deployment of logistics elements designated for use in support of the system in the field throughout its life cycle; and (2) the logistic support involved in the production process itself. The first category covers one of several phases in the total consideration of logistics from program inception to system operational use and ultimate equipment phase-out from the inventory. This constitutes the design, development, and production of logistic support elements on a concurrent basis with the development of prime equipment. The second category basically constitutes industrial logistics which is well covered in the literature through other references. This facet of logistics is primarily oriented to the production phase only and does not deal with the overall system life cycle.

Both aspects of logistic support as discussed in this chapter are necessary in the transition from a fixed design configuration of some system to a finished product delivered to the user. In both instances, the concepts of application are comparable; that is, we are dealing with the test and support equipment, personnel and training, spare parts and inventories, data, facilities, and resources required to accomplish the goal of producing an entity. In many cases, the actual resources required are identical even though the applications may vary somewhat. In any event, the concepts employed in the identification of requirements, design, evaluation and test, and production are directly related.

QUESTIONS AND PROBLEMS

1. The initial requirements for production/construction are based on what factors?

2. Define logistic support in the context of the production/construction phase. What are the elements of logistic support?

3. What considerations are necessary in the design of a production capability? What are the basic production design functions?

4. If an equipment is to be produced in multiple quantities, what considerations are necessary in the design of a production capability?

5. In the production of multiple quantities of a given item, what are the advantages of continuous production over discontinuous production? How is logistic support affected?

6. What is the basic difference between a job-shop operation and a flow-shop operation? How is logistic support affected?

7. How are production standards established and maintained?

8. How would you measure and assess the effectiveness of a production capability?

9. What are the differences in producing Assembly Part 231 as installed in the prime equipment and Assembly Part 231, which is designated as a spare part? Comment on manufacturing standards, quality standards, and inspection processes.

10. Can test and support equipment designated for operational use in the field be employed in the production process? If so, how, and what benefits are derived?

11. In what ways are functions performed in the production process similar to operational and maintenance functions which are anticipated for the field?

12. How does quality control affect logistic support in the field? Give some specific examples.

13. How does the evaluation of production functions relate to LSA?

14. Can the production operation affect the inherent characteristics of reliability and maintainability in the equipment? How?

15. How would you determine the level of quality control that should be applied to a given product? Discuss the factors that should be considered.

16. Why is configuration control important to logistic support? What happens to logistic support when the proper level of control is not maintained?

17. You are considering a design change in the prime equipment. What factors should be evaluated in the decision-making process?

18. How would a design change in the prime equipment affect test and support equipment? Spare/repair parts? Facilities? Personnel and training? Technical data? Why is change control important?

19. Why is the transition process from production/construction to user operation so important?

20. What are the logistic support considerations in the transition from production/construction to user operation? Discuss the elements of support.

21. Is the level of logistic support provided when the system/equipment is initially deployed to the various user operational sites the same as or consistent with that recommended for subsequent periods in the life cycle? Why?

22. What is "producibility"?

23. What is "phased logistic support"? What is the major consideration involved?

24. Figure 9-7 represents a reliability characteristic curve for an equipment item. The current delivery requirements and production process results in an item whose reliability characteristics are represented at point A. Assuming that you are allowed to extend the delivery schedule, what would you do to produce an item with a reliability value as represented at point B?

25. What is the main objective of production planning?

26. In the accomplishment of equipment assembly/disassembly tasks as part of production operations (i.e., during the repair and rework cycle), it was noted

that the equipment design lacked certain necessary inherent diagnostic and accessibility features. What would you do to correct the situation?

SYSTEM OPERATION AND SUPPORT

Experience has indicated that when systems first become fully operational, a number of problems are likely to occur, and that significant modifications and procedural adjustments are often required to correct deficiencies. Many of these problems in the past have been related to the inadequacies of support, and fall into any one of the following categories:[1]

1. One or more of the individual elements of logistics is incompatible with the prime equipment (e.g., the prescribed test and support equipment will not perform the proper functions in verifying prime equipment operation or in the performance of maintenance).
2. The depth and extent of support provided is insufficient (e.g., there are not enough of the required type of spares available; the personnel assigned to operate and maintain the equipment are inadequately trained for the job; etc.).
3. The level of support in certain areas is higher than what is actually required (e.g., facilities, personnel, and support equipment are not being fully utilized or there are too many spare parts of a certain type, which results in a higher inventory cost than necessary).

---

[1]Inadequacy in this instance can mean too much support as well as not enough support, both of which are costly.

10

4. The elements of logistic support are incompatible with each other (e.g., the maintenance procedures do not cover the tasks being performed at a given level and the support equipment used in task accomplishment).

Because of the inherent problems at this stage in the life cycle, the number of procedural adjustments and/or equipment modifications required to correct the deficiencies noted has in some instances been extensive and costly. In other words, a major program modification effort has had to be initiated to bring the system up to the level of operation required. In other cases, this has not been technically or economically feasible at this late stage and the system has never been able to fulfill its intended mission objective(s); thus, the results of all of the previously conducted design and development effort have been ineffective.

Realization of these rather conventional problems of the past, particularly with regard to large-scale systems, has caused an increased emphasis in logistic support early in the life cycle. Previous chapters have discussed the level of emphasis required, and implementation of the steps involved has produced beneficial results on many occasions. With the necessary steps accomplished to date, it is hoped that the majority of the problems falling in one or more of the above-defined categories have been eliminated and will not occur when the system becomes fully operational. Certainly, it is unrealistic to assume that *all* related problems have been eliminated, but it is not unrealistic to assume that many of the typical discrepancies occurring in the past have been designed out of the system with application of the proper effort. If this overall objective is met, the functions remaining will consist of (1) operating and supporting the system in the prescribed manner for the life cycle, (2) providing an assessment of system operation and support in terms of performance and effectiveness, and (3) initiating any corrective action as necessary for improvement.

This chapter deals primarily with system/product life-cycle support, and with the continuing assessment and corrective-action process. Specifically, the discussion relates to the establishment of a data collection and analysis function, and the subsequent improvement of the elements of the system as necessary.

10.1. System/Product Support

The requirements for the sustaining day-to-day support of a system are initially identified through the maintenance concept defined in Chapter 4, and subsequently refined through logistic support analysis (LSA), described in Chapter 6. The results of LSA in terms of maintenance levels, personnel quantities and skills, test and support equipment, and so on, are usually included in a formal logistic support plan prepared prior to the start of the production phase, and used as a basis for implementing a life-cycle support capability for the system throughout its operational-use period (refer to Section 9.6A and Chapter 11).

The formal logistic support plan will (1) describe what maintenance activities are to be accomplished, (2) reference the maintenance procedures to be followed, and (3) will identify the resources required. The plan will also identify the number and location of consumer operational sites, the number of customer service representatives (or field service engineers) and their assigned geographical areas of reponsibility, and the number and location of intermediate maintenance shops and the consumer activities supported by each. Further, the plan will designate maintenance reponsibilities by organization (e.g., producer responsibility, user or consumer responsibility, or a combination thereof).

When addressing system/product support responsibilities, a number of different policies may be adopted depending on the type of system, the duration of the operational life cycle, the extent of support anticipated, and the capabilities of the user (consumer) and the producer organizations. Example approaches are noted.

1. All system maintenance activities (at each level of maintenance) will be accomplished by the producer throughout the planned life cycle.
2. All system maintenance activities (at each level of maintenance) will be accomplished by the producer for a x period of time after the system first becomes operational. Subsequently, the user organization will accomplish all maintenance activities.
3. All system maintenance activities (at each level of maintenance) will be accomplished by an outside contractor, under the guidance of the user organization.
4. The user organization will accomplish all maintenance activities designated at the organizational and intermediate levels, while the producer organization will accomplish all maintenance activities designated at the manufacturer or depot levels.
5. The producer will accomplish all maintenance activities associated with items A, B, C and D; the user will accomplish all maintenance activities covering all other items.
6. All system maintenance activities (at each level of maintenance) will be accomplished by the user organization.

In essence, the day-to-day maintenance activities for a given system may be accomplished entirely by the user organization, by the producer, by an outside contractor, or a combination thereof. The decision will be based on a number of factors such as the anticipated maintenance work load, contractual warranty provisions associated with certain elements of the system, the legal implications of product liability, and the general interest on the part of the producer (or user) to provide the services required. In addition, the responsibilities for maintenance may change as the user becomes more familiar with the system and is able to provide the support required. Maintenance and support for a system may be handled any number of ways, either through an existing function within the user's or producer's organization(s) or through a subcontracting arrangement with an outside agency.

10.2. Data Collection, Analysis, and System Evaluation

The assessment of performance and effectiveness of a system requires the availability of operational and maintenance histories of the various system elements. Performance and effectiveness parameters are established early in the life cycle with the development of operational requirements and the maintenance concept. These parameters describe the characteristics of the system that are considered paramount in fulfilling the need objectives.

Now with system deployed and in full operational status, the following questions arise.

1. What is the *true* performance and effectiveness of the system?
2. What is the *true* effectiveness of the logistic support capability?
3. Are the initially specified requirements being met?

Providing answers to these questions requires a formalized data information feedback subsystem with the proper output. A data subsystem must be designed, developed, and implemented to achieve a specific set of objectives, and these objectives must relate directly to the foregoing questions and/ or whatever other questions the system manager needs to answer. The establishment of a data subsystem capability is basically a two-step function to include (1) the identification of requirements and the applications for such, and (2) the design, development, and implementation of a capability that will satisfy the identified requirements.

A. REQUIREMENTS

The purpose of the data information feedback subsystem is twofold.

1. It provides ongoing data that are analyzed to evaluate and assess the performance, effectiveness, operations, maintenance, logistic support capability, and so on, for the system in the field. The system manager needs to know exactly how the system is doing and needs the answer relatively soon. Thus, certain types of information must be provided at designated times throughout the system life cycle.
2. It provides historical data (covering existing systems in the field) that are applicable in the design and development of new systems/ equipments having a similar function and nature. Our engineering growth and potential in the future certainly depends on our ability to capture experiences of the past and subsequently be able to apply the results in terms of "what to do" and "what not to do" in the new design.

Supporting such a subsystem requires a capability that is both responsive to a repetitive need in an expeditious and timely manner (i.e., the manager's need for assessment information), and that incorporates the provisions for data storage and retrieval. It is necessary to determine the specific elements of data required, the frequency of need, and the associated format for data reporting. These factors are combined to identify total volume requirements for the subsystem and the type, quantity, and frequency of data reports.

The elements of data identified are related to the operational and support requirements for the system. An analysis of these elements will provide

Table 10-1. DATA INFORMATION SYSTEM APPLICATIONS (REQUIREMENTS)

1. *General Operational and Support Factors*
   (a) Evaluation of mission requirements and performance measures.
   (b) Verification of system utilization (modes of operation and operating hours).
   (c) Verification of cost/system effectiveness, operational availability, dependability, reliability, maintainability.
   (d) Evaluation of levels and location of maintenance.
   (e) Evaluation of function/tasks by maintenance level and location.
   (f) Verification of repair level policies.
   (g) Verification of frequency distributions for unscheduled maintenance actions and repair times.
2. *Test and Support Equipment*
   (a) Verification of support equipment type and quantity by maintenance level and location.
   (b) Verification of support equipment availability.
   (c) Verification of support equipment utilization (frequency of use, location, percent of time utilized, flexibility of use).
   (d) Evaluation of maintenance requirements for support equipment (scheduled and unscheduled maintenance, downtime, logistic resource requirements).
3. *Supply Support (Spare/Repair Parts)*
   (a) Verification of spare/repair part types and quantities by maintenance level and location.
   (b) Evaluation of supply responsiveness (is a spare available when needed?).
   (c) Verification of item replacement rates, condemnation rates, attrition rates.
   (d) Verification of inventory turnaround and supply pipeline times.
   (e) Evaluation of maintenance requirements for shelf items.
   (f) Evaluation of spare/repair part replacement and inventory policies.
   (g) Identification of shortage risks.
4. *Personnel and Training*
   (a) Verification of personnel quantities and skills by maintenance level and location.
   (b) Verification of elapsed times and manhour expenditures by personnel skill level.
   (c) Evaluation of personnel skill mixes.
   (d) Evaluation of personnel training policies.
   (e) Verification of training equipment and data requirements.
5. *Transportation and Handling*
   (a) Verification of transportation and handling equipment type and quantity by maintenance level and location.
   (b) Verification of availability and utilization of transportation and handling equipment.
   (c) Evaluation of delivery response times.
6. *Facilities*
   (a) Verification of facility adequacy and utilization (operation, maintenance, and training facilities).
   (b) Evaluation of logistics resource requirements for support of operation, maintenance, and training facilities.
7. *Technical Data*
   (a) Verification of adequacy of data coverage (level, accuracy, and method of information presentation) in operating and maintenance manuals.
   (b) Verification of adequancy of field data, collection, analysis, and corrective action sub-system.

certain evaluative and verification type functions covering the characteristics of the system that are to be assessed. A listing of sample applications appropriate in the assessment of system support characteristics is presented in Table 10-1.

Referring to the table, when determining the reliability of an item (i.e., the probability that an item will operate satisfactorily in a given environment for a specified period of time), the data required will include the system operating time-to-failure and the time-to-failure distribution which can be generated from a history of that particular item or a set of identical and independent items. When verifying spare/repair part demand rates, the data required should include a history of all item replacements, system/equipment operating time at replacement, and disposition of the replaced items (whether the item is condemned or repaired and returned to stock). An evaluation of organizational effectiveness will require the identification of assigned personnel by quantity and skill level, the tasks accomplished by the organization, and the manhours and elapsed time expended in task accomplishment. Assessment objectives such as these (comparable to those listed in the table) serve as the basis for the identification of the specific data factors needed.

B. DESIGN, DEVELOPMENT, AND IMPLEMENTATION
OF A DATA SUBSYSTEM CAPABILITY

With the overall subsystem objectives defined, the next step is to identify the specific data factors that must be acquired and the method for acquisition. A format for data collection must be developed and should include both *success* data and *maintenance* data. Success data constitutes information covering system operation and utilization on a day-to-day basis, and the information should be comparable to the factors listed in Table 10-2.

Maintenance data covers each event involving scheduled and unscheduled maintenance. The events are recorded and referenced in system operational information reports, and the factors recorded in each instance are illustrated in Table 10-3.

Table 10-2. SYSTEM SUCCESS DATA

System Operational Information Report
1. Report number, report date, and individual preparing report.
2. System nomenclature, part number, manufacturer, serial number.
3. Description of system operation by date (mission type, profile, and duration).
4. Equipment utilization by date (operating time, cycles of operation, etc.).
5. Description of personnel, transportation and handling equipment, and facilities required for system operation.
6. Recording of maintenance events by date and time (reference maintenance event reports).

Table 10-3. SYSTEM MAINTENANCE DATA

Maintenance Event Report

1. *Administrative data*
   (a) Event report number, report date, and individual preparing report.
   (b) Work order number.
   (c) Work area and time of work (month, day, hour).
   (d) Activity (organization) identification.
 2. *System factors*
   (a) Equipment part number and manufacturer.
   (b) Equipment serial number.
   (c) System operating time when event occurred (when discovered).
   (d) Segment of mission when event occurred.
   (e) Description of event (describe symptom of failure for unscheduled actions).
 3. *Maintenance factors*
   (a) Maintenance requirement (repair, calibration, servicing, etc.).
   (b) Description of maintenance tasks.
   (c) Maintenance downtime (MDT).
   (d) Active maintenance times (Mct_i and Mpt_i)
   (e) Maintenance delays (time awaiting spare part, delay for test equipment, work stoppage, awaiting personnel assistance, delay for weather, etc.).
 4. *Logistics factors*
   (a) Start and stop times for each maintenance technician by skill level.
   (b) Technical manual or maintenance procedure used (procedure number, paragraph, date, comments on procedure adequacy).
   (c) Test and support equipment used (item nomenclature, part number, manufacturer, serial number, time of item usage, operating time on test equipment when used).
   (d) Description of facilities used.
   (e) Description of replacement parts (type and quantity).
     i. Nomenclature, part number, manufacturer, serial number, and operating time on replaced item. Describe disposition.
     ii. Nomenclature, part number, manufacturer, serial number, and operating time on installed item.
 5. *Other information*
 Include any additional data considered appropriate and related to the maintenance event.

The format for data collection may vary considerably, as there is no set method for the accomplishment of such, and the information desired may be different for each system. However, most of the factors in Tables 10-2 and 10-3 are common for all systems and must be addressed in the design of a new data subsystem. In any event, the following provisions should apply.

1. The data collection forms should be simple to understand and complete (preferably on single sheets) as the task of recording the data may be accomplished under adverse environmental conditions by a variety of personnel skill levels. If the forms are difficult to under-

stand, they will not be completed properly (if at all) and the needed data will not be available.

2. The factors specified on each form must be clear and concise, and not require a lot of interpretation and manipulation to obtain. The right type of data must be collected.

3. The factors specified must have a meaning in terms of application. The usefulness of each factor must be verified.

These considerations are extremely important and cannot be over-emphasized. All of the analytical methods, prediction techniques, models, and so on, discussed earlier have little meaning without the proper input data. Our ability to evaluate alternatives and predict in the future depends on the availability of good historical data, and the source of such stems from the type of data information feedback subsystem developed at this stage. The subsystem must not only incorporate the forms for recording the right type of data, but must consider the personnel factors (skill levels, motivation, etc.) involved in the data recording process. The person who must complete the appropriate form(s) must understand the system and the purposes for which the data are being collected. If this person is not properly motivated to do a good thorough job in recording events, the resulting data will of course be highly suspect.

Once that the appropriate data forms are distributed and completed by the responsible line organizations, a means must be provided for the retrieval, formatting, sorting, and processing of the data for reporting purposes. Field data are collected and sent to a designated centralized facility for analysis and processing. The results are disseminated to management for decision making and entered into a data bank for retention and possible future use.

C. SYSTEM EVALUATION AND CORRECTIVE ACTION

Figure 10-1 illustrates the system evaluation and corrective-action loop. The evaluation aspect responds to the type of subjects listed in Table 10-1, and can address both the system as an entity or individual segments of the system on an independent basis. Figure 10-2 presents some typical examples of evaluation factors. The evaluation approach and the analytical techniques (i.e., tools) used are basically the same as described in Chapter 6 and Appendix C with the only difference being the data input. The evaluation effort can be applied on a continuing basis to provide certain system measures at designated points throughout the life cycle (see *A* and *C* of Figure 10-2), or it may constitute a *one-time* investigation.

Problem areas are identified at various stages in the evaluation, and are reviewed in terms of the necessity for corrective action. Referring to Figure 10-2(*B*), Subsystem *E* is a likely candidate for investigation since the MMH/

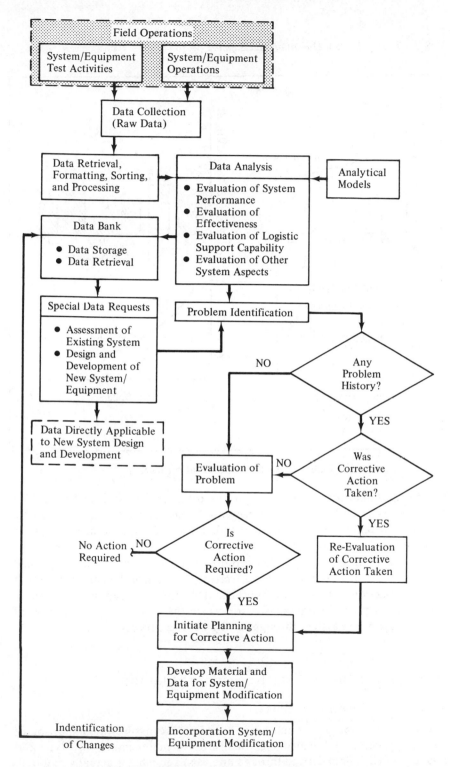

Figure 10-1. System evaluation and corrective action loop.

297

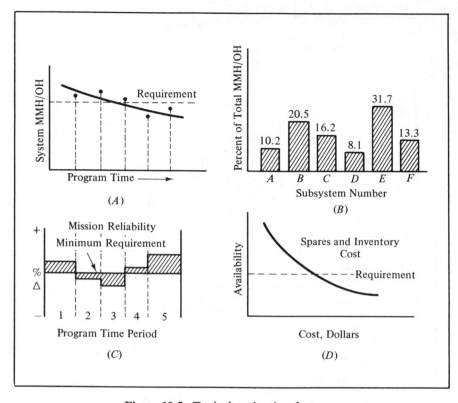

Figure 10-2. Typical evaluation factors.

OH for that item constitutes 31.7% of the total system value. In Figure 10-2 (*C*), one may wish to investigate Program Time Period 3 to determine why the mission reliability was so poor at that time. Corrective action may be accomplished in response to a system/equipment deficiency (i.e., the equipment fails to meet the specified requirements), or may be accomplished to improve system performance, effectiveness, and/or logistic support. If corrective action is to be accomplished, the necessary planning and implementation steps are a prerequisite to ensure the complete compatibility of all elements of the system throughout the change process.

10.3. Evaluation of Logistic Support Elements

A. TEST AND SUPPORT EQUIPMENT

The evaluation of test and support equipment involves a comparison of what is procured and available at each level of maintenance (i.e., type and quantity of each item derived through analysis) and what is actually required.

The initial determination of requirements in this area is accomplished in LSA discussed in Chapter 6. These requirements are based on the following (as applicable).

1. Random equipment arrival rates or the predicted quantity of items returned for maintenance. This factor is generally determined from an exponential distribution for major items (e.g., Unit *A* of System *XYZ*) considering primary failures, secondary failures, suspected failures, and so on. A Poisson probability distribution can be used as a density function to predict the quantity of returns within each major item.
2. Equipment item active maintenance times. The time required to test the arriving items is also predicted through the use of a probability density function. Automatic testing is essentially constant, but the other aspects of the maintenance cycle follow a log-normal distribution.
3. Support equipment design characteristics. This includes support equipment availability, equipment warm-up time, test setup time, and the ease in performing the actual maintenance operations.
4. The external work and environmental factors to include the length of the workday, personnel effectiveness, noise, temperature, and related human factors.

Through the use of a Monte Carlo sampling process, a model may be generated to simulate time demands on an item of support equipment. Probabilities are developed to cover queue length (i.e., waiting line) and the turnaround time of a typical item scheduled for maintenance. Loading studies are accomplished and an optimum quantity of support equipment is recommended and provisioned for operational use.

When the system becomes operational, it is imperative that an assessment of the above factors be made. Historical data are collected using a recording format similar to Table 10-4. After a designated period of time, arrival rates, the queue length or waiting time, and support equipment utilization are determined from actual field experience. In addition, support equipment

Table 10-4. SUPPORT EQUIPMENT USAGE RECORD

Item Returned for Maintenance or Requiring Support	Time in Work Area		Time on Support Equipment		Time Off Support Equipment	
	Date	Hour	Date	Hour	Date	Hour
Unit *A*	12/10/72	10:30 a.m.	12/11/72	11:30 a.m.	12/11/72	1:45 p.m.
Assembly 2345	1/3/73	2:30 p.m.	1/3/73	2:30 p.m.	1/3/73	3:52 p.m.

availability and the logistics resources required for support equipment maintenance can be evaluated.

If an existing item of support equipment at a given level of maintenance is not adequately utilized, it may be appropriate to recommend a change in the detailed maintenance plan. With a lower number of arrivals than initially anticipated, it might be feasible to shift the repair of the applicable items to a higher level of maintenance (e.g., from intermediate to depot). This will reduce the quantity of support equipment in the field and thus affect a probable savings in life-cycle cost. The final determination will result from a level of repair analysis (see Chapter 6) using the actual field data collected. On the other hand, if the queue is long and the support equipment availability is inadequate, then it may be feasible to procure an additional quantity of like items for the same geographical installation. The intent is to evaluate each facet of system operation and maintenance and verify that the proper type and quantity of support equipment are available at the right location. The results of this evaluation must be consistent with the overall system performance and effectiveness requirements, and yet support an approach that reflects the lowest life-cycle cost.

B. Supply Support

Supply support constitutes all materials, data, personnel, and related activities associated with the requirements, provisioning, and acquisition of spare/repair parts and the sustaining maintenance of inventories for support of the system throughout its life cycle. Specifically, this includes:

1. Initial and sustaining requirements for spares, repair parts, and consumables for the prime equipment. Spares are major replacement items and are repairable while repair parts are nonrepairable smaller components. Consumables refer to fuel, oil, lubricants, liquid oxygen, nitrogen, and so on.
2. Initial and sustaining requirements for spares, repair parts, material, and consumables for the various elements of logistic support (i.e., test and support equipment, transportation and handling equipment, training equipment, and facilities).
3. Facilities required for the storage of spares, repair parts, and consumables. This involves consideration of space requirements, location, and environment.
4. Personnel requirements for the accomplishment of supply support activities such as provisioning, cataloging, receipt and issue, inventory management and control, shipment, and disposal of material.
5. Technical data requirements for supply support to include initial and sustaining provisioning data, catalogs, material stock lists, receipt and issue reports, material disposition reports, and so on.

Supply support is applicable to the early test and evaluation activities (described in Chapter 8), sustaining system/equipment operations, and during equipment phase-down (or phase-out) toward the end of the life cycle. Supply support is *dynamic* and must be responsive to changes in system operation, deployment, utilization, effectiveness requirements, repair policies, and environment. It also must be responsive to prime equipment modifications.

1. Determination of requirements. Initial requirements for spares, repair parts, and consumables stem from the logistic support analysis (described in Chapter 6 and Appendix B). LSA supports the maintenance concept in identifying functions and tasks by level, repair policies (i.e., repair or discard at failure), individual spare/repair part types, and item replacement frequencies. These factors are combined to indicate supply support requirements for each geographical location and for the system as an entity. Major considerations include (a) spares and repair parts covering actual item replacements occurring as a result of corrective and preventive maintenance actions; (b) an additional stock level of spares to compensate for repairable items in the process of undergoing maintenance; (c) an additional stock level of spares and repair parts to compensate for the pipeline and procurement lead times required for item acquisition; and (d) an additional stock level of spares to compensate for the condemnation or scrapage of repairable items.

Addressing spare/repair part requirements from an optimum standpoint consists of solving three basic problems: (1) determine the range or variety of spares; (2) determine the optimum quantity for each line item; and (3) evaluate the impact of item selection and quantities on the effectiveness of the system. Items must be justified by establishing a demand prediction and identifying the consequences of not having the spare/repair part in stock. Demand predictions are based on the Poisson distribution approach discussed in Chapter 2. Some items are considered more critical than others in terms of impact on mission success. The criticality of an item is generally based on its function in the equipment and not necessarily its acquisition cost. However, the justification for these critical items may vary somewhat depending on the type of system and the nature of its mission.

The objectives in determining spare/repair part requirements are to identify item replacements; determine item replacement and repair frequencies, repair and resupply cycle times, condemnation factors, unit cost; and to develop a supply support capability that will:

a. Not impair the effectiveness of the system by having equipment on a nonoperationally ready status due to supply.
b. Reflect a least cost inventory profile by not having unnecessary items in the inventory, and minimize outstanding back orders. Large inventories may be costly.

In the early design and development stages of the system life cycle, the objectives listed above are evaluated through analyses and the use of models (see Chapter 6 and Appendix C). The supply support capability is simulated with the intent of arriving at an optimum balance between a stock-out situation and the proper level of inventory. Stock-out conditions promote the cannibalization of parts from other equipments (which may have further detrimental effects on the system), and/or the necessity of initiating high priority orders from the supplier (requiring expeditious and special handling). Both options are costly.

The purpose of the analysis and simulation effort is to evaluate the best among a number of alternative approaches. When arriving at a recommended solution, the results are used in the initial provisioning of spares, repair parts, and consumables. In other words, the appropriate material items are acquired for support of the system for a specified period of time when the system first becomes operation. Reprovisioning is then accomplished as appropriate, using experience data from the field, to cover successive periods throughout the life cycle.

2. Provisioning and acquisition of material.   Given the basic requirements for spare/repair parts and consumables, a plan is developed as part of the formal logistic support plan for the provisioning of the appropriate material. Provisioning constitutes the source coding of items, the preparation of stock lists and procurement documentation, and the acquisition and delivery of material.[2] Usually it is not feasible to provision enough support for the entire life cycle of the system as too much capital would be tied up in inventory. The cost of inventory maintenance is high and much waste could occur, particularly if equipment changes are implemented and certain components become obsolete. In addition, initial provisioning is generally based on the estimated maintenance factors provided in LSA (i.e., replacement rates, repair and recycle times, pipeline times, etc.). These are only estimates derived from predictions and as such may be in error.[3] Estimation errors will of course have a significant impact on the quantity of items in inventory; thus,

---

[2]Source coding basically applies to the determination of whether an item is repairable or nonrepairable and, if repairable, where it is to be repaired. This information is determined by the logistic support analysis (see Chapter 6 and Appendix B), and the results are coded and included in the provisioning documentation. Procurement documentation includes identification of suppliers, pricing information, scheduling data, lead times, and so on.

[3]Experience on many systems has indicated that the correlation between predicted maintenance factors and actual field results has been rather low. As we acquire more data and experience relative to the input requirements and their relationships, it is hoped that our predictions will continue to improve in the future as they have in the past decade.

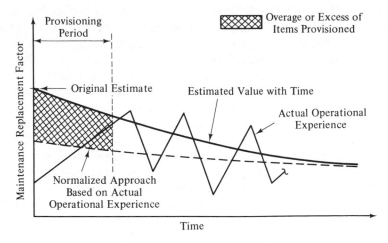

Figure 10-3. Maintenance replacement factors.

provisioning should be accomplished at shorter intervals to allow for the necessary adjustments based on actual field experience.

Figure 10-3 illustrates the possible differences between an early estimate of the maintenance replacement factor, actual operational experience, and a normalized set of values based on the operational experience. The figure shows the variation of estimates over time. An original estimate and its anticipated variation with time is made and used in LSA and associated simulation efforts involving supply support. Initial provisioning is accomplished using this estimate as the basis for determining the quantity of different items in the inventory.[4] The system is then deployed and operational field data may indicate a different level of item usage. Actual usage may be erratic at first, but ultimately may be represented by a normalized curve as shown in the figure. Assuming that initial provisioning is based on the period of time indicated, there will be an excess of items in the inventory. Maintenance factors can be adjusted for the next provisioning period and the excess stockage can be used during that time. On the other hand, the provisioning of too little support results in the probability of causing the system to be inoperative due to stock-out, which can also be costly.

Generally, a realistic period of time is specified (e.g., 6 months, 1 year, 2 years, etc.) and enough spare/repair parts are procured to cover the demand requirements anticipated. Sometimes the quantities of different items procured will be adjusted for economic reasons. For instance, it may be feasible to acquire a set quantity of an item in order to realize a price break or to avoid excessive supplier production startup and shutdown costs. If the quantity is

---

[4]Each item type may be represented by a different curve (as illustrated in Figure 10-3).

excessive and the applicable items are not consumed during the selected support period, the residue may be carried into the next period of support.

The provisioning concept will vary somewhat between major high value items and smaller repair parts.[5] In addition, the procurement policies may differ for items with different usage rates. Fast-moving items may be procured locally near the point of usage such as the intermediate maintenance shop, while slower moving items stocked at the depot may be acquired from a remotely located supplier as the pipeline and procurement lead times are not as critical.

The planning for major high-value items is quite detailed and generally receives management scrutiny at every step in the process. This is required for both strategic and economic reasons. First, the supply status of these items influences to a great extent the supply levels of a large portion of the smaller repair parts in the inventory. Second, the dollar value of the larger items is significant and may even exceed the total value of the hundreds of repair parts and accessories needed for their continued support. In other words, a relatively small number of items may represent a large percentage of the total inventory value. Thus, greater emphasis is placed in the computation of replacement factors and consumption rates to arrive at a *true demand*. In addition, the provisioning time periods may vary from item to item to assure an economic order quantity that is compatible with the actual usage rate. In some instances, a given quantity of items are maintained in stock to compensate for repair and recycle times, pipeline and procurement lead times, and so on, and new quantities are ordered on a one-for-one basis as existing items are withdrawn from the inventory.

For other items such as common spares and repair parts, particularly where large quantities are involved over the life cycle, the economic order principle is applied. The ultimate goal is to have the correct amount and type of supplies available for the lowest total cost. Procurement costs vary with the quantity of orders placed. The principle involves the optimization between the placing of many orders resulting in high material acquisition costs and placing orders less frequently while maintaining a higher level of inventory causing increasing inventory maintenance and carrying costs. In other words, ordering creates procurement cost while inventory creates carrying cost. The economic order principle equates the *cost to order* to the *cost to hold*, and the point at which the combined costs are at a minimum indicates the desired size of order. The economic order principle and inventory profiles were discussed in Section 2.3.

---

[5]High value items are those components with a relatively high unit acquisition cost, and should be provisioned on an individual basis. In addition, special packing and handling may be required. The classification of high value items will vary with the program, and may be established at a certain dollar value (i.e., all components whose unit cost exceeds x dollars are considered as high-value items).

The illustration in Figure 2-17 is a theoretical representation of an inventory cycle for a given item. Actually, demands are not always constant and quite often the reorder cycle changes with time. Figure 2-18 presents a situation that is more realistic.

In the accomplishment of provisioning, the most feasible approach is to employ the theoretical EOQ model illustrated in Figure 2-17 for each applicable class of items until such time that enough data are collected to enable a definition of an actual inventory profile. When this is available, the factors in Figure 2-17 can be adjusted as applicable to fit the actual situation.

The demand for spare/repair parts and the provisioning factors illustrated in Figures 2-17 and 2-18 lead to the preparation of stock item lists, procurement data, inventory records, and so on. These data items are oriented to the line organization responsible for system support. The factors used will be different for the intermediate shop and the depot since the demands, procurement lead times, pipeline, and so on, vary.

3. Inventory maintenance and control. As the system progresses through its life cycle, data are collected and analyzed to assess the effectiveness of the supply support capability. The object is to establish a historical base for individual item demand rates and to adjust the provisioning factors as required to improve supply support.

The operational demand based on experience may assume a jagged plot as illustrated in Figure 10-3. Trends and averages may be identified using statistical techniques (e.g., exponential smoothing, method of least squares, etc.), and the results are included in an updating of the provisioning data for future spare/repair part reorders. At the same time, the inventory is evaluated in terms of current assets, average months of supply on hand, costs to procure material and maintain the inventory, quantity of orders, and so on. A sample data sheet format is presented in Table 10-5. Inventory status for each item at each supply point is maintained on a continuing basis.

In the event that historical experience indicates that the level of inventory is insufficient to support operational needs, the EOQ and quantity of

Table 10-5. INVENTORY STATUS RECORD

Item	Annual Demands (D)	Average Months of Supply on Hand (Month)	Quantity of Orders per Year (N)	Average Active Inventory ($)	Cost to Procure ($)	Cost of Inventory Maintenance ($)
Part 234	12	0.3	2	721	35	21
Assembly *A*	18	6.7	3	681	72	43

orders are recomputed and the required additional stock is procured. On the other hand, if it appears that the stock level is excessive, either one of two actions may be required. First, the provisioning factors are adjusted and future orders are curtailed until the inventory is depleted to a desired level. Second, a destockage plan may be implemented to remove a designated quantity of the serviceable assets on hand. In any event, criteria should be established covering both the desired upper and lower levels of inventory, and the evaluative and control aspects should employ this criteria in the measurement of supply support effectiveness.

4. Disposition of material.   Repairable spares that are condemned (for one reason or another) and nonrepairable parts, when removed from the system and replaced, are generally shipped to the depot or the supplier facility for disposition. These items are inspected, disassembled where possible, and the items that may have further use will be salvaged, reclaimed, and recycled. The residue will be disposed of in an expedient and economical manner consistent with environmental and ecological requirements.

C. PERSONNEL AND TRAINING

Personnel and training requirements are initially derived through (1) an operator and maintenance functional analysis, (2) a detailed task analysis identifying the quantity and skills required, and (3) a comparison of the personnel requirements for the system with the personnel quantities and skills available in the user organization. Operator personnel requirements are usually derived from a human factors task analysis, and maintenance personnel requirements are identified in LSA. The difference between system requirements and the user personnel skill levels scheduled to operate and maintain the system in the field is covered through a combination of formal and on-the-job (OJT) training. Training requirements include both the training of personnel initially assigned to the system and the training of replacement personnel throughout the life cycle. Training in both operator and maintenance functions (at all levels) is accomplished.

When the system becomes operational, data are collected at all levels for each organization responsible for the accomplishment of system operation and maintenance functions. The object is to assess organizational effectiveness on a continuing basis. Specifically, we are interested in the quantity of personnel required to do the job, the maintenance manhours expended, the attrition rate and whether it increases or decreases with time, error rates in the performance of job functions, and general morale. An analysis of such data will indicate whether the initial personnel selection criteria are adequate and whether the training program as designed is satisfactory. If error rates are high, then either additional training is required or a change in the basic system/equipment design is necessary. High attrition rates may necessitate a continuous formal training effort. On the other hand, if the system is not complex and attrition and error rates are low, then it may be feasible to eliminate the program for formal training and maintain only the requirement for a specified amount of OJT. Personnel operations in the field are evaluated using the same approach as the industrial engineering and quality control organizations use in monitoring production and/or construction operations (see Chapter 9).

D. TECHNICAL DATA

Technical data include all operating and maintenance procedures, special test procedures, installation instructions, checklists, change notices and change procedures, and so on, for the prime equipment, support equipment, training equipment, transportation and handling equipment, and facilities. The requirements for data coverage stem from engineering design data and LSA. Operator and maintenance functions by organization, repair policies, and logistic support resource requirements are identified. Technical data are prepared to cover all system operations and logistic support requirements in the field.

Subsequent to data preparation, the appropriate documentation is used in support of test and evaluation activities (Types 1, 2, 3, and 4 testing described in Chapter 8), production/construction functions (Chapter 9), and field operations. Problems are noted relative to actual documentation errors, and difficulties concerning prime equipment and logistic support activities are recorded. For instance, if a particular function is difficult to accomplish, it may be due to the fact that the documented procedure is inadequate relative to the scope of coverage; thus, additional information should be prepared and incorporated through a change notice. In addition, technical data should be updated as required to cover prime equipment modifications, revised maintenance policies, and changes in the elements of logistic support.

E. SUMMARY

The preceding paragraphs discuss some of the major factors involved in the evaluation of the elements of logistic support. Although not all elements are covered, the information presented does cover facets that require particular attention. The objective is to design and implement a data information feedback subsystem that will enable a true assessment of the logistic support capability. All elements of logistics must be evaluated both individually and on an integrated basis. Each individual element directly impacts the others; thus, when changes occur (to correct deficiencies and/or for system improvement), the impact of the change must be reflected throughout.

10.4. System Modification

When a change occurs in a procedure, the prime equipment, or an element of logistic support, the change in most instances will affect many different elements of the system. Procedural changes will impact personnel and training requirements and necessitate a change in the technical data (equipment operating and/or maintenance instructions). Hardware changes will affect spare/repair parts, test and support equipment, technical data, and training requirements. Each change must be thoroughly evaluated in terms of its impact on other elements of the system prior to a decision on whether or not to incorporate the change. The feasibility of incorporating a change will depend on the extensiveness of the change, its impact on the system's ability to accomplish its mission, the time in the life cycle when the change can be incorporated, and the cost of change implementation. A minimum amount of evaluation and planning are required in order to make a rational decision on whether the change is feasible.

If a change is to be incorporated, the necessary change control procedures must be implemented. The various components of the system (including all of the elements of logistic support) must track. Otherwise, the probability of inadequate logistic support and unnecessary waste is high. The configuration change control and the change cycle are discussed in Section 9.5. The concepts and concerns in the production/construction stage are equally as appropriate in the operational phase. In fact, a change involving the operational system is more critical since we are dealing with a later stage in the life cycle. Changes will usually be more costly as the life-cycle progresses.

10.5. System Retirement and Material Disposal

System retirement, phase-out, and the disposal of material no longer required in the operational inventory is a subject not too well covered in the literature. It is common to address the design and development of a system and the operation of that system; however, quite often the phase-out and subsequent disposition of that system is not adequately considered until the time arrives to do something about it!

Realistically, system phase-out and the disposal of material is a definite part of the life cycle. In fact, nonrepairables are removed from the inventory as equipment failures occur in the field. The phase-out and disposition of material should be considered in the early conceptual and advanced development phases of a program. The planning for phase-out and disposal should be responsive to the following questions.

1. What should be done to equipment phased out of the inventory and where should it be accomplished?

2. At what rate should obsolete items be phased out of the inventory?
3. How is disposability considered in the system/equipment design process and what measures are used?
4. How much of the equipment can be salvaged and used for other purposes? Can the material be processed, converted, and used in the manufacture of another product?
5. Is the method of disposal consistent with ecological and environmental requirements? What are the effects on the environment?
6. What logistic support requirements are necessary to accomplish phase-out and disposal functions?

System/equipment phase-out and material disposal is another significant stage in the life cycle. There are functions to be accomplished involving transportation and handling, disassembly, decomposition, processing, and so on. Associated with the completion of these functions are the requirements for logistic support (i.e., transportation and handling equipment, personnel, facilities, and technical procedures). These requirements are identified through a functional analysis and LSA as applied to this stage of the life cycle. Depending on the type of system and the quantity of equipment in the inventory, the logistic support requirements can be significant; thus, the system program manager must address system phase-out and material disposal in the same level of detail as with any other stage in the life cycle. This area is initially covered in the early system design stage (through the establishment of design disposability criteria), and is subsequently included in the formal logistic support plan prepared in the detail design and development phase.

QUESTIONS AND PROBLEMS

1. Assuming that the objectives of logistic support have been met in a satisfactory manner in the earlier program phases, what are the logistic support functions in the operational use phase?
2. How would you verify the adequacy of the following:
   (a) Spare and repair parts?
   (b) Test and support equipment?
   (c) Frequency distributions for unscheduled maintenance actions?
   (d) Personnel quantities and skill levels?
   (e) Operating and maintenance procedures?
3. What data are required to measure the following:
   (a) Cost effectiveness?
   (b) System effectiveness?
   (c) Operational availability?
   (d) Life-cycle cost?
4. A good field data subsystem serves what purposes?

5. Why is system success data important? What type of information is required?

6. Why is change control so important? How do system changes affect logistic support?

7. How does the design of test and support equipment affect the quantity of same?

8. How does the type and quantity of support equipment available affect spare and repair part requirements?

9. What is a "queue"? How does it influence spare and repair part requirements?

10. How do the maintenance requirements for support equipment affect prime equipment availability?

11. What considerations must be addressed in determining the proper quantity of spares and repair parts for a given stock location? How are spare part requirements justified?

12. Some spare/repair parts are considered to have a higher priority (in importance) than others. What factor(s) determines this priority?

13. If the cannibalization of items from other equipment is practiced on a regular basis, what will be the likely effects on the system?

14. How are maintenance replacement factors determined? How are they adjusted to reflect a realistic support posture? How do replacement factors relate with MTBM and MTBF?

15. Referring to Figure 2-17, what happens to the EOQ when the demand increases? What happens when there are outstanding backorders? What factors are included in production lead time?

16. What factors determine the level of safety stock?

17. What are "high-value items"? How are they classified?

18. How would you measure organizational effectiveness?

19. How would you measure human reliability?

20. Select a system of your choice and develop a data collection and feedback capability. Include an example of the data collection format proposed. Describe the data analysis, evaluation, and corrective action loop. How would you make it work?

21. How would you consider equipment disposability in the design process? How would you determine the cost of disposal?

22. Determine the economic order quantity of an item for inventory replenishment when
    (a) The cost per unit is $100.
    (b) The cost of preparing a shipment and sending a truck to the warehouse is $25.
    (c) The estimated cost of holding the inventory, including capital tied up, is 25% of the inventory value.
    (d) The annual demand is 200 units. Assume that the cost per order and the inventory carrying charge are fixed.

23. Refer to Figure 2-17 and assume that production of an item occurs incrementally and that inventory replenishment is accomplished as each item is produced. The inventory level for the economic lot size model follows the illustration below.

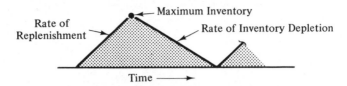

Assume that d is the annual rate of demand for the item and is constant, p the annual rate of production for the item and is constant, Q the size of the production lot (quantity of units), and L lead time and is constant. Write the equation (in terms of the above factors) for

(a) The rate of inventory replenishment.

(b) The rate of inventory depletion.

(c) Maximum inventory value.

(d) Average inventory value.

(e) Total annual cost.

24. What is meant by "spare/repair parts provisioning"?

LOGISTIC SUPPORT MANAGEMENT

Logistic support management involves the planning, organization, direction, and control of all functions and activities discussed in previous chapters. Management responsibilities commence with the early phases of logistics planning at system inception and extend through system operational use and the ultimate equipment retirement from the inventory. The form or activity emphasis in management throughout the system life cycle will vary from program to program depending on the type of system and its mission, whether new design and development are required, schedule and budget constraints, and many other related factors. For the purposes of discussion, five basic program phases are assumed.

1. *Conceptual Phase.* The need for a system is defined and the technical basis for an acquisition program is established through feasibility studies. Basic operation and support concepts are identified, and early logistic support planning commences.
2. *Advance Development Phase.* The system configuration is defined along with program objectives, performance parameters, major areas of risk, system alternatives, and acquisition strategy. Logistic support analyses are accomplished to verify early design concepts, and a preliminary logistic support plan is developed.
3. *Detail Design and Development Phase.* The system, including all

11

items necessary for its support, is designed and tested from a set of specifications. Reliability, maintainability, human factors, and logistics are major considerations in the design process. Engineering models and prototype equipments are fabricated and tested to determine expected operational effectiveness, the degree of supportability, and producibility. A formal logistic support plan is developed.

4. *Production and/or Construction Phase.* The system with its associated support (e.g., test and support equipment, spare/repair parts, training equipment, software, data, etc.) is produced for operational use. Personnel are trained and assigned to perform system operator and maintenance functions. Further, those activities which support material flow, product distribution, and warehousing functions are implemented (i.e., the activities classified under "industrial" or "business" logistics).

5. *Operational Use Phase.* The operating system with associated elements of logistic support is deployed for operational use by the consumer and sustained by remote field units. The system mission is accomplished.

6. *System Retirement Phase.* The system is retired from operational use and equipment is phased out of the inventory, recycled, and/or dispositioned as appropriate.

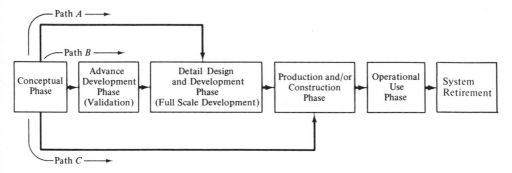

Figure 11-1. Typical program phases.

The program phase relationship may assume a variety of patterns as illustrated in Figure 11-1.

The extent that a system is processed through the various phases is dependent on the degree of system definition and the associated risks involved. If there is a need for a highly sophisticated system where the technical state of the art is being advanced (i.e., there are many unknowns and the risks are high), system development may proceed through all phases with a program review being scheduled after each of the early phases. The proper checkpoints are provided at designated times in the program (i.e., end of conceptual, advance development, and detail design and development phases) to allow for decisions on whether to proceed to the next phase. In other words, a system development effort can be closely evaluated in terms of progress toward meeting the need objectives. Contractual arrangements may be based on a phase-by-phase policy, allowing the consumer to stop the program in the event that the system design and development effort is not meeting expectations.

On the other hand, the system configuration may be well enough defined during a conceptual effort to allow for an early transition directly into production. In this instance, there may be a minimum of system design required and most of the lower indenture equipment items may be off-the-shelf. In other words, the risks are low and processing a system through all of the program phases is unnecessary. The program phasing should be tailored to the system, and the depth of coverage required is determined during the conceptual phase as a result of feasibility studies and associated planning.

11.1. Logistics Planning

As a major element of a program, logistics is associated with each of the six program phases. The tasks to be performed during each phase are defined in Figure 11-2. When a system is processed through all of the phases (path *B*, Figure 11-1), these tasks are fairly representative of what should be accom-

Conceptual Phase	Advance Development Phase	Detail Design and Development Phase	Production and/or Construction Phase	Operational Use Phase
A1. Identify need and accomplish feasibility studies. A2. Define system operational requirements—mission definition, performance parameters, deployment, life-cycle, utilization, effectiveness factors (R, M, A), environment. A3. Define support (maintenance) concept—echelons, maintenance site locations, support effectiveness factors (R, M, Logistics), environment. A4. Define basic logistic support goals/constraints—test and support equipment, spare/repair parts, personnel, facilities, data. A5. Accomplish initial logistics planning—define program tasks, schedules, acquisition sources, funding, organizational structure. A6. Participate in conceptual program/design review.	B1. Accomplish functional analysis, optimization, synthesis, and system definition—operator functions, maintenance functions. B2. Accomplish allocation of reliability, maintainability, human factors, and logistic support requirements. B3. Establish supportability design criteria (R, M, H.F., Logistics). B4. Accomplish preliminary logistic support analysis—evaluation of alternatives using cost effectiveness, life-cycle cost, maintenance analysis, and logistics modeling techniques. B5. Accomplish design liaison and support services—reliability and maintainability analysis, design consultation, project training, design data review, predictions. B6. Prepare preliminary logistic support plan—program tasks, schedules, funding, organization, direction, control methods. Include reliability, maintainability, and human factors program plans. B7. Participate in system design reviews.	C1. Accomplish design liaison and support services—application of design criteria, trade-off studies, project training, reliability and maintainability predictions, utilization of design aids, design data review, feedback and corrective action. C2. Accomplish logistic support analysis—system/equipment design evaluation and determination of logistic support requirements (test and support equipment, spare/repair parts, personnel and training transportation and handling, technical data, facilities). C3. Prepare provisioning data for the acquisition of logistic support elements. C4. Plan, implement, and participate in test and evaluation (Types 1 and 2 tests)—data collection, analysis, and corrective action. C5. Prepare formal logistic support plan (individual logistic element plans). C6. Participate in formal equipment design reviews.	D1. Fabricate, assembly, test, inspect and deliver prime equipment, and associated elements of logistic support (hardware and software)—test and support equipment, spare/repair parts, training equipment, data, facilities. D2. Prepare operational sites for receipt of production items—initial personnel training, supply support, facility development, etc. D3. Plan, implement, and participate in test and evaluation (Types 2 and 3 tests)—data collection, analysis, and corrective action. D4. Update logistic support analysis data to enable evaluation of the system and verify logistic factors for use in reprovisioning. D5. Initiate transition from producer to consumer operation.	E1. Operate and support (maintain) prime equipment and associated elements of logistic support in the field. E2. Provide interim support capability (as required) until full operational capability is attained—field service engineers, specialized repair capability, preliminary data, etc. E3. Initiate and maintain field data collection system—data analysis evaluation, and corrective action. E4. Evaluate impact of system/equipment modifications in the field. Plan and implement modification program as necessary. E5. Update logistic support analysis and accomplish reprovisioning as required to support the system throughout its life-cycle. E6. Plan and implement equipment phase-out and disposition program.

Figure 11-2. Typical program tasks for logistic support.

plished. However, the depth of coverage will certainly be less for a small radar system than for a large airplane. Again, the proper tailoring is extremely important. The objective is to accomplish the right task to the depth necessary at the time required—not too late or too early. Figure 11-3 presents a flow process showing the input–output relationships of the tasks identified in Figure 11-2.

When a system is fairly well defined and all phases are not necessary (path *A* or *C*, Figure 11-1), many of the tasks indicated in Figure 11-2 are still considered appropriate but may be shifted in schedule. For example, analyses and predictions may be appropriate during the conceptual phase prior to entering production (see path *C*, Figure 11-1). Therefore, a reallocation of tasks will be necessary to adjust to this specific condition.

Since logistics is a major facet of the overall system and interrelates with many other program activities, it is difficult to separate *pure logistic* tasks from some of the program functions which are often considered as *nonlogistic* oriented. Logistic activities complement the basic system design and development process from the beginning. The tasks listed in Figure 11-2 are presented in such a manner that logistics-oriented functions are directly tied in with the overall activities of a typical program.

Logistic activities primarily constitute planning and support in the analyses and design functions during the early program phases. Design alternatives are evaluated and a preferred approach is selected. A major impact on the selection process is the effect of the various configurations being considered on total logistic support. This effect must be a major consideration in decision making in order to produce effective results. The impact of logistics on the design process is primarily realized through formalized reliability, maintainability, and human factors program functions. This approach is reflected in Figure 11-2.

As the program progresses and the design configuration becomes relatively fixed, logistics assumes the more conventional role of (1) determining logistic support requirements from available system design data, (2) accomplishing the provisioning and acquisition of those items identified through analysis, and (3) providing the necessary support of the system throughout its life cycle. These functions have been recognized for some time.

The concept presented herein is based on the initial planning for logistic support during the early conceptual phase (Figure 11-2, task *A*5). As program requirements and associated plans are developed, it is necessary to accomplish logistics planning to ensure the proper consideration of the prime equipment and its associated support on an integrated basis. Logistics planning functions are to:

1. Interpret system requirements for design supportability and ultimate logistic support. This is accomplished through feasibility studies and definition of the maintenance concept and support policies.

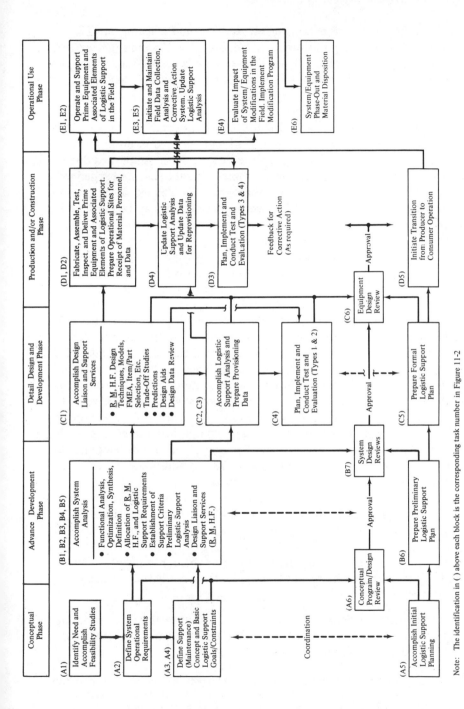

Figure 11-3. System life-cycle process.

Note: The identification in ( ) above each block is the corresponding task number in Figure 11-2

2. Identify program functions/tasks, and develop a listing of tasks in a manner similar to the presentation in Figure 11-2. As indicated earlier, the tasks may vary somewhat depending on the type of system and the overall requirements. The list should be supported by a detail description of each task.

3. Schedule each task in terms of levels of activity and specific milestones for task completion. A milestone chart, an example of which is presented in Figure 11-4, should be prepared and included in program planning documentation. The milestones for the tasks to be accomplished during the conceptual and advance development phases should be accurately defined, whereas subsequent efforts may be more generally defined at this time. The same tasks may be indicated in several phases and may be iterative in nature, varying only in terms of depth of accomplishment. Again, the extent of task definition will vary from program to program.

4. Project the tasks identified in Figure 11-4 (as appropriate) into activity networks to facilitate subsequent program monitoring and control functions. A partial summary activity network is illustrated in Figure 11-5.[1] The data presented constitute an oversimplification intended to convey the concept of network development. Actually, an overall program network is constructed covering major events (specific milestones in the program schedule) and the time frame for event completion. The circled tasks in Figure 11-5 represent start and/or completion points and the lines indicate task times and the proper sequencing of events (input–output requirements). Based on the overall program network, individual subnetworks may be developed to provide better control of program activities in specific areas. Program monitoring and control with networks can be accomplished rather effectively using computer techniques. The subject of program network development is fairly extensive and the student is advised to review additional material for a thorough understanding of the principles involved.

5. For the tasks listed, identify funding sources and prepare cost estimates. The estimated costs should be compatible with the identification of detail work packages and the program work breakdown structure (described in Section 11.2).

6. Define the organizational structure responsible for implementation of the tasks identified in Figures 11-2 and 11-4. Organization is discussed further in Section 11.2.

The initial logistics planning information is included in the basic program management documentation, and covers the effort required through conceptual and advance development phases.

---

[1] There are several program management techniques used which employ networks for monitoring and control purposes. A common approach is the *program evaluation and review technique* (PERT), which is described in a number of management textbooks.

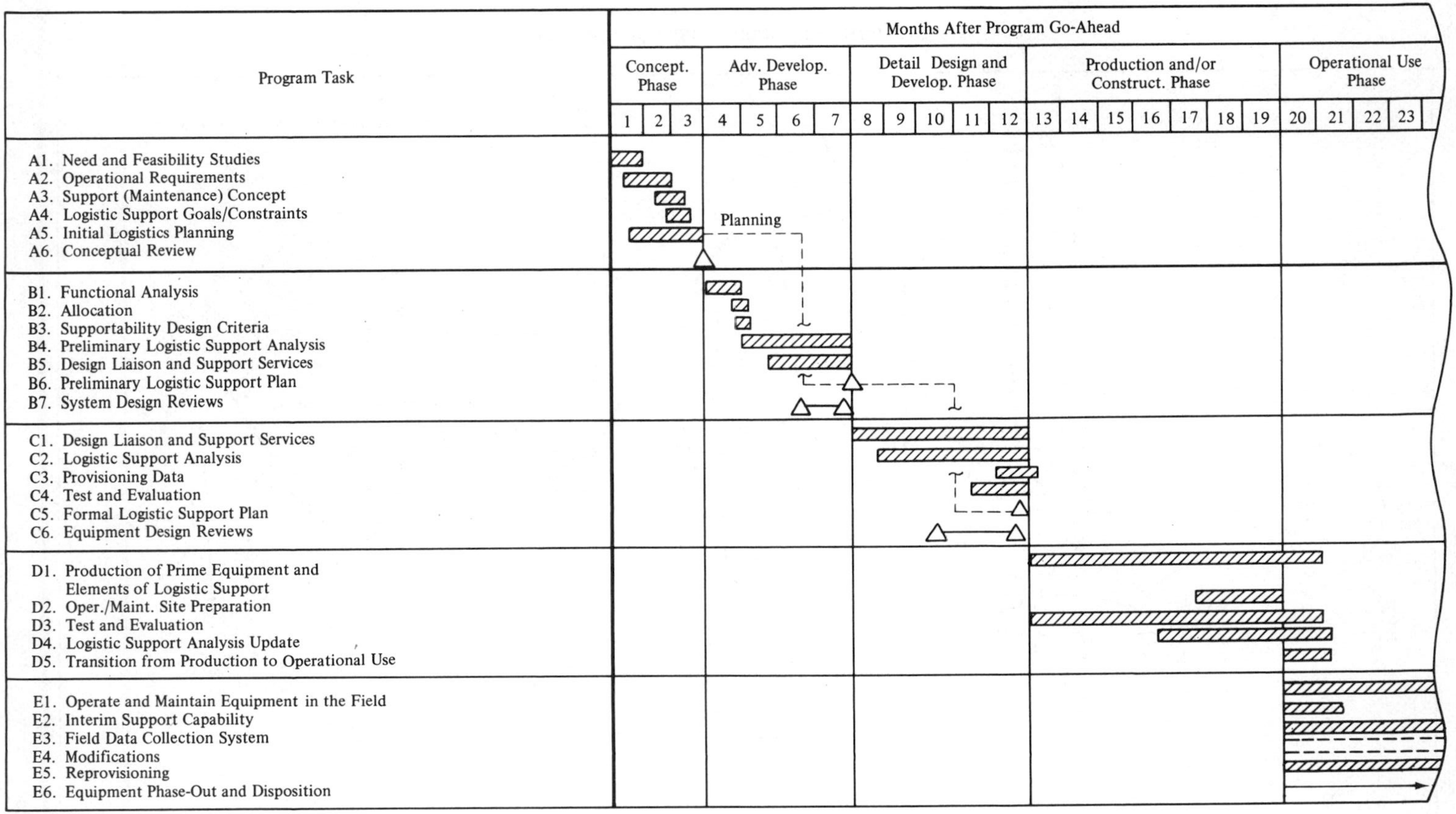

Figure 11-4. Basic milestone chart.

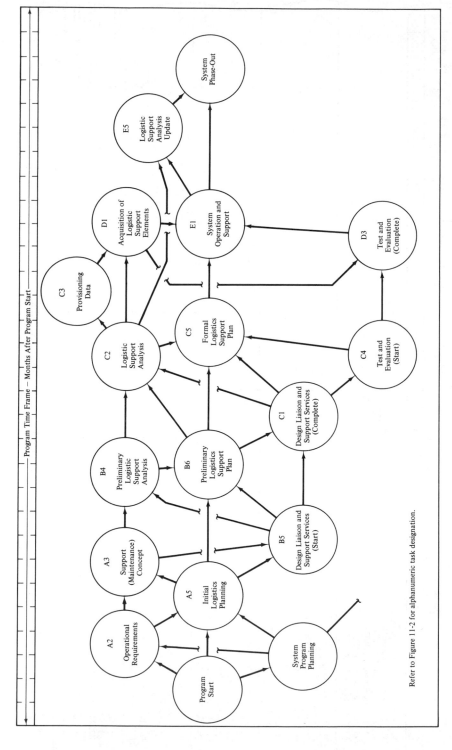

Figure 11-5. Partial summary program network.

Refer to Figure 11-2 for alphanumeric task designation.

Program Time Frame – Months After Program Start

The next major step in planning is the development of a *Preliminary Logistic Support Plan* (see Figure 11-2, task *B*6) toward the end of the advance development phase. This plan is primarily an update of the initial logistics planning information developed at program inception (see Figure 11-2, task *A*5), except that emphasis is placed on the tasks, scheduled program networks, and cost estimates associated with the detail design and development phase. This is not to say that planning information covering subsequent program phases is not included, but that design oriented tasks are detailed to a considerable degree. This includes reliability, maintainability, and human factors planning information as well as logistic support analysis and provisioning activities. Provisioning is a management process related to the acquisition of the logistic support items necessary to operate and maintain the prime equipment for a designated period of time. Provisioning must be timely and in many instances must be accomplished on a concurrent basis with design. Provisioning and all other logistics oriented program activities during system/equipment design, and test and evaluation (Types 1 and 2 testing) are monitored and controlled on the basis of the Preliminary Logistic Support Plan.

The third major element of planning is the *Formal Logistic Support Plan* prepared during the detail design and development phase (see Figure 11-2, task *C*5). This plan, representing a significant expansion of the Preliminary Logistic Support Plan (see Figure 11-2, task *B*6) covers all subsequent logistic support activity through the system life cycle. Specifically, this plan includes at least the following.

1. A detail *maintenance plan* is developed from logistic support analysis (LSA) data and the maintenance concept, and specific logistic support resources required at each level of maintenance are defined. The plan is actually a summary of the data presented in the Maintenance Analysis Summary (Figure *B*-5) described in Appendix B. This information serves as the *technical baseline* for all other sections of the logistic support plan.

2. A *reliability and maintainability plan* is developed earlier as part of the overall program plan for engineering activity and includes analysis and prediction data. These data, as applicable to the maintenance concept and logistic support, are included or referenced herein. In addition, reliability and maintainability requirements during the production and/or construction and the operational use phases are included. This may constitute Types 3 and 4 testing; data collection, analysis, and corrective action; evaluation of the impact of system/equipment modifications on reliability and maintainability; and so on.

3. A plan for the acquisition (whether make or buy) of *test and support and/or handling equipment* is prepared. Logistic support analysis (LSA), with supporting technical justification, identifies the requirements for support

equipment while this plan conveys the methods for acquisition, test, and deployment in the field. Specifically, this includes:

    a. A summary listing of test and support equipment requirements.
    b. Make-or-buy decisions.
    c. Acquisition plan for newly designed support equipment (basic flow process, special facility requirements, special tooling, production control methods, in-process testing, quality assurance provisions, etc.).
    d. Acquisition plan for off-the-the-shelf support equipment items.
    e. Compatibility testing approach, activity flow, and schedule.
    f. Delivery schedule and geographical point of delivery (hardware and software).

An illustration of the test and support equipment development process is presented in Figure 11-6.

    4. A *supply support plan* is generated to cover both preoperational support and full operational support, and the transition from one to the other. Preoperational support refers to the spare/repair parts and inventory requirements during a Type 3 test program or during system operations prior to the time when the user has acquired a complete operational support capability. The plan, covering both situations as applicable, includes:

    a. A summary listing of spare/repair part and consumable requirements by level of maintenance to include organizational, intermediate, depot, and/or supplier. This listing is based on logistic support analysis (LSA) data.
    b. Acquisition plan for new (nonstocklisted) spares and consumables for prime equipment, test and support/handling equipment, and training equipment. This shall consider manufacturing test approach, production control, quality assurance provisions, and delivery requirements.
    c. Acquisition plan for common standard (stocklisted) spares and consumables for prime equipment, test and support/handling equipment, and training equipment.
    d. Warehousing and accountability functions associated with maintenance support. This not only includes the initial cataloging, stocking, inventory maintenance and control, provisioning cycles, but also covers the disposition of residual assets.
    e. A plan for data collection, analysis, and the updating of spare/repair part demand factors necessary to improve provisioning cycles and reduce waste.

Figure 11-7 covers the spare/repair parts development process.

    5. A *transportation and handling plan* is prepared to identify:

    a. Proposed methods of packaging (type of containers—reusable versus nonreusable).
    b. Proposed mode(s) of transportation based on anticipated demand rates, weight and size of items, cost-effectiveness criteria, and so on. This

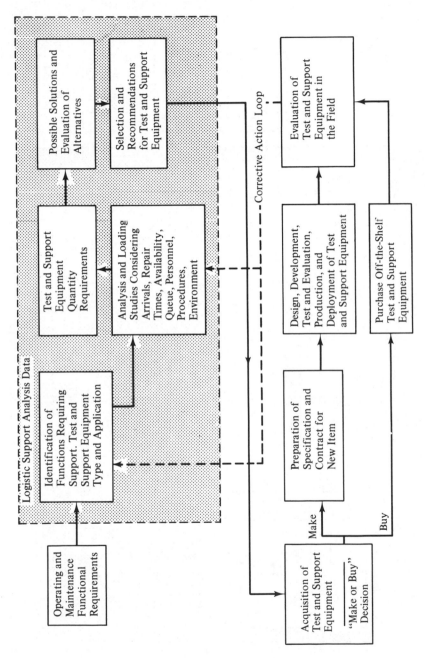

Figure 11-6. Test and support equipment development process.

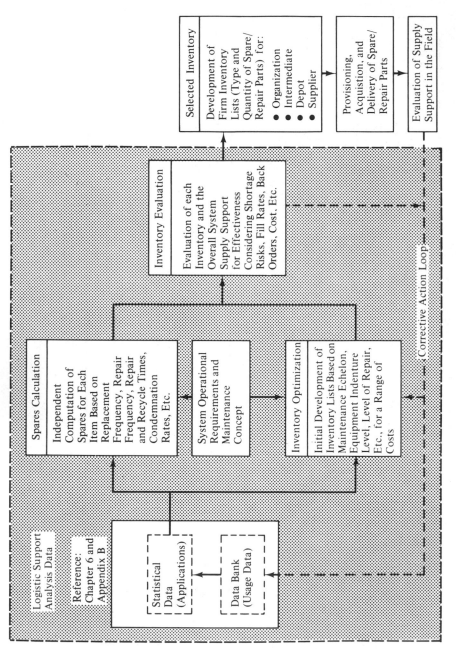

Figure 11-7. Spare/repair parts development process.

shall consider both first destination requirements as dictated by material delivery schedules and recurring transportation requirements based on anticipated maintenance support needs.

   c. Safety criteria, precautions, and provisions for handling, storage, and preservation.

The acquisition of transportation and handling equipment is included with test and support equipment.

   6. A *technical data plan* is prepared to include:

     a. A summary of technical data requirements (operating, maintenance, servicing, inspection, overhaul instructions) for each level of maintenance by equipment type. This covers prime equipment, test and support equipment, and training equipment.

     b. Technical data development schedule (major milestones).

     c. Plan for data verification and validation.

     d. Plan for incorporation of changes/revisions to the data, and the preparation of change documentation.

Figure 11-8 illustrates an overall technical data flow.

   7. A *facilities plan* is developed to identify all real property and equipment required to support system testing (Types 3 and 4), training, operation and logistic functions. The plan must contain sufficient qualitative and quantitative information to allow facility planners to:

     a. Initially assess and allocate requirements.

     b. Analyze existing facilities to determine adequacies/deficiencies.

     c. Determine requirements for new facilities and/or modifications to existing facilities. This includes utility needs such as power, telephone, environmental controls, water, and so on. Determine schedule requirements.

     d. Estimate the cost of construction or modification projects required to meet the needs of the system.

The facilities plan should include appropriate criteria to ensure that facility design is completely compatible with the prime equipment and its support elements. The plan must include the necessary scheduling information to permit the proper and timely implementation of any required civil engineering activity,

   8. A *personnel and training plan* should be developed to cover:

     a. Operator training (training of system operators)—type of training, basic entry requirements, and brief course outline.

     b. Maintenance training at all levels of maintenance—type of training, basic entry requirements, and brief course outline.

     c. Training equipment, devices, aids, and data required to support operator and maintenance training activity.

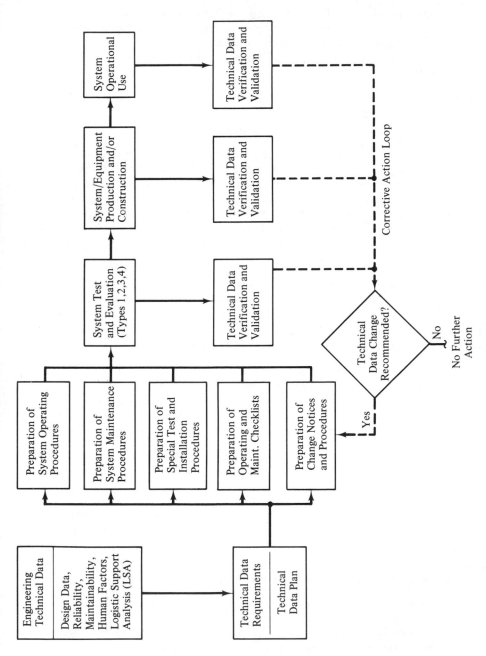

Figure 11-8. Technical data development.

    d. Proposed schedule for initial operator and maintenance training.

    e. Proposed approach for the accomplishment of replenishment training throughout the system life cycle.

Specific training requirements, derived from logistic support analysis (LSA) data, depends on the quantities and skills of the personnel defined for the system. Figure 11-9 shows basic training and training equipment development.

    9. A system *retirement plan* is outlined to cover the phase-out of equipment, the reclamation of items as appropriate, and the ultimate disposal of residue material. The plan should identify the requirements for transportation and handling, test and support equipment, personnel, facilities, and data necessary for the processing of items out of the inventory.

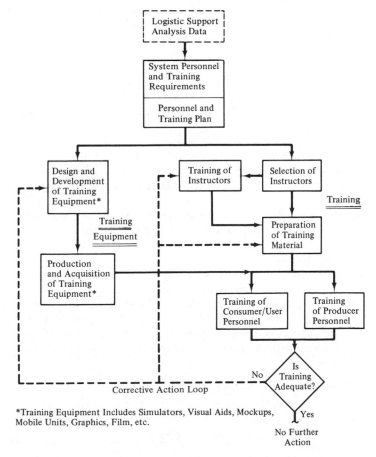

Figure 11-9. Personnel and training equipment development.

10. A detailed *management plan* should be prepared to include:

    a. Applicable tasks by program phase (see Figure 11-2).
    b. Milestone schedules, program networks, and work breakdown structure (see Figures 11-4 and 11-5).
    c. Organizational structure and responsibilities.
    d. Program monitoring and control procedures.
    e. Cost estimates by task.

This plan should cover all management aspects of provisioning, contracting, procurement, supplier monitoring and control, supplier/contractor sustaining support requirements, and the plans for phased-logistic support. Incentive and penalty provisions for contracting are also covered. Planning associated with the transition of logistic support from the producer to the ultimate user is critical to the success of system operation in the field and must be well defined at this point in time. In addition, the management plan should define and relate the procedures for the implementation of a data collection, feedback and corrective-action system. Specifically, the data collection and feedback system shall cover:

    a. Data recording, collection, processing, storage, and retrieval.
    b. Data analysis and system evaluation (including the elements of logistic support).
    c. Data reporting (assessment measures).
    d. Data integration and the upgrading of historical data for the provisioning of future logistic support requirements (e.g., updating of spare/repair part demand rates, test and support equipment utilization factors, etc.).
    e. Recommendations for corrective action as required for product improvement and/or to correct system deficiencies.
    f. Methods for incorporating equipment modifications and associated data changes.
    g. Procedures for maintaining configuration change control. A program should be initiated to maintain strict control and configuration accounting for all changes to ensure that the changes are effectively implemented and that complete compatibility exists between prime equipment, test and support equipment, spare/repair parts, training equipment, and technical data. A change in one area impacts the other areas to some degree.

The Formal Logistic Support Plan composition is reflected in Figure 11-10. When completed, the plan serves as the basic logistic support planning document for all associated activities during the production and/or construction phase and the operational use phase.

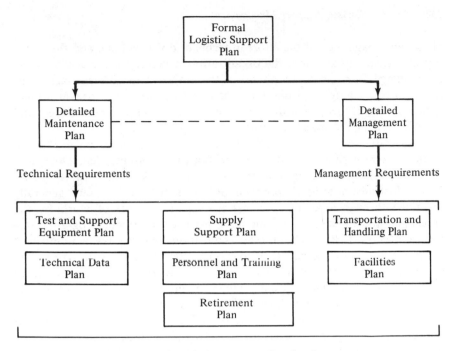

Figure 11-10. Logistic support plan development.

11.2. Organization for Logistic Support

Major management functions include the definition and establishment of objectives, organizing and implementing tasks necessary to achieve the desired results, and directing and controlling activities to ensure that these results are ultimately attained.[2]

The initial aspect of establishing objectives is accomplished through the planning effort described in the previous section. Logistics planning commences early in the program life cycle and constitutes the definition of tasks and establishing milestone schedules and input/output requirements. These tasks, tailored to the needs, support the primary overall objective of producing a system that will conform to a set of requirements in performing a designated mission in an effective manner.

The next step is organizing and implementing a program to meet the objectives defined through planning. Organization may assume a number of different approaches depending on the type of system, schedule, program

---

[2]These functions are compatible with the basic principles of managing by objectives (i.e., finding the objective, setting the objective, validating the objective, implementing the objective, and controlling and reporting status of the objective). A good reading source is Mali, P., *Managing by Objectives*, Wiley–Interscience, John Wiley & Sons, Inc., New York, 1972.

phase, and magnitude of the effort in terms of dollar volume and the quantity of systems. In addition, the organization structure for a given program may change from phase to phase as the emphasis in different task areas will shift (e.g., design and development to production). The organizational approach established, regardless of the program, should be tailored and must be dynamic to meet the needs.

An initial step in organizational development requires an evaluation of the current organization structure of both the consumer (customer) and producer, and establishing a relationship on a task-by-task basis. Figure 11-11 illustrates a sample approach. Program requirements are generally identified through a set of specifications and statements of work by the consumer, and an acquisition manager is assigned to provide program direction and control. Reporting to the acquisition manager are a number of functions providing the expertise to ensure that program requirements are met and the ultimate user will receive the product desired. These individual functional areas provide ongoing program monitoring, control, and approval of task efforts associated with their areas of expertise.

On the other side, the producer should establish an organization that will effectively respond to consumer requirements. Ideally, the producer's organization will relate directly to that of the consumer in such a manner that the extent and levels of communication are simplified. In other words, activities should be grouped and related on a comparable basis between producer and consumer.

In the area of logistics, there are many contributing functions and program tasks which must be accomplished in providing an effective output. These include planning and organizing, analysis, system and equipment design, test and evaluation, production, and life-cycle maintenance and support. Logistics represents a broad spectrum of activity cutting across many organizations. In the past, these various logistic activities have operated somewhat independently, and the results have been less than effective. The proper integration of the various elements of logistics and the communication between the organization entities responsible have been inadequate resulting in problems of the following type.

1. Each of the elements of logistic support are not developed from the same maintenance concept and/or policy.

   a. Test and support equipment is not compatible with the tasks scheduled to be accomplished at the level of maintenance for which it is intended.
   b. Spare/repair parts stocked at each level are not compatible with the removal and replacement requirements or repair–discard decisions anticipated.
   c. The facilities are not adequate for the operating and maintenance tasks scheduled to be performed.

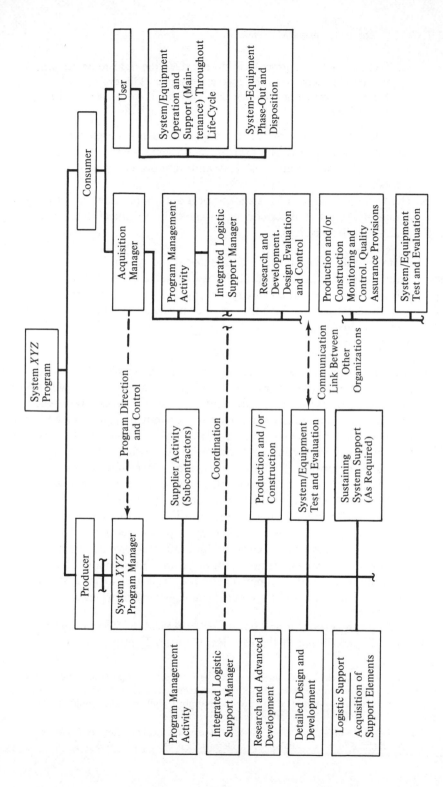

Figure 11-11. Producer-consumer organizational relationship.

d. Technical data and procedures do not track the tasks to be performed and are not prepared to the correct personnel skill levels.

e. The equipment design characteristics are not compatible with the support policy.

2. The various elements of logistic support are not developed in the proper order (e.g., the preparation of final maintenance procedures prior to the identification of test and support equipment requirements).

3. The various elements of logistic support are not provided in a timely manner (e.g., test and support equipment and technical data are not available when needed).

Problems of this nature must be eliminated if the system is to be ideally designed and supported in the field. This can be accomplished through the proper planning and recognition of logistic support at an appropriate level in the organization structure. Response to this approach has been recognized in many circles through the concept of *integrated logistic support* (ILS), which can be defined as[3]

1. A management function providing the controls which help to assure that the ultimate customer or user will receive a system that will not only meet performance requirements, but one that can be expeditiously and economically supported throughout its programmed life cycle. ILS assures the integration of the various elements of support with other system requirements and with each other.

2. ILS is a composite of all the support considerations necessary to assure the effective and economical support of a system for its life cycle. It is an integral part of all other aspects of system acquisition and operation. ILS is characterized by harmony and coherence among all the logistics elements. The principal elements of ILS related to the overall system life cycle include maintenance planning, test and support equipment, supply support, transportation and handling, technical data, facilities, personnel and training, logistic support resource funds, and logistic support management information.[4]

Within both the producer and consumer organization structure, logistic support must be recognized at the top. Referring to Figure 11-11, a major

---

[3]The author prefers the first definition, as ILS is a *management philosophy* and not a single individual organizational entity per se. It is not to be considered as an answer to all things. The second definition could be interpreted to imply a single organizational function, or an approach by which an organization should be structured.

[4]TM 38-710, APF-800-7, NAVMAT P-4000, *Integrated Logistic Support Implementation Guide for DOD Systems and Equipments*, Department of Defense, Washington, D.C., 1972.

program management function (designated as ILS manager or logistic support manager, or equivalent) is established high enough in the organization to gain recognition by the program manager and the acquisition manager, and to provide the planning, monitoring, and project management control functions for each of the individual organization entities performing logistic support tasks. This is not to say that this function controls or owns all of the necessary resources, but the individual assigned must effectively work with other managers to get the job done.

Ideally, both the consumer and the producer organizations should identify a prime logistic support manager responsible to ensure the proper planning and integration of all elements of logistic support. These managers should discuss requirements and communicate on a day-to-day basis. Likewise, the other program elements should establish comparable communication links. Basically, program direction and control progresses from the top, but a great deal of communication is facilitated if the consumer–producer organizations can be related on a task-by-task basis, and the method for accomplishing such should be included in the initial program planning documentation.

Within the producer's operation, there may be several approaches depending on the size of the project. For large projects, where funding is adequate, an organization structure similar to the one presented in Figure 11-12 may be established. In this instance, all the functions indicated are totally committed to System *XYZ*. An ILS manager, reporting to the program manager, must plan, coordinate, manage, and control all logistic support tasks which are accomplished by a number of lower-level organizations. This function, to properly operate and be effective, must have the total committment and backing of the program manager. With that committment, the ILS manager (with the support of lower-level project managers) can plan and establish logistic support objectives, milestones, and procedures for task accomplishment. Good planning is essential, particularly with the large number of lower level organizations involved and the span of control required. The ILS manager provides project-oriented direction, whereas the individual lower-level group managers provide technical direction.

For smaller projects, the task requirements and funding may not warrant the organizational approach conveyed in Figure 11-12. Personnel required for logistic support functions may be obtained on a loan basis from a staff unit to perform one or more project tasks before returning to staff work. The same personnel may be then assigned to another project to perform comparable or related tasks, and so on. Total committment to any single project is usually for a short term only. Figure 11-13 illustrates the two program approaches.[5]

---

[5]Additional information on project organization may be found in Blanchard, B. S., *Engineering Organization and Management*, Prentice-Hall, Inc., Englewood Cliffs, N.J., 1976.

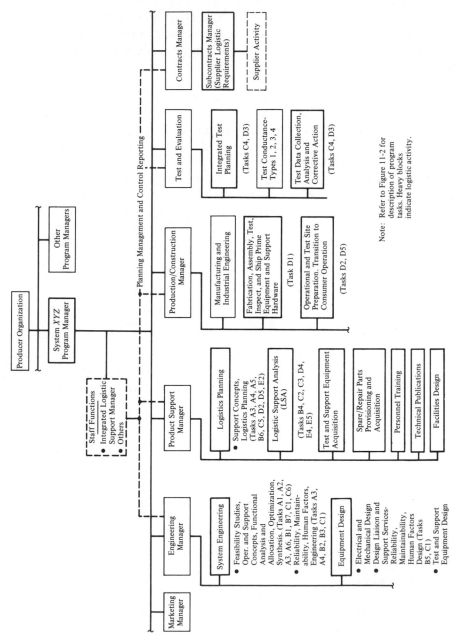

Figure 11-12. Producer's project organization-large project (example).

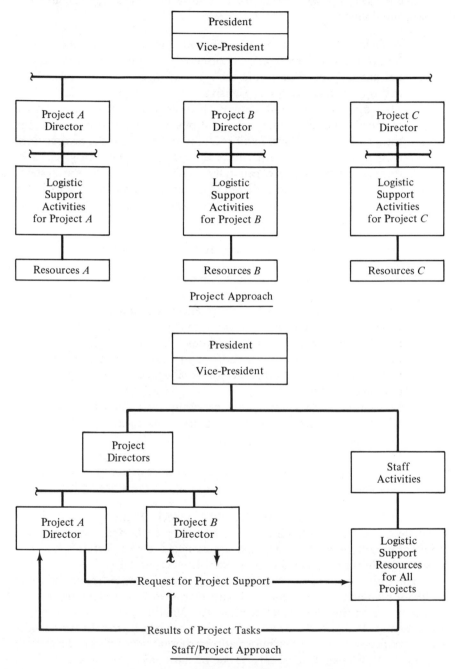

Figure 11-13. Producer organizational approaches.

The project approach (presented in Figure 11-12) is advantageous from several standpoints.

1. Assigned personnel are totally committed to the project. Their attention is undivided, motivation is oriented to the project (each individual has only one boss), and their knowledge of project procedures and the customer is fairly extensive.
2. The communication link between project personnel and between the producer and consumer organizations is usually good since the assigned personnel have in all probability been with the project since its inception. This in turn affects the quality output of a given task.
3. Assigned personnel are generally quite familiar with the system/ equipment requirements, design charateristics, and so on, and are in a favorable position to make the necessary design and support decisions.

On the other hand, there are advantages to the staff/project approach.

1. Personnel in staff units (when assigned to different projects) are able to study and apply new scientific and management techniques in completing certain tasks in a more effective manner. The transfer of experience and information from one project to another can be readily accomplished. These personnel, particularly in the field of logistic support, are often more up-to-date with technology and management functions than personnel assigned to a given project for a number of years.
2. Personnel in this category are generally more versatile and better adapted to solve different types of problems because of their broad experience on different programs.
3. When the producer is involved in many small programs, the staff/ project approach generally provides a more effective utilization of personnel and a greater degree of security at the working level.

Actually, both of the approaches illustrated in Figure 11-13 are beneficial under certain conditions. Quite often, it may be feasible to provide a mix of each; that is, some personnel are assigned to a project on a full-time basis and others are assigned only to complete certain tasks.

The ultimate decision concerning project organization stems from the program planning requirements and data discussed in the previous section, and is based on the best overall method for fulfilling the established objectives. Figures 11-2 and 11-4 present a listing of basic tasks and the major milestones, respectively. From this information program networks are developed. Specific work packages, consisting of one or more tasks, are developed from a combination of the task listing and the program network. Each work package is then analyzed in terms of the method and resources required for accomplishment. The individual work packages are then combined and identified in a work breakdown structure.

A task is made up of one or more events and associated activities. There are starting events, ending or terminating events, interface events, etc. Events are indicated by circles in a program network (see Figure 11-5) and the lines between the events represent activities. A task is an easily definable set of events. One or more tasks may constitute a work package. Figure 11-14 illustrates work packages in a program network.[6]

The identified work packages are evaluated from the standpoint of task type, complexity, and the required completion schedule. Tasks may be of a long-term nature and somewhat repetitive or short-term and relatively complex. For instance, reliability and maintainability design liaison and accomplishing a life-cycle cost analysis (part of the logistic support analysis) are quite different, with the former being somewhat long-term and the latter being short-term. Engineers may be assigned to a project on a full-time basis for the reliability and maintainability function while the life-cycle cost analysis may be accomplished by a specialist from a staff unit on a loan basis. In addition, the background and the capabilities of the personnel assigned to a task will vary.

The individual work packages are ultimately combined and integrated with the project *work breakdown structure* (WBS). The WBS links objectives and activities with resources, and is an excellent management tool for program planning, monitoring, and control. A partial sample WBS is presented in Figure 11-15.

The WBS is a logical separation of work related units. Work packages are identified against each block (see block 3A1100, Figure 11-15, for an example of package identification by block). These packages and blocks are then related to organizational groups, branches, departments, subprojects, suppliers, and so on. Cost estimating is accomplished for each work

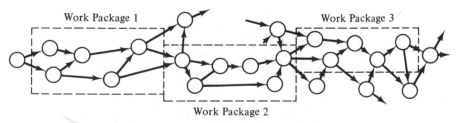

Figure 11-14. Program network and work packages.

---

[6]The development of program networks and work packages is described in Mali, Paul, *Managing by Objectives*, Wiley–Interscience, John Wiley & Sons, Inc., New York, 1972.

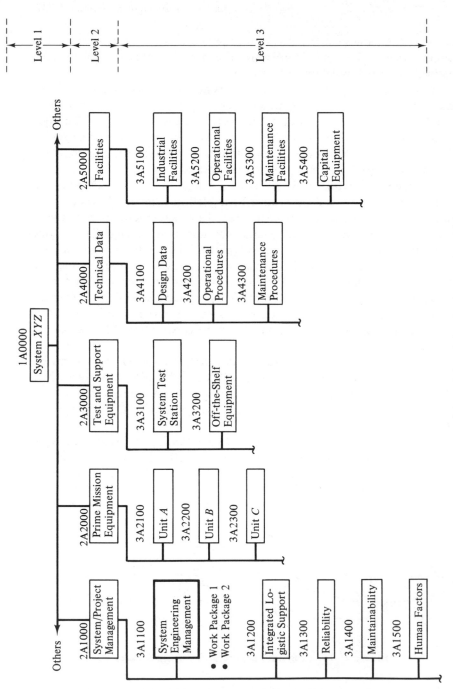

Figure 11-15. Partial work breakdown structure (sample).

package and identified by WBS block. The WBS is structured and coded in such a manner that program costs may be initially targeted and then collected against each block.[7] Costs may be accumulated both vertically and horizontally to provide summary figures for various categories of work. These cost data combined with the program networks provide management with the necessary tools for project evaluation and control.

The various tasks associated with logistic support are identified using the above approach, and an organization structure is established to provide the necessary response. As indicated earlier, the organization is a composite of departments, groups, functions, and so on, covering a wide spectrum of activity. Within the organization structure, the right type and quantity of personnel must be selected to do the job. Personnel manning will vary with the program phase and the task requirements. However, assuming that a full-scale program is required invoving all phases (see Figure 11-1, path *B*), program manning requirements might assume a profile such as the one presented in Figure 11-16.

For discussion purposes, four (4) basic job categories are assumed: (1) logistic support planning, (2) system/equipment design support, (3)

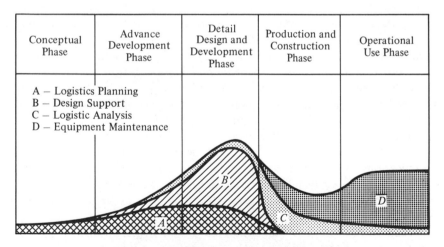

Figure 11-16. Typical manloading curve.

---

[7]In terms of cost collection, the WBS and cost breakdown structure used in life-cycle cost analyses are quite similar. The WBS serves as a program management tool and is often used for contracting purposes. The cost breakdown structure is an analytical device used in performing system/equipment analysis. Although their purposes are quite different, many of the same cost input factors are the same. The two efforts should be coordinated to the maximum extent possible to ensure compatibility where applicable.

logistic support analysis, and (4) system/equipment maintenance.[8] The planning function commences early in the program and basically extends through completion of the Formal Logistic Support Plan. System/equipment design support (refer to Chapter 7) commences late in the conceptual stage and continues until design is fixed. The analysis effort starts with participation in the initial system trade-off studies (preliminary LSA) and continues well into the operational use phase when data are collected and the system is being assessed in terms of effectiveness. Equipment maintenance support is required from the start of Type 1 testing, during production, and throughout the operational use phase until the system is phased out of the inventory.

Given the four categories, the program manager must find and place the right personnel in each category. This is a difficult assignment, particularly when manning the logistic planning, design support, and analysis functions. There is no sure way of selecting the right individual for a particular job. The manager must rely on his ability to properly assess the applicant's history, experience, education, and personal traits, and must substantiate his findings through techniques of interviewing. As a guide, the four job categories are as follows.

1. *Logistic Support Program Planning*—a management-oriented person who can visualize the impact of logistics on the total system/equipment life cycle, and who is aware of the interrelationships between the elements of logistic support with each other and with other facets of the program. Specifically, this person must understand the system design and development process, consumer/user operations and organization, and must know the basic principles of management (i.e., planning, organizing, cost estimating, task implementation, and control). This person should possess the following general attributes: (1) approach work in a logical and organized manner; (2) have a good understanding of the numerous functions and activities required to make a program successful; (3) be able to analyze specifications and work statements and design a program that will be responsive; (4) be diplomatic and apply good judgment in planning and performing logistic support functions; and (5) possess some prior experience in program planning functions.

The qualifications of an individual in the logistic support planning function appear to be quite constraining since the desired individual attributes are many. However, it should be recognized that logistic representatives in the past, particularly in the early program phases, have in essence been considered in the class of "second-rate citizens." When system acquisi-

---

[8]The number and nomenclature assigned to the job categories discussed is the author's way of conveying that the tasks associated with logistic support and the types of personnel selected are quite varied. Readers may adopt their own categories to fit the situation.

tion costs are anticipated as being high, logistic planning and the associated early program tasks are the first to be eliminated. Many program managers are not concerned with logistics at an early stage since they do not have to worry about it until later, and they feel that someone else will inherit any resulting problems that may occur; thus, a person who has experience, has visualization, possesses good judgement, and is persistent (not easily discouraged) is desired.

2. *System/Equipment Design Support*—a design-oriented person, preferably with some design experience, plus an in-depth knowledge of consumer/user operations, organization, environment, facilities, personnel skills, and so on. This person must be able to converse fluently with the design engineer (on the latter's terms), and must be able to translate system requirements and field experience into design criteria. He or she is inclined to be a specialist in a given equipment area and must be up to date relative to state-of-the-art advances in that field. The person in this area works with the design engineer on a day-to day basis, and should possess a high degree of ingenuity, intelligence, precision, and general technical ability. This function is generally accomplished by reliability, maintainability, and/or human factors engineers.

3. *Logistic Support Analysis*—a combination of maintenance analysts and system analysis specialists. The maintenance analyst must have the capability to review and evaluate design data and determine (through the application of prediction and analysis techniques) maintenance functions and logistic support requirements to include test and support equipment, spare/repair parts, personnel and training, technical data, and facilities (see Appendix B). He or she must be thoroughly familiar with user operating and maintenance procedures, organization structure, levels of maintenance, environment, and should have actual *hands-on* equipment maintenance experience. The maintenance analyst must be able to visually project (into the future) a system or equipment item and its support, and to capture that projection in writing. Persons selected must be analytically inclined and possess the ability to write.

The system analysis specialist (as defined here) aids in developing the analytical tools necessary to support the conductance of trade-off studies and the evaluation of alternatives. These tools include models, computer subroutines, and the development of data formats and processing requirements. The specialist also aids in the analysis and interpretation of test and field data. A person qualified in this area should be somewhat familiar with user operations and environment, and should have a good background in mathematics, statistics, modeling techniques, and computer applications. He or she must be able to accurately replicate an operational situation through use of a combination of analytical techniques.

4. *System/Equipment Maintenance*—a technician who will maintain and

support the equipment throughout testing and when the equipment is deployed in the field. This is the typical hardware-oriented person who, through formal and on-the-job training becomes an expert on the system/ equipment being acquired. Trade-school background and some field experience on comparable equipments are desired.

When the appropriate manning levels have been established, it is necessary to conduct formal training to ensure that each individual is thoroughly familiar with program requirements, the system/equipment being developed, and the particular tasks for which he or she is responsible. One or more familiarization courses may best serve this need.

11.3. Direction and Control of Logistic Support Activities

Program direction deals with the identification of responsibilities and the enforcement of procedures to ensure that the proper channels of communication are established to implement logistic support plans. The aspects of planning and organization have been discussed, and the next step is to provided the mechanism for applying the resources in the fulfillment of program objectives. Program control is that ongoing (sustaining) management activity that will guide, monitor, and evaluate accomplishments in terms of these objectives. Corrective action is initiated as appropriate to rectify problem areas. In summary, the program manager should assign task responsibilities, establish the necessary procedures for task completion, and should monitor and control activities in terms of schedule and budget commitments.

The ILS manager, in conjunction with the other functional managers, should initially establish cost and schedule targets along with the allocated performance and effectiveness requirements discussed in earlier chapters. Cost targets are identified by cost-estimating projections for each individual work package and the elements of the WBS. Schedules are established by milestone charts and program networks (see Figures 11-4 and 11-5, respectively). Cost projections are then related to network events as illustrated in Figure 11-17. For the completion of a preliminary logistic support analysis (task $B4$, Figure 11-2), a cost projection of $25,675 is established and the estimated rate of expenditure is illustrated by the projection curve in Figure 11-17. This is accomplished for each applicable logistic support task. As the program progresses, major activities are monitored for task status, expended funds, and schedule. The results are evaluated both individually and on an overall basis. Figure 11-18 presents a sample program summary.

Referring to the figure, four program milestone reviews ($M1$, $M2$, $M3$, $M4$) are established at critical points in the program schedule. The times

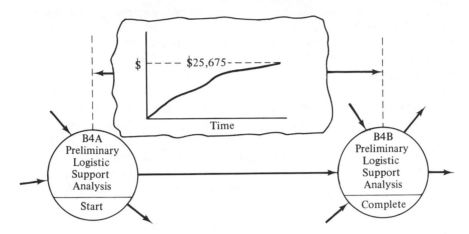

Figure 11-17. Event-cost projection.

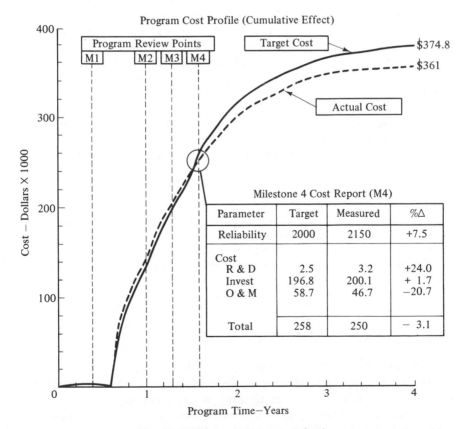

Program Cost Profile (Cumulative Effect)

Milestone 4 Cost Report (M4)

Parameter	Target	Measured	%Δ
Reliability	2000	2150	+7.5
Cost			
R & D	2.5	3.2	+24.0
Invest	196.8	200.1	+ 1.7
O & M	58.7	46.7	−20.7
Total	258	250	− 3.1

Figure 11-18. Program cost projection.

selected may or may not coincide with the system/equipment formal design reviews (discussed in Chapter 7), but are usually tied to a major decision point, a budget period, or a contractual commitment. The costs expended are summarized by the WBS and the result is compared against the initial target projection.

The intent of the program review is to assess all program elements at a specified point in time. Figure 11-18 illustrates a summary cost projection. An analysis of the projections and expenditures at a lower level can be readily accomplished by reviewing each WBS block in a like manner. In addition, projections of system performance parameters and effectiveness factors are evaluated with comparable values derived from predictions and analyses. These evaluations may be reviewed on an individual parameter basis as illustrated in Figure 11-19.

The extent that a manager will be able to control the program depends on the visibility he or she had to assess the various program elements, particularly those involving high risk. This visibility is based on the WBS makeup, the depth of initial cost estimating, the accounting or cost collection system, and the design and effectiveness of the management information and reporting system. Assurance that the proper tools are available for adequate program control stems from the initial planning effort conducted during the early part of conceptual phase. The planner needs to respond to two basic questions.

1. What are the program requirements and what does the manager need to know to ensure that these requirements are met?
2. How will the manager obtain the information needed at the proper time?

Answering these questions should lead to the development of a management information system which will provide the right data at the time needed. Included in these requirements are the needs of the ILS manager, who must be aware of the status of each logistic support task at all times. Such awareness is necessary if one is to assure that program requirements will be met.

11.4. Supplier Management

Earlier sections of this chapter covered the management requirements for logistic support and the general relationship between the producer and the consumer. In the event that portions of the system/equipment are subcontracted by the producer to one or more suppliers, the same philosophy may exist between producer and supplier. Supplier requirements are estab-

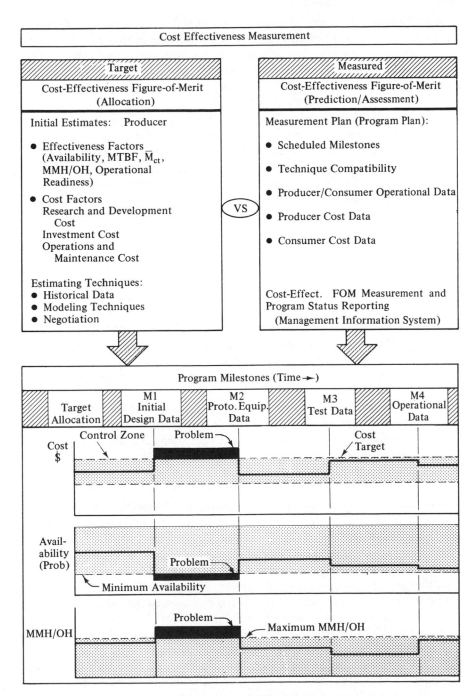

Figure 11-19. Parameter measurement and evaluation.

lished, program tasks and schedules are identified, organization relationships are defined, and program monitoring and control functions are accomplished in accordance with planning information. The supplier is responsible to the producer in the same manner that the producer is responsible to the customer.

Emphasis in logistic support can be acquired through the proper definition of system design requirements and program activities/tasks combined with the initiation of appropriate contractual arrangements. Contractually, an effective method for ensuring that logistics receives the right level of attention constitutes the establishment of a well-defined incentive–penalty structure. It may be feasible to establish significant incentive payment factors (in dollars) on certain key logistic parameters to encourage the supplier to improve his performance above and beyond that which was initially agreed upon without sacrificing other requirements (e.g., performance, effectiveness). For instance:

1. If the supplier is to be held responsible for the supply support of his equipment throughout the system life cycle, a target may be established in the contract for spare/repair part availability at a given level of life-cycle spares and inventory cost (i.e., the aspect of life-cycle cost which covers total supply support). If, during the implementation of the contract, the supplier improves performance relative to spares availability at a lower projected life-cycle cost, then he or she is entitled to a preestablished incentive payment at a designated point in time.
2. If the supplier improves the design of equipment for supportability, beyond that which was initially contracted, to effect a reduction in the need for new test and support equipment at lower life-cycle cost, he or she would be entitled to receive an incentive payment of significant magnitude to warrant the effort involved.

These and comparable contractual incentive considerations can be applied to other areas such as improving the reliability and maintainability characteristics in design, increasing the use of standard parts in equipment design, improving maintenance facility design to effect better equipment turnaround time, etc. To be effective, established incentive payments must be of significant magnitude to encourage the supplier to initiate the necessary activity to seek improvement. In addition, the payments must be established early enough in the program to be meaningful in terms of allowing the supplier to do a better job in defining equipment and assessing the possible risks involved in contract fulfillment.

On the other hand, if the supplier falls short in meeting the specified minimum contractual requirements, he or she should be penalized. Again, penalty factors of significant magnitude should be established to ensure that the supplier will do everything possible (from program inception on) to meet the minimum requirements.

Our experience relative to the application of incentive–penalty factors is somewhat limited to date; however, this area should be considered further if the goals and objectives discussed throughout this text are to be met.

11.5. Summary

The successful accomplishment of the objectives defined throughout this text is dependent on:

1. Proper planning for logistic support in all program phases.
2. Incorporation of appropriate supportability characteristics in system design and development.
3. Identification, provisioning, and timely acquisition of support elements required for prime equipment operation and maintenance.
4. Continued assessment of the overall effectiveness of the system throughout its life cycle, and the initiation of modifications for corrective action and/or product improvement (as required).

Logistic support must be considered on an equivalent basis along with performance, schedule, and cost implications. The appropriate trade-offs must be accomplished early in the life cycle and the proper balance attained if the output product is to be effective.

Logistic support must be recognized by all levels of program management as being a major ingredient in each phase of system development. The elements of support must be properly identified, and item acquisition should be accomplished in a timely manner. The contracting for logistic support should consider the application of incentive and penalty clauses in areas where special emphasis is required. Logistic support covers a broad spectrum of interests and should be properly integrated with all other facets of program activity.

QUESTIONS AND PROBLEMS

1. What are the basic requirements of program management? List components and criteria.
2. Assume that you are a manager responsible for the development of a system for operational use. Set up a program plan in outline form, identify the applicable program phases and major functions by phase, and develop a basic milestone chart.

3. Using the milestones identified in Problem 2, prepare a summary program network.

4. Define "integrated logistic support" (ILS).

5. Assume that you are a manager responsible for the development of a new system. How would you organize for and ensure that logistic support requirements are considered in a proper and timely manner? Draw an organization chart showing the relationship of logistic support functions with other program elements and briefly describe operating procedures. What problems do you perceive?

6. What is included in a formal logistic support plan?

7. Define "management by objectives" and discuss how the principles can be applied to logistic support.

8. Identify some of the problems that can develop if logistic support is not properly planned and implemented.

9. Integrated logistic support (ILS) should be identified by a single organization within a consumer's or producer's organizational structure. True or false? Why?

10. What is a "work package"? What is the purpose of a WBS? How do work packages relate to WBS?

11. How does the WBS relate to the cost breakdown structure utilized in cost-effectiveness analyses?

12. What is the functional relationship between system engineering and logistic support?

13. What type of personnel are needed to perform logistic support functions? Is a college degree a necessary prerequisite in the performance of logistic tasks? If so, in what area(s)?

14. When managing logistic support activities throughout program implementation, what measures would you employ to ensure that logistic support is being properly addressed?

15. In Problem 14, if an unsatisfactory condition is detected, how would you initiate corrective action? List and briefly discuss the steps involved.

16. Describe the major functions of logistic support during the production and/or construction and operational use phase.

17. Through what functions does logistic support impact system/equipment design?

18. How would you emphasize logistics in contracting for an item?

19. What factors are important in the application of incentive and penalty factors for logistics?

APPENDIX A

COST ANALYSIS DATA

When budgeting, contracting, or evaluating a system or equipment item, the aspect of total life-cycle cost (cost of acquisition, ownership, and ultimate disposal) should be considered and not just procurement price alone. Life-cycle cost includes all future costs associated with research and development, investment (production/construction), installation and check-out, operation and maintenance, and ultimate system phase-out. It covers all hardware, software, data, and associated logistic support.

Life-cycle costing, an inherent part of the LSA process, has many applications as discussed in Chapters 2 and 6. Common to each application are certain fundamental concepts covering cost breakdown structures, cost factors and estimating relationships, discounting and inflation, and cost modeling. These concepts are briefly discussed in the following sections.[1]

A. Cost Breakdown Structure (Cost Categories).

When accomplishing a life-cycle cost analysis, the analyst must develop a cost breakdown structure (i.e., cost tree) showing the numerous categories

---

[1]Life-cycle costing is covered further in (a) Blanchard, B. S., *Design and Manage to Life Cycle Cost*, M/A Press, International Scholarly Book Services, Inc., Forest Grove, Oreg., 1978; and (b) Seldon, M. R., *Life Cycle Costing: A Better Method of Government Procurement*, Westview Press, Inc., Boulder, Colo., 1979.

that are combined to provide the total cost. There is no set method for breaking down cost as long as the method used can be tailored to the specific application. However, the cost breakdown structure should exhibit the following basic characteristics.

1. *All* system cost elements must be considered.

2. Cost categories are generally identified with a significant level of activity or some major item of hardware. Cost categories must be well defined. The analyst, manager, customer, supplier, and so on, must all have the *same* understanding of what is included in a given category and what is not! Cost doubling (i.e., counting the same cost in two or more categories) and omissions must be eliminated. Lack of adequate definition causes inconsistencies in the evaluation process, and could lead to a wrong decision.

3. The cost structure and categories should be coded in such a manner as to allow for the analysis of certain specific areas of interest (e.g., system operation, energy consumption, equipment design, spares, and maintenance personnel and support) while virtually ignoring other areas. In some instances, the analyst may wish to pursue a designated area in depth while covering other areas with gross top-level estimates. This will certainly occur from time to time as a system evolves through the different phases of its life-cycle. The areas of concern (for decision-making purposes) will vary.

4. When related to a specific program, the cost structure should be compatible (through cross-indexing, coding, etc.) with the program work breakdown structure (WBS) and with the management accounting procedures used in collecting costs. Certain costs are derived from accounting records and should be a direct input into the life-cycle cost analysis.

5. For programs where subcontracting is prevalent, it is often desirable and necessary to separate supplier costs (i.e., initial bid price and follow-on program costs) from the other costs. The cost structure should allow for the identification of specific work packages that require close monitoring and control.

An example of a cost breakdown structure is presented in Figure A-1.[2] The particular categories in the structure are supported by the descriptive material and quantitative expressions in Table A-1. A summary listing of terms is presented in Table A-2.

Referring to Figure A-1, costs may be accumulated at the different levels depending on the areas of interest and the depth of detail required. In some instances, the analyst may wish to thoroughly investigate maintenance cost (C_{OM}) while roughly estimating operations cost (C_{OO}). On the other hand, engineering design cost (C_{RE}) may be amplified while looking at opera-

---

[2]Figure 2-20 illustrates a different example, applicable to a different problem and where certain sensitivities to cost are required for decision-making purposes.

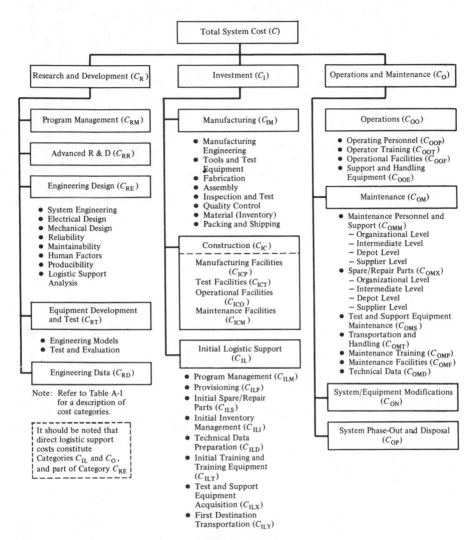

Figure A-1. Cost breakdown structure.

tions and maintenance cost (C_O) in terms of an estimated total value. The cost breakdown structure should incorporate the flexibility to allow for cost collection both horizontally and vertically. This can readily be accomplished through the use of computer methods and the proper coding.

Referring to Table A-1, the quantitative expressions which represent the costs in each of the categories define the requirements for cost estimating. In some instances, specific known cost factors are used while in other cases the establishment of cost estimating relationships is needed.

Table A-1. DESCRIPTION OF COST CATEGORIES

Cost Category (Reference Figure A-1)	Method of Determination (Quantitative Expression)	Cost Category Description and Justification
Total system cost (C)	$C = [C_R + C_I + C_O]$ $C_R = R$ and D cost $C_I =$ Investment cost $C_O =$ Operations and maintenance cost	Includes all future costs associated with the acquisition, utilization, and subsequent disposition of the system/equipment.
Research and development (C_R)	$C_R = [C_{RM} + C_{RR} + C_{RE} + C_{RT} + C_{RD}]$ $C_{RM} =$ Program management cost $C_{RR} =$ Advanced R and D cost $C_{RE} =$ Engineering design cost $C_{RT} =$ Equipment development and test cost $C_{RD} =$ Engineering data cost	Includes all costs associated with conceptual/feasibility studies, basic research, advanced research and development, engineering design, fabrication and test of engineering prototype models (hardware), and associated documentation. Also covers all related program management functions. These costs are basically nonrecurring.
Program management (C_{RM})	$C_{RM} = \sum_{i=1}^{N} C_{RM_i}$ $C_{RM_i} =$ Cost of specific activity i $N =$ Number of activities	Costs of management oriented activity applicable (across-the-board) to conceptual/feasibility studies, research, engineering design (including logistic support in the design process), equipment development and test, and related data/documentation. Such costs cover the program manager and his administrative staff; marketing; contracts; procurement; configuration management; logistics management; data management; etc. Management functions relate to C_{RR}, C_{RE}, C_{RT}, and C_{RD}.
Advanced research and development (C_{RR})	$C_{RR} = \sum_{i=1}^{N} C_{RR_i}$ $C_{RR_i} =$ Cost of specific activity i	Advanced research includes conceptual/feasibility studies conducted to determine and/or justify a need for a specific requirement. This includes

Table A-1. DESCRIPTION OF COST CATEGORIES (Continued)

Cost Category (Reference Figure A-1)	Method of Determination (Quantitative Expression)	Cost Category Description and Justification
	N = Number of activities	effort oriented to defining mission scenarios, system operational requirements (Chapter 3), preliminary maintenance concept (Chapter 4), etc., accomplished early in a program.
Engineering design (C_{RE})	$$C_{RE} = \sum_{i=1}^{N} C_{RE_i}$$ C_{RE_i} = Cost of specific design activity i N = Number of design activities	Includes all initial design effort associated with system/equipment definition and development. Specific areas include system engineering; design engineering (electrical, mechanical, drafting); reliability and maintainability engineering; human factors; functional analysis and allocation (Chapter 5); logistic support analysis (Chapter 6); components; producibility; standardization; safety; etc. Design associated with modifications is covered in C_{ON}.
Equipment development and test (C_{RT})	$$C_{RT} = [C_{RDL} + C_{RDM} + \sum_{i=1}^{N} C_{RDT_i}]$$ C_{RDL} = Cost of prototype fabrication and assembly labor C_{RDM} = Cost of prototype material C_{RDT_i} = Cost of test operations and support associated with specific test i N = Number of identifiable tests	The fabrication, assembly, test and evaluation of engineering prototype models (in support of engineering design activity–C_{RE}) is included herein. Specifically, this constitutes fabrication and assembly; instrumentation; quality control and inspection; material procurement and handling; logistic support (personnel, training, spares, facilities, support equipment, etc.); data collection; and evaluation of prototypes. Initial logistic support for operational system/equipment is covered in C_{IL}.

Table A-1. DESCRIPTION OF COST CATEGORIES (Continued)

Cost Category (Reference Figure A-1)	Method of Determination (Quantitative Expression)	Cost Category Description and Justification
Engineering data (C_{RD})	$$C_{RD} = \sum_{i=1}^{N} C_{RD_i}$$ C_{RD_i} = Cost of specific data N = Number of data items	This category includes the preparation, printing, publication, and distribution of all data/documentation associated with C_{RM}, C_{RE}, and C_{RT}, C_{RR}. This covers program plans; R and D reports; design data; test plans and reports; analyses; preliminary operational and maintenance procedures; and all effort related to a specific documentation requirement.
Investment (C_I)	$C_I = [C_{IM} + C_{IC} + C_{IL}]$ C_{IM} = System/equipment manufacturing cost C_{IC} = System construction cost C_{IL} = Cost of initial logistic support	Includes all costs associated with the acquisition of systems/equipment (once that design and development has been completed). Specifically this covers manufacturing (recurring and nonrecurring); manufacturing management; system construction; and initial logistic support.
Manufacturing (C_{IM})	$C_{IM} = [C_{IN} + C_{IR}]$ C_{IN} = Nonrecurring manufacturing cost C_{IR} = Recurring manufacturing cost	This covers all recurring and nonrecurring costs associated with the production and test of multiple quantities of prime systems/equipments. Facility construction, capital equipment, and facility maintenance are covered under C_{IC}.
Nonrecurring manufacturing cost (C_{IN})	$$C_{IN} = [C_{INM} + C_{INT} + C_{INA} + C_{INP} + \sum_{i=1}^{N} C_{INQ} + \sum_{j=1}^{N} C_{INS}]$$ C_{INM} = Manufacturing engineering cost C_{INT} = Tools and factory test equipment cost (excluding capital equipment) C_{INA} = Quality assurance cost	Includes all fixed *nonrecurring* costs associated with the production and test of operational systems/equipments. Specifically, this covers manufacturing management; manufacturing engineering; initial tooling and factory test equipment; quality assurance; first article qualification test (reliability test, maintainability

Table A-1. DESCRIPTION OF COST CATEGORIES (Continued)

Cost Category (Reference Figure A-1)	Method of Determination (Quantitative Expression)	Cost Category Description and Justification
	C_{INP} = Manufacturing management cost C_{INQ} = Cost of qualification test i C_{INS} = Cost of production sampling test j N = Number of individual tests	demonstration, support equipment compatibility, technical data verification, personnel test and evaluation, interchangeability, environmental test) and related support; production sampling tests and related support. Logistic support for each individual qualification and sampling test is included in the cost of the individual test.
Recurring manufacturing cost (C_{IR})	$C_{IR} = [C_{IRE} + C_{IRL} + C_{IRM} + C_{IRI} + C_{IRT}]$ C_{IRE} = Recurring manufacturing engineering support cost C_{IRL} = Production fabrication and assembly labor cost C_{IRM} = Production material and inventory cost C_{IRI} = Inspection and test cost C_{IRT} = Packing and initial transportation cost	This category covers all *recurring* production costs to include fabrication; subassembly and assembly; material and inventory control; inspection and test; packing and shipping to the point of first destination. Sustaining engineering support required on a recurring basis is also included. Costs are associated with the production of prime equipment. Operational test and support equipment, training equipment, and spare/repair parts material costs are included in C_{IL}. Manufacturing management cost is included in C_{IN}.
Construction cost (C_{IC})	$C_{IC} = [C_{ICP} + C_{ICT} + C_{ICO} + C_{ICM}]$ C_{ICP} = Manufacturing facilities cost C_{ICT} = Test facilities cost C_{ICO} = Operational facilities acquisition cost C_{ICM} = Maintenance facilities acquisition cost	Includes all initial acquisition costs associated with manufacturing, test, operational and/or maintenance facilities (real property, plant, and equipment), and utilities (gas, electric power, water, telephone, heat, air conditioning, etc.). Facility costs cover the development of new building projects, the modification of existing

Table A-1. DESCRIPTION OF COST CATEGORIES (Continued)

Cost Category (Reference Figure A-1)	Method of Determination (Quantitative Expression)	Cost Category Description and Justification
	For each item, one should consider the following. $C_{IC(\ )} = [C_{ICA} + C_{ICB} + C_{ICU} + C_{ICC}]$ $C_{ICA} =$ Construction labor cost $C_{ICB} =$ Construction material cost $C_{ICU} =$ Cost of utilities $C_{ICC} =$ Capital equipment cost	facilities, and/or the occupancy of existing facilities without modification. Work areas plus family housing are considered. Category costs include preliminary surveys; real estate; building constructions; roads and pavement; railroad sidings; etc. Cost items include construction labor, construction material, capital equipment, and utility installation. (a) Manufacturing facilities support the operations described in C_{IM}, C_{IN}, C_{IR}. Initial and sustaining costs are included. (b) Test facilities cover any peculiar requirements (beyond that covered under existing categories) for evaluation test. (c) Operational facilities are required for system operation throughout its life-cycle. Sustaining costs are covered in C_{OOF}. (d) Maintenance facilities are required to support the maintenance needs of the system throughout its life-cycle. Sustaining costs are covered in C_{OMF}.
Initial logistic support cost (C_{IL})	$C_{IL} = [C_{ILM} + C_{ILP} + C_{ILS} + C_{ILI} + C_{ILD}$ $\quad + C_{ILT} + C_{ILX} + C_{ILY}]$ $C_{ILM} =$ Logistic program management cost $C_{ILP} =$ Cost of provisioning $C_{ILS} =$ Initial spare/repair part material cost	Includes all integrated logistic support planning and control functions associated with the development of system support requirements, and the transition of such requirements from supplier(s) to the applicable operational site. Elements cover (a) Logistic program management cost—man-

Table A-1. DESCRIPTION OF COST CATEGORIES (Continued)

Cost Category (Reference Figure A-1)	Method of Determination (Quantitative Expression)	Cost Category Description and Justification
	C_{ILI} = Initial inventory management cost C_{ILD} = Cost of technical data preparation C_{ILT} = Cost of initial training and training equipment C_{ILX} = Acquisition cost of operational test and support equipment C_{ILY} = Initial transportation and handling cost	agement, control, reporting, corrective action system, budgeting, planning, etc. (b) Provisioning cost—preparation of data which is needed for the procurement of spare/repair parts and test and support equipment. (c) Initial spare/repair part material cost—spares material stocked at the various inventory points to support the maintenance needs of prime equipment, test and support equipment, and training equipment. Replenishment spares are covered in C_{OMX}. (d) Initial inventory management cost—cataloging, listing, coding, etc., of spares entering the inventory. (e) Technical data preparation cost—development of operating and maintenance instructions, test procedures, maintenance cards, tapes, etc. Also includes reliability and maintainability data, test data, etc., covering production and test operations. (f) Initial training and training equipment cost—design and development of training equipment, training aids/data, and the training of personnel initially assigned to operate and maintain the prime equipment, test and support equipment, and training equipment. Personnel training costs include instructor time; supervision; student pay and allow-

Table A-1. DESCRIPTION OF COST CATEGORIES (Continued)

Cost Category (Reference Figure A-1)	Method of Determination (Quantitative Expression)	Cost Category Description and Justification
		ances; training facilities; and student transportation. Training accomplished on a sustaining basis throughout the system life-cycle (due to personnel attrition) is covered in C_{OOT} and C_{OMP}.
		(g) Test and support equipment acquisition cost —design, development, and acquisition of test and support equipment plus handling equipment needed to operate and maintain prime equipment in the field. The maintenance of test and support equipment throughout the system life-cycle is covered in C_{OOB} and C_{OMS}.
		(h) Initial transportation and handling cost (first destination transportation of logistic support elements from supplier to the applicable operational site).
		Initial facility costs are identified in C_{IC}.
		Specific logistic support requirements are defined in the Logistic Support Analysis (LSA) accomplished during engineering design as discussed in Chapter 6 and Appendix B.
Operations and maintenance cost (C_O)	$C_O = [C_{OO} + C_{OM} + C_{ON} + C_{OP}]$ C_{OO} = Cost of system/equipment life-cycle operations C_{OM} = Cost of system/equipment life-cycle maintenance	Includes all costs associated with the operation and maintenance support of the system throughout its life-cycle subsequent to equipment delivery in the field. Specific categories cover the cost of system operation, maintenance, sustaining

Table A-1. Description of Cost Categories (Continued)

Cost Category (Reference Figure A-1)	Method of Determination (Quantitative Expression)	Cost Category Description and Justification
	$C_{ON} =$ Cost of system/equipment modifications $C_{OP} =$ Cost of system/equipment phase-out and disposal	logistic support, equipment modifications, and system/equipment phase-out and disposal. Costs are generally determined for each year throughout life-cycle.
Operations cost (C_{OO})	$C_{OO} = [C_{OOP} + C_{OOT} + C_{OOF} + C_{OOE}]$ $C_{OOP} =$ Operating personnel cost $C_{OOT} =$ Cost of operator training $C_{OOF} =$ Cost of operational facilities $C_{OOE} =$ Cost of support and handling equipment	Includes all costs associated with the actual operation (not maintenance) of the system throughout its life-cycle. Specific categories cover the costs of system/equipment operational personnel (system operator); the formal training of operators; operational facilities; and support and handling equipment necessary for system operation.
Operating personnel cost (C_{OOP})	$C_{OOP} = [(T_O)(C_{PO})(Q_{PO})(N_{PO}) \times$ (% allocation)] $T_O =$ Hours of system operation $C_{PO} =$ Cost of operator labor $Q_{PO} =$ Quantity of operators/system $N_{PO} =$ Number of operating systems	This category covers the costs of operating personnel as allocated to the system. A single operator may operate more than one system, but costs should be allocated on an individual system basis. Such costs include base pay or salary and allowances; fringe benefits (insurance, medical, retirement); travel; clothing allowances; etc. Both direct and overhead costs are included.
Operator training cost (C_{OOT})	$C_{OOT} = [(Q_{SO})(T_T)(C_{TOP})]$ $Q_{SO} =$ Quantity of student operators $T_T =$ Duration of training program (weeks) $C_{TOP} =$ Cost of operator training ($/student-week)	Initial operator training is included in C_{ILT}. This category covers the *formal* training of personnel assigned to operate the system. Such training is accomplished on a periodic basis throughout the system life-cycle to cover personnel replacements due to attrition. Total costs include instructor

Table A-1. DESCRIPTION OF COST CATEGORIES (Continued)

Cost Category (Reference Figure A-1)	Method of Determination (Quantitative Expression)	Cost Category Description and Justification
		time; supervision; student pay and allowances while in school; training facilities (allocation of portion of facility required specifically for formal training); training aids, equipment, and data; and student transportation as applicable.
Operational facilities cost (C_{OOF})	$C_{OOF} = [(C_{PPE} + C_U)(\% \text{ Allocation}) \times (N_{OS})]$ C_{PPE} = Cost of operational facility support ($/site) C_U = Cost of utilities ($/site) N_{OS} = Number of operational sites *Alternate Approach* $C_{OOF} = [(C_{PPF})(N_{OS})(S_O)]$ C_{PPF} = Cost of operational facility space ($/square foot/site). Utility cost allocation is included. S_O = Facility space requirements (square feet)	Initial acquisition cost for operational facilities is included in C_{ICO}. This category covers the annual recurring costs associated with the occupancy and maintenance (repair, paint, etc.) of operational facilities throughout the system life-cycle. Utility costs are also included. Facility and utility costs are proportionately allocated to each system.
Support and handling equipment cost (C_{OOE})	$C_{OOE} = [C_{OOO} + C_{OOU} + C_{OOS}]$ C_{OOO} = Cost of operation C_{OOU} = Cost of equipment corrective maintenance C_{OOS} = Cost of equipment preventive maintenance	Initial acquisition cost for operational support and handling equipment is covered in C_{ILX}. This category includes the annual recurring usage and maintenance costs for those items which are required to support system operation throughout the life-cycle (e.g., launchers, dollies, vehicles, etc.). The costs specifically cover equipment operation (not covered elsewhere); equipment corrective maintenance; and preventive main-

Table A-1. DESCRIPTION OF COST CATEGORIES (Continued)

Cost Category (Reference Figure A-1)	Method of Determination (Quantitative Expression)	Cost Category Description and Justification
	$C_{OOU} = [(Q_{CA})(M_{MHC})(C_{OCP}) + (Q_{CA})(C_{MHC}) + (Q_{CA})(C_{DC})](N_{OS})$ Q_{CA} = Quantity of corrective maintenance actions (M_A). Q_{CA} is a function of (T_O) (λ). M_{MHC} = Corrective maintenance manhours/M_A. C_{OCP} = Corrective maintenance labor cost ($\$/M_{MHC}$) C_{MHC} = Cost of material handling/ corrective M_A C_{DC} = Cost of corrective maintenance documentation/M_A N_{OS} = Number of operational sites $C_{OOS} = [(Q_{PA})(M_{MHP})(C_{OPP}) + (Q_{PA})(C_{MPH}) + (Q_{PA})(C_{DP})](N_{OS})$ Q_{PA} = Quantity of preventive maintenance actions (M_A). Q_{PA} relates to fpt M_{MHP} = Preventive maintenance manhours/M_A C_{OPP} = Preventive maintenance labor cost ($\$/M_{MHP}$) C_{MHP} = Cost of material. handling/ preventive M_A C_{DP} = Cost of preventive maintenance documentation/M_A N_{OS} = Number of operational sites	tenance. Spares and consumables are included included in C_{OMX}. Corrective and preventive maintenance requirements are derived from the Logistic Support Analysis (LSA) discussed in Chapter 6 and Appendix **B**.

Table A-1. DESCRIPTION OF COST CATEGORIES (Continued)

Cost Category (Reference Figure A-1)	Method of Determination (Quantitative Expression)	Cost Category Description and Justification
Maintenance cost (C_{OM})	$C_{OM} = [C_{OMM} + C_{OMX} + C_{OMS} + C_{OMT} + C_{OMP} + C_{OMF} + C_{OMD}]$ $C_{OMM} = $ Maintenance personnel and support cost $C_{OMX} = $ Cost of spare/repair parts $C_{OMS} = $ Test and support equipment maintenance cost $C_{OMT} = $ Transportation and handling cost $C_{OMF} = $ Cost of maintenance facilities $C_{OMD} = $ Cost of technical data	Includes all sustaining maintenance labor, spare/repair parts, test and support equipment, transportation and handling, replenishment training, support data, and facilities necessary to meet the maintenance needs of the prime equipment throughout its life-cycle. Such needs include both corrective and preventive maintenance requirements at all echelons—organizational, intermediate, depot, and factory.
Maintenance personnel and support cost (C_{OMM})	$C_{OMM} = [C_{OOU} + C_{OOS}]$ $C_{OOU} = $ Cost of equipment corrective maintenance $C_{OOS} = $ Cost of equipment preventive maintenance Total cost is the sum of the C_{OMM} values for each echelon of maintenance.	Includes corrective and preventive maintenance labor, associated material handling, and supporting documentation. When a system/equipment malfunction occurs or when a scheduled maintenance action is performed, personnel manhours are expended, the handling of spares and related material takes place, and maintenance action reports are completed. This category includes all directly related costs.
Corrective maintenance cost (C_{OOU})	$C_{OOU} = [(Q_{CA})(M_{MHC})(C_{OCP}) + (Q_{CA})(C_{MHC})$ $+ (Q_{CA})(C_{DC})](N_{MS})$ $Q_{CA} = $ Quantity of corrective maintenance actions (M_A). $Q_{CA} = (T_O)(\lambda)$ $M_{MHC} = $ Corrective maintenance manhours/M_A $C_{OCP} = $ Corrective maintenance labor cost ($\$/M_{MHC}$)	This category includes the personnel activity costs associated with the accomplishment of corrective maintenance. Related spares, test and support equipment, transportation, training, and facility costs are covered in C_{OMX}, C_{OMS}, C_{OMT}, and C_{OMF}, respectively. Total cost includes the sum of individual costs for each maintenance action multiplied by the quantity of

Table A-1. DESCRIPTION OF COST CATEGORIES (Continued)

Cost Category (Reference Figure A-1)	Method of Determination (Quantitative Expression)	Cost Category Description and Justification
	C_{MHC} = Cost of material handling/corrective M_A C_{DC} = Cost of documentation/corrective M_A N_{MS} = Number of maintenance sites Determine C_{OOU} for each appropriate echelon of maintenance.	maintenance actions anticipated over the entire system life-cycle. A maintenance action includes any requirement for corrective maintenance resulting from catastrophic failures, dependent failures, operator/maintenance induced faults, manufacturing defects, etc. The cost per maintenance action considers the personnel labor expended for direct tasks (localization, fault isolation, remove and replace, repair, verification), associated administrative/logistic delay time, material handling, and maintenance documentation (failure reports, spares issue reports). The corrective maintenance labor cost, C_{OCP}, will of course vary with the personnel skill level required for task performance. Both direct labor and overhead costs are included.
Preventive maintenance cost (C_{OOS})	$C_{OOS} = [(Q_{PA})(M_{MHP})(C_{OPP}) + (Q_{PA})(C_{MHP})$ $+ (Q_{PA})(C_{DP})](N_{MS})$ Q_{PA} = Quantity of preventive maintenance actions (M_A). Q_{PA} relates to fpt M_{MHP} = Preventive maintenance manhours/M_A C_{OPP} = Preventive maintenance labor cost (\$/M_{MHP}) C_{MHP} = Cost of material handling/preventive M_A	This category includes the personnel activity costs associated with the accomplishment of preventive or scheduled maintenance. Related spares/consumables, test and support equipment, transportation, training, and facility costs are covered in C_{OMX}, C_{OMS}, C_{OMT}, and C_{OMF}, respectively. Total cost includes the sum of individual costs for each preventive maintenance action multiplied by the quantity of maintenance actions anticipated over the system life-cycle. A maintenance action includes servicing, lubrica-

Table A-1. DESCRIPTION OF COST CATEGORIES (Continued)

Cost Category (Reference Figure A-1)	Method of Determination (Quantitative Expression)	Cost Category Description and Justification
	C_{DP} = Cost of documentation/preventive M_A N_{MS} = Number of maintenance sites Determine C_{OOS} for each appropriate echelon of maintenance.	tion, inspection, overhaul, calibration, periodic system check-outs, and the accomplishment of scheduled critical item replacements. The cost per maintenance action considers the personnel labor expended for preventive maintenance tasks, associated administrative/logistic delay time, material handling, and maintenance documentation. The preventive maintenance labor cost, C_{OPR}, will of course vary with the personnel skill level required for task performance. Both direct labor and overhead costs are included.
Spare/repair parts cost (C_{OMX})	$C_{OMX} = [C_{SO} + C_{SI} + C_{SD} + C_{SS} + C_{SC}]$ C_{SO} = Cost of organizational spare/repair parts C_{SI} = Cost of intermediate spare/repair parts C_{SD} = Cost of depot spare/repair parts C_{SS} = Cost of supplier spare/repair parts C_{SC} = Cost of consumables $$C_{SO} = \sum_{N_{MS}} [(C_A)(Q_A) + \sum_{i=1} (C_{Mi})(Q_{Mi}) + \sum_{i=1} (C_{Hi})(Q_{Hi})]$$ C_A = Average cost of material purchase order ($/order) Q_A = Quantity of purchase orders C_M = Cost of spare item i	Initial spare/repair part costs are covered in C_{ILS}. This category includes all replenishment spare/repair parts and consumable materials (e.g., oil, lubricants, fuel, etc.) that are required to support maintenance activities associated with prime equipment, operational support and handling equipment (C_{OOE}), test and support equipment (C_{OMS}), and training equipment at each echelon (organizational, intermediate, depot, supplier). This category covers the cost of purchasing; the actual cost of the material itself; and the cost of holding or maintaining items in the inventory. Costs are assigned to the applicable level of maintenance. Specific quantitative requirements for spares (Q_M) are derived from the Logistic Support Analysis (LSA) discussed

Table A-1. DESCRIPTION OF COST CATEGORIES (Continued)

Cost Category (Reference Figure A-1)	Method of Determination (Quantitative Expression)	Cost Category Description and Justification
	Q_M = Quantity of i items required or demand C_H = Cost of maintaining spare item i in the inventory ($\$/\$$ value of the inventory) Q_H = Quantity of i items in the inventory N_{MS} = Number of maintenance sites C_{SI}, C_{SD}, and C_{SS} are determined in a similar manner.	in Chapter 6 and Appendix B. These requirements are based on the criteria described in Chapter 2, Section 2E3. The optimum quantity of purchase orders (Q_A) is based on the EOQ criteria described in Section 2E3. Support equipment spares are based on the same criteria used in determining spare part requirements for prime equipment.
Test and support equipment cost (C_{OMS})	$C_{OMS} = [C_{SEO} + C_{SEI} + C_{SED}]$ C_{SEO} = Cost of organizational test and support equipment C_{SEI} = Cost of intermediate test and support equipment C_{SED} = Cost of depot test and support equipment $C_{SEO} = [C_{OOU} + C_{OOS}]$ C_{OOU} = Cost of equipment corrective maintenance C_{OOS} = Cost of equipment preventive maintenance $C_{OOU} = [(Q_{CA})(M_{MHC})(C_{OCP}) + (Q_{CA})(C_{MHC}) + (Q_{CA})(C_{DC})](N_{MS})$ Q_{CA} = Quantity of corrective maintenance actions (M_A) or $Q_{CA} = (T_O)(\lambda)$	Initial acquisition cost for test and support equipment is covered in C_{ILX}. This category includes the annual recurring life-cycle maintenance cost for test and support equipment at each echelon. Support equipment operational costs are actually covered by the tasks performed in C_{OMM}. Maintenance constitutes both corrective and preventive maintenance, and the costs are derived on a similar basis with prime equipment (C_{OOU} and C_{OOS}). Spares and consumables are included in C_{OMX}. In some instances, specific items of test and support equipment are utilized for more than one (1) system, and in such cases, associated costs are allocated proportionately to each system concerned.

Table A-1. DESCRIPTION OF COST CATEGORIES (Continued)

Cost Category (Reference Figure A-1)	Method of Determination (Quantitative Expression)	Cost Category Description and Justification
	M_{MHC} = Corrective maintenance manhours/M_A	
	C_{OCP} = Corrective maintenance labor cost ($/$M_{MHC}$)	
	C_{MHC} = Cost of material handling/corrective M_A	
	C_{DC} = Cost of documentation/corrective M_A	
	N_{MS} = Number of maintenance sites (involving organizational maintenance)	
	$C_{OOS} = [(Q_{PA})(M_{MHP})(C_{OPP}) + (Q_{PA})(C_{MHP}) + (Q_{PA})(C_{DP})](N_{MS})$	
	Q_{PA} = Quantity of preventive maintenance actions (M_A). Q_{PA} = fpt	
	M_{MHP} = Preventive maintenance manhours/M_A	
	C_{OPP} = Preventive maintenance labor cost ($/$M_{MHP}$)	
	C_{MHP} = Cost of material handling/preventive M_A	
	C_{DP} = Cost of documentation/preventive M_A	
	N_{MS} = Number of maintenance sites (involving organizational maintenance)	
	C_{SEI} and C_{SED} are determined in a similar manner.	

Table A-1. DESCRIPTION OF COST CATEGORIES (Continued)

Cost Category (Reference Figure A-1)	Method of Determination (Quantitative Expression)	Cost Category Description and Justification
Transportation and handling cost (C_{OMT})	$C_{OMT} = [(C_T)(Q_T) + (C_P)(Q_T)]$ C_T = Cost of transportation C_P = Cost of packing Q_T = Quantity of one-way shipments $C_T = [(W)(C_{TS})]$ W = Weight of item (lb) C_{TS} = Shipping cost ($/lb) C_{TS} will of course vary with the distance (in miles) of the one-way shipment. $C_P = [(W)(C_{TP})]$ C_{TP} = Packing cost ($/lbs) Packing cost and weight will vary depending on whether reusable containers are employed.	Initial (first destination) transportation and handling costs are covered in C_{ILY}. This category includes all sustaining transportation and handling (or packing and shipping) between organizational, intermediate, depot, and supplier facilities in support of maintenance operations. This includes the return of faulty material items to a higher echelon; the transportation of items to a higher echelon for preventive maintenance (overhaul, calibration); and the shipment of spare/repair parts, personnel, data, etc., from the supplier to forward echelons.
Maintenance training cost (C_{OMP})	$C_{OMP} = [(Q_{SM})(T_T)(C_{TOM})]$ Q_{SM} = Quantity of maintenance students C_{TOM} = Cost of maintenance training ($/student-week) T_T = Duration of training program (weeks)	Initial maintenance training cost is included in C_{ILT}. This category covers the *formal* training of personnel assigned to maintain the prime equipment, test and support equipment, and training equipment. Such training is accomplished on a periodic basis throughout the system life-cycle to cover personnel replacements due to attrition. Total costs include instructor time; supervision; student pay and allowances while in school; training facilities (allocation of portion of facility required specifically for formal training); training aids and data; and student transportation as applicable.

Table A-1. DESCRIPTION OF COST CATEGORIES (Continued)

Cost Category (Reference Figure A-1)	Method of Determination (Quantitative Expression)	Cost Category Description and Justification
Maintenance facilities cost (C_{OMF})	$C_{OMF} = [(C_{PPM} + C_U) \times (\% \text{ allocation})(N_{MS})]$ $C_{PPM} =$ Cost of maintenance facility support (\$/site) $C_U =$ Cost of utilities (\$/site) $N_{MS} =$ Number of maintenance sites *Alternate approach* $C_{OMF} = [(C_{PPO})(N_{MS})(S_O)]$ $C_{PPO} =$ Cost of maintenance facility space (\$/square foot/site). Utility cost allocation is included. $S_O =$ Facility space requirements (square feet) Determine C_{OMF} for each appropriate echelon of maintenance.	Initial acquisition (construction) cost for maintenance facilities is included in C_{ICM}. This category covers the annual recurring costs associated with the occupancy and support (repair, modification, paint, etc.) of maintenance shops at all echelons throughout the system life-cycle. On some occasions, a given maintenance shop will support more than one (1) system, and in such cases, associated costs are allocated proportionately to each system concerned.
Technical data cost (C_{OMD})	$C_{OMD} = \sum_{i=1}^{N} C_{OMDi}$ $C_{OMDi} =$ Cost of specific data item i $N =$ Number of data items	Initial technical data preparation costs are covered in C_{ILD}. Individual data reports covering specific maintenance actions are included in C_{OOE}, C_{OMM}, and C_{OMS}. This category includes any other data (developed on a sustaining basis) necessary to support the operation and maintenance of the system throughout its life-cycle.
System/equipment modification cost (C_{ON})	$C_{ON} = \sum_{i=1}^{N} C_{ONi}$ $C_{ONi} =$ Cost of specific modification i	Throughout the system life-cycle after equipment has been delivered in the field, modifications are often proposed and initiated to improve system performance, effectiveness, or a combination of

Table A-1. DESCRIPTION OF COST CATEGORIES (Continued)

Cost Category (Reference Figure A-1)	Method of Determination (Quantitative Expression)	Cost Category Description and Justification
	N = Number of system/equipment modifications	both. This category includes modification kit design (R and D); material; installation and test instructions; personnel and supporting resources for incorporating the modification kit; technical data change documentation; formal training (as required) to cover the new configuration; spares; etc. The modification may affect all elements of logistics.
System phase-out and disposal cost (C_{OP})	$C_{OP} = [(F_C)(Q_{CA})(C_{DIS} - C_{REC})]$ F_C = Condemnation factor Q_{CA} = Quantity of corrective maintenance actions C_{DIS} = Cost of system/equipment disposal C_{REC} = Reclamation value	This category covers the liability or assets incurred when an item is condemned or disposed. This factor is applicable throughout the system/equipment life-cycle when phase-out occurs. This category represents the only element of cost that may turn out to have a negative value—resulting when the reclamation value of the end item is larger than the disposal cost.

Table A-2. SUMMARY OF TERMS

C	Total system life-cycle cost
C_A	Average cost of material purchase order (\$/order)
C_{DC}	Cost of maintenance documentation/data for each corrective maintenance action (\$/M_A)
C_{DIS}	Cost of system/equipment disposal
C_{DP}	Cost of maintenance documentation/data for each preventive maintenance action (\$/M_A)
C_H	Cost of maintaining spare item i in the inventory or inventory holding cost (\$/dollar value of the inventory)
C_I	Total investment cost
C_{IC}	Construction cost
C_{ICA}	Construction fabrication labor cost
C_{ICB}	Construction material cost
C_{ICC}	Capital equipment cost
C_{ICM}	Maintenance facilities acquisition cost
C_{ICO}	Operational facilities acquisition cost
C_{ICP}	Manufacturing facilities cost (acquisition and substaining)
C_{ICT}	Test facilities cost (acquisition and sustaining)
C_{ICU}	Cost of utilities
C_{IL}	Initial logistic support cost
C_{ILD}	Cost of technical data preparation
C_{ILI}	Initial inventory management cost
C_{ILM}	Logistics program management cost
C_{ILP}	Cost of provisioning (preparation of procurement data covering spares, test and support equipment, etc.)
C_{ILS}	Initial spare/repair part material cost
C_{ILT}	Cost of initial training and training equipment
C_{ILX}	Acquisition cost of operational test and support equipment
C_{ILY}	Initial transportation and handling cost
C_{IM}	Manufacturing cost
C_{IN}	Nonrecurring manufacturing/production cost
C_{INA}	Quality assurance cost
C_{INM}	Manufacturing engineering cost
C_{INP}	Manufacturing management cost
C_{INQ}	Cost of qualification test (first article)
C_{INS}	Cost of production sampling test
C_{INT}	Tools and factory equipment cost (excluding capital equipment)
C_{IR}	Recurring manufacturing/production cost
C_{IRE}	Recurring manufacturing engineering support cost
C_{IRI}	Inspection and test cost
C_{IRL}	Production fabrication and assembly labor cost
C_{IRM}	Production material and inventory cost
C_{IRT}	Packing and initial transportation cost
C_M	Cost of spares item i
C_{MHC}	Cost of material handling for each corrective maintenance action (\$/M_A)
C_{MHP}	Cost of material handling for each preventive maintenance action (\$/M_A)
C_O	Operations and maintenance cost

Table A-2. SUMMARY OF TERMS (Continued)

C_{OCP}	Corrective maintenance labor cost ($/$M_{MHC}$)
C_{OM}	Cost of system/equipment life-cycle maintenance
C_{OMD}	Cost of technical data
C_{OMF}	Cost of maintenance facilities
C_{OMM}	Maintenance personnel cost
C_{OMP}	Cost of replenishment maintenance training
C_{OMS}	Test and support equipment maintenance cost
C_{OMT}	Transportation and handling cost
C_{OMX}	Spare/repair parts cost (replenishment spares)
C_{ON}	Cost of system/equipment modifications
C_{OO}	Cost of system/equipment life-cycle operations
C_{OOE}	Cost of support and handling equipment
C_{OOF}	Cost of operational facilities
C_{OOO}	Cost of operation for support and handling equipment
C_{OOP}	Operating personnel cost
C_{OOS}	Cost of equipment preventive (scheduled) maintenance
C_{OOT}	Cost of replenishment training
C_{OOU}	Cost of equipment corrective (unscheduled) maintenance
C_{OP}	Cost of system/equipment phase-out and disposal
C_{OPP}	Preventive maintenance labor cost ($/$M_{MHP}$)
C_P	Cost of packing
C_{PO}	Cost of operators labor ($/hour)
C_{PPE}	Cost of operational facility support ($/operational site)
C_{PPF}	Cost of operational facility space ($/square foot/site)
C_{PPM}	Cost of maintenance facility support ($/maintenance site)
C_{PPO}	Cost of maintenance facility space ($/square foot/site)
C_R	Total research and development cost
C_{RD}	Engineering data cost
C_{RDL}	Prototype fabrication and assembly labor cost
C_{RDM}	Prototype material cost
C_{RDT}	Prototype test and evaluation cost
C_{RE}	Engineering design cost
C_{REC}	Reclamation value
C_{RM}	Program management cost
C_{RR}	Advanced research and development cost
C_{RT}	Equipment development and test cost
C_{SC}	Cost of consumables
C_{SD}	Cost of depot spare/repair parts
C_{SED}	Cost of depot test and support equipment
C_{SEI}	Cost of intermediate test and support equipment
C_{SEO}	Cost of organizational test and support equipment
C_{SI}	Cost of intermediate spare/repair parts
C_{SO}	Cost of organizational spare/repair parts
C_{SS}	Cost of supplier spare/repair parts
C_T	Cost of transportation
C_{TOM}	Cost of maintenance training ($/student-week)
C_{TOT}	Cost of operator training ($/student-week)
C_{TP}	Packing cost ($/pound)
C_{TS}	Shipping cost ($/pound)

Table A-2. SUMMARY OF TERMS (Continued)

C_U	Cost of utilities ($/operational site)
fc	Condemnation factor (attrition)
fpt	Frequency of preventive maintenance (actions/hour of equipment operation)
λ	System/equipment failure rate (failure/hour of equipment operation)
M_{MHC}	Corrective maintenance manhours/maintenance action (MA)
M_{MHP}	Preventive maintenance manhours/maintenance action (MA)
N_{MS}	Number of maintenance sites
N_{OS}	Number of operational sites
N_{PO}	Number of operating systems
Q_A	Quantity of purchase orders
Q_{CA}	Quantity of corrective maintenance actions (MA)
Q_H	Quantity of i items in the inventory
Q_M	Quantity of i items required or demanded
Q_{PA}	Quantity of preventive maintenance actions (MA)
Q_{PO}	Quantity of operators/system
Q_{SM}	Quantity of maintenance students
Q_{SO}	Quantity of student operators
Q_T	Quantity of one-way shipments
S_O	Facility space requirements (square feet)
T_O	Hours of system operation
T_T	Duration of training program (weeks)
W	Weight of item (pounds)

B. COST ESTIMATING.

A cost estimate is an opinion or judgment concerning the expected cost to be accrued in the acquisition and/or utilization of an item. Cost estimates are derived from:

1. Known factors or rates.
2. Estimating relationships (analogous and/or parametric).
3. Expert opinion.

The first category is fairly straightforward. The analyst (or cost estimator) uses the current cost of an incremental unit of some commodity or service and multiplies it by the quantity of units involved. Some examples are presented in Table A-3.

The second category (estimating relationships) seeks to establish some higher level of estimating. Estimating relationships are analytic tools that relate various cost categories to cost generating or explanatory variables. For instance, it may be feasible to relate life-cycle cost in terms of unit weight, cost per mile of range, cost per maintenance action, cost per equip-

Table A-3. TYPICAL COST FACTORS*

1.	**PERSONNEL LABOR**	
	Operators (C_{PO})	$17.50/hour
	Preventive maintenance (C_{OPP})	
	Organizational	11.98/hour
	Intermediate	14.81/hour
	Depot	15.80/hour
	Corrective maintenance (C_{OCP})	
	Organizational	11.98/hour
	Intermediate	13.81/hour
	Depot	15.80/hour
2.	**TRANSPORTATION**	
	Shipping (C_{TS})	$63/pound-mile
	Packing (C_{TP})	65/pound-mile
3.	**TRAINING**	
	Operational (C_{TOT})	$275/student week
	Maintenance (C_{TOM})	350/student week
4.	**FACILITIES**	
	Operational (C_{PPF})	$35/sq. ft.
	Maintenance (C_{PPO})	50/sq. ft.
5.	**INVENTORY**	
	New item entry	
	Repairable	$335/item
	Nonrepairable	272/item
	Maintenance	20% of inventory value ($/$/year)
6.	**DATA**	
	Technical manuals	$350/page
	Maintenance documentation	200/MA
7.	**CONSUMABLES**	
	Oil	$1.55/quart
	Gasoline	1.30/gallon

Note: Symbols and subscripts (C_{PO}, C_{OCP}, etc.) are derived from Table A-1.
*Referring to the information in Table A-3, it is obvious that the analyst must be continually aware of changing prices or rates, particularly in view of current inflationary trends.

ment module, quantity of maintenance support personnel in terms of quantity of operating personnel, cost per unit of volume, cost per unit of reliability, and so on.

Cost estimating relationships may assume numerous forms, varying from informal rules of thumb or simple analogies to a more formal mathematical relationship derived through a statistical analysis of empirical data. Generally, cost and related data are collected on existing systems in the inventory, analyzed, converted to the form of some relationship, and applied to a new system (which is similar in form and function) as a predicting tool. Given an identifiable data base, the analyst assumes some theoretical relationship and then proceeds to test that relationship for validity (hypotheses testing). Testing may range from the use of simple graphics to a complex statistical test using well defined data samples.

The estimating relationship may be a simple linear function identified by the equation.

$$\text{cost} = (\text{some constant})(\text{variable } X) \tag{A.1}$$

From a series or mass of data points, a relationship can be established through curve fitting techniques such as least squares or through a conventional linear regression analysis.

Nonlinear cost relationships may be stated in the form of some distribution such as normal, log-normal, exponential, and so on. Sometimes the relationship assumes one form between two discrete values of a variable and another form between other values of the same variable. A simple example is the *step function*, where cost is constant over a certain range, then suddenly jumps to higher level before becoming once again constant over another range of values. Determining production costs for a varied quantity of equipment items is a good example of the step-function concept.

Still another form of the estimating relationship is the multivariate function. In all situations it may not be possible or feasible to express cost in terms of a single variable. Cost may be expressed as a function of system range and weight, utilization and the number of system elements, spare parts and inventory level, and so on. The cost function may take the form

$$\text{cost} = 100 + (K_1)(\text{variable } X_1) + (K_2)(\text{variable } X_2) \tag{A.2}$$

where K is some fixed constant.

The cost-estimating relationship must be reasonable and it must have predictive value. It is a highly significant factor in the analysis and, when improperly applied, can lead to the introduction of a great deal of error in the results. The type of technique used is dependent on the problem being solved and the type of data available to the analyst. If unsure of this area, the student is advised to review additional material before proceeding.[3]

The last category of cost estimating is the one dictated by expert opinion. Although argumentive, it is often the only method available to the analyst since backup data are sometimes scarce, if they exist at all. In such instances, when expert opinion is used in the analysis, the analyst should be sure to include assumptions and rationale that support his or her position.

C. Discounting

Discounting relates to the time value of money. Time is valuable, and the analyst cannot treat benefits and costs as being equal without considering

---

[3]Fisher, G. H., *Cost Considerations in System Analysis*, American Elsevier Publishing Co., Inc., New York, 1971, chap. 6.

the time element. When comparing two or more alternatives, a common base is necessary to ensure a fair evaluation. Since the common base is the present point in time, all future costs must be adjusted to the present value. Discounting refers to the application of a selected rate of interest to a cost stream such that each future cost is adjusted to the present time, the point when the decision is made.

The procedure for discounting is simple; however, selecting the proper discount rate is often difficult. The proper choice of a discount rate used in comparing future dollars with today's dollars depends on the options available for exchanging one for the other. In other words, all the investment opportunities should be evaluated. Through using the present-value concept, these opportunities are evaluated on a comparable basis.

Thus, when accomplishing a life-cycle cost analysis, costs are determined by category (see Table A-1) for each year in the life cycle. A discount rate may be applied to adjust those costs to back the decision point. An example of the calculation for discounting is presented in Section 2.9 and typical present-value factors are presented in Table 2-9.

D. INFLATION

The persistent trend toward inflation in recent years creates an awareness of another way which the aspect of time can affect costs (i.e., the changing value of the dollar). Consideration of inflation is necessary in the performance of a life-cycle analysis.

E. LEARNING CURVES

When accomplishing a process on a repetitive basis, learning takes place and the experience gained often results in reduced cost. This is particularly true in the production of a large quantity of a given item. The cost of the first unit is generally higher than the cost of the 50th unit, which may be higher than the cost of the 100th unit, and so on. This is primarily due to job familiarization by workmen in the production facility, development of more efficient methods of assembly, use of more efficient tools, improvement in overall management, and so on. This continues until a leveling off takes place.

In such instances, it may be appropriate to apply a learning curve in order to promote a more realistic cost profile. For example, if the cost of producing the 10th unit is 80% of the first unit cost, the cost of producing the 20th unit is 80% of the 10th unit cost, and the cost of producing the 40th unit is 80% of the 20th unit cost, then the production process is said to follow an 80% *unit* learning curve. This cost learning curve can be applied to the manufacturing cost category under investment. An illustration of several learning curves is presented in Figure A-2.

If it turns out that the average cost of producing the first 20 units is

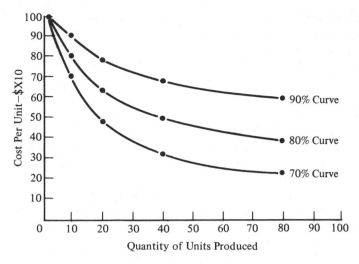

Figure A-2. Unit learning curves.

80% of the average cost of producing the first 10 units, then the process follows an 80% *cumulative average* learning curve.

The application of learning curves must not only consider labor cost but also should cover material costs which may vary due to shifts in procurement methods (large lot quantity purchases) and inventory policies. There are many factors involved and different learning curves may be applied depending on the situation. To gain more insight on the subject, the review of additional material is recommended.[4]

F. COST MODELS

As defined in Chapter 6, a model is a simplified representation of a real-world situation, and is an analytical tool employed in the decision-making process. Cost models can be classified in a number of ways—according to the function they serve, according to the anticipated repetitive type usage in terms of the subject area they are intended to represent, etc.[5]

With reference to the material covered in this text, the model is the analytic tool which combines the effectiveness elements and cost categories in Table A-1 to generate life-cycle cost data in a timely manner for evaluation purposes. The model application is discussed rather thoroughly in Chapter 6. Additional applications are included in the summary information presented in Appendix C.

---

[4]Fabrycky, W. J., Ghare, P. M., and Torgersen, P. E., *Industrial Operations Research*, Prentice-Hall, Inc., Englewood Cliffs, N.J., 1972.

[5]Fisher, G. H., *Cost Considerations in System Analysis*, American Elsevier Publishing Co., Inc., New York, 1971.

APPENDIX B

MAINTENANCE ANALYSIS DATA

The maintenance analysis is an inherent part of logistic support analysis (LSA), described in Chapter 6. The analysis provides an engineering data package covering all scheduled and unscheduled maintenance functions, tasks, and associated logistic support requirements for the system or equipment being analyzed. The type of information output provided by the analysis is presented in Figure 6-5.[1]

Maintenance analysis data cover:

1. All significant repairable items (i.e., system, subsystem, assembly, and subassembly). Items, identified through the level of repair analysis, which are relatively complex and require an analysis to determine the type and extent of support needed should be addressed.
2. All maintenance requirements (i.e., troubleshooting, remove and replace, repair, servicing, alignment and adjustment, functional test and check-out, inspection, calibration, overhaul, etc.).

---

[1]Several source documents covering the maintenance analysis are (a) AMCP 700-4, NAVMAT-P-4000-1, AFLCM/AFSCM 400-4, *Standard Integrated Support Management System* (*SISMS*), Department of Defense, Washington, D.C., March 1969. (b) MIL-STD-1388, Military Standard, "Logistic Support Analysis," Department of Defense, Washington, D.C., October 1973.

The maintenance analysis is developed on an iterative basis throughout system definition and design. The development cycle is illustrated in Figure 7-6. Basically, the analysis stems from the maintenance concept and is dependent on engineering design data, reliability and maintainability analyses and predictions, human factors data, and so on. Maintenance analysis data are used to support design decisions and to serve as the basis for the subsequent provisioning and acquisition of specific logistic support items needed for the operation and maintenance of the system when deployed in the field.

The maintenance analysis data format is by no means fixed. It varies from program to program, and is tailored to the specific information desired and the time in the life cycle when needed. When developing analysis data in support of early design decisions (involving the evaluation of alternatives— see Chapter 6), the amount of information needed is less precise and not as extensive as the data required for a fixed configuration going into a final design review. In addition, the early analysis efforts must provide the right information expeditiously as the designer is required to make many decisions in a relatively short period of time. If this information is not available in a timely manner, the decisions will be made anyway and the results may not prove to be as beneficial. Thus, the maintenance analysis may assume several different postures as system/equipment development progresses.

In the interest of illustrating the maintenance analysis and the methods for data generation, a few sample (representative) forms are included and discussed in terms of the requirements for completion. The maintenance task analysis form (Figures B-1 and B-3) is completed for each major requirement associated with a given repairable item. The data summary form (Figure B-5) combines the various requirements and covers the repairable as an entity.

A. MAINTENANCE TASK ANALYSIS (SHEET 1), FIGURE B-1

The following instructions should be followed when completing sheet 1 of the maintenance task analysis form.[2]

1. *Block 1—System.* Enter the proper nomenclature of the system or end item covered by the overall analysis.
2. *Block 2—Item Name/Part Number.* Enter the name and manufacturer's part number for the repairable item being covered by this task analysis sheet. This may constitute a subsystem, assembly, subassembly, and so on.
3. *Block 3—Next Higher Assembly.* Include the name and part number of the next higher assembly. This constitutes one higher indenture level of

---

[2]Many of these same requirements are described in Blanchard, B. S., and Lowery, E. E., *Maintainability—Principles and Practices*, McGraw-Hill Book Company, New York, 1969.

1 SYSTEM	2 ITEM NAME/PART NO.	3 NEXT HIGHER ASSY.	4 DESCRIPTION OF REQUIREMENT:
Ship Steering	Hydraulic System /A12345	Ship Steering /A45400	A faulty starboard automatic valve in the hydraulic system must be repaired to restore ship's steering to full operational capability. Repair is accomplished on shipboard.

5 REQ. NO.	5 REQUIREMENT	7 REQ. FREQ.	8 MAINT. LEVEL	9 MA CONT. NO.
02	Repair	0.000486	Intermediate	A10000

10 TASK NUMBER	11 TASK DESCRIPTION	ELAPSED TIME-MINUTES (2–38)	13 TOTAL ELAP. TIME	14 TASK FREQ.	15 R	16 I	17 S	18 TOTAL
0010	Actuate Valve 2, Shut-off Pressure From Stbd. Pump.	①	2	0.000486	–	2	–	2
0020	Operate Emergency Handpump		23		23	–	–	23
0030	Remove 1½" External Tubing		10		10	10	–	20
0040	Remove 3/4" External Tubing		4		4	4	–	8
0050	Remove Automatic Valve Assy. From System		2		2	2	–	4
0060	Install Flanges On Tubing. Stop Handpump. Actuate Valve 3. Start Port Pump (Pressure On Syst.)		7		–	7	–	7
0070	Transport Valve Assy. To Intermediate Shop		13		13	13	–	26
0080	Disassemble Valve Assy. & Remove Valve Rod & Piston. Remove Valve P/N 16742-1.	(cycle 2)	18		–	18	–	18
0090	Transport Valve To Machine Shop		8		8	–	–	8
0100	Machine & Clean Valve	(cycle 3)	33		–	–	33	33
0110	Clean Valve Rod, Piston, Spring Assy.		19		–	19	–	19
0120	Install Valve, Valve Rod, Piston, Spring, Gaskets & O-Rings Into Valve Assy.	(cycle 4)	17		–	17	–	17
0130	Checkout Automatic Valve Assy.		12		12	12	–	24
0140	Transport Valve Assy. To System		13		13	13	–	26
0150	Stop Port Pump. Actuate Valve 3 & Start Handpump.	(cycle 5)	23		18	5	–	23
0160	Remove Flanges From Tubing. Install Valve Assy.		6		6	6	–	12
0170	Connect 3/4" External Tubing		5		5	5	–	10
0180	Connect 1½" External Tubing		7		7	7	–	14
0190	Stop Handpump. Actuate Valve 2. Start Stbd. Pump		4	0.000486	4	4	–	4
			Σ 184		Σ 121	Σ 144	Σ 33	Σ 298

Prepared By: Blanchard   Date: 10/1/xx

Figure B-1. Maintenance task analysis (sheet 1).

hardware above the item listed in block 2. If a subassembly is being analyzed, the assembly should be identified in block 3.

4. *Block 4—Description of Requirement.* A technical description and justification for the maintenance requirement identified in block 6 should be included. The need for performing maintenance must be clearly established. Include references to related requirements.

5. *Block 5—Requirement Number.* A number is assigned for each requirement applicable to the item being analyzed. Requirements are identified in block 6, and may be sequentially numbered from 01 to 99 as necessary.

6. *Block 6—Requirement.* The requirement nomenclature should be entered in this block. Generally, maintenance requirements fall into one of the following areas.

> a. *Adjustment/alignment*—to line up, balance, or alter as necessary to make an item compatible with system requirements. This is a maintenance requirement when the primary cause of the maintenance action is to adjust or align, or to verify adjustment/alignment of an item. Adjustment/alignment accomplished subsequent to repair of a given item is not considered as a separate requirement, but is included as a task in the repair requirement.
>
> b. *Calibration*—a maintenance requirement whenever an item is checked against a working standard, a secondary standard, or a primary standard. Calibration generally applies to precision measurement equipment (PME) and can be accomplished either on a scheduled basis or on an unscheduled basis subsequent to the accomplishment of a repair action on a PME item. Calibration provides the necessary test accuracy and traceability to the National Bureau of Standards (e.g., a working standard is checked against a secondary standard that in turn is checked against a primary standard).
>
> c. *Functional test*—a system or subsystem operational checkout either as a condition verification after the accomplishment of item repair or as a periodic scheduled requirement.
>
> d. *Inspection*—a maintenance requirement when the basic objective is to ensure that a requisite condition or quality exists. In order to inspect for a desired condition, it may be necessary to remove the item, to gain access by removing other items, or to partially disassemble the item for inspection purposes. In such instances, these associated actions which are necessary to accomplish the required inspection would be specific tasks.
>
> e. *Overhaul*—a maintenance requirement whenever an item is completely disassembled, refurbished, tested, and returned to a serviceable condition meeting all requirements set forth in applicable specifications. Overhaul may result from either a scheduled or unscheduled requirement and is generally accomplished at the depot maintenance facility or the producer's facility.

f. *Remove*—a maintenance requirement when the basic objective is to remove an item from the next-higher assembly.

g. *Remove and reinstall*—a maintenance requirement when an item is removed for any reason, and the same item is later reinstalled.

h. *Remove and replace*—constitutes the removal of one item and replacement with another like item (i.e., spare part). Such action can result from a failure or from a scheduled replacement of a critical-useful-life item.

i. *Repair*—constitutes a series of corrective maintenance tasks required to return an item to a serviceable condition. This involves the replacement of parts, the alteration of material, fixing, sealing, filling-in, etc.

j. *Servicing*—includes the maintenance operations associated with the application of lubricants, gas, fuel, oil, and so on. Servicing may require removal, disassembly, reassembly, adjustment, installation, or a lesser number of these tasks. Servicing may also be included as a task under a requirement to repair, calibrate, or test an item; however, it will not be classified under servicing in this instance.

k. *Troubleshooting*—involves the logical process (series of tasks) which leads to the positive identification of the cause of a malfunction. It includes localization and fault isolation. Troubleshooting is best illustrated by the logic troubleshooting flow diagram illustrated in Figure B-4.

Whenever one of the foregoing requirements is the basic underlying cause, purpose, or objective to be satisfied, the operation becomes a maintenance requirement.

7. *Block 7—Requirement Frequency.* The frequency at which the requirement is expected to occur is entered in this block. If the requirement is "Repair" and the item is the "Hydraulic System," the analyst must determine or predict how often repair of the hydraulic system is to be accomplished. This value is dependent on the task frequencies in block 14, and is generally expressed either in number of actions per hour of equipment operation or in terms of a given calendar time period.

The need for establishing a frequency factor for a requirement is to provide a basis for determining associated logistics resource demands. In other words,

a. How often do we expect to need a spare/repair part?

b. How often do we need test and support equipment for maintenance?

c. How often will maintenance personnel be required?

d. How often will an equipment item be down for maintenance?

e. How often will servicing be required?

f. How often will overhaul be accomplished?

Once these questions are answered, it becomes possible to project downtime and determine logistics resource requirements.

When determining the intervals or frequencies representing unscheduled maintenance actions, the inherent reliability characteristics of an item may be significant, but they are not necessarily dominant considerations. For some equipment, field data have indicated that less than one-third of all unscheduled maintenance actions are attributed to random catastrophic (primary) failures; therefore, it is obvious that consideration must be given to other contributing factors as well. On the other hand, there are many instances where reliability failure rates dominate all considerations. In this event, a proportional amount of attention must be given to the significance of random failures. In either case, the maintenance frequency factor must consider the following.[3]

> a. *Inherent reliability characteristics.* This category covers primary failures based on the physical makeup of the item and the stresses to which the item is subjected. Part catastrophic failures and out-of-tolerance conditions are included. Primary failures are derived through reliability prediction data and are usually based on a constant failure rate.
>
> b. *Manufacturing defects or burn-in characteristics.* Quite often when an equipment item first comes off the production line, there are a rash of failures until the system is operated for a short period of time and a constant failure rate is realized. This is particularly true for electronic equipment when certain corrective actions are necessary to attain system stabilization. The extent of difficulty at this early point in the operational use phase is dependent on the amount of equipment operation and the type of testing accomplished in the production/construction phase. If enough hours of equipment operation are attained through testing, the quantity of failures after delivery will probably be less. In any event, when new equipment first enters the inventory, there may be more initial failures than indicated by the predicted reliability failure rate, and this factor must be considered in determining the requirements for initial system support.
>
> c. *Wear-out characteristics.* After equipment has been in operational use for a period of time, various individual components begin to wear out. Some components (i.e., mechanical linkages, gears) wear out sooner than others. When this occurs, the resultant frequency of failure and corrective maintenance will increase.
>
> d. *Dependent failures (chain effect).* This category includes those secondary failures which occur as a result of a primary catastrophic failure. In other words, the failure of one item may cause other items to fail. The frequency of dependent failures is based on the extent of fail-safe characteristics inherent in the design. In electronic equipment, circuit protection provisions may be incorporated to reduce the probability of

---

[3]The extent of reliability, maintainability, and human factors influence in the design will significantly affect the factors used in determining this value. Refer to Chapter 7.

dependent failures. The reliability failure mode and effect analysis (FMEA) is the best data source for reflecting dependent failure characteristics.

e. *Operator-induced failures.* Overstress of equipment due to operator human error is a possibility and is very significant in determining frequency factors. Unplanned stresses can be placed on the equipment as a result of different operating methods (by different operators or by the same operator), and these stresses can accumulate to the extent that the equipment will fail more frequently. Hopefully, conditions such as this can be minimized or eliminated through the proper emphasis on human factors in the design process.

f. *Maintenance-induced failures.* Damage to equipment caused by human error during maintenance actions may result from not following the proper maintenance procedures, improper application and use of tools and test items, losing components or leaving parts out when reassembling items after repair, forcing replacement items to fit when physical interferences are present, causing physical damage to components lying adjacent to or near the item being repaired, and many others. Induced faults of this type may occur due to improper maintenance envi onment (inadequate illumination, uncomfortable temperatures, high noise level), personnel fatigue, inadequately trained personnel performing the maintenance tasks, equipment sensitivity or fragility, poor internal accessibility to components, and not having the right elements of logistic support available when needed. Maintenance-induced faults are possible both during the accomplishment of corrective maintenance and preventive maintenance. For instance, during a scheduled calibration when performing a fine adjustment, a screwdriver slip may cause damage in another area resulting in corrective maintenance.

g. *Equipment damage due to handling.* Another important aspect is the probability of equipment damage due to bumping, dropping, shoving, tossing, and so on. These factors are particularly relevant during transportation modes and often contribute to subsequent equipment failures. The extent to which consideration is given toward transportability in the equipment design will influence the effects of handling on the equipment failure rate. The analyst should evaluate anticipated transportation and handling modes, review the design in terms of effects, and assign an appropriate frequency factor.

System failures (of one type or another) may be detected through built-in self-test go/no-go indicators, performance monitoring devices, and/or through actual visual indication of a faulty condition. Performance monitoring devices may allow for the measurement of certain designated system parameters on a periodic basis; thus permitting the observation of trends. The concept of performance monitoring is illustrated in Figure B-2, where measurement points are indicated in terms of system operating time. When cer-

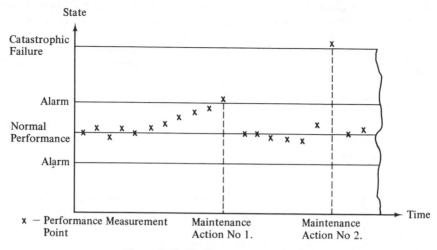

Figure B-2. Performance monitoring.

tain failure trends are noted, maintenance actions may be initiated even though an actual catastrophic failure has not occurred. In other words, the anticipation of future maintenance causes a maintenance action to be accomplished at an earlier time. These instances must also be considered in determining requirement frequency.

The foregoing considerations are reviewed on an individual basis and may be combined to provide an overall factor for a given corrective maintenance action.

Consideration	*Assumed Factor (Instances/Oper. Hour)*
(a) Inherent Reliability Failure Rate	0.000392
(b) Manufacturing Defects	0.000002
(c) Wearout Rate	0.000000
(d) Dependent Failure Rate	0.000072
(e) Operator-Induced Failure Rate	0.000003
(f) Maintenance-Induced Failure Rate	0.000012
(g) Equipment Damage Rate	0.000005
Total Combined Factor	0.000486

The frequency factor in block 7 represents the overall number of instances per equipment operating hour (or calendar period) for the maintenance requirement defined in block 6. The factor is determined from the frequency of the individual tasks identified in blocks 10 and 11. The maintenance requirement may constitute a series of tasks, each one of which is accomplished whenever the requirement exists. In this instance, the frequency factor for each task (block 14) will be the same as the factor entered in block 7. This is illustrated in Figure B-1. On the other hand, it may be feasible to include a series of *either–or* tasks on a single maintenance task analysis sheet. For instance, when a troubleshooting requirement exists, tasks may be identified as follows:

[10]*Task Number*	[11]*Task Description*	[14]*Task Frequency*
0010	Localize fault to Unit *A*	0.000486
0020	Remove Unit *A* access cover	0.000486
X030	Isolate to Assembly *A*	0.000133
X040	Isolate to Assembly *B*	0.000212
X050	Isolate to Assembly *C*	0.000141
0060	Install Unit *A* access cover	0.000486
0070	Check out Unit *A*	0.000486

The troubleshooting requirement will apply to Assembly *A* in 0.000133 instance per equipment operating hour, Assembly *B* in 0.000212 instance, and so on. The sum of the various alternatives (*x* tasks) will constitute the overall frequency, or the value in block 7 is 0.000486. Tasks 0010, 0020, 0060, and 0070 are applicable for each occurrence of Tasks X030, X040, and X050. This method of data presentation provides a simplified approach for covering the numerous possible alternatives often applicable to the diagnostic aspects of corrective maintenance, particularly for electronic equipment. A clearer picture of the alternative courses of action is illustrated in the logic troubleshooting flow diagram in Figure B-4.

8. *Block 8—Maintenance Level.* The level of maintenance at which the requirement will be accomplished is identified. This may be organizational, intermediate, depot, or supplier. Refer to Chapter 4 for a description of the levels of maintenance.

9. *Block 9—MA Control Number.* Enter the maintenance analysis (MA) control number for the item identified in block 2. The control numbering sequence is a numerical breakdown of the system by hardware indenture level and is designed to provide traceability from the highest maintenance significant item to the lowest repairable unit. An example of MA control number assignment is as follows:

Equipment Item	*MA Control Number*
System *XYZ*	A0000
Unit *A* (in System *XYZ*)	A1000
Assembly 2 (in Unit *A*)	A1200
Subassembly *C* (in Assy. 2)	A1230

A MA control number is assigned to each maintenance significant item. Maintenance tasks and logistic support resource requirements are identified against each control number and may be readily tabulated from the lowest item to the system level. MA control numbers are assigned by function and not necessarily by part number. If a modification of Assembly 2 is accomplished or an alternate configuration of Assembly 2 is employed, the manufacturer's part number changes, but the MA control number remains the same as long as the basic function of the applicable item is unchanged.

10. *Block 10—Task Number.* A four-digit alphanumeric designation is assigned to each task. Sequential tasks (those applicable each time that the maintenance requirement is accomplished) are identified with a "0" as the first digit. Tasks which are optional (either–or) depending on their applicability are designated with an x. The last three digits indicate the sequence of task accomplishment (e.g., 0010, 0020, 0030, etc.). Subtasks may be identified further, if desired, through the use of the fourth digit (e.g., 0021, 0022, etc.). The alphanumeric designation simplifies task identification when maintenance analysis data are computerized.

11. *Block 11—Task Description.* Tasks should be stated in a concise technical manner, and should be defined to the extent necessary to enable development of a complete maintenance checklist. Significant tasks include those whose accomplishment requires a spare, an item of support equipment, or some related element of logistic support. Including an extensive amount of detail is not necessary; however, enough detail should be provided to enable the identification of logistic support requirements.

12. *Block 12—Elapsed Time (Minutes).* For each task listed in blocks 10 and 11, an elapsed time line should be projected. If two or more people are involved in a task, it may be feasible to construct a separate time line for each individual (e.g., ▨ ① for worker 1, ▨ ② for worker 2, etc.). If the task extends beyond the 40-minute period indicated on the form, the time line is continued on the next line commencing at zero and a new cycle is indicated. In instances where times are extensive (hours instead of minutes), the basic scale can readily be converted to hours. The benefit of the layout of time lines included in Figure B-1 is to allow for the evaluation of manpower utilization and task sequencing. There may be a number of tasks which can be accomplished in parallel, or in other instances a series relationship may exist. If several equipments require maintenance at the same time, the time-line analysis in block 12 will aid the analyst in determining schedule and manpower requirements. By pictorially presenting timeline data, it is possible to evaluate a number of sequences, arriving at an optimum arrangement. The objective is to minimize both elapsed time and man time, and to make greater use of lower skilled personnel where possible.

13. *Blocks 13 and 19—Total Elapsed Time.* The numerical values of elapsed time (represented by the time lines in block 12) are entered in block

13 and totaled in block 19. This constitutes the time between task start and task completion. Do not total the times of the various task segments.

14. *Block 14—Task Frequency.* The frequency of each task, in terms of instances per equipment hour of operation, is recorded. This represents the number of times that a certain maintenance action is expected to occur or the anticipated demand rate for a given spare/repair part in a remove and replace action.

15. *Blocks 15–18 and 20–23 (Man-minutes).* Enter the total man-minutes required per task for each of three basic skill levels. These skill levels may be defined as follows.[4]

a. *Basic skill level (blocks 15 and 20).* A basic skill level is assumed to be a technician with the following characteristics.
Age—18 to 21 years.
Experience—no regular work experience prior to training.
Educational level—high school graduate.
General reading/writing level—9th grade.
After a limited amount of specialized training, these personnel can perform routine checks, accomplish physical functions, use basic hand-tools, and follow clearly presented instructions where interpretation and decision making is not necessary. Workers in this class usually assist more highly skilled personnel, and require constant supervision. For military applications, service pay grades E3 and E4 generally fall in this category.

b. *Intermediate skill level (blocks 16 and 21).* These personnel have had a more formalized education, consisting of approximately 2 years of college or equivalent course work in a technical institute. In addition, they have had some specialized training, and 2 to 5 years of experience in the field related to the type of equipment in question. Personnel in this class can perform relatively complex tasks using a variety of test instruments, and are able to make certain decisions pertaining to maintenance and the disposition of equipment items. Military personnel grade E5, or civilian equivalent, falls in this category.

c. *Supervisory or high skill level (blocks 17 and 22).* These personnel have had 2 to 4 years of formal college or equivalent course work in a technical institute, and possess 10 years or more of related on-the-job experience. They are assigned to supervise and train intermediate and basic-skill-level personnel, and are in the position to interprete proce-

---

[4]There may be other classifications of personnel skills depending on the user's organization structure. The intent is to define specific classifications that will be applicable in system operational use, and to evaluate maintenance tasks in terms of these classifications. Some examples of personnel classification may be found in civil service job descriptions and in the following military documentation: (a) AFM 39-1, *U.S. Air Force Personnel Manual;* (b) NAVPERS 18068, *Navy Personnel Information;* and (c) AR 611-201, *Army Personnel Selection and Classification.*

dures, accomplish complex tasks, and make major decisions affecting maintenance policy and the disposition of equipment. They are knowledgeable in the operation and use of highly complex precision (calibration) equipment. Military personnel grades of E6 and above, or equivalent civilian classifications, are included.

Each task in block 11 is analyzed from the standpoint of complexity and requirement for task accomplishment relative to human sensory and perceptual capacities, motor skills, mobility coordination, human physical dimensions and muscular strength, and so on. In some instances, the conductance of a human factors detailed task analysis will be necessary to provide the detail required for a skill-level assignment. An appropriate skill level is assigned to each task and the man-minutes by skill level are entered in blocks 15–18. A total of personnel labor time for the requirement (identified in block 6) is included in blocks 20–23.

Once the personnel skill levels have been assigned by task, it is necessary to compare these with the skills of user personnel scheduled (in the future) to maintain the equipment in the field. The results will dictate formal training requirements. For example, user personnel scheduled for assignment to maintain System *XYZ* in the field are currently classified as basic, and the task analysis indicates a requirement for intermediate skills. In this instance, it is obvious that some formal/on-the-job training is required to upgrade the personnel from basic to the intermediate level. Through a review of all maintenance requirements at each echelon, the analyst can determine the number of personnel required, the skill levels, and the areas that must be covered through formal training.

B. Maintenance Task Analysis (Sheet 2), Figure B-3

The instructions below should apply when completing sheet 2 of the maintenance task analysis form. Sheet 2 supplements sheet 1 (Figure B-1) through the assignment of common task numbers in block 7.

1. *Blocks 1–6.* Enter the applicable data from sheet 1.
2. *Block 7—Task Number.* Identify (by use of the appropriate four-digit alphanumeric designation) each task from sheet 1 where replacement parts, test and support equipment, facilities, and/or special data instructions are required. If a task requires the replacement of an item, a spare-part need should be identified along with the anticipated frequency of replacement. Similarly, if a task requires the use of an item of support equipment, the task should be entered in block 7. Whenever a logistic support requirement is anticipated, the applicable task(s) must be included.
3. *Blocks 8–11—Replacement Parts.* This category identifies all anticipated replacement parts and consumables associated with scheduled and unscheduled maintenance. Blocks 9 and 11 define the item by nomenclature

Maintenance Task Analysis

1. ITEM NAME/PART NO.	2. REQ. NO.	3. REQUIREMENT	4. REQ. FREQ.	5. MAINT. LEVEL	6. MA CONT. NO.
Hydraulic System/A12345	02	Repair	0.000484	Intermediate	A10000

7. TASK NUMBER	8. QTY PER ASSY	9/11. PART NOMENCLATURE / PART NUMBER	10. REP. FREQ.	12. QTY	13/15. ITEM NOMENCLATURE / ITEM PART NUMBER	14. USE TIME (MIN)	16. DESCRIPTION OF FACILITY REQUIREMENTS	17. SPECIAL TECHNICAL DATA INSTRUCTIONS
0010								Handpump Operating Instructions
0020								Hydraulic System Maintenance Procedures (MP3201) →
0030				1	Wrench-1½"/600120-2	10		
0040				1	Wrench-3/4"/645809-1	4		
0050				1	Handling Dolly/S101-4	2		
0060				1	1½" Flange/AA123	150		
				1	3/4" Flange/AB142	150		
0070				1	Handling Dolly/S101-4	13	Intermediate Maint. Shop →	
0080				1	Wrench-1/4"/632111-1	18		
				1	Screwdriver/732102	18		
0090								
0100				1	Grinder/BN101(S&Co)	33	Machine Shop (With Cleaning Facilities)	Grinder/Sander Operating Instructions (OP3104 & OP3107)
					Sander/C32101(PMN)	33		Hydraulic System Maintenance Procedures (MP3201)
0110	1 Gal.	Solvent/SA123	0.000484				Intermediate Maint. Shop →	
0120	1	Gasket/AN11B-1	0.000484					
0130	2	"O"Ring/AN9001-2	0.000484		Pneu.Test Set/HPT-162	12		Pneu.Test Set Oper. Instructions
0140					Handling Dolly/S101-4	13		Hydraulic System Maintenance Procedures (MP3201) →
0150								
0160					Wrench-1½"/600120-2	6		
0170	1	3/4" Gasket/AN912	0.000484		Wrench-3/4"/645809-1	6		
0180	1	1½" Gasket/AN877-1	0.000484		Wrench-3/4"/645809-1	5		
0190					Wrench-1½"/600120-2	7		

Prepared By: Blanchard   Date: 10/1/xx

Figure B-3. Maintenance task analysis (sheet 2).

and manufacturer's part number. Block 8 indicates the quantity of items used (actually replaced or consumed) in accomplishing the task. Block 10 specifies the predicted replacement rate based on a combination of primary and secondary failures, induced faults, wear-out characteristics, condemned items scrapped, or scheduled maintenance actions. If an item is replaced for any reason, it should be covered in this category. This forms the basis for determination of MTBR.

In the event that an either–or situation exists (identified by an x task number in block 7, sheet 1) the listing of replacement parts should follow the task listing.

		Replacement Parts		
Task Number	Task Description	Qty. per Assy.	Part Nomenclature Part Number	Rep. Freq.
0010	Localize fault to Unit A	. . . .	. . . .	. . . .
0020	Remove Unit A access cover	. . . .	. . . .	. . . .
X030	Isolate to Assy. A	. . . .	. . . .	. . . .
X031	Remove and Replace Assy. A	1	Ampl.-Modular Assy. A160189-1	0.000133
X040	Isolate to Assy. B	. . . .	. . . .	. . . .
X041	Remove and Replace	1	Power Converter Assy. A180221-2	0.000212
X050	Isolate to Assy. C	. . . .	. . . .	. . . .
X051	Remove and Replace Assy. C	1	Power Supply Assy. A21234-10	0.000141
0060	Install Unit A access cover	. . . .	. . . .	. . . .
0070	Check out Unit A	. . . .	. . . .	

The replacement parts are identified for all maintenance requirements at each level, and the replacement frequencies (replacements per hour of equipment operation) indicate the demand for each part application. When these factors are integrated at the system level, it is possible to determine spare/repair part requirements.

4. *Blocks 12–15—Test and Support/Handling Equipment.* Enter all tools, test and support equipment, and handling equipment required to accomplish the tasks listed in block 7. Blocks 13 and 15 define the item by

nomenclature and manufacturer's part number. Block 12 indicates the quantity of items required per task, and block 14 specifies item utilization.

When determining the type of test and support equipment, the analyst should address the following in the order presented.

   a. Determine that there is a definite need for the test and support/handling equipment. Can such a need be economically avoided through a design change?
   b. Given a need, determine the environmental requirements. Is the equipment to be used in a sheltered area or outside? How often will the equipment be deployed to other locations? If handling equipment is involved, what item(s) is to be transported, and where?
   c. For test equipment, determine the parameters to be measured. What accuracies and tolerances are required? What are the requirements for traceability? Can another test equipment item at the same location be used for maintenance support or does the selected item have to be sent to a higher level of maintenance for calibration? It is desirable to keep test requirements as simple as possible and to a minimum. For instance, if 10 different testers are assigned at the intermediate level, it would be preferable to be able to check them out with one other tester (with higher accuracy) in the intermediate shop rather than send all 10 testers to the depot for calibration. The analyst should define the entire test cycle prior to arriving at a final recommendation.
   d. Determine whether an existing off-the-shelf equipment item will do the job (through review of catalogs and data sheets) rather than contract for a new design, which is usually more costly. If an existing item is not available, solicit sources for design and development.
   e. Given a decision on the item to be acquired, determine the proper quantity. Utilization or use time is particularly important when arriving at the number of test and support equipments assigned to a particular maintenance facility. When compiling the requirements at the system level, there may be 24 instances when a given test equipment item is required; however, the utilization of that item may be such that a quantity of two will fulfill all maintenance needs at a designated facility. Without looking at actual utilization and associated maintenance schedules, there is a danger of specifying more test and support equipment than what is really required. This, of course, results in unnecessary cost. The ultimate objective is to determine overall use time, allow enough additional time for support equipment maintenance, and procure just enough items to do the job.

Test and support equipment requirements are listed in blocks 12–15. However, the justification and backup data covering each item is provided in a specification defining need, functions, and recommended technical approach. This may be presented in the form of a design specification if a new development effort is required, or in the form of a procurement specification if an off-the-shelf item is identified. In any event, once the maintenance analysis identifies a need for a support equipment item, action is taken to acquire the item in time for system evaluation and test (preferably for Type 2 testing).

5. *Block 16—Description of Facility Requirements.* When evaluating each task, the analyst must determine where the task is to be accomplished and the facilities required. This includes the determination of space requirements, capital equipment needs, equipment layout, storage space, power and light, telephone, water, gas, environmental controls, and so on. If a "clean room" is required for the accomplishment of precise maintenance and calibration, it should be specified. The analyst should solicit assistance from system design and human factors personnel and generate a facilities plan showing a complete layout of all essential items. The type of facility, a brief summary description, and reference to the facilities plan are included in block 16.

6. *Block 17—Special Technical Data Instructions.* The reference procedure describing the task(s) identified in block 7 is listed in block 17. In addition, enter any special instructions (where specific detailed coverage is required), safety or caution notices, or other information which should be conveyed to the maintenance technician.

C. Logic Troubleshooting Diagram, Figure B-4

In the performance of corrective maintenance, the analyst must visualize what the maintenance technician will experience in the field. At random points in time when the system is operating, failures are likely to occur and will be detected by the operator through visual, audio, and/or physical means. The operator proceeds to notify the appropriate maintenance organization that a problem exists.

The maintenance technician assigned to deal with the problem must analyze the situation and verify that the system is indeed faulty. In some instances, the fault will be obvious, particularly in dealing with mechanical or hydraulic systems when a structural failure has occurred or a fluid leak takes place. On other occasions, the technician must operate the system and attempt to repeat the condition leading to failure occurrence. This is often the case for electronic equipment when the failure is not always obvious.

In any event, corrective maintenance generally commences with the identification of a failure symptom such as the system does not work, the hydraulic system leaks, the engine does not respond in terms of power output, no voltage indication on the front panel meter, and so on. Based on a symptom of this nature, the maintenance technician proceeds to troubleshoot and accomplish the necessary repair actions.

Troubleshooting may be extremely simple or quite complex. If a hydraulic leak is detected, the source of the leak is often quite easily traced. On the other hand, the failure of a small component in a radar or computer equipment is not readily identified. In this instance, the technician must accom-

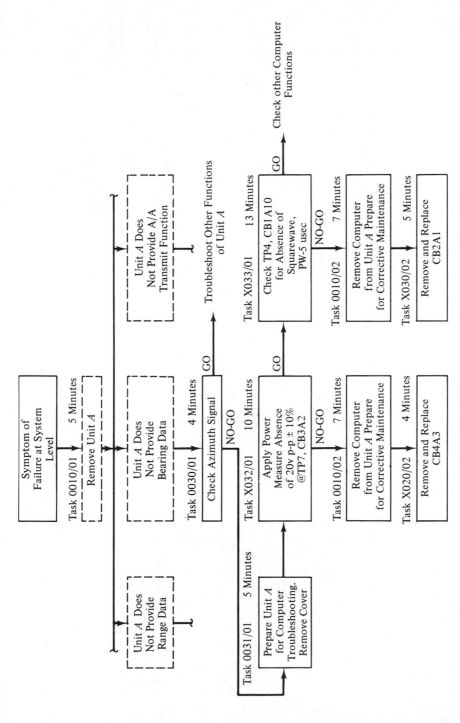

Figure B-4A. Logic troubleshooting flow diagram (example).

393

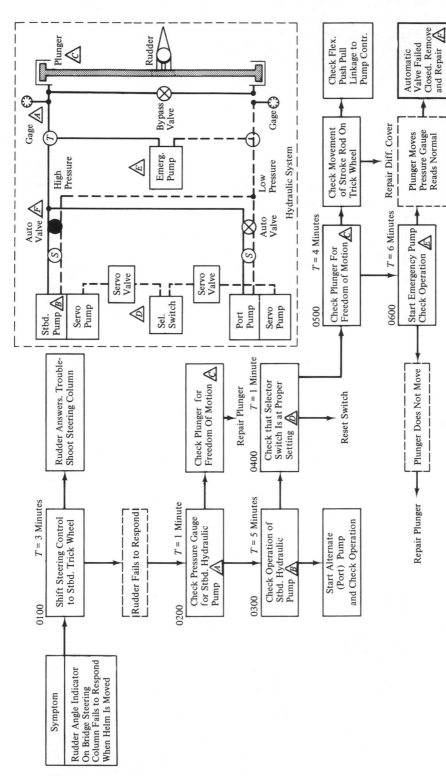

Figure B-4B. Logic troubleshooting flow for ship steering system (example). (B. Blanchard and E. Lowery, *Maintainability—Principles and Practices*, McGraw-Hill Book Co., 1969.)

plish a series of steps in a logical manner which will lead him or her directly to the faulty item. At times, these steps are not adequately defined and the technician is forced into a trial-and-error approach to maintenance. A good example is when the technician starts replacing parts on a mass basis (without analyzing cause-and-effect relationships) hoping that the problem will disappear in the process. This, of course, affects maintenance downtime and spare/repair part needs, as the technician may replace many parts when only one of them is actually faulty.

To preclude the possibility of wasting time and resources when the system is deployed in the field, the equipment design must provide the necessary characteristics to enable the maintenance technician to proceed in an accurate and timely manner in identifying the cause of failure. Such characteristics may constitute a combination of go/no-go lights, test points, meters, and other readout devices providing the necessary information which allows the technician to go from step to step with a high degree of confidence that he or she is progressing in the right direction. This objective is one of the goals of the maintainability design effort. Given a design approach, the maintenance analysis is accomplished to verify that the design is compatible. This facet of the analysis (i.e., the diagnostic aspect) is best accomplished through the development of logic troubleshooting flow diagrams, including go/no-go solutions on a step-by-step basis. Two examples are presented in Figure B-4.

The analyst should review reliability failure mode and effect analysis data to determine cause and effect relationships, and then proceed to list all of the major symptoms which a system is likely to experience.[5] For each symptom, various troubleshooting approaches are analyzed in terms of maintenance time and logistics resources, and the best approach is selected.[6] The analysis process is accomplished through the generation of logic trouble shooting flow diagrams in conjunction with the completion of maintenance task analysis sheets 1 and 2 for the troubleshooting requirement.

Figure B-4 presents two examples of a partial logic troubleshooting flow. Task numbers and elapsed times are indicated at the top of each block. In some instances tasks are sequenced in series and in other cases the either–or situation exists. The logic troubleshoot flow presents a clear picture of how the maintenance technician should approach the diagnostic aspect of corrective maintenance, and the results are used in maintenance procedures for support of equipment deployed in the operational use phase.

---

[5]It may be impossible to cover all symptoms of failure; however, the analyst should be able to identify the major ones or those occurring most frequently.

[6]The preferred approach is the one which is consistent with performance and effectiveness requirements and which reflects the lowest life-cycle cost.

D. MAINTENANCE ANALYSIS SUMMARY, FIGURE B-5

The maintenance analysis data summary (Figure B-5) presents a composite coverage of all maintenance requirements for each significant repairable item. The data summary includes a brief discription of the item function, definition of the maintenance concept, and a listing of predicted quantitative factors covering the applicable scheduled and unscheduled maintenance requirements. The summary presents an overview of the information included in the maintenance task analysis sheets (Figure B-1 and B-3).

1. *Block 1—System.* Enter the proper nomenclature of the system or end item covered by the overall analysis.

2. *Block 2—Item Name/Part Number.* Enter the name and manufacturer's part number for the repairable item being covered by this analysis.

3. *Block 3—Next Higher Assembly.* Include the name and part number of the next higher assembly.

4. *Block 4—Design Specification.* Enter the applicable design or performance specification covering the description and design requirements for the item listed in block 2. The document listed serves to tie maintenance support requirements with basic design criteria.

5. *Block 5—MA Control Number.* Enter the maintenance analysis (MA) control number for the item identified in block 2.

6. *Block 6—Functional Description.* For the item identified in block 2, briefly describe the function performed (its purpose). The description should be complete enough to ascertain what the item is and what function it serves, and should tie in with the functional analysis described in Chapter 5.

7. *Block 7—Maintenance Concept Description.* Briefly describe the maintenance concept or policy for the item covered in block 2. This should include reference to the levels or echelons of maintenance, the depth of maintenance, the maintenance environment, and any additional information considered appropriate. Both scheduled and unscheduled requirements should be summarized in a narrative form. The description should support the information defined in Chapter 4.

8. *Block 8—Requirement Number.* Enter the appropriate two-digit number for each maintenance requirement applicable to the item covered by the analysis. This may include troubleshooting, repair, servicing, inspection, and so on.

9. *Block 9—Requirement.* Include the nomenclature for each requirement number listed in block 8.

10. *Block 10—Maintenance Level.* The level or echelon of maintenance at which the requirement will be accomplished is identified. This may be organizational, intermediate, depot, or supplier.

11. *Block 11—Requirement Frequency.* The frequency (in terms of

1 SYSTEM	2 ITEM NAME/PART NO.	3 NEXT HIGHER ASSY.	4 DESIGN SPECIFICATION	5 MA CONTROL NO.
CXxx Aircraft	Unit A Synchronizer/PN1345	System XYZ	ZA 88446 (10/2/72)	B12000

6 FUNCTIONAL DESCRIPTION: System XYZ is an airborne navigation subsystem installed in the CXxx Aircraft. Unit A of the navigation subsystem provides finite range and bearing information for the overall aircraft. Unit A includes Assembly A, a power supply, and Circuit Boards 2A1 and 3A2.

7 MAINTENANCE CONCEPT DESCRIPTION: Unscheduled Maintenance -- Upon detection of a fault at the system level, the applicable fault is isolated to Unit A, Unit B, or Unit C (as applicable) through built-in self-test. The unit is removed and replaced at the avionraft, and the faulty item is returned to the Intermediate Shop for corrective maintenance. Fault isolation is accomplished to CB2A1, CB3A2, Assy A, or Pwr. Supply. Assy A & Pwr. Supply are repairable while CB's are non-repairable. Scheduled Maintenance -- Periodic calibration.

8 REQ. NO.	9 REQUIREMENT	10 MAINT. LEVEL	11 REQ. FREQ.	12 ELAP. TIME	13 PER. SKILLS	14 MAN-MIN	15 REPL. PARTS	16 TEST & SUPPORT EQUIP.
01	Troubleshooting	Intermediate	0.00184	27	Intermediate / Basic	27 / 27		Oscilloscope/HPI-34, Voltmeter/BN-33, Squarewave Gen./CPP33
02	Repair	Intermediate	0.00184	18	Basic	18	Assy A/A12345, CB3A2/BN1456, Pwr.Supply/PP320, CB2A1/BN1576	Screwdrive, Soldering Gun, Wireclippers
03	Functional Test	Intermediate	0.00184	6	Intermediate	6		Oscilloscope/HPI-34, Precision VTVM/AIr-13, WS Bridge/SU-123, Oscilloscope/Tek462, Common Handtools
04	Calibration	Depot	0.00139	480	Supervisory	590		
TOTAL			0.00321	531		668		

17 NOTES: ⚠ Refer to Addendum A for specific type and quantity of spare/repair parts. ⚠ Refer to Addendum B for a detailed listing of test and support equipment.

Prepared By: _Blanchard_ Date: _10/1/xx_ Figure B-5. Maintenance analysis summary.

instances per equipment operating hour or calendar time period) at which the requirement is expected to occur is entered. This information is derived from block 7 of the maintenance task analysis, sheet 1 (Figure B-1).

12. *Block 12—Elapsed Time.* The total elapsed clock time for each requirement, included in block 13 of the maintenance task analysis, sheet 1, is entered.

13. *Blocks 13 and 14—Personnel Skills and Man-Minutes.* The information in these blocks provides an overview of the personnel skill levels (basic, intermediate, and supervisory) and maintenance labor time anticipated for each requirement and for the end item itself. This information is derived from blocks 20–23, maintenance task analysis, sheet 1.

14. *Blocks 15 and 16—Replacement Parts/Test and Support Equipment.* To provide an overview of spare/repair part and support equipment requirements, a summary listing is presented in blocks 15 and 16, respectively. The information presented is certainly not all inclusive in the space allowed, but serves as a checklist of major items of logistic support. More in-depth data are obtained from the maintenance task analysis, sheet 2 (Figure B-3), and from related supporting reports and program planning documentation.

15. *Block 17—Notes.* Reference any additional information as appropriate to amplify and support the entries in any of the other blocks. Use an addendum sheet if the space allowed is inadequate.

The maintenance analysis summary is developed to cover each repairable item from the lowest applicable indenture hardware component to the system level. At the system level, the requirements for logistic support are summarized for evaluative purposes.

E. DATA ANALYSIS AND EVALUATION

Figure 6-5 presents a summary listing of output factors desired from the logistic support analysis, of which the maintenance analysis is an integral part. Many of these factors (primarily those which do not represent cost values), are derived from the data sheets described above. The data items presented as related to the elements of logistic support are summarized in Figure B-6.

Relative to system operational and maintenance effectiveness factors, many of the system figures of merit described in this text may be calculated from the data presented in the analysis. For instance,

$$A_o = = \frac{\text{MTBM}}{\text{MTBM} + \text{MDT}} \tag{B.1}$$

MTBM is the reciprocal of the frequency of maintenance, which is derived from the factors in block 11 of the maintenance analysis summary (Figure

Areas of Logistic Support	Data Source		
	Maintenance Task Analysis-Sheet 1	Maintenance Task Analysis-Sheet 2	Maintenance Analysis Summary
1. Test and Support/Handling Equipment	Blocks 4, 8, 11	Blocks 12, 13, 14, 15	Blocks 6, 7, 16
2. Spare/Repair Parts	Blocks 8, 11, 14	Blocks 5, 8, 9, 10, 11	Blocks 7, 15
3. Personnel and Training	Blocks 8, 11, 12, 15, 16, 17, 18, 19, 20, 21, 22, 23	Block 17	Blocks 7, 13, 14
4. Facilities	Blocks 8, 11	Block 16	Blocks 6, 7
5. Technical Data	Blocks 4, 8, 11, 12, 15, 16, 17	Blocks 3, 5, 8, 9, 11, 12, 13, 15, 16, 17	Blocks 6, 7, 9, 10, 13, 15, 16
6. Operational and Maintenance Effectiveness Factors	Blocks 7, 8, 13, 14, 18, 23	Blocks 4, 5, 10, 14	Blocks 7, 10, 11, 12, 14
7. Maintenance Concept and Policy Definition	Blocks 4, 6, 8, 11, 15, 16, 17	Blocks 3, 5, 9, 11, 13, 15, 16, 17	Blocks 7, 9, 10, 13, 15, 16

Figure B-6. Maintenance analysis data application.

B-5). MDT is the mean elapsed downtime, which can be determined from block 12 (of the same data sheet).

$$A_a = \frac{\text{MTBM}}{\text{MTBM} + \bar{\text{M}}} \tag{B.2}$$

$$A_i = \frac{\text{MTBF}}{\text{MTBF} + \bar{\text{M}}\text{ct}} \tag{B.3}$$

MTBF is the reciprocal of the failure rate, which is based on equipment inherent reliability characteristics, and can be determined from a breakout of the data in blocks 7 and 14 of the maintenance task analysis, sheet 1. $\bar{\text{M}}$ and $\bar{\text{M}}$ct constitute active maintenance elapsed times and can be determined from block 13 of the maintenance task analysis, sheet 1, and/or block 12 of the maintenance analysis summary.

$$\text{MMH/OH} = \frac{\text{total maintenance manhours}}{\text{equipment operating hour}} \tag{B.4}$$

MMH/OH can be derived from the factors in block 23 of the maintenance task analysis, sheet 1, or block 14 of the maintenance analysis summary, depending on the end item being evaluated.

These and other system quantitative measures can be derived from maintenance analysis data. However, the student must have a good understanding of how the various data elements are to be applied to provide meaningful results. If there is a question concerning the meaning of some of these factors, the student is advised to review Chapter 2. Review of maintenance analysis data is accomplished to determine (analytically) whether system requirements have been met. Areas where problems exist are readily identified and should be brought to the attention of the design engineer for possible corrective action. In other words, maintenance analysis is a tool that serves as a check on the design process to ensure the development of a system configuration which can be effectively and economically supported. Also, the analysis serves as the basis for the subsequent provisioning and acquisition of all logistic support elements.

APPENDIX C
LOGISTIC SUPPORT MODELS

Chapter 6 introduces the subject of models and indicates typical model applications. A model constitutes a simplified representation of a real-world situation, and is employed to aid the decision maker in addressing and analyzing certain problem areas. Models can vary from a basic mathematical expression to a complex computer program. The type of model required is a function of the quantity of variables, the number of alternatives, and the complexity of the operation. The decision maker must analyze the problem at hand, select techniques that can be used to resolve individual segments of the problem, and select or develop a model that properly employs these techniques. Typical problem applications may fall into any one of the following four categories.

1. *Conceptual design and advanced system development*—comparing alternative operational concepts, utilization rates, performance parameters, logistic support policies, and related factors.

During the early phase of system development (at program inception), the system designer must initially establish an overall repair philosophy. He or she may wish to determine whether an equipment will be repaired or discarded-at-failure, whether intermediate and/or depot maintenance will be required, whether preventive maintenance will be feasible, and so on. The designer will not be able to establish a firm policy at this point but must start somewhere. Feasible approaches are identified and included as part of the maintenance concept (see Chapter 4). These approaches will later be refined and a preferred policy will be selected. Models may be effectively used to aid in the evaluation of the many possible alternatives identified for consideration.

2. *Detail equipment design*—comparing alternative design configurations.

Equipment packaging schemes, testing approach, accessibility, size and weight, standardization and other related reliability, maintainability, and human factors design characteristics significantly impact the various elements of logistic support. Models may be employed to aid the designer in defining the ultimate equipment design configuration.

3. *Determination of specific logistic support requirements*—comparing alternative logistic postures and specific support items for an established equipment design configuration.

As equipment design matures, it is necessary to evaluate the various alternative methods for supporting the equipment in the field. This includes the numerous and wide variety of approaches which become evident through the accomplishment of life-cycle cost analyses and maintenance analyses (refer to Appendices A and B, respectively). The use of logistic support models facilitates this evaluation.

4. *Assessment of logistic support effectiveness*—evaluation of equipment supportability and the effectiveness of logistic support throughout system/equipment operation in the field.

After initial deployment of the prime equipment and its associated elements of logistic support in the field, it is necessary to measure overall cost/system effectiveness. Are the elements of logistic support which have been acquired adequate (in terms of type, quantity, and location)? How should logistic support provisioning factors used in reprocurements be changed to better meet the needs? What is the impact of a prime equipment change on the various elements of logistic support? These and other factors need to be evaluated on a continuing basis to ensure that the required degree of system operational effectiveness is maintained, and logistic models may be employed accordingly.

When addressing problems of this type, we may ask "Why models?" Models are useful for the following reasons.

1. There are numerous interrelated elements of a system which must be treated on an integrated basis. The interactions between reliability, maintainability, performance, effectiveness, logistic support, and so on, are many, and a variation in any one will affect the others in differing degrees. A model can be developed to represent these conditions in a realistic integrated manner, and will allow for a productive analysis effort.
2. There may be many different alternatives available for consideration and requiring evaluation. A model may be developed to assess each alternative in a timely manner. The decision maker is provided the opportunity to investigate many more situations than would be possible through other means.
3. The use of models often permits the solution to problems that are impossible to solve by other means.
4. The use of appropriate models aids in rapidly identifying high-risk areas (i.e., problems).
5. Models often facilitate the processing and handling of historical and statistical data in an effective manner.
6. Models may be employed to readily assess alternative corrective actions in terms of impact on the total system.

Modeling in general has tremendous educational benefits as well as being an effective tool in decision making. The analyst can readily identify relationships between system parameters, and is better prepared to respond to the "What if?" questions. For instance, what is the impact on spare/repair parts if the equipment reliability is degraded? What is the impact on support equipment if the prime equipment packaging design changes? What is the impact on overall system maintenance if the equipment is utilized to a greater extent than initially planned? There are many questions of this nature to which an analyst with experience can readily respond, and in many instances these intuitive rapid responses are necessary to avoid possible future problems.

Models may be developed by applying a variety of analytical techniques.[1] For instance, we may employ simulation to analyze the overall behavior of a system over time under a specified set of constraints. Functional relationships exist between the solution parameters and the control variables in the model, and in many instances the solutions are stated in terms of a range of values (not point estimates) or one or a set of intervals that contain the correct answer. On the other hand, straight analytical methods

---

[1]For a better understanding of available analytical techniques and their specific applications, the student should review additional material covering the use of operations research methods.

may be used to provide a single answer or a unique set of answers for any given set of input variables.

Models are often categorized by the analytical method(s) used to solve the problem.[2] There are reliability models based on the probability of occurrence of various events. Given the configuration, certain basic probabilities, and a distribution, such models may be used in the prediction of failure rates and the quantity of maintenance actions. In a similar manner, maintainability models may be employed to determine anticipated maintenance times.

Network models are useful in evaluating the characteristics of systems that involve the movement of material, and may be employed in evaluating the movement of prime equipment, spare/repair parts, and repairables shipped to a higher level maintenance facility (e.g., intermediate shop to depot) for corrective maintenance support. A number of network models use probabilistic considerations in determining which path to take when choosing one from a number of alternatives.

Optimization techniques are used when an optimal system design or support policy is desired and there are a number of constraints. Linear programming can be employed in optimizing with linear constraints while nonlinear programming is used when the applicable functions and constraints are nonlinear. Dynamic programming is a technique utilized if the solution involves a discrete set of possible alternatives with sequentially related constraints. This method is particularly suitable when the problem at hand involves a large number of variables.

Accounting models are used when the functions involved are basically additive. A good example is the determination of life-cycle cost which is structured for the purpose of adding up numerous individual component costs.

There are many quantitative methods available for application in the development of models. Often, a model will incorporate a number of different analytical methods. For instance, optimization will be used along with linear and nonlinear programming, queueing techniques, probabilistic functions, accounting methods, and so on, in a given model. The selection of techniques is tailored to the specific problem areas being addressed and becomes dominant in the development of a model.

When developing models, certain cautions must be exercised. First, a single, complex, all-inclusive model cannot offer some of the advantages which are available through the use of multiple models designed to function as an integrated set. Computer storage may be quickly exceeded; it may be difficult to acquire the required time on the computer; the model may not incorporate the desired flexibility and/or growth potential; it becomes

---

[2]Paulson, R. M., Waina, R. B., and Zacks, L. H., *Using Logistics Models in System Design and Early Support Planning*, Report R-550-PR, RAND Corporation, February 1971.

difficult and costly to incorporate changes in the model; and the model may not provide timely results. On the other hand, developing a set of models (each model in the set having the capability of evaluating a specific class of problems) does provide the necessary flexibility required to solve the large variety of problems listed above. Individual models can be tailored and are more responsive to evaluating the impact of a design change on spare/repair parts, the impact of a waiting line or repairable item demands on support equipment loading and utilization, and other similar lower-level problems. If changes to the model are required, the necessary changes can be incorporated without affecting other models in the set. Thus, when developing models, the modular approach is preferable. Both individual evaluations and the total system evaluation effort must be considered such that different models in the set may be employed singly or on a combined basis.

As a second point, in developing the model, the usual dangers inherent in abstraction are present. A mathematically feasible model or series of expressions may require gross oversimplifications. There is no guarantee that the time and effort invested in model development will provide the results desired. The analyst must be careful to ensure that the model does indeed reflect a realistic situation.

Finally, there is the danger that the analyst, after playing with the model for a long period of time, will become too attached to the model. Some analysts will become so attached that they will insist that the model *is* the real world and/or is directly applicable to *all* problems at hand. Again, care must be exercised to ensure that the model selected or developed is compatible with the problem(s) being solved.

Models are only a tool used in decision making and cannot be considered as a substitute for experience and judgment. As such, the use of models in a variety of situations has produced successful results. Five excellent references which further discuss the use and application of models are:

1. Schuchman, A., *Scientific Decision Making in Business—Readings in Operations Research for Non-Mathematicians*, Holt, Rinehart and Winston, New York, 1963.
2. Paulson, R. M., Waina, R. B., and Zacks, L. H., *Using Logistics Models in System Design and Early Support Planning*, Report No. R-550-PR, The RAND Corporation, 1700 Main Street, Santa Monica, Calif. 90406, 1971.
3. NAVFAC P-443, *Catalog of Navy Systems Commands, Systems Analysis/Operations Research Models*, Department of the Navy, NFEC, Washington, D. C. 20390, 1972.
4. *Department of Defense Catalog of Logistics Models*, Defense Logistics Studies Information Exchange (DLSIE), U.S. Army Logistics Management Center, Ft. Lee, Va. 23801.

5. Fabrycky, W. J., Ghare, P. M., and Torgersen, P. E., *Industrial Operations Research*, Prentice-Hall, Inc., Englewood Cliffs, N.J., 1972.

Models may be categorized for different applications and include inventory models, allocation models, queueing models, sequencing models, routing models, replacement models, gaming models, search models, and cost estimating models. Four classes of models and specific examples are briefly discussed for illustration.

A. SYSTEM OPERATIONAL ANALYSIS AND LOGISTIC SUPPORT MODELS

1. Support availability multisystem operations model (SAMSON). This model simulates operational events (alert requirements, aircraft flight capabilities, and readiness postures) and associated logistic support requirements (personnel, equipment, facilities, and spares) for one or more aircraft at one or more operational sites. The model takes into account weather, resource shortages, flying schedules, alert commitments, flight configuration requirements, abort rates, attrition estimates, and operating policies governing flight cancellation and makeup practices. The model can be used to evaluate the impact of changes in concepts, policies, and resource mixes upon operational capability. It is used in conceptual design for performance/support trade-off analysis, and in support planning.

Reference: *User's Manual for SAMSON II*, Report No. RM-4923-PR, November 1967, The RAND Corporation, 1700 Main Street, Santa Monica, Calif. 90406.

2. Logistics composite model (LCOM). LCOM is a large-scale computer simulation model that simulates aircraft operation and main supporting functions that are represented by a mix of sortie types, flight line and shop repair processes for both aircraft and components, and supply functions. It has three main programs: a preprocessor that translates input data into a format compatible with requirements of the simulation program; a simulation program that represents flight and base support processes in response to mission requirements; and a postprocessor that produces displays depicting results of the simulation program. The simulation program may be run many times, with systematic changes being made in the data base, according to particular study objectives. A unique feature of LCOM is the task network that describes base processes to be simulated by identifying particular tasks and the sequence for completing them. This model is suitable for conducting studies that relate to logistics, operations, and manpower.

Reference: AF Regulation 25–8, Department of the Air Force, Headquarters U.S. Air Force, Washington, D.C. 20330.

3. Computer analysis of maintenance policies (COAMP). This model estimates the support costs of an end item consisting of *n* similar assemblies for 20 basic maintenance postures. Including all the stockage options, there are 80 distinct four-echelon, three-indenture postures that can be analyzed. Support equipment requirements are estimated by computing the number of service channels required to handle the material flows at the various repair points. COAMP can analyze complex decisions including various types of built-in test equipment; however, in order to handle such postures, COAMP must approximate optimal stock levels and optimal support equipment requirements. The model supplies default values for all variables. Thus, one can start runs initially with very little information, and then become more precise as valid data becomes available. Sensitivity tests can be automatically run for a number of specified variables. This model can be used in concept evaluation, detailed design, and support planning.

Reference: *Evaluating the Economics of Integrated Logistic Support*, Radio Corp. of America, Defense Electronics Products, SEER, ATE-8-612, September 1968, Moorestown, N.J. 08057.

B. LEVEL-OF-REPAIR ANALYSIS

1. Optimum repair level analysis (ORLA) model. ORLA evaluates alternative support postures (i.e., discard at failure, intermediate-level repair, or depot-level repair) in terms of total life-cycle cost. Also, it allows for the trade-off evaluation of any two or more elements of logistic support. The model is used in the conceptual and early design process to make repair level decisions.

Input data include equipment deployment, system utilization, maintenance rates and times, and operation and maintenance cost factors. ORLA approaches the data uncertainty problem by considering several levels of variable factors (i.e., parametric analysis approach) such as system utilization, item costs, and so on.

Reference: U.S.Air Force AFLCM/AFSCM 800–4, *Optimum Repair Level Analysis (ORLA)*, June 1971, Air Force Logistics Command, Wright-Patterson AFB, Ohio 45433.

2. System cost and operational resource evaluation (SCORE) model. This model provides estimates of life-cycle cost (research and development, investment, operations and maintenance) for up to 15 years for various component estimates, and aggregates these into a total cost for a system. Cost estimates are based on historical accounting records and on cost-estimating relationships. Costs are arranged in a two-dimensional matrix (program element and time).

Reference: *SCORE Executive Routine, Phase I*, Report No. NADC-AW-6734, February 1969, Naval Air Development Center, Johnsville, Warminister, Pa. 18974.

3. Level of repair for aeronautical material (LORAM). LORAM is used for making level of repair decisions (i.e., discard at failure, intermediate-level repair, or depot repair) for assemblies, modules, and other elements of a system. The model also includes screening methods and noneconomic criteria, and is used for design decisions and support planning. The model ties in closely with the maintenance analysis.

Reference: MIL-STD-1390A, Military Standard, "Level of Repair," Department of the Navy, Washington, D.C. 20360, April 1974.

C. LIFE-CYCLE COST MODELS FOR PROCUREMENT AND PROGRAM EVALUATION

1. Acquisition based on consideration of logistics effects (ABLE). ABLE computes life-cycle cost by item by cost type (storage, repair, etc.), and sums cost for all items in the system. The model could be used in support of detailed design, but is intended primarily for developing and specifying contract incentives regarding logistics.

Reference: *Project ABLE*, Operations Analysis Report No. 8, May 1969, Operations Analysis Office, Air Force Logistics Command, Wright-Patterson AFB, Ohio 45433.

2. Life-cycle cost model (LCCM). LCCM calculates life-cycle costs by item by period. Costs can be entered directly into the model or calculated by cost-estimating relationships, standard formulas, or by summation of other costs. Learning curves are considered and costs are discounted to the present value. This model is used in program management.

Reference: *Life-Cycle Cost Model Final User's Manual and Operating Instructions*, Vol. I, April 1969, Planning Research Corporation, PRC-R-1225, Arlington, Va.

3. Programmed review of information for costing and evaluation (PRICE). PRICE is a family of cost-predicting models. The basic PRICE model predicts development and production costs for proposed electromechanical devices or systems while they are still in the concept stage. PRICE L, the PRICE life-cycle cost model, is a supplement to, and operates in conjunction with the basic PRICE model to rapidly compute support costs for many varieties of systems. PRICE S, the PRICE software model, applies the PRICE parametric modeling methods to the problems of computer software costing. It is designed to cover the complete range of systems and applications programming. All PRICE models are exercised interactively through commercial time-sharing computer networks.

Reference: Director, PRICE Systems, RCA, Cherry Hill, N.J. 08000.

D. SPARES AND INVENTORY POLICY MODELS

1. Base depot stockage model (BDSM). This model determines intermediate base and depot stock levels that will minimize back orders within a fixed spares budget. The model assumes a compound Poisson demand at n identical bases. The model considers basing posture, failure rates, repair-cycle times, condemnation rates, procurement costs, procurement lead times, reorder quantities, and cost constraints.

Reference: *Base Depot Stockage Model*, Operations Research, Report ERR-FW-621, December 1967, General Dynamics, Ft. Worth, Tex. 76100.

2. Spares kit evaluator model (SKEM). This model determines optimum types and quantities of spare parts for the support of a deployed unit, subject to multiple constraints. Also, the model computes supply effectiveness in terms of *probability of no stock-out* or *expected time to stock-out*. The model is used in support planning.

Reference: Product Support Report P.S. 447, 26 February, 1968, Advanced Logistics Dept. 501, McDonnell-Douglas Corp., St. Louis, Mo. 63100.

3. Spares provisioning model (SPM). SPM computes spare part levels and fill rates and investment for each station in an airlift network. The model is oriented to commercial airline operations, and is used in support planning.

Reference: *Total Airline Profit and Simulation Models*, ER-10110, June 1969, Lockheed-Georgia Company, Commercial Systems Integration, Marietta, Ga. 30000.

APPENDIX D

SYSTEM DESIGN REVIEW CHECKLIST

On a periodic basis throughout the design and development process, it is beneficial to accomplish an informal review to assess (1) whether necessary tasks have been accomplished, and (2) the extent that supportability characteristics have been considered and incorporated in the equipment design. Questions, presented in a checklist format, have been developed to reflect certain features. Reliability, maintainability, human factors, and logistic support considerations are included. Not all questions are applicable in all reviews; however, the answer to those questions that are applicable should be YES to reflect desirable results. For many questions, a more in-depth study of applicable reliability, maintainability, and human factors criteria documentation will be required prior to arriving at a decision. These questions directly support an abbreviated checklist presented in Figure 7-5.

GENERAL

1.0 System Operational Requirements

1.1. Has the mission been defined? Mission scenarios?
1.2. Have all basic system performance parameters been defined?
1.3. Has the planned operational deployment been defined (quantity of systems per location)?
1.4. Has the system life cycle been defined?

1.5. Have system utilization requirements been defined? This includes hours of system/equipment operation or quantity of operational cycles per a given time period. Define an operational cycle if used.

1.6. Has the operational environment been defined in terms of temperature extremes, humidity, shock and vibration, storage, transportation, and handling?

2.0 Effectiveness Factors

2.1. Have system availability, dependability, readiness, or equivalent operational effectiveness factors been identified?

2.2. Have quantitative reliability and maintainability factors been specified? This includes MTBF, MTBM, λ, MDT, $\bar{M}$, $\bar{M}ct$, $\bar{M}pt$, M_{max}, MMH/OH, Cost/OH, Cost/MA, and so on.

3.0 System Maintenance Concept

3.1. Have the echelons or levels of maintenance been specified and defined?

3.2. Have basic maintenance functions been identified for each level?

3.3. Have quantitative parameters been established for turnaround time (TAT) at each level and logistics pipeline time between level?

3.4. Has the logistics pipeline time between levels been minimized to the extent feasible considering cost? The lack of adequate supply responsiveness has a major detrimental effect on total logistic support.

3.5. Have level of repair policies been established? All assemblies and subassemblies should be classified as repairable or discard at failure.

3.6. Has the criteria for level of repair decisions been adequately defined?

3.7. Has the level of maintenance (organizational, intermediate, depot, or supplier) been defined for each repairable item?

3.8. Have criteria been established for test and support equipment at each level of maintenance?

3.9. Have criteria been established for personnel quantities and/or skills at each level of maintenance?

4.0 Functional Analysis and Allocation

4.1. Have system operational and maintenance functions been defined?

4.2. Have reliability and maintainability factors been allocated to the appropriate system elements (e.g., unit, assembly, subassembly, etc.)?

4.3. Have cost factors been allocated to the appropriate system elements?

5.0 Logistic Support Annlysis

5.1. Have trade-off evaluations and analyses been accomplished to support all logistic support requirements?

5.2. Is the response to all questions in Figure 6-6 (analysis checklist) positive? These questions cover life-cycle cost analyses, maintenance analyses, and logistics modeling.

5.3. Have trade-off evaluations and analyses been adequately documented?

6.0 Logistic Support Operational Plan

6.1. Has a plan been developed for the design, production, acquisition, deployment, and integration of the prime equipment and logistic support elements in the field? This includes a preliminary logistic support plan and a formal logistic support plan.
6.2. Has a plan been developed for the handling of system modifications in the field?
6.3. Has a plan been developed covering system/equipment phaseout?

LOGISTIC SUPPORT ELEMENTS

1.0 Test and Support Equipment

1.1. Have the test and support equipment requirements been defined for each level of maintenance?
1.2. Have standard test and support equipment items been selected? Newly designed equipment should not be necessary unless standard equipment is unavailable.
1.3. Are the selected test and support equipment items compatible with the prime equipment? Does the test equipment do the job?
1.4. Are the test and support equipment requirements compatible with logistic support analysis?
1.5. Have test and support equipment requirements (both in terms of variety and quantity) been minimized to the greatest extent possible?
1.6. Are the reliability and maintainability features in the test and support equipment compatible with those equivalent features in the prime equipment? It is not practical to select an item of support equipment which is not as reliable as the item it supports.
1.7. Have logistic support requirements for the selected test and support equipment been defined? This includes maintenance tasks, test equipment, spare/repair parts, personnel and training, data, and facilities.
1.8. Is the test and support equipment selection process based on cost-effectiveness considerations (i.e., life-cycle cost)?

2.0 Supply Support (Spare/Repair Parts)

2.1. Are the types and quantity of spare/repair parts compatible with the level of repair analysis?
2.2. Are the types and quantity of spare/repair parts designated for a given location appropriate for the estimated demand at that location? Too many or too few spares can be costly.
2.3. Are spare/repair part provisioning factors consistent with logistic support analysis?
2.4. Are spare/repair part provisioning factors directly traceable to reliability and maintainability predictions?

2.5. Are the specified logistics pipeline times compatible with effective supply support? Long pipeline times place a tremendous burden on logistic support.

2.6. Have spare/repair parts been identified and provisioned for pre-operational support activities (e.g., interim supplier support, test programs, etc.)?

2.7. Have spare/repair part requirements been minimized to the maximum extent possible?

2.8. Have test and acceptance procedures been developed for spare/repair parts? Spare/repair parts should be processed, produced, and accepted on a similar basis with their equivalent components in the prime equipment.

2.9. Have the consequences (risks) of stock-out been defined in terms of effect on mission requirements and cost?

2.10. Has an inventory safety stock level been defined?

2.11. Has a provisioning or procurement cycle been defined (procurement or order frequency)?

2.12. Has a supply availability requirement been established (the probability of having a spare available when required)?

3.0 Personnel and Training

3.1. Have operational and maintenance personnel requirements (quantity and skill levels) been defined?

3.2. Are operational and maintenance personnel requirements minimized to the greatest extent possible?

3.3. Are operational and maintenance personnel requirements compatible with logistic support analysis and with human factors data? Personnel quantities and skill levels should track both sources.

3.4. Are the planned personnel skill levels at each location compatible with the complexity of the operational and maintenance tasks specified?

3.5. Has maximum consideration been given to the use of existing personnel skills for new equipment?

3.6. Have personnel attrition rates been established?

3.7. Have personnel effectiveness factors been determined (actual time that work is accomplished per the total time allowed for work accomplishment)?

3.8. Have operational and maintenance training requirements been specified? This includes consideration of both initial training and replenishment training throughout the life cycle.

3.9. Have specific training programs been planned? The type of training, frequency of training, duration of training, and student entry requirements should be identified.

3.10. Are the planned training programs compatible with the personnel skill level requirements specified for the performance of operational and maintenance tasks?

3.11. Have training equipment requirements been defined? Acquisitioned?
3.12. Have maintenance provisions for training equipment been planned?
3.13. Have training data requirements been defined?
3.14. Are the planned operating and maintenance procedures (designated for support of the system throughout its life cycle) utilized to the maximum extent possible in the training program(s)?

4.0 Technical Data (Operating and Maintenance Procedures)

4.1. Have operating and maintenance procedure requirements been defined? Have the necessary procedures been prepared?
4.2. Are operating and maintenance procedures compatible with logistic support analysis data? This pertains particularly to the logic trouble-shooting flow diagrams, task sequences, and support requirements defined in the maintenance analysis described in Appendix B.
4.3. Are operating and maintenance procedures as brief as possible without sacrificing necessary information?
4.4. Are operating and maintenance procedures adequate from the standpoint of presenting simple step-by-step instructions; including appropriate use of illustrations; and including tables for presenting data?
4.5. Are operating and maintenance procedures compatible with the level of activity performed at the location where the procedures are used? Depot maintenance instructions should not be included in manuals which are used at the intermediate level of maintenance. The maintenance procedures should be compatible with the level of repair analysis and the maintenance concept.
4.6. Are operating and maintenance procedures written to the skill level of the individual accomplishing the functions covered by the procedures? Procedures should be written in a simple, clear, and concise manner for low-skilled personnel.
4.7. Do the operating and maintenance procedures specify the correct test and support equipment, spare/repair parts, transportation and handling equipment, and facilities?
4.8. Do the procedures include special warning notices in areas where safety is a concern?
4.9. Are the designated operating and maintenance procedures used in system/equipment test programs?

5.0 Facilities and Storage

5.1. Have facility requirements (space, volume, capital equipment, utilities, etc.) necessary for system operation been defined?
5.2. Have facility requirements (space, volume, capital equipment, utilities, etc.) necessary for system maintenance at each level been defined?
5.3. Have operational and maintenance facility requirements been minimized to the greatest extent possible?

5.4. Have environmental system requirements (e.g., temperature, humidity, and dust control) associated with operational and maintenance facilities been identified?

5.5. Have storage or shelf-space requirements for spare/repair parts been defined?

5.6. Have storage environments been defined?

5.7. Are the designated facility and storage requirements compatible with the logistic support analysis and human factors data?

6.0 Transportation and Handling

6.1. Are transportation and handling requirements for both operational and maintenance functions defined? This includes transportation of prime equipment, test and support equipment, spares, personnel, and data.

6.2. Are transportation and handling environments (temperature, shock and vibration, exposure to dust and salt spray, storage, etc.) defined?

6.3. Are the modes (air, ground vehicle, rail, sea, or a combination) of transportation known? A profile or scenario, similar to that accomplished for mission definition, should be developed showing the various transportation and handling requirements.

6.4. Are the requirements for reusable containers known? Design information should be developed on reusable containers.

6.5. Are the requirements for packing known? This includes labor, material, preservation, storage limitations, and the processing of an item for shipment.

DESIGN FEATURES[1]

1.0 Selection of Parts

1.1. Have appropriate standards been consulted for the selection of components?

1.2. Have all component parts and materials selected for the design been adequately evaluated prior to their procurement and application? Evaluation should consider performance parameters, reliability, maintainability, and human factors.

1.3. Have supplier sources for component part procurement been established?

1.4. Are the established supplier sources reliable in terms of quality level, ability to deliver on time, and willingness to accept part warranty provisions?

1.5. Have the reliability, maintainability, and human factors engineers been consulted in the selection and application of parts? Reliabil-

---

[1]Many similar areas of design criteria coverage are described in Blanchard, B. S. and Lowery, E. E., *Maintainability—Principles and Practices*, McGraw-Hill Book Company, New York, 1969.

ity is concerned with part failure rates, stresses, tolerances, allowable temperature extremes, signal ratings, and so on. Maintainability and human factors are concerned with the part effects on maintenance times, mounting provisions, human interfaces, and so on.

2.0 Standardization

2.1. Are standard equipment items and parts incorporated in the design to the maximum extent possible (except for items not compatible with effectiveness factors)? Maximum standardization is desirable.

2.2. Are the same items and/or parts used in similar applications?

2.3. Are the number of different part types used throughout the design minimized? In the interest of developing an efficient supply support capability, the number of different item spares should be held to a minimum.

2.4. Are identifying equipment labels and nomenclature assignments standardized to the maximum extent possible?

2.5. Are equipment control panel positions and layouts (from panel to panel) the same or similar when a number of panels are incorporated and provide comparable functions?

3.0 Test Provisions

3.1. Have self-test provisions been incorporated where appropriate?

3.2. Is the extent or depth of self-testing compatible with the level of repair analysis?

3.3. Are self-test provisions automatic?

3.4. Have direct fault indicators been provided (either a fault light, an audio signal, or a means of determining that a malfunction positively exists)? Are continuous performance monitoring provisions incorporated where appropriate?

3.5. Are test points provided to enable check-out and fault isolation beyond the level of self-test? Test points for fault isolation within an assembly should not be incorporated if the assembly is to be discarded at failure. Test point provisions must be compatible with the level of repair analysis.

3.6. Are test points accessible? Accessibility should be compatible with the extent of maintenance performed. Test points on the operator's front panel are not required for a depot maintenance action.

3.7. Are test points functionally and conveniently grouped to allow for sequential testing (following a signal flow), testing of similar functions, or frequency of use when access is limited?

3.8. Are test points provided for a direct test of all replaceable items?

3.9. Are test points adequately labeled? Each test point should be identified with a unique number, and the proper signal or expected measured output should be specified on a label located adjacent to the test point.

3.10. Are test points adequately illuminated to allow the technician to see the test point number and labeled signal value?

3.11. Can every equipment malfunction (degradation beyond specification tolerance limits) which could possibly occur in the equipment be detected through a no-go indication at the system level? This is a measure of test thoroughness.

4.0 Packaging and Mounting

4.1. Is functional packaging incorporated to the maximum extent possible? Interaction affects between modular packages should be minimized. It should be possible to limit maintenance to the removal of one module (the one containing the failed part) when a failure occurs and not require the removal of two, three, or four modules.

4.2. Is the packaging design compatible with level of repair analysis decisions? Repairable items are designed to include maintenance provisions such as test points, accessibility, plug-in components, and so on. Items classified as discard at failure should be encapsulated and relatively low in cost. Maintenance provisions within the disposable module are not required.

4.3. Are disposable modules incorporated to the maximum extent practical? It is highly desirable to reduce overall support through a no-maintenance design concept as long as the items being discarded are relatively high in reliability and low in cost.

4.4. Are plug-in modules and components utilized to the maximum extent possible (unless the use of plug-in components significantly degrades the equipment reliability)?

4.5. Are accesses between modules adequate to allow for hand grasping?

4.6. Are modules and components mounted such that the removal of any single item for maintenance will not require the removal of other items? Component stacking should be avoided where possible.

4.7. In areas where module stacking is necessary because of limited space, are the modules mounted in such a way that access priority has been assigned in accordance with the predicted removal and replacement frequency? Items requiring frequent maintenance should be more accessible.

4.8. Are modules and components, not of the plug-in variety, mounted with four fasteners or less? Modules should be securely mounted, but the number of fasteners should be held to a minimum.

4.9. Are shock-mounting provisions incorporated where shock and vibration requirements are excessive?

4.10. Are provisions incorporated to preclude installation of the wrong module?

4.11. Are plug-in modules and components removable without the use of tools? If tools are required, they should be of the standard variety.

4.12. Are guides (slides or pins) provided to facilitate module installation?

4.13. Are modules and components labeled?

4.14. Are module and component labels located on top or immediately adjacent to the item and in plain sight?

4.15. Are the labels permanently affixed and unlikely to come off during a maintenance action or as a result of environment? Is the information on the label adequate? Disposable modules should be so labeled.

4.16. In equipment racks, are the heavier items mounted at the bottom of the rack? Unit weight should decrease with the increase in installation height.

4.17. Are operator panels optimally positioned? For personnel in the standing position, panels should be located between 40 and 70 inches above the floor. Critical or precise controls should be between 48 and 64 inches above the floor. For personnel in the sitting position, panels should be located 30 inches above the floor.

5.0 Interchangeability

5.1. Are modules and components having similar functions electrically, functionally, and physically interchangeable?

6.0 Accessibility

6.1. Are access doors provided where appropriate? Are hinged doors utilized?

6.2. Are access openings adequate in size and optimally located for the access required?

6.3. Are access doors and openings labeled in terms of items that are accessible from within?

6.4. Can access doors that are hinged be supported in the open position?

6.5. Are access door fasteners minimized?

6.6. Are access door fasteners of the quick-release variety?

6.7. Can access be attained without the use of tools?

6.8. If tools are required to gain access, are the number of tools held to a minimum? Are the tools of the standard variety?

6.9. Are accesses between modules and components adequate?

6.10. Are access requirements compatible with the frequency of maintenance? Accessibility for items requiring frequent maintenance should be greater than that for items requiring infrequent maintenance.

7.0 Handling

7.1. For heavy items, are hoist lugs (lifting eyes) or base-lifting provisions for fork-lift-truck application incorporated? Hoist lugs should be provided on all items weighing more than 150 pounds.

7.2. Are hoist and base lifting points identified relative to lifting capacity? Are weight labels provided?

7.3. Are packages, units, components, or other items weighing over 10 pounds provided with handles? Are the proper-size handles used, and are they located in the right position? Are the handles optimally located from the weight-distribution standpoint? (Handles should be located over the center of gravity.)

7.4. Are packages, units, or other items weighing more than 40 pounds provided with two handles (for two-person carrying capability)?

7.5. Are containers, cases, or covers provided to protect equipment vulnerable areas from damage during handling?

8.0 Fasteners

8.1. Are quick-release fasteners used on doors and access panels?

8.2. Are the total number of fasteners minimized?

8.3. Are the number of different type of fasteners held to a minimum? This relates to standardization.

8.4. Have fasteners been selected based on the requirement for standard tools in lieu of special tools?

9.0 Panel Displays and Controls

9.1. Are controls standardized?

9.2. Are controls sequentially positioned?

9.3. Is control spacing adequate?

9.4. Is control labeling adequate?

9.5. Have the proper control/display relationships been incorporated?

9.6. Are the proper type of panel switches used?

9.7. Is the control panel lighting adequate?

9.8. Are the controls placed according to frequency of use?

9.9. Has a human factors engineer been consulted relative to controls and panel design?

10.0 Adjustments and Alignments

10.1. Are adjustment requirements and frequencies known?

10.2. Have adjustment requirements been minimized?

10.3. Are adjustment points accessible?

10.4. Are adjustment-point locations compatible with the maintenance level at which the adjustment is made?

10.5. Are adjustment interaction effects eliminated?

10.6. Are factory adjustments specified?

10.7. Are adjustment points adequately labeled?

11.0 Cables and Connectors

11.1. Are cables fabricated in removable sections?

11.2. Are cables routed to avoid sharp bends?

11.3. Are cables routed to avoid pinching?

11.4. Is cable labeling adequate?

11.5. Is cable clamping adequate?

11.6. Are connectors of the quick-disconnect variety?

11.7. Are connectors that are mounted on surfaces far enough apart so that they can be firmly grasped for connecting and disconnecting?

11.8. Are connectors and receptables labeled?

11.9. Are connectors and receptables keyed?

11.10. Are connectors standardized?

11.11. Do the connectors incorporate provisions for moisture prevention?

12.0 Servicing and Lubrication

12.1. Have servicing requirements been held to a minimum?

12.2. When servicing is indicated, are the specific requirements identified? This includes frequency of servicing and the materials needed.

12.3. Are procurement sources for servicing materials known?

12.4. Are servicing points accessible?

12.5. Have personnel and equipment requirements for servicing been identified? This includes handling equipment, vehicles, carts, and so on.

12.6. Does the design include servicing indicators?

13.0 Calibration

13.1. Are calibration requirements known?

13.2. Are calibration frequencies known?

13.3. Are calibration tolerances known?

13.4. Are standards available for calibration?

13.5. Are calibration procedures prepared?

13.6. Is traceability to the National Bureau of Standards possible?

13.7. Have the facilities for calibration been identified?

13.8. Are the calibration requirements compatible with logistic support analysis and the maintenance concept?

14.0 Environment

14.1. Has the equipment design considered the following: temperature, shock, vibration, humidity, pressure, wind, salt spray, sand and dust, rain, fungus, and radiation? Have the ranges and extreme conditions been specified and properly addressed in design?

14.2. Have provisions been made to specify and control noise, illumination, humidity, and temperature in areas where personnel are required to perform operating and maintenance functions?

15.0 Storage

15.1. Can the equipment be stored for extended periods of time without excessive degradation (beyond specification limits)?

15.2. Have scheduled maintenance requirements for stored equipment been defined?

15.3. Have scheduled maintenance requirements for stored equipment been eliminated or minimized?

15.4. Have the required maintenance resources necessary to service stored equipment been identified?

15.5. Have storage environments been defined?

16.0 Transportability

16.1. Have transportation and handling requirements been defined?

16.2. Have transportation requirements been considered in the equipment design? This includes consideration of temperature ranges, vibration and shock, humidity, and so on. Has the possibility of equipment degradation been minimized if transported by air, ground vehicle, ship, or rail?

16.3. Can the equipment be easily disassembled, packed, transported from one location to another, reassembled, and operated with a minimum of performance and reliability degradation?

16.4. Have container requirements been defined?

16.5. Have the requirements for ground handling equipment been defined?

16.6. Was the selection of handling equipment based on cost-effectiveness considerations?

17.0 Producibility

17.1. Has the design stabilized (minimum change)?

17.2. Has the design been verified through prototype and qualification testing?

17.3. Is the design such that many models of the same item can be produced with identical results?

17.4. Are the production drawings and material lists adequate?

17.5. Are common materials used (in lieu of special materials)?

17.6. Can standard tooling and existing facilities be used for fabrication, assembly, and test operations?

17.7. Is the design such that rework requirements are minimized? Are spoilage factors held to a minimum?

17.8. Are standard fabrication, assembly, test, and inspection procedures applicable?

17.9. Is the design such that automated manufacturing processes (e.g., numerical control techniques) can be applied for repetitive functions?

17.10. Is the design definition such that two or more suppliers can produce the equipment from a set of drawings with identical results?

18.0 Safety

18.1. Have fail-safe provisions been incorporated in the design?

18.2. Have protruding devices been eliminated or are they suitably protected?

18.3. Have provisions been incorporated for protection against high voltages? Are all external metal parts adequately grounded?

18.4. Are sharp metal edges, access openings, and corners protected with rubber, fillets, fiber, or plastic coating?

18.5. Are electrical circuit interlocks employed?

18.6. Are standoffs or handles provided to protect equipment from damage during the performance of bench maintenance?

18.7. Are tools that are used near high-voltage areas adequately insulated at the handle or at other parts of the tool which the maintenance person is likely to touch?

18.8. Are the environments such that personnel safety is ensured? Are noise levels within a safe range? Is illumination adequate? Is the air relatively clean? Are the temperatures at a proper level?

18.9. Has the proper protective clothing been identified for areas where the environment could be detrimental to human safety? Radiation, intense cold or heat, gas, and loud noise are examples.

18.10. Are safety equipment requirements identified in areas where ordnance devices and the like are activated?

19.0 Reliability

19.1. Has the system/equipment wear-out period been defined?

19.2. Have failure modes and effects been identified?

19.3. Are item failure rates known?

19.4. Have parts with excessive failure rates been identified?

19.5. Has mean life been determined?

19.6. Have adequate derating factors been established and adhered to where appropriate?

19.7. Has equipment design complexity been minimized?

19.8. Is protection against secondary failures (resulting from primary failures) incorporated where possible?

19.9. Has the use of adjustable components been minimized?

19.10. Has the use of friction or pressure contacts in mechanical equipment been avoided?

19.11. Have all critical-useful-life items been eliminated from the equipment design?

19.12. Have cooling provisions been incorporated in design "hot spot" areas? Is cooling directed toward the most critical items?

APPENDIX E

NORMAL DISTRIBUTION TABLES

Table E-1. AREAS UNDER THE NORMAL CURVE

Proportion of total area under the curve that is under the portion of the curve from $-\infty$ to $\dfrac{X_i - \bar{X}'}{\sigma'}$. ($X_i$ represents any desired value of the variable X)

$Z = \dfrac{X_i - \bar{X}'}{\sigma'}$	0.09	0.08	0.07	0.06	0.05	0.04	0.03	0.02	0.01	0.00
−3.5	0.00017	0.00017	0.00018	0.00019	0.00019	0.00020	0.00021	0.00022	0.00022	0.00023
−3.4	0.00024	0.00025	0.00026	0.00027	0.00028	0.00029	0.00030	0.00031	0.00033	0.00034
−3.3	0.00035	0.00036	0.00038	0.00039	0.00040	0.00042	0.00043	0.00045	0.00047	0.00048
−3.2	0.00050	0.00052	0.00054	0.00056	0.00058	0.00060	0.00062	0.00064	0.00066	0.00069
−3.1	0.00071	0.00074	0.00076	0.00079	0.00082	0.00085	0.00087	0.00090	0.00094	0.00097
−3.0	0.00100	0.00104	0.00107	0.00111	0.00141	0.00118	0.00122	0.00126	0.00131	0.00135
−2.9	0.0014	0.0014	0.0015	0.0015	0.0016	0.0016	0.0017	0.0017	0.0018	0.0019
−2.8	0.0019	0.0020	0.0021	0.0021	0.0022	0.0023	0.0023	0.0024	0.0025	0.0026
−2.7	0.0026	0.0027	0.0028	0.0029	0.0030	0.0031	0.0032	0.0033	0.0034	0.0035
−2.6	0.0036	0.0037	0.0038	0.0039	0.0040	0.0041	0.0043	0.0044	0.0045	0.0047
−2.5	0.0048	0.0049	0.0051	0.0052	0.0054	0.0055	0.0057	0.0059	0.0060	0.0062
−2.4	0.0064	0.0066	0.0068	0.0069	0.0071	0.0073	0.0075	0.0078	0.0080	0.0082
−2.3	0.0084	0.0087	0.0089	0.0091	0.0094	0.0096	0.0099	0.0102	0.0104	0.0107
−2.2	0.0110	0.0113	0.0116	0.0119	0.0122	0.0125	0.0129	0.0132	0.0136	0.0139
−2.1	0.0143	0.0146	0.0150	0.0154	0.0158	0.0162	0.0166	0.0170	0.0174	0.0179
−2.0	0.0183	0.0188	0.0192	0.0197	0.0202	0.0207	0.0212	0.0217	0.0222	0.0228
−1.9	0.0233	0.0239	0.0244	0.0250	0.0256	0.0262	0.0268	0.0274	0.0281	0.0287
−1.8	0.0294	0.0301	0.0307	0.0314	0.0322	0.0329	0.0336	0.0344	0.0351	0.0359
−1.7	0.0367	0.0375	0.0384	0.0392	0.0401	0.0409	0.0418	0.0427	0.0436	0.0446
−1.6	0.0455	0.0465	0.0475	0.0485	0.0495	0.0505	0.0516	0.0526	0.0537	0.0548
−1.5	0.0559	0.0571	0.0582	0.0594	0.0606	0.0618	0.0630	0.0643	0.0652	0.0668
−1.4	0.0681	0.0694	0.0708	0.0721	0.0735	0.0749	0.0764	0.0778	0.0793	0.0808
−1.3	0.0823	0.0838	0.0853	0.0869	0.0885	0.0901	0.0918	0.0934	0.0951	0.0968
−1.2	0.0985	0.1003	0.1020	0.1038	0.1057	0.1075	0.1093	0.1112	0.1131	0.1151
−1.1	0.1170	0.1190	0.1210	0.1230	0.1251	0.1271	0.1292	0.1314	0.1335	0.1357
−1.0	0.1379	0.1401	0.1423	0.1446	0.1469	0.1492	0.1515	0.1539	0.1562	0.1587
−0.9	0.1611	0.1635	0.1660	0.1685	0.1711	0.1736	0.1762	0.1788	0.1814	0.1841
−0.8	0.1867	0.1894	0.1922	0.1949	0.1977	0.2005	0.2033	0.2061	0.2090	0.2119
−0.7	0.2148	0.2177	0.2207	0.2236	0.2266	0.2297	0.2327	0.2358	0.2389	0.2420
−0.6	0.2451	0.2483	0.2514	0.2546	0.2578	0.2611	0.2643	0.2676	0.2709	0.2743
−0.5	0.2776	0.2810	0.2843	0.2877	0.2912	0.2946	0.2981	0.3015	0.3050	0.3085
−0.4	0.3121	0.3156	0.3192	0.3228	0.3264	0.3300	0.3336	0.3372	0.3409	0.3446
−0.3	0.3483	0.3520	0.3557	0.3594	0.3632	0.3669	0.3707	0.3745	0.3783	0.3821
−0.2	0.3859	0.3897	0.3936	0.3974	0.4013	0.4052	0.4090	0.4129	0.4168	0.4207
−0.1	0.4247	0.4286	0.4325	0.4346	0.4404	0.4443	0.4483	0.4522	0.4562	0.4602
−0.0	0.4641	0.4681	0.4721	0.4761	0.4801	0.4840	0.4880	0.4920	0.4960	0.5000

From E. L. Grant and R. S. Leavenworth, *Statistical Quality Control*, 4th Edition, McGraw-Hill Book Company, 1972. Reproduced by permission.

Table E-1. AREAS UNDER THE NORMAL CURVE (Continued)

$Z=\dfrac{X_i-\bar{X}'}{\sigma'}$	0.00	0.01	0.02	0.03	0.04	0.05	0.06	0.07	0.08	0.09
+0.0	0.5000	0.5040	0.5080	0.5120	0.5160	0.5199	0.5239	0.5279	0.5319	0.5359
+0.1	0.5398	0.5438	0.5478	0.5517	0.5557	0.5596	0.5636	0.5675	0.5714	0.5753
+0.2	0.5793	0.5832	0.5871	0.5910	0.5948	0.5987	0.6026	0.6064	0.6103	0.6141
+0.3	0.6179	0.6217	0.6255	0.6293	0.6331	0.6368	0.6406	0.6443	0.6480	0.6517
+0.4	0.6554	0.6591	0.6628	0.6664	0.6700	0.5736	0.6772	0.6808	0.6844	0.6879
+0.5	0.6915	0.6950	0.6985	0.7019	0.7054	0.7088	0.7123	0.7157	0.7190	0.7224
+0.6	0.7257	0.7291	0.7324	0.7357	0.7389	0.7422	0.7454	0.7486	0.7517	0.7549
+0.7	0.7580	0.7611	0.7642	0.7673	0.7704	0.7734	0.7764	0.7794	0.7823	0.7852
+0.8	0.7881	0.7910	0.7939	0.7967	0.7995	0.8023	0.8051	0.8079	0.8106	0.8133
+0.9	0.8159	0.8186	0.8212	0.8238	0.8264	0.8289	0.8315	0.8340	0.8365	0.8389
+1.0	0.8413	0.8438	0.8461	0.8485	0.8508	0.8531	0.8554	0.8577	0.8599	0.8621
+1.1	0.8643	0.8665	0.8686	0.8708	0.8729	0.8749	0.8770	0.8790	0.8810	0.8830
+1.2	0.8849	0.8869	0.8888	0.8907	0.8925	0.8944	0.8962	0.8980	0.8997	0.9015
+1.3	0.9032	0.9049	0.9066	0.9082	0.9099	0.9115	0.9131	0.9147	0.9162	0.9177
+1.4	0.9192	0.9207	0.9222	0.9236	0.9251	0.9265	0.9279	0.9292	0.9306	0.9319
+1.5	0.9332	0.9345	0.9357	0.9370	0.9382	0.9394	0.9406	0.9418	0.9429	0.9441
+1.6	0.9452	0.9463	0.9474	0.9484	0.9495	0.9505	0.9515	0.9525	0.9535	0.9545
+1.7	0.9554	0.9564	0.9573	0.9582	0.9591	0.9599	0.9608	0.9616	0.9625	0.9633
+1.8	0.9641	0.9649	0.9656	0.9664	0.9671	0.9678	0.9686	0.9693	0.9699	0.9706
+1.9	0.9713	0.9719	0.9726	0.9732	0.9738	0.9744	0.9750	0.9756	0.9761	0.9767
+2.0	0.9773	0.9778	0.9783	0.9788	0.9793	0.9798	0.9803	0.9808	0.9812	0.9817
+2.1	0.9821	0.9826	0.9830	0.9834	0.9838	0.9842	0.9846	0.9850	0.9854	0.9857
+2.2	0.9861	0.9864	0.9868	0.9871	0.9875	0.9878	0.9881	0.9884	0.9887	0.9890
+2.3	0.9893	0.9896	0.9898	0.9901	0.9904	0.9906	0.9909	0.9911	0.9913	0.9916
+2.4	0.9918	0.9920	0.9922	0.9925	0.9927	0.9929	0.9931	0.9932	0.9934	0.9936
+2.5	0.9938	0.9940	0.9941	0.9943	0.9945	0.9946	0.9948	0.9949	0.9951	0.9952
+2.6	0.9953	0.9955	0.9956	0.9957	0.9959	0.9960	0.9961	0.9962	0.9963	0.9964
+2.7	0.9965	0.9966	0.9967	0.9968	0.9969	0.9970	0.9971	0.9972	0.9973	0.9974
+2.8	0.9974	0.9975	0.9976	0.9977	0.9977	0.9978	0.9979	0.9979	0.9980	0.9981
+2.9	0.9981	0.9982	0.9983	0.9983	0.9984	0.9984	0.9985	0.9985	0.9986	0.9986
+3.0	0.99865	0.99869	0.99874	0.99878	0.99882	0.99886	0.99889	0.99893	0.99896	0.99900
+3.1	0.99903	0.99906	0.99910	0.99913	0.99915	0.99918	0.99921	0.99924	0.99926	0.99929
+3.2	0.99931	0.99934	0.99936	0.99938	0.99940	0.99942	0.99944	0.99946	0.99948	0.99950
+3.3	0.99952	0.99953	0.99955	0.99957	0.99958	0.99960	0.99961	0.99962	0.99964	0.99965
+3.4	0.99966	0.99967	0.99969	0.99970	0.99971	0.99972	0.99973	0.99974	0.99975	0.99976
+3.5	0.99977	0.99978	0.99978	0.99979	0.99980	0.99981	0.99981	0.99982	0.99983	0.99983

APPENDIX F

SELECTED BIBLIOGRAPHY

When addressing the subject of logistics engineering, one should become familiar not only with the available literature in the field of logistics itself, but with some of the subject areas closely aligned to logistics, particularly as related to the engineering process. With this in mind, the author has included a number of key references pertaining to systems engineering and analysis, reliability and maintainability, human factors, engineering economy and life-cycle costing, quality control, and management. These subject areas have been discussed extensively throughout this text, and hopefully the references listed will prove to be beneficial. This list is certainly not to be considered as being all-inclusive.

A. LOGISTICS

[1] *Annual Department of Defense Bibliography of Logistics Studies and Related Documents*, Defense Logistics Studies Information Exchange (DLSIE). U.S. Army Logistics Management Center, Fort Lee, Va.

[2] BALLOU, R. H., *Business Logistics Management*. Englewood Cliffs, N.J.: Prentice-Hall, Inc., 1973.

[3] BLEUEL, W. H. AND J. D. PATTON, *Service Management—Principles and Practices*. Pittsburgh, Pa.: Instrument Society of America, 1978.

[4] BOWERSOX, D. J., *Logistical Management*. New York: Macmillan Publishing Co., Inc., 1974.

[5] COYLE, J. J. AND E. J. BARDI, *The Management of Business Logistics*. New York: West Publishing Co., 1976.

[6] DANIEL, N. E. AND J. R. JONES, eds., *Business Logistics Concepts and Viewpoints*. Boston: Allyn and Bacon, Inc., 1969.

[7] DAVIS, G. M. AND S. W. BROWN, *Logistics Management*. Lexington, Mass.: Lexington Books, D. C. Heath and Company, 1974.

[8] DOD Directive 5000.39, "Acquisition and Management of Integrated Logistic Support for Systems and Equipment." Department of Defense, Washington, D.C., January 1980.

[9] GLUCK, F., ed., Technical Report No. 5, *A Compendium of Authenticated Logistics Terms and Definitions*. School of Systems and Logistics, U.S. Air Force Institute of Technology, WPAFB, Ohio, 1970.

[10] HESKETT, J. L., N. A. GLASKOWSKY, AND R. M. IVIE, *Business Logistics*, 2nd ed. New York: The Ronald Press Company, 1973.

[11] *Logistics Spectrum*, Journal of the Society of Logistics Engineers (SOLE). Park Plaza, Suite 922, 303 Williams Avenue, Huntsville, Ala. 35801.

[12] MAGEE, J. F., *Industrial Logistics*. New York: McGraw-Hill Book Company, 1968.

[13] MAGEE, J. F., *Physical Distribution Systems*. New York: McGraw-Hill Book Company, 1967.

[14] MIL-STD-1388, Military Standard, "Logistic Support Analysis." Department of Defense, Washington, D.C., October 1973.

[15] ROSE, W., *Logistics Management: Systems and Components*. Dubuque, Iowa: William C. Brown Company, Publishers, 1978.

[16] TM 38–710, APF 800–7, NAVMAT P-4000, *Integrated Logistics Support Implementation Guide for DOD Systems and Equipments*. Department of Defense, Washington, D.C., 1972.

B. SYSTEMS ENGINEERING AND ANALYSIS

[1] BLANCHARD, B. S. AND W. J. FABRYCKY, *Systems Engineering and Analysis*. Englewood Cliffs, N.J.: Prentice-Hall, Inc., 1981.

[2] CHASE, W. P., *Management of System Engineering*. New York: John Wiley & Sons, Inc., 1974.

[3] CHESTNUT, H., *Systems Engineering Methods*. New York: John Wiley & Sons, Inc., 1967.

[4] CHESTNUT, H., *Systems Engineering Tools*. New York: John Wiley & Sons, Inc., 1965.

[5] FABRYCKY, W. J., P. M. GHARE, AND P. E. TORGERSEN, *Industrial Operations Research*. Englewood Cliffs, N.J.: Prentice-Hall, Inc., 1972.

[6] MIL-STD-499A, Military Standard, "Engineering Management." Department of Defense, Washington, D.C., May 1974.

[7] OSTROFSKY, B., *Design Planning and Development Methodology*. Englewood Cliffs, N.J.: Prentice-Hall, Inc., 1977.

C. RELIABILITY AND MAINTAINABILITY

[1] AMCP 706–133, *Engineering Design Handbook-Maintainability Engineering Theory and Practice.* U.S. Army Materiel Command, Department of the Army, January 1976.

[2] AMCP 706–134, *Engineering Design Handbook—Maintainability Guide for Design.* U.S. Army Materiel Command, Department of the Army, Washington, D.C., October 1972.

[3] AMSTADTER, B. L., *Reliability Mathematics: Fundamentals, Practices, Procedures.* New York: McGraw-Hill Book Company, 1971.

[4] BAZOVSKY, I., *Reliability Theory and Practices.* Englewood Cliffs, N.J.: Prentice-Hall, Inc., 1961.

[5] BLANCHARD, B. S. AND E. E. LOWERY, *Maintainability Principles and Practices.* New York: McGraw-Hill Book Company, 1969.

[6] CALABRO, S. R., *Reliability Principles and Practices.* New York: McGraw-Hill Book Company, 1962.

[7] CUNNINGHAM, C. E. AND W. COX, *Applied Maintainability Engineering.* New York: John Wiley & Sons, Inc., 1972.

[8] DOD Directive 5000.40, "Reliability and Maintainability." Department of Defense, Washington, D.C., July 1980.

[9] GOLDMAN, A. AND T. SLATTERY, *Maintainability—A Major Element of System Effectiveness.* New York: John Wiley & Sons, Inc., 1967.

[10] HALPERN, S., *The Assurance Sciences—An Introduction to Quality Control and Reliability.* Englewood Cliffs, N.J.: Prentice-Hall, Inc., 1978.

[11] JARDINE, A. K. S., *Maintenance, Replacement, and Reliability.* New York: A Halsted Press Book, John Wiley & Sons, Inc., 1973.

[12] KAPUR, K. C. AND L. R. LAMBERSON, *Reliability in Engineering Design.* New York: John Wiley & Sons, Inc., 1977.

[13] KELLY, A. AND M. J. HARRIS, *Management of Industrial Maintenance.* London–Boston: Newnes–Butterworths, 1978.

[14] LANDERS, R. R., *Reliability and Product Assurance: A Manual for Engineering and Management.* Englewood Cliffs, N.J.: Prentice-Hall, Inc., 1963.

[15] LLOYD, D. K. AND M. LIPOW, *Reliability: Management, Methods, and Mathematics,* 2nd ed. Published by the authors, Defense and Space Systems Group, TRW Systems and Energy, Redondo Beach, Calif., 1977.

[16] MIL-HDBK-217C, Military Standardization Handbook, *Reliability Prediction of Electronic Equipment.* Department of Defense, Washington, D.C., April 1979.

[17] MIL-STD-470, Military Standard, "Maintainability Program Requirements (for Systems and Equipments)." Department of Defense, Washington, D.C., March 1966.

[18] MIL-STD-471A, Military Standard, "Maintainability Verification, Demonstration, Evaluation." Department of Defense, Washington, D.C., March 1973.

[19] MIL-STD-781C, Military Standard, "Reliability Design Qualification and Production Acceptance Tests: Exponential Distribution." Department of Defense, Washington, D.C., October 1977.

[20] MIL-STD-785A, Military Standard, "Reliability Program for Systems and Equipment." Department of Defense, Washington, D.C., March 1969.

[21] SANDLER, G. H., *System Reliability Engineering.* Englewood Cliffs, N.J.: Prentice-Hall, Inc., 1963.

[22] SHOOMAN, M. L., *Probabilistic Reliability: An Engineering Approach.* New York: McGraw-Hill Book Company, 1968.

[23] VON ALVEN, W. H., ed., *Reliability Engineering.* Englewood Cliffs, N.J.: Prentice-Hall, Inc., 1964.

D. HUMAN FACTORS

[1] DEGREENE, K. B., ed., *Systems Psychology.* New York: McGraw-Hill Book Company, 1970.

[2] MCCORMICK, E. J., *Human Factors in Engineering and Design*, 4th ed. New York: McGraw-Hill Book Company, 1976.

[3] MEISTER, D., *Human Factors: Theory and Practice.* New York: John Wiley & Sons, Inc., 1971.

[4] MIL-STD-1472B, Military Standard, "Human Engineering Design Criteria for Military Systems, Equipment, and Facilities." Department of Defense, Washington, D.C., 1974.

E. ENGINEERING ECONOMY AND LIFE-CYCLE COST

[1] BLANCHARD, B. S., *Design and Manage to Life Cycle Cost.* Oreg.: M/A Press, International Scholarly Book Services, Inc., Forest Grove, 1978.

[2] BROWN, R. J. AND R. R. YANUCK, *Life Cycle Costing—A Practical Guide for Energy Managers.* Atlanta, Ga.: The Fairmont Press, Inc.

[3] DARCOM P700–6, NAVMAT P5242, AFLCP/AFSCP 800–19, *Joint Design-to-Cost Guide—Life Cycle Cost as a Design Parameter.* Department of Defense, Washington, D.C., October 1977.

[4] ENGLISH, J. M., ed., *Cost Effectiveness—The Economic Evaluation of Engineered Systems.* New York: John Wiley & Sons, Inc., 1968.

[5] FABRYCKY, W. J. AND G. J. THUESEN, *Economic Decision Analysis*, 2nd ed. Englewood Cliffs, N.J.: Prentice-Hall, Inc., 1980.

[6] FISHER, G. H., *Cost Considerations in System Analysis.* Englewood Cliffs, N.J.: Prentice-Hall, Inc., 1971.

[7] GRANT, E. L., W. G. IRESON, AND R. S. LEAVENWORTH, *Principles of Engineering Economy*, 6th ed. New York: The Ronald Press Company, 1976.

[8] OSTWALD, P. F., *Cost Estimating for Engineering and Management.* Englewood Cliffs, N.J.: Prentice-Hall, Inc., 1974.

[9] SELDON, M. R., *Life Cycle Costing: A Better Method of Government Procurement*. Boulder, Colo.: Westview Press, Inc., 1979.

[10] THUESEN, H. G., W. J. FABRYCKY, AND G. J. THUESEN, *Engineering Economy*, 5th ed. Englewood Cliffs, N.J.: Prentice-Hall, Inc., 1977.

F. PRODUCTION AND QUALITY CONTROL

[1] BUFFA, E. S., *Modern Production Management*, 5th ed., New York: John Wiley & Sons, Inc., 1977.

[2] GRANT, E. L. AND R. S. LEAVENSORTH, *Statistical Quality Control*, 4th ed. New York: McGraw-Hill Book Company, 1972.

[3] JURAN, J. M., ed., *Quality Control Handbook*, 2nd ed. New York: McGraw-Hill Book Company, 1962.

[4] STARR, M. K., *Operations Management*. Englewood Cliffs, N.J.: Prentice-Hall, Inc., 1978.

G. MANAGEMENT

[1] BLANCHARD, B. S., *Engineering Organization and Management*. Englewood Cliffs, N.J.: Prentice-Hall, Inc., 1976.

[2] CLELAND, D. I. AND W. R. KING, *Systems Analysis and Project Management*. New York: McGraw-Hill Book Company, 1968.

[3] JOHNSON, R. A., F. E. KATZ, AND J. E. ROSENZWEIG, *The Theory and Management of Systems*, 3rd ed. New York: McGraw-Hill Book Company, 1973.

[4] KARGER, D. AND R. MURDICK, *Managing Engineering and Research*. New York: Industrial Press, Inc., 1969.

[5] KOONTZ, H. AND C. O'DONNELL, *Principles of Management—An Analysis of Management Functions*, 3rd. ed., New York: McGraw-Hill Book Company, 1964.

INDEX